AFRICAN CHRISTIAN GOD-TALK

Matthew Ajuoga's Johera Narrative

George F. Pickens

Brihtrie,
It has been a blessing to know you, and I pray God's richest blessings upon you!
George F. Pickens
12/14/17

University Press of America,® Inc.
Dallas · Lanham · Boulder · New York · Oxford

Copyright © 2004 by
University Press of America,® Inc.
4501 Forbes Boulevard
Suite 200
Lanham, Maryland 20706
UPA Acquisitions Department (301) 459-3366

PO Box 317
Oxford
OX2 9RU, UK

All rights reserved
Printed in the United States of America
British Library Cataloging in Publication Information Available

Copublished by arrangement with the American Society
of Missiology and George F. Pickens

Library of Congress Control Number: 2004103438
ISBN 0-7618-2921-0 (paperback : alk. ppr.)
ISBN 0-7618-2920-2 (cloth: alk. ppr.)

To Deb
for twenty-three years of encouragement

Contents

Preface   vii

Chapter 1 Introduction   1

Formation of the Study and Text

Chapter 2 Towards an Inside Understanding of the *Johera Narrative*   9

Chapter 3 Sources Available for the Study of the *Johera Narrative*   27

Chapter 4 The Gestation of the *Johera Narrative*   35

Presentation of the Contexts and Text

Chapter 5 The Kenyan Legacy   53

Chapter 6 The Christian Legacy   81

Chapter 7 The Luo Legacy	111
Chapter 8 A Literary Survey	139
Chapter 9 A Theological Assessment	155
Chapter 10 A Listener's Guide	189
Chapter 11 A Last Look	217
Appendix 1 The *Johera Narrative*	221
Appendix 2 A Chronology of Significant Events	293
Endnotes	297
Reference List	317
Index	335

Preface

This study represents the academic fruit of my sustained encounters with African Instituted Churches (AICs) over a fourteen year period. Because I have had the privilege of sharing in the Christian experiences of numerous AICs from three African nations, I have benefited spiritually. This study, however, reflects mostly the theological reflections my participation with one particular AIC (the Church of Christ in Africa-Johera) has provoked.

I acknowledge the impact these relationships with AICs have had on my personal Christian pilgrimage. In 1983 I began the academic study of AICs, being introduced to the vast and ever-increasing literature of the field. In January 1985, my family and I travelled to Africa for the first time, and during the next four years I grounded my academic study of AICs in direct experience. I began to listen to their "God-Talk"—their oral and narrative theologizing—and to participate otherwise in the lives of numerous AICs in Abidjan, Ivory Coast through a Bible teaching program I had been asked by them to develop. I was rarely comfortable, often shocked, always surprised, yet ever challenged, stretched, educated, and inspired. Very soon, I became so fascinated by the vitality and sincerity of these Christians and their "God-Talk," that I desired to continue and deepen my involvement with their vital Christian communities.

During the summer of 1990 my family relocated to Nairobi, Kenya where I began teaching at Daystar University. In one of my classes that first year was Mrs. Milcah Ajuoga, whom I soon came to know as the wife of Matthew Ajuoga, the founder and presiding Bishop of the Church of Christ in Africa-Johera (CCA). Even though we had not yet met, I was aware of Bishop Ajuoga and his leadership of the CCA and the Organization of African Instituted Churches. One day I mentioned to Milcah that I would welcome the opportunity to meet her husband, and I eventually met Matthew Ajuoga in early 1991. Upon my encouragement, two years later Bishop Ajuoga agreed to allow me to oversee the recording, transcription, and translation of his story of his Christian experiences—his personal "God-Talk"—within the CCA. He desired that his narrative be preserved for his community's sake, but he also related that he would like the wider world to understand him, the CCA, and other AICs better. Toward that end, he kindly agreed to allow me to complete this study based on his narrative.

The recording of Matthew Ajuoga's *Johera Narrative* began in earnest in mid 1993, and during my visits to his home in Kisumu, I was able to convince Bishop Ajuoga to find time in his demanding daily schedule to complete his narration. Thus, this study would not have been possible without the persistent efforts of Matthew Ajuoga to record his narrative, and without his kind cooperation and permission that have allowed me to complete this study. I also thankfully acknowledge my debt to Bishop Ajuoga for teaching me about the struggle to be Christian in Africa, and for telling and consigning his story to me. I am also grateful to Milcah for her wise insights and generous hospitality.

I must also acknowledge my debts to several other individuals whose imprints on this study I recognize. In the U. S. I am indebted to Dr. Gifford B. Doxsee, now retired but when I encountered him between 1983-85, he was Professor of History and Director of the African Studies Program, Ohio University, Athens, Ohio. By him I was first introduced to the academic study of Africa, and in him I first observed a sincere desire to understand and appreciate that continent that has been so misunderstood and maltreated by the rest of the world.

In Ivory Coast I acknowledge my debts to two men. In Abidjan, Dr. David A. Shank became my mentor, introducing me to the materials and methods of the study of African Instituted Churches. He was also able to persuade me that nothing I had learned or experienced before had prepared me to understand their "God-Talk," and so I must start afresh and learn yet another theological "language." Yet, perhaps most importantly, Dr. Shank modelled the humility and willingness to listen and learn which I believe to be necessary for a fruitful encounter with AICs. In Divo, James Krabill encouraged me in my pursuit of deeper knowledge of AICs, and his own Birmingham thesis on the hymnody of the Dida Harrist Churches (Krabill 1989) has been helpful in the organization of this study.

Preface

In Kenya, besides Matthew and Milcah Ajuoga, I have benefited from the encouragement, wisdom, and experience of John Padwick. John's long affiliation with Kenyan AICs, as well as his long-term acquaintance with Matthew Ajuoga, have been invaluable. I have also been rescued—more times than I care to remember—by the computer wizardry of two close friends, Don Ertley and Ron Navamanie; that we are still friends demonstrates their charity.

In England, I wish to thank the Faculty of Arts and the Department of Theology at the University of Birmingham for granting me five bursaries that have allowed me to complete this study. I am particularly grateful for the wise, kind, and gently affirming guidance and criticisms of my advisor at the University of Birmingham, Professor Werner Ustorf. I do not believe a more faithful and encouraging advisor exists anywhere. His excitement over this project was contagious, and it has helped to sustain the efforts and focus necessary to see it to completion.

At Kentucky Christian College, I would like to thank those who have assisted in the project to prepare my manuscript for publication: Scott Asbury, Andy May, Andrew Walters, Josh Lane, John Harvey, and Terry Golightly. I would also like to thank the college's administration for their encouragement and support.

I have been given the time and supportive environment necessary to complete this study only through the patience, discipline, industry, and encouragement of my wife Debbie, and our sons George-Mark and John-Michael. This study is also theirs.

Finally, I acknowledge my debt to the thousands of Johera, living and dead, who have bestowed upon me perhaps the greatest honour yet responsibility possible: they have entrusted their most prized possession—their story—to me. I am humbled, I express my deepest appreciation, and despite my attempts explained in this study to do otherwise, if I have mishandled their story, I ask for forgiveness; it has not been intentional. As from a fellow pilgrim in the Way, I now return their story for their reflection.

Chapter 1

Introduction

In late 1957, in the midst of the fervour of the East African Revival, a schism within the Anglican Church "more considerable in scale than any other separation this century" (Hastings 1979, 127) occurred in the Nyanza Province of Kenya. This exodus was led by seven duly ordained African clergy, and involved at least sixteen thousand communicants from some 130 congregations (Barrett 1968, 12). This company called themselves *Johera*, a Dholuo word meaning "people of love," and they soon established the Church of Christ in Africa- Johera (CCA). By the time of its official registration in early January 1958, CCA membership had swelled to twenty thousand led by only nine priests (Welbourn and Ogot 1966, 56).

One of the original seven Johera clergy, as well as the initial leader from the very first rumblings of schism, was Matthew Ajuoga. After the CCA was formally established, Ajuoga was elected as its chairman, then later he became the new church's first bishop. By early 1958, as the new bishop of a large, expanding, yet infant African Instituted Church (AIC),[1] Matthew Ajuoga's standing as a significant Christian leader in Kenya was solidified. Ajuoga's influence continued to increase, and when he was elected chairman of the Organization of African Instituted Churches (OAIC) in 1982, his influence was felt even further afield.

Even so, Matthew Ajuoga's voice has rarely been heard outside African Instituted Church circles, and his personal reflections regarding his spiritual pilgrimage and the CCA have until recently been the private property of that community. For most of his life and for various reasons, Matthew Ajuoga had been reluctant to offer his full and unmediated story to outsiders.[2] Yet by late 1993, in his sixty-seventh year and no longer fearing the consequences, Matthew Ajuoga recounted his "official" version of the origins and subsequent development of the Church of Christ in Africa- Johera. Ajuoga's story, the *Johera Narrative*, also narrates his personal Christian pilgrimage spanning sixty-seven years (1926-1993). Because the text thus conveys these oral theological reminiscences, Ajuoga's "God-Talk" (Kalu 1993, 176) expresses the Christian reflections of an African Christian patriarch, the spiritual father of Johera.

The purpose of this study is to describe and demonstrate an effective collection and presentation of Matthew Ajuoga's *Johera Narrative*. Foundational to this task is the conviction that Ajuoga's text is a significant source for the study of African Christianity, and more specifically, African Instituted Churches. Two major reasons for the text's significance arise from its contents, and a third area of significance results from what the text itself represents. Because of their foundational nature, these issues will be introduced in general here, then they will be developed in more detail throughout this study.

THE CONTENT SIGNIFICANCE OF THE *JOHERA NARRATIVE*
An Untold Story

The contents, or specifically **what** is said by Ajuoga in his *Johera Narrative*, are significant because they include a particular perspective and insight on events that have hitherto been publicly unavailable. In his text Ajuoga presents his version of the events that led up to and followed the 1957 schism, and this is the first time Ajuoga's view has been offered to a wider audience in its complete and unmediated form.[3]

Other versions of the CCA schism have been offered. Welbourn and Ogot (1966) have based their interpretation of the 1957 schism on CCA sources and on information provided by the Joremo, the opponents of Johera within the revival (Welbourn and Ogot 1966, 1-3). However, Welbourn and Ogot's conclusions, while valuable, reflect the interpretations of "outsiders" after consulting "inside" sources; their assessment is not Johera's.[4]

David B. Barrett (1968, 8-17, 254-263) provides a cursory analysis of the Johera schism, yet he also does so in a biased way. Barrett attempts to explain the schism of 1957 within the broader context of his theories of the "tribal zeitgeist" of religious tension (1968, 108ff). Barrett's assessment presents many difficulties, yet the point to be made here is that his brief and superficial analysis of the CCA schism reflects a general lack of openness to the perspectives of Johera.[5]

A third version of the CCA schism will potentially become available to the interested researcher when the Church Missionary Society's archives for the relevant period are opened. Even so, while the official CMS version will be extremely valuable and necessary for a balanced understanding of the origins of the CCA, it nevertheless will not reflect Johera's version.[6]

These interpretations of Johera are all valuable, and have been helpful in the pursuit of this study.[7] However, a version of events from within the CCA itself has hitherto been unavailable, and consequently the story of the thousands of Johera has not been heard outside their community. Matthew Ajuoga's "Johera Narrative" finally provides that version of the story for a wider audience.

An Inside Story

The contents of Matthew Ajuoga's *Johera Narrative* are also significant because they provide an "inside" view of an African Christian community. As already noted above, the *Johera Narrative* provides the official CCA version of the 1957 schism, yet more importantly for this study, it also provides insight into the spiritual life of an African Instituted Church. Of great significance is not only what happened and why, that is, the actual narration of events, but also Johera's perceptions and impressions of those events, and the way these perceptions formed Christian experience within Johera. One version of these experiences and perceptions within the CCA over thirty-six years of its history, that of Matthew Ajuoga, is revealed in the *Johera Narrative*.

This uncovers yet another limitation of the "outside" interpretations of the CCA schism mentioned above. Not only have Welbourn and Ogot and Barrett not taken Johera's version of events seriously, they also have given little attention to religious life within Johera itself. After reading Welbourn and Ogot and Barrett's accounts, one wonders about the internal dynamics of Johera, and numerous questions arise. What made the group so attractive to so many? What were the individual and corporate experiences of Christianity reflected among Johera? How did they appropriate Christianity, and what innovations, if any, did they make from the Faith they had received? Also, what were the central themes which formed or resulted from their experiences of schism and subsequent developments? To put it more succinctly, what was and is the phenomenology of Johera? Until 1993 the answers to these questions were not available outside the CCA. However, with the birth of the *Johera Narrative*, an "inside" version of the life of an African Christian community has become available, and answers to such questions are offered.

To date most studies of African Instituted Churches have focused on the issues of their origins; this field has been well investigated, and overly emphasized.[8] Consequently, this study is not limited to the historical arguments surrounding the origins of the CCA. Not only would it be impossible to complete a balanced historical analysis of the origins of the CCA at present even if one desired,[9] but it is a premise of this study that the *Johera Narrative* is valuable because of the extra-historical information it offers; it provides an "inside" narration of the Christian experiences of the CCA before and after its secession. The text presents the concerns or themes that have dominated the life of the CCA—at least according to Matthew Ajuoga—over the thirty-six years covered in the *Johera Narrative*. The primary focus of this study, therefore, will be upon the phenomenology of Johera as revealed in Ajuoga's narrative.

The text also provides yet another inside perspective. It reveals the spiritual and theological development of Matthew Ajuoga himself, as narrated by himself, and thus the text provides an inside interpretation of the Christian development of the founder/leader of an African Instituted Church. Not only does Ajuoga focus on his communal experiences within the CCA, but the *Johera Narrative* also invites us into the spiritual and theological sanctum of an African Christian patriarch. Ajuoga's appropriations and innovations of Christianity are revealed, justified, and legitimated. This personal and retrospective explanation of Christian experience within an African Instituted Church is a rare and rich source for African Christian scholarship, and is consequently another reason for the significance of the *Johera Narrative*.

THE REPRESENTATIVE SIGNIFICANCE OF THE "JOHERA NARRATIVE"

Not only is the *Johera Narrative* a significant text for the study of African Christianity because of its contents, but it is also significant because of what the text itself represents. The *Johera Narrative* was born as a result of a particular type of theological activity within the Christian experience of Matthew Ajuoga, and the text provides insights into these developments.

A Level of "Interpretative Depth"

In a recent article the African theologian, Kwame Bediako, argues that one of the most important future tasks for African Christian scholarship is "the scholarly penetration of African Christianity" (Bediako 1995, 55). Bediako recalls,

> Historically, the Christian faith has developed as a religion savante, continually stimulating an intellectual tradition through a process of inward and outward self-definition which it produces in its converts (Bediako 1995, 55).

He then notes that, while the earliest concerns of African theologians related to the relationship between the primal religions and Christianity, now there is a need to move on from this necessary foundation to the understanding of Christianity as it relates to broader issues of daily experience in Africa. To accomplish this, according to Bediako, what is needed is not only access to more information about daily African Christian experience, "but more important still, greater depth" (Bediako 1995, 56).

Matthew Ajuoga's *Johera Narrative* provides such a deeper level of assessment of the experiences of himself and Johera. He not only narrates but goes further to explain, justify, and legitimate the actions, beliefs, and experiences of himself and others. His account is inward looking, and what results goes a long way towards producing a self-definition of himself and the CCA.

This is done because Matthew Ajuoga has himself moved from the foundations of his Christian theology, that is from his understanding of the relationship between his primal religion and Christianity, towards a deeper reflection upon the wider meaning of Christianity for his individual and corporate experiences. In fact, the *Johera Narrative* says surprisingly little about Ajuoga's primal past;[10] what *is* said reflects a further development in his theologizing. Accordingly, the *Johera Narrative* represents a significant level of "interpretative depth."

Because Matthew Ajuoga's text reflects this deeper level of theological reflection, it can be viewed as an "intermediate" theological source which represents a particular stage of theological development that has been neglected in the study of African Instituted Churches.[11] The *Johera Narrative* contains the retrospective, systematic, and well-reasoned reflections of Matthew Ajuoga, and it suggests an "intermediate" stage in the theological development of Ajuoga and the CCA: a move from a primal, oral stage which focused on issues related to the relationship between the inherited and adopted pasts (Walls 1980), to a stage where the focus is on the telling and analysis of the formative stories of their experiences. This stage can be called "intermediate" because it is not the final stage, as Ajuoga and the CCA continue to develop their "intellectual penetration" (Bediako 1995, 55) of their own experiences. Consequently, the *Johera Narrative* represents a significant genre of theological material.

In his text Matthew Ajuoga speaks openly, with minimal mediation, to recount an unavailable, inside, and intermediate perspective of a personal experience of African Christian independency. Indeed, the *Johera Narrative* breaks the long silence of an African Christian patriarch, and Ajuoga offers his understanding and particular innovation of Christianity that arises from his long experience as the founder/leader of a large African Instituted Church.

These contributions of the *Johera Narrative*, however, cannot be accessed easily. Given the singular and non-standard, oral nature of Ajuoga's "God-Talk," the potential listener/reader must be "converted" from the bias towards more conventional sources and against non-traditional records of theologizing (Pobee 1989, 92). This study intends to assist in this conversion process by providing a guide for understanding and properly appropriating Ajuoga's text. This will be accomplished through the three requisite tasks of the handler of oral materials (Henige 1982, 6):
1. Describing and demonstrating an effective collection of Ajuoga's "God-Talk";
2. Providing a thorough assessment of the text in light of the relevant literature;
3. And, identifying the major contributions of the text through interpretations in light of its formative contexts.

The first procedure is the focus of Part One, which describes the formation of the study and text. The methodology and types of source materials utilized will be discussed (Chapters 2 and 3), then a description of the transmission of the *Johera Narrative* will be presented (Chapter 4). The second and third processes will be accomplished in Part Two, which concerns the presentation of the text. Three chapters will seek to describe the text's most formative contexts, and interpretations of the narrative in view of these backgrounds will be offered (Chapters 5-7). The singular nature of the *Johera Narrative* is the subject of Chapter 8, and an assessment of the text as a theological source is presented in Chapter 9. An index for a deeper understanding of Matthew Ajuoga's "God-Talk" is provided in Chapter 10, then the study concludes with suggestions for further examinations of the text.

The purpose throughout this study is to understand, respect, appreciate, and amplify this "inside" and "intermediate" narrative of African Christian experience. Through the text, an African Christian's "God-Talk" is heard; in the following pages it is our intention to listen and learn.

Chapter 2

Towards an Inside Understanding of the *Johera Narrative*

This study is based on the assumption that Matthew Ajuoga's *Johera Narrative* is a significant source for the study of African Christianity. However, Ajuoga's text, though a potentially rich source, must be approached with care if its treasures are to be uncovered. Accordingly, in order to handle this text responsibly a particular study design has been developed, and this chapter sets forth this basic approach towards the *Johera Narrative*.

Considering the fact that the *Johera Narrative* is primarily a text arising from and about one case of African Christian independency, the study design described here is based upon methods widely recognized for the study of African Instituted Churches. Though the literature on African Christian independency—including issues of methodology— is now vast, this study has benefited most from the approaches of two of the pioneers of the study of African Instituted Churches, Drs. Bengt Sundkler and Harold W. Turner. Their particular contributions to this study's methodology are described below.

BENGT SUNDKLER AND THE PROPER MANAGEMENT OF AIC TEXTS

By his own admission, Bengt Sundkler's (1948) pioneering volume on Zulu Christian independency was based on faulty methodology (Sundkler 1976, 305), and perhaps this self-analysis allowed Dr. Sundkler to be especially sensitive towards methodological issues in the study of African Instituted Churches. In his critique of G. C. Oosthuizen's (1967) analysis of Nazaretha hymns, Sundkler maintained that Oosthuizen had "mismanaged" the texts, and consequently the study's conclusions were inaccurate (Sundkler 1976, 186-205). Professor Sundkler thus alerted researchers of African Instituted Churches to the dangers of source misuse, and to reduce this risk of textual mishandling, Sundkler prescribed a particular orientation towards source materials emerging from these Christian communities.

Sundkler argued that an African Instituted Church text would be "mismanaged" (Sundkler 1976, 190) unless primary attention by the researcher was given to the "inside" understanding of the text, and it is for this lack of focus on the "inside" understanding of Shembe's hymns that Oosthuizen was criticized (Sundkler 1976, 186-205). Dr. Sundkler maintained that Shembe's hymns must be interpreted in light of the Nazaretha understanding, not within the context of some outside framework.

> These lovely songs of his [Shembe's] must be interpreted, not from the presuppositions of Luther's catechism or of that of Heidelberg, but out of their own milieu, on a basis of their own presuppositions, out of the needs and aspirations of the Zulu in the context of race-ridden South Africa.
> It is with this hermeneutical principle as a key that one must try to open the locks of the shrine (Sundkler 1976, 195).

For Professor Sundkler, a text emerging from an African Instituted Church must be approached and interpreted with the intents and understandings of the source(s) of the text; otherwise the text would be mishandled and its interpretations distorted.

Sundkler also offered that, in order to approach this "inside" understanding of an AIC text, the researcher must be fully aware of the broader context from which the particular text emerged. More specifically for the case of Shembe's hymnal, Sundkler argued that any interpretation must take into account the broader concerns of the worship and struggles of the Nazaretha (Sundkler 1976, 192). He also maintained that, especially for a text arising from one individual source such as Shembe's hymns, the life of that individual must be considered in any interpretation of that text. Sundkler argued that texts arising from an individual's life experiences must be interpreted using a biographical approach (Sundkler 1976, 281).

Proper Management of the Johera Narrative

Because this study seeks to avoid the mismanagement of the *Johera Narrative*, its approach towards the text is based upon Dr. Sundkler's recommendations. In order to manage properly Ajuoga's text it will be assessed and analyzed with regard to Matthew Ajuoga's intentions, and the broader historical and religious contexts of the *Johera Narrative* will be given serious consideration.

Even so, discovering the original intentions for the *Johera Narrative* is problematic. As noted, a partial understanding of the sources' intentions for a particular text can be gained from the broader historical and religious contexts, and these are given due consideration in Chapters 5-7. Yet, in order to arrive at Sundkler's "inside" understanding of the original intentions of the text, especially a text that arises from one individual source, one must discover and consider the intentions of the person from whom the text originates.

In order to move towards the original intention of Shembe's hymn, Sundkler asked "What was Shembe's concern" (Sundkler 1976, 204)? Since the hymns originated with Shembe himself, emerging from his own experiences and appropriations of Christianity, a proper interpretation could be approached only by being sensitive to Shembe's purposes for the hymns (Sundkler 1976, 281ff).

Consistent with this approach, this study seeks to present Matthew Ajuoga's *Johera Narrative* with sensitivity towards his intentions for the text. However, how are Matthew Ajuoga's intentions for the *Johera Narrative* to be uncovered? His presuppositions must be taken into account, yet how are these presuppositions to be known? In answering these questions, I have benefited from the methodologies advocated by Harold W. Turner.

HAROLD W. TURNER AND THE WAY INSIDE THE TEXT

Harold W. Turner is considered one of the pioneers of the academic, religious study of African Instituted Churches, and he has been called "'The founder of prophet movements and the phenomenology of religion" (Greschat 1990, 19). Turner's methodology is detailed in his (1967a and b) monumental two-volume study of the Church of the Lord (Aladura),[1] and his approach initially grew out of the relationship he was able to develop with leaders of that African Instituted Church. In describing Turner's general methodology Andrew Walls notes.

> The mode of investigation...grew naturally out of the first encounter. He [Turner] took his new acquaintance in the

> Church of the Lord seriously for what they were and for what they claimed to be: as fellow believers seeking to worship God and to experience the divine presence and power. This enabled him to build trust and friendship with Church of the Lord leaders and members and to share freely with them in their activities. This form of "participant observation" was not role play but deliberate sharing, as far as the participant was able, in what he took in good faith to be Christian worship by other believers. ...So Harold Turner accepted the risks and the personal vulnerability involved in such openness (Walls 1990a, 5).

Turner based this approach on principles borrowed from the phenomenology of religion,[2] and the basic assumptions of the phenomenological method utilized by Turner have been summarized by Hans-Jurgen Greschat.

> We are to keep ourselves from taking a phenomenon apart, from analyzing it, subjecting it to texts, experimenting with it, defining it, explaining it etymologically, rethinking it into a concept or into a theory. In other words, phenomenologists are to imitate neither scientist nor scholar. Putting aside for the time being all they have ever heard or read or thought about a religious matter, they are to become aware of the phenomenon, of what appears (Greschat 1990, 27).

Among other benefits, this orientation allowed Turner to move towards an "inside" understanding of the Church of the Lord (Aladura). Resulting from the relationship of mutual trust and respect which he had cultivated, was the opportunity to approach the Church of the Lord (Aladura) and minimize his "outsider" status. Turner developed free and open communication with leaders and members of the Church of the Lord (Aladura) (Turner 1967a, 209), and this allowed his interpretations to approach those held within the community.

In attempting to move towards an inside understanding of the *Johera Narrative*, I have followed five principles advocated by Harold Turner.

Sympathy
Harold Turner approached his study of the Church of the Lord (Aladura) from a position of sympathy.

Towards an Inside Understanding of the Johera Narrative

> One cannot avoid learning in one direction or another, and we have preferred that, if at all, we should be found to lean towards sympathy with the community that has engaged our respect and affection, rather then to thrust forward at every point with the criticisms that spring too easily to Western minds (Turner 1967b, vi).

Turner viewed the members and leaders of the Church of the Lord (Aladura) as Christians who believed and practiced their faith with sincerity. This general orientation and attitude paved the way for openness and dialogue, and Turner was consequently able to access sources that would no doubt have otherwise been denied him.

This study begins with, indeed it has resulted from, sympathy towards African Instituted Churches in general and Matthew Ajuoga and the Church of Christ in Africa-Johera in particular. My sympathy towards Matthew Ajuoga and the CCA result from two crucial factors. First, this approach is a product of my training and experience with African Instituted Churches since 1983.[3] I learned to approach AICs with humility and sympathy, and not to confuse agreement with understanding. I was taught that it was not—at least initially—my role to agree or disagree, but to seek understanding. Within this framework sympathy towards AICs was necessary, and consequently my four years of ministry alongside AICs in Cote d'Ivoire was approached from this perspective.

Upon arrival in Nairobi, my involvement with and sympathy towards AICs had been communicated through the OAIC, and thus when I approached Matthew Ajuoga about his participation in this project, he agreed.[4] Throughout the course of this project I attempted to take Matthew Ajuoga and the CCA seriously, to consider them as fellow believers and pilgrims, to trust in their sincerity, to admire and respect their experiences, and to learn from them.

Not only has the sympathetic approach been taken in this study because it naturally flows from my past training and experiences, but it has also been utilized for one very practical reason. Without such an approach based on mutual respect, trust, and sincerity, Matthew Ajuoga would never have consented to share his narrative with me. Like many leaders of African Instituted Churches Matthew Ajuoga is suspicious of "outsiders" who show interest in his community.[5] Well acquainted with the less than noble motives of many would-be researchers, Ajuoga was at first hesitant to cooperate in the *Johera Narrative* project. However, based upon his knowledge of my past involvement with AICs and my sympathetic attitudes towards them, he consented to give me access to his narrative. Thus, it was only after Ajuoga was fully convinced of my sympathy towards himself and the CCA that he gave me free and unlimited access to the resources of his community. Without this sympathetic approach, this study would not have been possible.

Even so, Turner's sympathetic approach is not without its difficulties, and this must be confronted. One of its greatest dangers is that it can jeopardize objectivity. Yet, Harold Turner has argued that

> the approach to objectivity depends not on the assumption of a neutral or external position, but on a resolute attempt to become aware of all the factors at work in the relationship between the observer and the church with which he is concerned (Turner 1979, 43).

Objectivity is thus not an issue of attitude, but rather one of thoroughness, and in this study sympathy and thoroughness have been utilized in pursuit of an inside interpretation of the *Johera Narrative*. No other approach would have provided access to or proper management of the text.

Participation

A second methodological device advocated by Turner to move towards an inside understanding of the religious phenomenology of African Christian independency is participation. Turner's pioneering work (1967a and b) was based heavily upon information gathered from his participation in the life of the Church of the Lord (Aladura). Turner maintained that "one cannot appreciate the religion of a religious community without some genuine participation in its activities" (Turner 1967b, vi).

Participation in the life of an African Christian community is required for approaching an intramural understanding of that community, because many dynamics—for example, central beliefs and values—are not so much articulated as demonstrated. Most African Instituted Churches place great emphasis upon ritual, event, and ceremony, and these communicate the theology of the community. If the researcher fails to participate in these rites, he is consequently separating himself from some of the richest sources of information available to him.

Turner also notes the most important value of participation as a research method. He argues that, given the importance of personal relationships in Africa, the inner depths of an individual or community's experience cannot be accessed without regular and sincere participation; it is participation which symbolizes relationships. Turner maintains that the development and maintenance of personal relationships are more important than technical methods in Africa, and "if this is recognized as important for other disciplines it is supremely so for the study of someone else's religion" (Turner 1979, 39).

In my attempt to move towards an inside understanding of the *Johera Narrative* I have participated in the communal life of the CCA, but more importantly, I shared in the daily schedule of Matthew Ajuoga himself.[6] I believe that one cannot begin to understand the *Johera Narrative* unless one first understands Matthew Ajuoga, its author. In order to understand better Ajuoga—his beliefs, values, motivations—I participated in his daily routine, and this participation has not only provided helpful insights into Ajuoga's inner world of Christian experience, but it has also symbolized my sincerity which in turn secured opportunity for still further participation.

Partnership

Participation, especially if it is merely observant rather than interactive, is of limited value as a research tool for the study of African Instituted Churches. Turner believed that participation should not be based on a distant and affected relationship, but that it should lead to or result from a genuine sense of partnership between the researcher and the members of the community being studied. For Turner the "chief procedure" in the study of an African religious community "consists of this encounter at the personal level and the establishment of a joint enterprise" (Turner 1979, 40). In his study of the Church of the Lord (Aladura) Turner recalled, "once there was a sense of partnership in this task, the most intimate personal religious history was often freely available..." (Turner 1979, 39). Turner had succeeded in developing a level of mutuality which led to the cultivation of a genuine partnership and even friendship.

> Friendship, then, is the only door to an understanding of the inner reality of an African religious movement, and in many cases this will mean that the enquiry becomes to some extent a joint enterprise wherein both parties gain a deeper and a clear comprehension (Turner 1979, 39).

Partnership resulting in friendship opened for him the inner sanctum of the religious community, and additionally stimulated the community to reflect upon and analyze its own story.

Yet there is a further, and for this study more important, element of partnership. Just as the opening and examining of resources was to be a joint enterprise between the researcher and the religious community, so also were the conclusions and interpretations to be arrived at in partnership. Turner argues,

> all that he [the researcher] finally has to say about the movement he is studying must commend itself to both the parties who have been involved together in the study in this intimate way (Turner 1979, 39).

Just as a sense of partnership and friendship guide the examination of sources, so must they also form the interpretations that emerge.

From its very inception the *Johera Narrative* project has been built on a partnership between myself, Matthew Ajuoga, and the CCA. This was so, not only because of my own convictions that Turner's methods were valid, but primarily because the project would not have been possible without it. Matthew Ajuoga was ready and determined to tell his story, yet he was not willing to act as a mere passive subject. He was not seeking an aloof researcher, but rather a genuine partner with whom he could share and examine the story of his experiences. Consequently it was only through the partnership approach that his narrative became available.

I have cultivated my partnership with Matthew Ajuoga at every stage of this project, and consistent with Turner's suggestions, even my conclusions have been shared, and to an extent, jointly formed. I have been conscious throughout of my indebtedness and responsibility to Matthew Ajuoga and the CCA, realizing that this is *their* story, not mine. I have attempted to handle their story with respect, mindful that this is a joint enterprise, and this study is intended to reflect this partnership.

Openness

Partnership cannot be realized if the researcher holds rigid presuppositions about the information s/he intends to uncover. Realizing this, Harold Turner counseled that the approach to the study of African religious movements must be "open,"

> "...for we do not know clearly in advance what we are observing, and we must allow the data to raise new questions, and suggest new categories and terminology" (Turner 1979, 24).

Turner was aware that to a great extent the researcher is able to find what s/he is looking for, and that information, especially in qualitative areas such as religious experience, can be interpreted in diverse ways. Therefore, the researcher must approach the information with an open mind, and with a humility and readiness to learn from those inside the religious community. If rigid presuppositions are held, if interpretations are preconceived, then the researcher's conclusions will be prejudiced; they will not approach the inside interpretation of the religious community under investigation.

In my desire to move towards an inside interpretation of the *Johera Narrative* I have approached the entire project with openness. I have tried to put away—as much as possible—my presuppositions regarding the nature of the CCA, the character of Matthew Ajuoga, and the content and forms of Ajuoga's religious experiences. My sympathy and partnership result in being able to approach my study of Ajuoga's text with a sincere desire to find what is truly there, not simply what I want to find. This openness is reflected in the methodologies I have employed in the transmission of the *Johera Narrative*,[7] and the combination of these approaches—sympathy, participation, partnership, and qualitative methods in accessing the *Johera Narrative*—has minimized the danger of finding what I am looking for.[8]

Listening

In pursuing my open approach to understanding the *Johera Narrative*, I have become a listener and have allowed and encouraged Matthew Ajuoga to speak for himself. In my openness I have not tried to presume to tell Ajuoga what he believes, or what actually happened. While I have questioned him and asked him to confront issues which I felt he was avoiding,[9] I have nevertheless allowed Ajuoga to provide the answers and I have attentively listened to *his* "God-Talk."

This approach is also consistent with the one advocated by Harold Turner. In his study of the Church of the Lord (Aladura) Turner relied heavily upon the community's own sources: letters, reports, programs, minutes, records, hymns, and sermons (Turner 1967b, 157). His primary reason for utilizing these resources was to "let the Church speak for itself" (Turner 1967a, xv). His openness led him to listen to the community speak for itself through its own materials.

A researcher's willingness to listen while the religious community speaks for itself is also advocated by at least one group of African

Instituted Churches, who proclaimed their weariness at outsiders telling them about themselves.

> Until now all the research and all the literature about the so-called "African Independent Churches" has been the work of outsiders.... . Each of them has had his or her own motives for studying us... .
> It is therefore not surprising that we do not recognize ourselves in their writings. We find them seriously misleading and often far from the truth. They are full of misunderstandings, misconceptions and falsehood (Ngada 1985, 5).

Consequently, the group decided to speak for themselves, and produced a booklet entitled "Speaking for Ourselves" (African Spiritual Churches Association 1985).

This general approach towards the *Johera Narrative*, borrowed from Harold Turner, was chosen to assist me in moving inside the text, to discover and present the narrative consistent with Matthew Ajuoga's designs. This phenomenological methodology has enabled me to determine Ajuoga's most basic intentions for the text, and as noted above, a proper handling of a text arising from one individual requires sensitivity to the original intentions of that source. What follows is a summary of my perception of Ajuoga's intentions for his *Johera Narrative*.

MATTHEW AJUOGA'S BASIC INTENTIONS FOR THE JOHERA NARRATIVE

Matthew Ajuoga had a definite set of intentions when he agreed to cooperate in the production of the *Johera Narrative*, and these intentions have been communicated to me by Ajuoga himself in the course of interviews. Direct statements were made by Ajuoga regarding his motivation for giving his narration, and his desires for the uses of the text, as well as his own assessments of its value, were also communicated.

If Sundkler's approach, as outlined above, is to be followed, the *Johera Narrative* can be properly handled only by giving serious regard to Ajuoga's intentions. It is thus necessary to identify and assess Ajuoga's clearly communicated intentions for his narrative, as well as their implications for the value and interpretation of the text. Arising from dialogue with Matthew Ajuoga, four dominant intentions for the *Johera Narrative* have been identified.

Recognition

Based on Matthew Ajuoga's clear statements given in interviews, as well as my vivid impressions resulting from my participation, it is clear that the *Johera Narrative* was narrated so that Ajuoga and the CCA could be more widely recognized. Ajuoga intends for the text to serve as a public relations tool, in order that his work and church should receive wider attention.

Matthew Ajuoga is more widely known and respected outside Kenya than he is within his homeland, with the exception of his home province of Nyanza.[10] Through Ajuoga's education in the United States, his wide and numerous travels, his ecumenical activities, and especially his leadership of the Organization of African Instituted Churches, his reputation as a leader among African Instituted Churches is widely recognized. However, within his own nation, Matthew Ajuoga is less known outside Nyanza and African Instituted Church circles.

Ajuoga's limited reputation is a direct result of his low profile in Kenya since independence. Chapter 5 will describe the general plight of the Nyanza Luo in independent Kenya, but here it is sufficient to note that Matthew Ajuoga has deliberately led a very private life since Kenya's independence. He has sought to avoid public attention, and consequently his lack of reputation in wider Kenya is not surprising.

Ajuoga has noted that, had he remained in the Anglican Church, he would certainly be better known in Kenya than is now the case.[11] He also believes that his efforts have borne fruits that at least equal those of his classmates from St. Paul's United Theological Seminary who remained with the "mainline" churches. He is proud of these achievements, and no sense of regret has been noted in my dialogue with Ajuoga. This being the case, it is not surprising that Matthew Ajuoga desires to be more widely known, especially in his own nation.

Even so, Matthew Ajuoga's intention for the *Johera Narrative* to assist him in achieving personal recognition is not the full story. He also desires that his church should receive the recognition it deserves. In the *Johera Narrative* Ajuoga boasts of the CCA's accomplishments in education, community health, and the advancement of women (pars. 265-285), and Ajuoga has just cause to feel a sense of accomplishment. Accordingly, he would like for these efforts to be duly recognized. From whom does Ajuoga desire recognition? It is clear that, having already established his own reputation and that of the CCA within African Instituted Church circles, he now seeks the recognition of those outside African Christian independency. More specifically, Ajuoga desires that he and his church be taken seriously within the broader

Christian community in Kenya. The *Johera Narrative* is intended to portray a growing, progressive, international denomination, that is every bit as "fit" to be recognized fully as the older, mission churches in Kenya.

Legitimacy

Closely related to Ajuoga's intention that the *Johera Narrative* should produce recognition, is the issue of legitimacy. It is clear to me that legitimization is one of the dominant themes found in the *Johera Narrative*, and this concern is discussed in Chapter 10. Here it is only necessary to note the presence and dominance of this intention, and consequently Ajuoga's search for legitimacy must be taken into account as the text is approached.

It must also be noted that what Ajuoga seeks is not primarily the production of legitimacy within his own mind or among the membership of the CCA.[12] Rather, as is the case with his desire for recognition, Ajuoga's concerns for legitimacy are focused on those outside African Instituted Church circles, where a generally negative view of AICs dominates. Even though African Instituted Churches have been the focus of Western academic and missiological attention for more than a generation, still in Kenya these communities are widely held in suspicion, even openly derided.

The myriad of reasons for this negative image cannot be discussed here, yet it is because of this situation that Matthew Ajuoga seeks to be considered as a legitimate "Christian" leader, and for the CCA to be viewed as a legitimate "Christian" Church. Ajuoga intends for the *Johera Narrative* to assist in his desire for outsiders to consider he and his work legitimate, and so to be accepted as legitimate members of the larger Christian community in Kenya.

Understanding

Directly related to Ajuoga's concerns for outside recognition and legitimacy are his intentions for understanding. To Matthew Ajuoga, outside recognition and legitimacy will result from understanding, and towards that end he narrates his *Johera Narrative*.

Matthew Ajuoga feels that African Instituted Churches have been misunderstood by almost everyone outside their communities. He acknowledges that the communities themselves are partially responsible for this misunderstanding, accordingly he believes that AICs should endeavour to promote understanding, and Ajuoga's own involvement in ecumenical pursuits must be viewed in this context.[13]

Ajuoga's intention to promote understanding by speaking for himself reflects the efforts of another group of African Instituted Churches already mentioned, who also desired to overcome the misunderstandings and misconceptions held by outsiders (African Spiritual Churches' Association 1985). The shared belief is that those outside African Instituted Church communities suffer from "serious handicaps" when they attempt to study these communities, and consequently if the communities are to be understood properly, in the contexts in which they understand themselves, then the churches must describe and explain themselves (Ngada 1985, 5).

Ajuoga desires to dispel the widely held views that he and the CCA are less than Christian,[14] and the *Johera Narrative* communicates his reasons for his community's orthodoxy, and the way in which he desires outsiders to understand himself and the CCA. Thus, Ajuoga's promotion of outside understanding emerges from the development of his own self-understanding.

Education

So far Matthew Ajuoga's intentions for his *Johera Narrative* have been identified in terms of those outside the CCA and African Instituted Church circles. His intentions for the text have been understood to be related to public relations, ecumenicism, and even mission. Ajuoga's concerns are largely external, targeting those outside the CCA.

Even so, Ajuoga has clearly communicated an additional and internal intention for his narrative, one which focuses on the CCA itself. At the earliest stages of my discussions with Matthew Ajuoga concerning the proposed *Johera Narrative* project, he related that he felt a great need to recount his experiences in a publicly accessible way. These feelings, he related, were because most of the "inner circle" during the formative stages of the CCA are now dead, and as he himself was growing older, if he did not record the story, it probably would never be preserved. Ajuoga's concern was to educate the membership, particularly the younger members, of their heritage. As the founder/leader of the church it was also appropriate that he be the one to produce the "official" version of the church's history. Ajuoga wanted the CCA members to be aware of their history, not merely from oral accounts or the versions produced by outsiders. He desired that the story be recorded by someone on the inside, someone who was a participant in all the most formative events in the church's history. Ajuoga's concern to educate his membership of their own history introduces the basic theme of identify formation which is woven throughout the *Johera Narrative*. This basic idiom employed by Ajuoga in his "God-Talk" is further discussed in Chapter 10, yet as we begin to approach the text, it is necessary to be aware of Ajuoga's intention to educate via Christian identity formation.

The general approach towards the *Johera Narrative* that has just been outlined was designed to move towards an inside understanding of the text. To do so, according to Sundkler, the author's intentions for the text must be considered. In order to determine Matthew Ajuoga's intentions for the text, research methods advocated by Harold Turner have been employed. This penetrating methodology will now be reviewed in order to highlight both its possibilities and limitations.

REVIEWING THE METHODOLOGY

The above discussion demonstrates that our methodology is concerned with subjectivity rather than objectivity. In the current academic climate it is widely acknowledged that objectivity does not exist. For example, it is now recognized that even within the traditionally perceived detached and unbiased study of history, subjectivity is necessarily involved.

> Here we need simply be reminded that in secular historiography as well as in the writing of church history the notion of objectivity has long since been recognized as an untenable fiction. The historian brings his own assumptions to his task, and the sooner he recognizes them the better (Gensichen 1976, 254).

Conversely, the previously perceived enemy of solid research—subjectivity—is not only now acknowledged as inevitable but also as indispensable. Particularly for investigating religious experience, subjectivity is regarded as essential. "Without the inevitable subjectivity of religious research, no human knowledge is possible" (A. Anderson 1995, 285).

Given such inevitability of subjectivity, we here acknowledge yet clarify our focus on subjectivity. Our purpose is to understand Matthew Ajuoga's religious subjectivity as narrated in his text, and accordingly our methodology is phenomenological and qualitative.[15] Our intention is to move "inside" the *Johera Narrative* to understand Matthew Ajuoga's religious testimony. This requires that we focus our attention on *what* Ajuoga says in his narrative, rather than upon disputes over his narration. We seek to understand Ajuoga's descriptions of his experiences rather than upon whether or not they were warranted. Thus, we intend to take Ajuoga at his word, to accept his perceptions as valid, and not enter into a debate on whether he had reason to perceive as he did. Given that actions result from what people believe rather than from what others think they should believe, only such an approach will illuminate Matthew Ajuoga's testimony of religious experience.

Within this methodological context we accept Ajuoga's perceptions as "fact" and "truth." In approaching the text I am aware of Ajuoga's production of history through a one-sided remembrance of actual events. Yet, I believe rather than reducing the value of his account, Ajuoga's subjectivity reflected in his narrative selectivity is extremely valuable. Indeed, it has been argued that "there are no `false' oral sources...[for] the diversity of oral history consists in the fact that `untrue' statements are still psychologically `true'..." (Portelli 1981, 100). We therefore accept the validity of what Matthew Ajuoga offers, convinced that his narrative expresses his "truth."

Moreover, the *Johera Narrative* is to a large degree a significant theological text because of its narration of these personal perceptions of reactions to missionary Christianity and broader historical events. The chronicles of colonial and mission history are now supplemented by one personal testimony of how these were experienced. Indeed, this perspective liberates Ajuoga's text so that it might make one of its most singular contributions. One of the greatest values of oral sources is their ability to communicate experiences of events rather than the actual order of events. "The first thing that makes oral history different...is that it tells us less about events as such than about their meaning." Oral sources "tell us not just what people did, but what they wanted to do, what they believed they were doing, [and] what they now think they did" (Portelli 1981, 99-100). By focusing on Matthew Ajuoga's perspective of events, we are able to trace his religious intentions and identify his fundamental concerns.

LIMITATIONS OF THIS STUDY

Given the study design that has just been presented, coupled with the realistic expectations of what can hoped to be accomplished in the following pages, this study proceeds with definite limitations.

Limitations of the Researcher: An Outsider

I have stated that my intention is to move towards an inside understanding of the *Johera Narrative*, to assess and interpret it in full awareness of the intentions of its author. Even so, it must be asked just how close can I hope to come to that goal of an intramural understanding? This question relates to my status as an outsider, hampered by my culture and experiences. Given such, how can I expect to achieve an inside understanding of the *Johera Narrative*?

It must be stated that throughout this study I have been fully aware of my limitations, yet I hope this study will be seen as what it professes to be: a pioneering study of a virgin text, not the final word on a text that has been widely analyzed over a long period of time. I cannot hope to gain the understanding of the *Johera Narrative* that is held by Matthew Ajuoga and those inside the CCA, but I can move *towards* such a position, and I am convinced that this process is also educative, and consequently worthy of our focus.

Moreover, I have again been instructed by Bengt Sundkler. After outlining his methods to move towards an intramural interpretation of Zulu Christian experience Sundkler concluded,

> And yet, I am fully conscious that my account does not reach the heart of the matter. I doubt whether any outsider can achieve that. However sympathetic an attitude the White observer may take, he remains--an outsider (Sundkler 1961, 16).

Likewise, the approach towards the *Johera Narrative* employed in this study is that of an outsider desiring to move inside, and while I am convinced of the necessity and value of that movement, my assessments and interpretations of Ajuoga's text reflect this status. While I hope to be able to speak *with* Matthew Ajuoga, I cannot speak *for* him.

Limitation of the Subject: Theological Studies in Africa

A second limitation of this study is related to its subject. Given the potential of the *Johera Narrative* as a scholarly source, it has been necessary to restrict the academic perspectives, methods, and resources utilized in this study. Because this study is concerned with African Christian experience, it will be limited to the perspectives of theological studies in Africa in its overall focus. While it is true that African Christian independency has been analyzed from a variety of academic disciplines, and even though it has been argued that African Instituted Churches can best be understood in their totality through multi-disciplinary approaches (Barrett 1971c and Fernandez 1978), this study is primarily concerned with the religious *qua* religious dimensions of Ajuoga's *Johera Narrative*.[16]

I am fully aware that in traditional African thought, life was understood to be unitary, and that it was impossible to separate the religious dimension of human experience from the social, political, or economic (Mbiti 1981, 10ff; 1989, 1ff). Indeed, Ogbu Kalu has argued that "in the African world, the religious is inextricably intertwined with the political, economic, ecological and other social forces" (Kalu 1993, 172). Even so, this study considers Matthew Ajuoga's *Johera Narrative* to be a text primarily about Christian experience, and its focus will consequently be theological, and this for three fundamental reasons.

First, in interpreting his narrative as essentially a theological text, I am being consistent with Matthew Ajuoga's own intentions for the text. Ajuoga, like many in a modern Africa that has been largely secularized, is able to divide his experiences into separate categories, and he identifies the religious dimension as the dominant theme in his text. Therefore, by focusing on the theological significance of the *Johera Narrative* I am not imposing a meaning on the text unrecognized by its author.

Second, even though African Instituted Churches have been analyzed using the materials and methods of various academic disciplines, such as the social sciences (Fernandez 1964 and Lanternari 1963) and history (Ranger and Kimambo 1972), it has been argued that African Christian independency is essentially a religious phenomenon, and can be best understood only when this fact is accepted.

Indeed, Harold Turner devoted much of his academic career to the religious study of African Instituted Churches, and he waged his own crusade for the recognition of African Christian independency as primarily a religious phenomenon. Turner's pioneering study (1967a & b) was a religious study, and Turner justified this approach by noting the importance of religion as a motivating force in Africa (1967a, xiv). His thesis was "that these movements [AICs] are fundamentally religious in nature, and must be so understood" (Turner 1967b, xiii).

In another place, speaking of African Instituted Churches, he argued that "it is essential that they be studied as Christian religious phenomena by means of the appropriate religious and theological disciplines" (Turner 1979, 35). Turner had enough experience with and respect for AICs to interpret them within the categories they had chosen for themselves—religious and Christian. This study accepts Turner's argument, and approaches the *Johera Narrative* as a text primarily about religious experience within an African Instituted Church.

Finally, this study is limited to a theological study of Matthew Ajuoga's *Johera Narrative*, because, based upon my own research, I am convinced that the text indeed is most significant as a source for theological inquiry. As a result of my participation and partnership with Matthew Ajuoga, I am persuaded that his basic goals, values, motivations, and orientation in life are theological, and to approach his text in any other way would be to mishandle it greatly. Over the years, Matthew Ajuoga has been accused of having various ignoble designs for his secession and subsequent activities, yet it seems illogical that if such perceptions were accurate, he should have continued on the course he set for himself in 1957. This study is based upon my desire to understand Ajuoga's text as he does, and so it would be inconsistent for me to fail to see the dominance and importance of the theological in Matthew Ajuoga's *Johera Narrative*.

These limitations, instead of restricting the quality of this study, will focus and direct our intention to move towards an inside understanding of Matthew Ajuoga's *Johera Narrative*. Accordingly, with our direction and methods so established, in the chapters which follow we begin listening to the "God-Talk" of an African Christian patriarch.

Chapter 3

Sources Available for the Study of the *Johera Narrative*

A multiplicity of sources are available for this study, and the different types of materials utilized is the subject of this chapter. The purpose here is not to list or describe every source; a complete list of sources is found in the reference list at the end of this study, and the uses of specific sources will become clear from the references. Rather, given the pioneering nature of this study, it is desirable to note and briefly evaluate the various types of sources employed.

The value of this chapter then, apart from its immediate purpose of explaining the materials used in completing this particular study, is that it denotes the types of sources available for the collection and presentation of personal faith stories for the study of African Christianity: a mixture of local and general, as well as oral and written sources. This chapter is also intended to provide a list and description of the sources available to future researchers who may also wish to study Matthew Ajuoga's *Johera Narrative*.

I have separated the sources available for this study into two categories: the principal source and the supplementary sources. Then, consistent with my concern for an inside understanding of the *Johera Narrative*, I have placed the supplementary sources into two groups: those emerging from inside and those originating outside the CCA.

THE PRINCIPAL SOURCE: THE JOHERA NARRATIVE

As stated in the Introduction, this purpose of this study is to demonstrate an effective collection and presentation of Matthew Ajuoga's *Johera Narrative*, and, consequently throughout, our focus will be upon the text itself. Ajuoga's narrative, therefore, is the principal source used in this study, and the one which provides the primary information for the assessments and interpretations that follow. However, in order to situate and interpret properly the *Johera Narrative* additional sources have been utilized. A description of these supplementary sources follows.

SUPPLEMENTARY SOURCES

Since the focus of this study is limited to Ajuoga's text itself, and since the concomitant methodology in assessing and examining the text is qualitative, the number of supplementary source materials I have consulted was limited.[1] The following list and description of materials includes those which have served to provide ancillary information for our study of Ajuoga's narrative. These sources are supplementary in the sense that they augment the understanding of Matthew Ajuoga's experiences as he relates them in his *Johera Narrative*.

Two broad categories of supplementary sources are identified: those originating from within the CCA, and those produced from outside.

Inside Supplementary Sources

In my attempt to move towards an intramural understanding of the *Johera Narrative*, I have relied upon supplementary materials emerging from within the CCA. Especially important for this study are Matthew Ajuoga's writings, with which I have compared his testimony presented in his narrative.

Matthew Ajuoga's Writings

In addition to the *Johera Narrative*, which is essentially an oral text, Matthew Ajuoga has written a number of materials during his lifetime, and I have consulted all of Ajuoga's writings that have been made available to me. One of the values of this project for Matthew Ajuoga has been that it has afforded reason and motivation for him to locate and collect his writings. I have served as the stimulus for these efforts, because I desired to consult Ajuoga's writings with his *Johera Narrative* for at least two reasons.

First, for comparative purposes, I desired to note the continuity and discontinuity in Ajuoga's thinking over the course of his lifetime; and second, for the purposes of understanding, I valued the elaboration and contextual information Ajuoga's writings could provide for my study of the *Johera Narrative*. Consequently, my concerns have prompted Matthew Ajuoga to appreciate anew his own productions.

Two types of written materials by Matthew Ajuoga have been located and utilized in this study: letters and one pamphlet.[2]

Letters

Not surprisingly for a Christian leader of his standing, Matthew Ajuoga has carried out a lively correspondence. Sadly however, most of his correspondence has been inaccessible for this study, either because of a failure to save it initially, because it cannot now be located, or because of Ajuoga's unwillingness to permit access. Even so, Ajuoga was able to locate and provide access to five of his early letters. These letters have been preserved and copied because Ajuoga himself realized their significance, and indeed they have proved valuable for this study.

The five letters are all from the crucial early period of Johera's existence, the period 1955-58, when that group's disillusionment and frustration with the Anglican leadership was first articulated and disseminated in written form. Ajuoga's first letter (1955) expresses his personal discontent concerning various issues related to the Anglican Church's training programs, while his letter to the Bishop of Mombasa (Ajuoga 1956a) questions the dismissal of Nathan Silas Awuor, a fellow cleric and leader of Johera. By July 1956 Ajuoga wrote concerning the Wahamaji, a revival inspired group which had left the Anglican Church in 1953 (Welbourn and Ogot 1966, 33-44), and in a later letter (1956b) he enumerated six unscriptural practices of that group. By 1958, after Johera's disillusionment and frustration had led to schism, Ajuoga wrote two letters to the Archbishop of Canterbury, G. F. Fisher. In his first (1958a) Ajuoga requested the Archbishop's blessings and assistance for the newly established CCA, and his second letter (1958b) was a reply to the Archbishop's letter (Fisher 1958) in which Ajuoga declared Johera's determination to proceed on their own.

These letters have provided helpful insight for this present study in two areas. First, they reveal both the depth and nature of Matthew Ajuoga's disillusionment with the Anglican leadership. They also reveal continuity in Ajuoga's concerns: the issues over which he expressed frustration in his letters are the same issues he focuses on almost forty years later in his *Johera Narrative*.[3]

The Light

In mid 1956, Matthew Ajuoga wrote a lengthy letter (1956c) addressed to the Vicar General of the Anglican Church in Nairobi. Ajuoga entitled his letter/pamphlet "The Light," and it provides a detailed list and explanation of Ajuoga's frustrations.[4] It is clear from this pamphlet that Ajuoga's difficulties were not with the Anglican Church as an institution, that is with its doctrines and traditions, but rather with the then current Anglican leadership. "The Light" then provides further insight into the content of Ajuoga's frustration, as well as an early example of his concerns for restitution and fidelity.[5]

Unstructured Interviews of Matthew Ajuoga

An especially valuable supplementary source utilized in this study was a series of "unstructured interviews" (Bogdan and Taylor 1975, 6ff) with Matthew Ajuoga. The purpose of these weekend sessions (Ajuoga 1993, 1994a, b, c) was twofold. First, these unstructured sessions provided insight into the daily life and perspectives of Matthew Ajuoga himself. Since Ajuoga's narrative is the focus of this study, it was necessary to begin to understand his daily life, and thus a general personal and biographical context in which to understand the *Johera Narrative* was approached in these interviews.

Second, these open sessions with Bishop Ajuoga helped me to address specific questions raised by my interactions with the *Johera Narrative*. Consistent with qualitative methodology, I was careful to avoid "leading" Ajuoga by introducing my agenda through direct questions, and I was, as well, careful not to encourage Ajuoga to question what he had previously narrated; I was interested in his original and "uncorrupted" text, not in his later revisions or his "second guesses."[6] Even though I had specific questions which I desired to be answered, I attempted to provide Ajuoga with the maximum freedom—both in terms of time and control—to provide answers in his time and intellectual and theological contexts. I was also open to accept whatever information Ajuoga offered, regardless of its immediate relevance to my own thinking.[7] Of all the supplementary sources employed in this study, these sessions with Matthew Ajuoga proved the most valuable.

Church of Christ in Africa-Johera Materials

A final supplementary source of information from inside Johera was a collection of miscellaneous materials produced by the CCA, the most significant of which are magazines of Nyanza Christian College (1976; 1984) and Regional Reports of the Central African Christian

Council (1975). These materials have proved valuable for my understanding of the nature and concerns of the CCA during the first twenty years of its existence.[8]

Outside Supplementary Sources

While the greatest attention in this study has been given to sources from inside Matthew Ajuoga's community, I have consulted relevant sources originating from outside the CCA, and these outside sources fall into four categories. Each will be described and evaluated below.

Archival Materials of the Church Missionary Society

This study is not intended to be one of missionary Christianity or mission history, and consequently, I have not desired to discover or recount the Church Missionary Society's "official" version of the CCA schism. In any event, this would have been impossible considering that the CMS archives for the period most crucial for this study, the 1950's and following, were not yet opened. Even so, the Church Missionary Society was the mission agency which brought to Nyanza the particular form of Anglicanism which Matthew Ajuoga accepted and to a large degree still practices, and accordingly CMS Anglicanism has been a crucial influence on Ajuoga's Christian spiritual formation. This legacy is examined in Chapter 6 below.

Because of this significance of the CMS for Ajuoga's text, I have consulted the Church Missionary Society's archives to situate and understand its influence on Matthew Ajuoga and his *Johera Narrative*. Of greatest value have been the documents related to the general policies of the CMS and its mission in Nyanza, specifically the official histories (Stock 1899, 1916; Hewitt 1971) and the relevant files for East Africa. These materials have been especially valuable in my assessment of the enduring impact of CMS-Anglicanism upon Ajuoga and his text, and of the difficulties he and Johera encountered with CMS personnel and policy in Nyanza (cf. Chapter 6).

Private Reflections and Letters

Due to the closure of the CMS archives for the period most crucial for this study, I was most eager to communicate with former CMS personnel in Kenya, individuals who may have known Matthew Ajuoga and who could provide valuable contextual information for understanding the *Johera Narrative*.

Unfortunately, however, I soon discovered that most of the principal CMS personalities named in the *Johera Narrative* are deceased, and others were either not located or were reluctant to offer assistance. I, therefore, have had access to few personal reflections from CMS personnel who were active in Nyanza in the 1950's, yet those I have obtained have been valuable.

Reflections of African Colleagues of Matthew Ajuoga

I have also sought the impressions of Matthew Ajuoga and his narrative from Ajuoga's colleagues, both within the CCA and within the OAIC. I initially was desirous of communicating with African Christian patriarchs, such as Meshack Owira, who had known Ajuoga from the earliest years and who obviously disagreed with him, yet I was unable. Owira and most others are now deceased, while still others were unavailable.

Even so, I have gathered many impressions of Ajuoga from within the CCA and the OAIC. Because my informants wished to remain anonymous—and so I suspect their candidness—these impressions have been especially valuable in understanding the man and Christian leader, Matthew Ajuoga.

Insights Gained from Participant Observation

The personal reflections from Matthew Ajuoga's colleagues within the CCA and the OAIC have been obtained from my participant observation of both communities. Above I have described the weekend open interview sessions I conducted with Matthew Ajuoga, yet these sessions also included wider participant observation at Ajuoga's home, Dala Hera, Kisumu. During these visits I was able to observe Ajuoga in his normal daily routines, and I was able to participate in some of his activities. I have also made numerous visits to the OAIC office in Nairobi, and have attended a number of their formal programs. Through these I was able to observe Matthew Ajuoga at work outside the CCA and away from Dala Hera.

I have utilized participant observation, however, as simply one source of information among the others that I have described. Because this study is based upon data received through other means, specifically via the *Johera Narrative* itself, the insights gained from participant observation are meant to be supplementary and not principal sources. I have employed participant observation merely to assist in providing contextual data for understanding the *Johera Narrative*.

Moreover, because this study seeks to move towards an inside understanding of Matthew Ajuoga's narrative, I have relied most heavily upon sources which could assist in this intent. Even though my participant observation has brought me into intense social interaction with Matthew Ajuoga and his communities, and so in a sense I have been given an "inside" glimpse of Matthew Ajuoga's world, still these are my own perceptions of Ajuoga's reality. Consequently, I consider them to be outside sources. Because this study seeks to describe and understand Matthew Ajuoga's own experiences as he has narrated them, my personal observations are important, yet of limited and merely supplementary value.

Monographs

A vast number of monographs have been helpful in the completion of this study, and these are listed in the appended reference list. Even so, two monographs need to be specifically mentioned here because both contain studies of Matthew Ajuoga and Johera, and consequently, they have been especially valuable for this study.

A Place to Feel at Home

F. B. Welbourn and B. A. Ogot's *A Place to Feel at Home* (1966) is the first and most detailed study of Johera to date, even though only one-half of the volume—barely seventy-one pages—is devoted to this topic. The purpose of this volume is to introduce two cases of African Christian independency from Kenya, based on the assumption that the story of African history "must be written as a story no longer of European adventure but of African experience" (Welbourn and Ogot 1966, viii). The book describes and examines the causes for the rise of the Church of Christ in Africa-Johera and the African Israel Church Nineveh. As is the case with all pioneering efforts, Welbourn and Ogot's study provides a necessary beginning by mapping the uncharted, yet it fails to provide a comprehensive assessment.

The Kenyan Luo historian, B. A. Ogot, wrote most of the section relating to the CCA, and his purpose was primarily historical rather than theological. His is an attempt to examine the historical factors in Nyanza which led to the CCA schism, and it was not meant to be a description or examination of the CCA itself. So, while the focus of the book is on African experience, it is not religious or theological experience, but rather the more general historical experience which is emphasized. Consequently, this volume has been of limited value for this study because of its lack of insight into the religious experiences of Johera or Matthew Ajuoga. In fact, Ogot's conclusions as to the reasons for the schism, namely the significance of tribalism (Welbourn and Ogot 1966, 40), reflect an all too common reductionism of the complex issues involved in this mostly religious controversy.

Even so, *A Place to Feel at Home* has been an extremely valuable source of background information necessary to complete this study.

Welbourn and Ogot have been very thorough in their historical chronicle of the CCA schism, particularly in the gathering of names, dates, and in the narration of events. This data has provided a foundation from which to begin my own research, as well as offering a version of events with which I could compare Ajuoga's perspective.

Schism and Renewal in Africa

Besides Welbourn and Ogot's study, the only other volume which offers a specific discussion of Matthew Ajuoga and Johera at any length is David B. Barrett's, Schism and Renewal in Africa (1968). Even so, Barrett devotes only fifteen pages to his analysis of Johera,[9] and he does so only to illustrate his thesis concerning the general causes of African Christian independency.

According to Barrett's theory, now widely discounted as too simplistic and general, certain African ethnic groups are more prone to Christian independency because of the presence of certain socio-historical and religious factors (Barrett 1968, 109). These factors form a tribe's zeitgeist, which is "the socio-religious climate of opinion favouring independency, protest or renewal in a given tribe at a given time" (Barrett 1968, 110). In the context of this theory, Barrett considers the Kenya Luo, the tribe of Matthew Ajuoga, to be extremely high on this scale, and so it is not surprising that so many AICs should have been formed among them.[10] Mostly because its approach is primarily sociological and now dated, Barrett's volume has been of only limited value for this study. However, Barrett provides necessary contextual information relating to the traditional culture of the Kenya Luo, Christian innovations among that tribe, and basic interpretations concerning the rise of Johera. These have been helpful in forming our discussions in Chapter 7. In addition, in spite of Barrett's caricatural portrayal of the Luo, he has provided a challenging mixture of fact and theory that has stimulated my thinking throughout this study.

The above categories of sources have been accessed in completing this study. Their mixture of local and general, oral and written, as well as inside and outside perspectives, have provided a montage through which I have approached my study of Matthew Ajuoga's *Johera Narrative*. By utilizing such a large and diverse collection of source materials, the danger of producing a myopic study through reliance upon "a limited repertoire" (Bodgan and Taylor 1975, 125) has been minimized.

Chapter 4

The Gestation of the *Johera Narrative*

In order to appreciate fully Matthew Ajuoga's *Johera Narrative*, it is necessary to understand the development of the text, that is, the gestation process through which the text was conceived and transmitted. The purpose of this chapter, therefore, is to describe the transmission of the text by identifying four gestational stages and the concomitant procedures which have led to the formation of Matthew Ajuoga's *Johera Narrative* in the form it appears in Appendix 1 of this study.

Besides providing necessary background information for the version of the text that is presented and examined in this study, this chapter also demonstrates a methodology for the consideration of future researchers also interested in recording personal religious histories within African Instituted Churches.

FOUR STAGES OF GESTATION

The first section of this chapter will focus on the formative stages through which the *Johera Narrative* passed in order to appear in its present form (Appendix 1).

Preparation

To use an apt Scriptural phrase, Matthew Ajuoga's *Johera Narrative* was born "in the fullness of time" (Galatians 4:4). The text's gestation occurred only after many years of preparation, both in the life of the narrator, Matthew Ajuoga, and of myself, the external human stimulus.

Matthew Ajuoga offered his in-depth and unmediated narrative in his sixty-seventh year, after the passing of thirty-six years of Johera history. This was the case, not because Ajuoga had never before been asked to relate his experiences, but because until 1993 Ajuoga himself was not ready; he was not sufficiently convinced that the "fullness of time" had come for him to offer his testimony to a broader, public forum. Based upon my conversations with Matthew Ajuoga, 1993 represented the "fullness of time" for his narration due to a mixture of factors, including personal and internal convictions coupled with external circumstances.

Wyatt MacGaffey has noted the difficulties members of African Instituted Churches face in "speaking for themselves" (MacGaffey 1969, 129-130). Likewise, Matthew Ajuoga delayed his narration largely due to obstacles which were a direct result of his role as the leader of a marginalized and misunderstood religious community. By his own admission, during the early history of Johera, Ajuoga was struggling to avert the community's enemies. Because his early energies were expended on shear ecclesiastical survival, Ajuoga did not have the leisure time nor the mental space required to reflect upon and narrate at length his Christian experiences. However, by 1993 Ajuoga felt his own reputation as well as Johera's existence was secure enough to provide him the opportunity to tell his story. Accordingly, 1993 represented the "fullness of time" in terms of Ajuoga's perceptions of his opportunity to redirect his attention from external concerns to historical and theological reflection.

A second factor which led Ajuoga to offer his story when he did was related to his advanced age,[1] and it has been observed that it is "mortality which gives the collection of oral history its singular urgency" (Isichei 1977, 7). Realizing this, Matthew Ajuoga has more than once stated that, because most of Johera's patriarchs and matriarchs are now dead, he is among the few remaining who could tell their complete story. Ajuoga is concerned that the history of the CCA be preserved in detail, and because he is perhaps the only living person who has been a participant in all phases of Johera's development, he felt a certain urgency and responsibility to relate his story while the opportunity still existed.

Finally, and again because of his advanced age, it was culturally appropriate for Matthew Ajuoga to play the role of *griot* and narrate his experiences only in later life.[2] In Luo culture it is the responsibility of the elders to instruct the young, in part through story-telling. The elders preserve and perpetuate the traditions of the people, and conversely it is the responsibility of the young to listen and learn.[3] By his sixty-seventh year Matthew Ajuoga was accepted as an elder, and he was consequently expected to tell stories, to preserve and perpetuate the traditions of his people, Johera. For him to have done so much earlier would have not only violated tradition, but more importantly ensured that his story would have had less communal appeal and authority.

The "fullness of time" for the *Johera Narrative* arrived in 1993 also in relation to my own readiness to act as the external human stimulus for the text's narration. The "birth" of the *Johera Narrative* came after at least ten years of preparation in my own experience with African Instituted Churches. Even if Matthew Ajuoga had been prepared to recount his story earlier, and even if I had encouraged his narration before, I am convinced Ajuoga would have refused to cooperate with me. Given the suspicions of most African Instituted Churches towards outsiders—especially white missionaries—without a high degree of credibility, I would have been considered unsuitable as a partner to whom the *Johera Narrative* could be entrusted. However, by 1993 I had ministered among AICs for eight years, and given the nature of my interaction, Ajuoga was willing to accept me as a trustworthy repository for his narrative. Just as Matthew Ajuoga had been prepared by the passing of time to recount his story, so I too was prepared to receive it.[4]

Stimulation

Almost thirty years ago, Richard Gray argued that if serious studies of the African contributions to Christianity were to be carried out, the encouragement and stimulation of external researchers would be necessary.

> If this dimension is to be studied at all adequately, a large-scale operation is an immediate priority...and the efforts...to encourage the preservation of Church records and private papers should be intensified. For if...the oral sources remain unrecorded, the essential evidence will soon be lost, and the possibility of a balanced understanding of...Christianity in Africa will disappear (Gray 1968, 27).

Because Gray was well informed about the nature of sources for the study of African Christianity, both human and written, he realized that directed outside efforts would be needed to ensure their preservation.

Twenty years later, the International Association for Mission Studies recommended that its members become actively involved in stimulating the preservation of local Christian histories.

> It is recommended that IAMS members take seriously... the recognition, gathering and utilization of Christian oral tradition and oral theology, everywhere, in all their forms, because this is the basic expression of the response of the people of God to the Gospel in the local situation (International Association for Mission Studies 1988, 153).

The US-American mission leader John R. Mott went even further, arguing that missionaries had a responsibility to assist in the creation of local Christian stories.

> It is a Christian, that is, a missionary *obligation* to collect, preserve, and protect the available data so that when the 'younger churches' begin to be interested in their own pre-history, this documentation is available (quoted in Irvine 1976, 189-190).

This same responsibility has been more recently echoed by H. L. Pretorius (1995, 53ff).

In sympathy with these understandings of the need for the outside researcher to act as a stimulus for the preservation of local Christian histories, I approached Matthew Ajuoga in early 1993 and suggested that he record his testimony. I also asked his permission to allow me access to his narration for my own academic interests. To my surprise Ajuoga agreed to cooperate, yet later I realized that my stimulation and encouragement for the project had been crucial in the formation of his decision.

In spite of Matthew Ajuoga's internal and cultural convictions that by 1993 the "fullness of time" had come for him to recount his story, he was nevertheless hesitant. His reluctance arose primarily from time constraints which led him to question if the recording of his story was worth the necessary expenditure of time. In order to overcome his doubts, Ajuoga required an external and personal stimulus, one who could gain his trust and convince him of the necessity of recounting his testimony. I was able to win not only his confidence, but also encourage him to make the investment of time and effort necessary to complete the *Johera Narrative*. Without this external stimulus Ajuoga may never have produced his testimony for a wider audience.

Narration

Matthew Ajuoga began the actual work of narration in November 1993, after we had spent a weekend together at his home. During our discussions I not only encouraged him to begin his narrative, but I also related that I felt he should tell his story as *he* believed it should be told. Ajuoga was, at first, uncomfortable with this lack of imposed structure, and he asked if I would not rather interview him, or at least tell him where to begin and how to proceed. He related that all the other researchers who had approached him in the past had suggested these methods.

However, I was firmly convinced that only a qualitative approach could best ensure the "purest" narration and appropriation of his experiences, and consequently I suggested that Ajuoga should simply recount his story as *he* wanted to tell it: starting from the point at which he believed the story began, treating the events and issues he considered formative, and provide as much detail as he deemed important. He only reluctantly agreed, yet he eventually came to appreciate the freedom to finally recount his story in such a complete and unmediated manner.

Because I desired his unmediated story and thus wanted to exert as little influence as possible, at the end of our November meeting I left with Ajuoga a small cassette recorder, an ample supply of fresh batteries, and several blank cassettes. Realizing his hectic daily schedules, and also understanding that he could most effectively narrate only during his few leisure periods, I encouraged him to record his narrations at his convenience. Even so, I suggested that he attempt to be finished telling his story by the following April.

Due to his very demanding daily routine Ajuoga was not able to complete his narration by April, yet again I was careful to affirm and encourage him without wanting to influence the form or contents of the narrative itself. In June 1994 Ajuoga contacted me to say that he had finally completed his story, and the next and final phase of the gestation of the *Johera Narrative* began.

Presentation

Matthew Ajuoga had filled nine hours of tape with his narration, and in late June 1994, I initiated the processes which would transform

Ajuoga's tapes into a written text that could be presented for deeper and wider examination. For these processes I secured the assistance of two Kenya Luo assistants, both final year undergraduates at Daystar University, and both approved for this service by Ajuoga himself.[5]

By early August 1994 Ajuoga's tapes had been transcribed and translated from Dholuo to English, and the written text was then passed to Ajuoga for his editing. I related to Ajuoga that he should not concern himself with the grammar, spelling, or sentence structure of the text, but rather concentrate on the contents. I wanted to ensure that the written text accurately expressed Ajuoga's original oral narration, so Ajuoga's editing was crucial. By late September 1994 Ajuoga had completed his editorial efforts, and the text was then given to me with his approval; he was convinced of its accuracy, and he sanctioned its public presentation.

Upon receipt of Ajuoga's approved written text, I began the arduous task of further editing to "clean up" the text. Two concerns were primary: I desired that the text be made more readable without fatally jeopardizing its orality or its meaning; and, the text needed to be divided into smaller units to facilitate its examination. In these efforts I have been guided by accepted procedures for the editing of oral texts, and specific details of my editorial methodologies and concerns are discussed in the following section.

Through these four stages the *Johera Narrative* was born. Like all births, the text's current form reflects a procession through crucial phases. Moreover, the development of Matthew Ajuoga's oral narration into its present, written form (Appendix 1) was a process born of necessity, yet it was not without hesitation and a degree of remorse. The very act of reducing an oral account into a written document is a compromise between the desire to protect the essential vitality of the text's orality and the need to preserve the text for posterity and a wider audience. Consequently, while this section has focused on the *stages* of the oral text's transformation into written form, the *procedures* of transmission, which forged this compromise, are also of crucial significance.

PROCEDURES OF TRANSMISSION

Our discussion of the transmission of the *Johera Narrative* here will first present the guiding objectives, then the methodologies employed and problems encountered will be described. Because it is believed that "the preparation of a good collection of sources is as much a part of the historian's craft as a printed publication" (Curtin 1968, 371), and because "the historical method essentially consists of gathering as well as interpreting data" (Pretorius 1995, 53), this focus on the actual transmission of the *Johera Narrative* is a crucial part of this study.

General Objectives

Matthew Ajuoga's *Johera Narrative* is essentially a personal reminiscence and the acquisition and use of this particular genre of material as a scholarly source is problematic. The difficulties in employing personal reminiscence are summarized in an excellent article by the historian of Africa, Terence Ranger, who lists three problems that often arise when accessing life histories: romanticism, manipulation, and authenticity (Ranger 1978, 46-47, 56). Because these potential difficulties are directly related to the transmission of life histories,[6] and especially because they can jeopardize the validity of studies based upon personal reminiscences, I have attempted to avoid these extremes in the transmission of the *Johera Narrative*.

Consequently, the opposites of these three common abuses of personal reminiscence listed by Ranger express the general objectives which have governed the transmission procedures employed for the *Johera Narrative*. These general objectives will be stated and discussed in three sets of opposites, thus highlighting the tension present throughout the transmission process. In addition, these sets identify the transmissive qualities that were solicited, and the abuses that were to be avoided.

Realism not Romanticism

A common abuse of life history material in scholarly enquiry is the tendency to romanticize. Ranger notes that in African history personal reminiscences have most often been used in the formation of revisionist accounts, that is, to recount versions that either have not yet been told, or to retell stories that have been mis-told. Consequently, those who utilize personal reminiscences commonly tend to romanticize both the narrators and the narratives, portraying each in an unbalanced and even gratuitous light. In such cases, one extreme is simply replaced by another, for while these inaccurate portrayals may serve the purposes of the researchers, they fail to accept objectively the narrators and their narratives for exactly whom and what they are (Ranger 1978, 46-47).

In this study's formation and presentation of the *Johera Narrative*, I have sought balance, attempting to avoid romanticizing Matthew Ajuoga and his text. Ajuoga is viewed for what he is: an African Christian patriarch who is greatly respected by some, yet who also has many antagonists. Admittedly, this balanced view has been difficult to obtain and maintain, given my personal admiration for Ajuoga. Yet, my use of a montage of sources for this study, including many who hold very different views from my own, has assisted in de-romanticizing Ajuoga. Even though Ajuoga presents himself and his church in an extremely complimentary fashion, I have attempted to understand why this is so, and interpret the *Johera Narrative* accordingly.

I have also battled against romanticizing the *Johera Narrative* itself, and this relates to two particular issues. First, I have attempted to avoid overemphasis of the orality of Ajuoga's text. The importance of oral materials for both African history and theology are commonly accepted,[7] and there seems to be in some circles a tendency to romanticize oral sources as somehow being "purer" and closer to the "heart" of issues than are written materials.[8] Given this intellectual climate, especially in the field of oral theology,[9] it is tempting to belabour the orality of the *Johera Narrative*. Even though Ajuoga's narrative first existed in oral form, still Ajuoga recorded his narration knowing and desiring that it would be written. While this fact does not diminish the value of the text, it does limit the degree to which Ajuoga's narrative can be lauded and interpreted as a purely oral text.

Secondly, I have struggled against romanticizing Ajuoga's text simply because it was born from African Christian independency, and because it narrates religious experience within an African Instituted Church. Among scholars of African Christian independency there often exists such a tendency, a predisposition which often regards African Instituted Churches as somehow more "African," and thus more "authentic" than "mission" churches.[10]

Although I have great sympathy for African Instituted Churches, still I have attempted to examine Ajuoga and the CCA fully aware of their significant contributions, yet also recognizing their shortcomings. While it can be argued that African Christian independency preserves certain aspects of historic African culture, it can also be argued that African Instituted Churches are especially prone to certain excesses. These immoderations are not simply limited to the much discussed struggle with syncretism, but, as in Ajuoga's case, they are extended to include preoccupations with self, reflected in obsessions with legitimacy and vindication. With these excessive tendencies in full view, I have attempted to examine the *Johera Narrative* realistically, struggling to avoid romantic notions of the text's value.

Freedom not Manipulation

A second pitfall often encountered when dealing with personal reminiscence is that of manipulation of the narrator and the resultant account. Again, Terence Ranger has noted this danger, arguing that commonly researchers—often unknowingly—exert various types of pressure on their informants in order to gain the desired information. He also warns that individual narratives can be manipulated, so that the researcher records or utilizes only that part of an account which supports the investigator's predispositions (Ranger 1978, 46ff). Because of this manipulation, the informants are prohibited from telling their own story, their complete story, or the story as they wish to tell it. Essentially, in such a situation the narrators simply serve to validate the researcher's biases, and the story-tellers are viewed as mere objects to be controlled, not subjects to whom narrative license should be granted.

Rather than seeking to manipulate Matthew Ajuoga into telling the story I wanted told, I was careful to extend to him the freedom to tell his own story, as he wanted it told, and ultimately even to allow him to determine freely the final version that was to be used in this study. This was accomplished by employing qualitative methods in the initial recording of the *Johera Narrative*, and was then reinforced by Ajuoga's free participation in all the subsequent transmissive processes.

As noted earlier, Ajuoga was initially uncomfortable with this freedom, and he first requested that I change my approach. However, because I had no desire to restrict his license to speak and compose as he desired, I resisted, and was able to convince him that I had no wish to manipulate him or his account through the use of questionnaires or even structured interviews. These approaches tend to minimize the input of the narrator which encourages manipulation by the researcher.

Because my objective was Ajuoga's complete freedom, my personal involvement in the first three stages of transmission was minimized. Consequently, the version of the *Johera Narrative* that forms the basis of this study is the result of Matthew Ajuoga's unhindered—yet not unaided—narration, transcription, translation, and editing.

Authenticity not Inaccuracy

A final general objective which guided the entire transmission of the *Johera Narrative* was authenticity, the third difficulty Ranger notes in relation to the uses of personal reminiscences (Ranger 1978, 46ff). I endeavored to ensure that the resultant text would indeed reflect Ajuoga's story in all its aspects: its beginning and ending points, its structure, style, contents, and even its idiomatic usage of English were all preserved and presented.

However, this concern for authenticity required a struggle with certain temptations. How closely should I edit the text, even after Ajuoga's emending? Should I rearrange the text topically to facilitate examination? Ajuoga's account is often repetitious; should I not delete all but the first narrations of repeated segments? These and others were temptations to seek the cleanliness of the text, yet they would have sacrificed accuracy and authenticity.[11] Authenticity would have been compromised because the resultant text would not truly be Ajuoga's, and inaccuracies would have been created through the introduction of external organizational and interpretative devices.

Four Transmissive Processes

The above mentioned general objectives guided the transmission of the *Johera Narrative*, and it now remains to note how these objectives were realized in the four transmissive processes of recording, transcription, translation, and editing. Each will be discussed, and the specific transmissive objectives, the particular methodologies employed, and the peculiar problems encountered will be summarized.

Recording[12]: Specific Objectives

Matthew Ajuoga desired to tell his story, and as the external stimulus my role was merely to "give a voice" (Plummer 1983, 1) to Ajuoga's intentions by assisting him in the recording of his narrative, so preserving it and facilitating its wider distribution.

Three specific recording objectives were dominant in eventually determining the particular method of recording employed. First, my concern was to allow Ajuoga maximum freedom to tell his story with minimal external input.[13] Second, because I was aware of my responsibilities as a collector and presenter of an oral text, I desired to employ methods which would produce a text that would have the greatest value for future researchers.[14] Third, given Ajuoga's age and demanding daily schedule, I was required to adopt a recording method which would make the greatest use of Ajuoga's infrequent and scarce leisure hours, and at the same time make allowance for Ajuoga's fading aptitude for "quick recall" (Henige 1982, 112).

Methods

The recording method which would incorporate these specific objectives was one widely used in the collection of oral sources in Africa,[15] and one which is recommended by Philip Curtin, a leading historian of Africa (Curtin 1968, 376ff). This method involves giving the informant a recording device, and allowing him/her to make the recordings on their own schedules, in private or in the company of only those whom they choose to be present.

Matthew Ajuoga, therefore, was given a small cassette recorder, and he was encouraged to record his testimony how and when he desired. All his recordings were made in private, usually alone, but sometimes in the company of his wife. This method allowed Ajuoga to organize his thoughts before the actual recordings, and he often wrote a basic outline of the events and issues he desired to narrate. Additionally, this method granted Ajuoga time and mental space so that his narrative might include his prolonged and organized retrospective reflections. The contents, style, and schema of the *Johera Narrative* thus reflects the recording methodology employed.

Problems

While the recording method employed minimized the most common problem of manipulation, still other problems were encountered in the recording phase of transmission. Some were of a technical nature, and were related to the operation of the recording equipment. Others were more practical, and concerned Ajuoga's readiness and time pressures.

The problem which most influenced the ultimate contents and style of the *Johera Narrative*, however, was Ajuoga's concern that his story be clear and well-organized. This concern resulted in his desire to re-record his narrative at certain points, because he believed the initial telling had not been sufficiently lucid. Because stories change over time, with each new telling (Bruner 1986b, 145ff), Ajuoga was therefore tempted to tell several stories instead of one.[16] His concern for textual cleanliness endangered textual authenticity by anticipating imported expectations. Consequently, he was advised to record his story only once, to resist doubting the lucidity of his original narration, and to refrain from anticipating the questions and concerns of outsiders. Ajuoga was, essentially, again encouraged to tell his story in his way.

A further challenge concerned the specific language Matthew Ajuoga would use in his recording. Like most Kenyans, Matthew Ajuoga is trilingual: he uses his mother tongue, Dholuo, in most local and familial settings; he speaks Kiswahili, Kenya's national language; and, he is fluent and comfortable using English, Kenya's official language. Potentially, Ajuoga could have used any of these three languages for his original recording, and he was given complete freedom to choose which he desired.

Matthew Ajuoga finally decided to narrate his story primarily in his mother tongue, Dholuo. However, he also narrated certain sections (e.g., pars. 1-15) in standard English, and often he would mix the vernacular with idiomatic English (see par. 15). This use of English and the vernacular, even within the same sentence, is common in modern Kenya, where a local pidgin is often used in relaxed settings. Ajuoga explained the use of this medium by highlighting the fact that many Johera would be unable to understand his story if it was not transmitted in Dholuo.[17] He also noted that his story was primarily "a Luo story," for it involved mostly the Luo, and so it should first be recounted in their language. Additionally, Ajuoga argued that the *Johera Narrative*, although recounted by one individual, was nevertheless essentially a communal narrative. It was meant to be the story of all *Johera*, and this intention reflects Ajuoga's understanding of corporate rather than private history.

Consequently, Matthew Ajuoga recorded his *Johera Narrative* in Dholuo, first preserving and disseminating his account for those who speak that language. Ajuoga's use of the vernacular additionally preserved and even revived that language, especially a particular usage of that language, for future generations whose understanding and use of the vernacular will be distinctly altered.

Transcription: Specific Objectives

After Matthew Ajuoga had recorded nine hours of narration, following his repeated confirmations that he was indeed finished with his story, and after making a set of backup copies of the tapes, the next process to be carried out was the transcription of the tapes into a written text. This process was required if the *Johera Narrative* was to be preserved and made available for a wider audience.

Three specific objectives determined the methods employed for the transcription of the text. The first objective resulted from time pressures, and required that the evolution from tape to written text be achieved as quickly as possible. However, a second objective, accuracy, required that the concern for time efficiency not jeopardize the exactness of the text; and, third, the objective of authenticity demanded that the transcribed text faithfully and correctly reproduce Ajuoga's recordings.

Methods

In order to realize these specific objectives, the transcription of the *Johera Narrative* was carried out carefully. In order to expedite the transcription as quickly as possible, the assistance of two Kenyan Luo assistants was secured.[18] These two worked on the transcription simultaneously, each concentrating on different tapes, and at the end of two months the process was completed; thus the objective of time efficiency was achieved.

Because "transcription is invention" (Portelli 1981, 97), because it was recognized that a written text can never replace a taped recording,[19] and yet because it was desired that the transcription be accurate, the transcribers were directed to reproduce exactly on paper what was recorded on tape. They were instructed to make a direct, word for word transcription, accomplishing the "first-line" in the "three- line system" commonly used in the collection of oral materials (Curtin 1968, 381). This required that punctuation marks, sentence structures, and paragraphing be introduced only when absolutely necessary for understanding. If possible, all hesitations and discernible emotions were also to be noted in the text, and these instructions were faithfully carried out by the two assistants.

Authenticity required that Matthew Ajuoga himself proofread the transcriptions, and he was encouraged to correct all inaccuracies. Because of Ajuoga's unhindered involvement and oversight during the entire transcription process, minimal compromises relating to the authenticity of the written text were conceded.

Problems

Apart from the common difficulties of transcription related above, two additional problems were encountered. The first related to the changing nature of the vernacular used as the initial medium for the *Johera Narrative*. Because Matthew Ajuoga first narrated in his mother tongue, Dholuo, the transcription was done in that language. However, even though the two transcribers were themselves native speakers of Dholuo, still their knowledge of the language was two generations removed from Ajuoga's. Consequently, the transcribers often encountered "classical" vernacular vocabulary and syntax which they could not transcribe. Usually the transcribers understood the basic meanings of the classical usages, yet the spellings were unclear. These problems, often humorous, reflect the differences in generational understandings of the language, yet they also underline the dynamic popular functionalism of the vernacular. Even so, these difficulties were resolved during Ajuoga's proofreading, as he would either make the necessary corrections from memory, or would consult his age-mates or the proper linguistic reference tools.

A final difficulty encountered, one perhaps unique to a study containing delicate information relating to an African Instituted Church, involved the possession, distribution, and eventual placement of the tapes and transcripts. Matthew Ajuoga was concerned that the materials should be used—at least initially—only for this project, and consequently he was adamant that they should remain his property. He agreed to allow me and the two transcribers access, and he also agreed that one set of backup copies of the tapes could be made. However, as soon as the transcribers and I were finished with the taped and written accounts, Ajuoga required that they be returned to him for safe-keeping. Ajuoga argued that these materials were not simply his private property, but ultimately they belonged to all Johera; they were not merely "his," but perhaps primarily "theirs." Obviously, Ajuoga's wishes were granted: his materials were not shown to anyone apart from we three researchers, and they were returned to his possession as soon as possible.[20]

Translation: Specific Objectives

After the Dholuo transcription of the *Johera Narrative* was completed, it was necessary to translate the written text into English. This was desirable in order that the text could be more easily examined by a wider audience. The translation of the *Johera Narrative* was guided by the same concerns for accuracy and authenticity that have already been noted. In addition, another objective was sought, namely that the English text might be understandable to those with little knowledge of the local context from which the *Johera Narrative* emerged, and to those who would not understand the literary styles of either the vernacular or Kenyan English. The goal, then, was that

> it should not be a fully literary translation that conveys the fullest possible sense of the original meaning to readers of the Western language. It is, rather, a translation that is grammatically correct and says as nearly as possible exactly what the original says (Curtin 1968, 381).

Methods

These objectives were realized by carrying out the remaining "two-lines" of the "three-line system" recommended for transcribing and translating oral materials. This called for, first, a literal English translation for each Dholuo word, and then for this overly awkward literal text to be translated into grammatically correct English, preserving the literal meaning, but not the literal wording, of the vernacular original (Curtin 1968, 381).

This method of translation was once more completed by the two Kenyan Luo assistants. After completing their literal, then basic, literary translations, these were given to Matthew Ajuoga for his proofreading. Because of his high degree of English fluency, Ajuoga was able to correct effectively all inaccuracies, preserving the correctness and authenticity of the English version which was handed to me for final editing.[21]

Problems

It is conceded that, in spite of the safeguards noted above, the English versions of the *Johera Narrative* cannot fully convey the emotions, nuances, and general richness of the original vernacular narration. Just as written texts cannot completely replace oral narrations, so, too, are translations limited linguistic vehicles at best. The most that can be hoped for is that the greatest part of the essential value of the oral originals will be preserved in translation, and this risk is necessarily taken for the sake of wider accessibility of the text.

For this study the problem of the inadequacy of translation, however, was depreciated through the applied linguistic abilities of Matthew Ajuoga. Curtin has noted that the ideal situation is for an oral informant to be fluent in the language with the widest distribution possibilities (Curtin 1968, 368-369), and even though Ajuoga originally spoke in the vernacular, still he was himself able to correct the English translation. Because of his formal academic studies in Kenya and the U. S., Ajuoga is fluent and very comfortable using the English language.[22] He was, therefore, able to skillfully correct the English translation of his *Johera Narrative*, and eventually sanction it as suitably conveying his vernacular original. Ajuoga's high degree of English language ability thus minimized the need for the linguistic assistance of myself and the two research assistants, at least in regards to forging an authentic translation.

Editing: Specific Objectives

Perhaps the only universally agreed upon premise of oral literature is that oral materials are essentially different from written sources. Beyond that, however, scholars differ widely in their views of the specific methods and mechanics to be applied for the collection of oral materials. This diversity of opinion is especially acute in relation to the editing of oral materials, where a lack of universal agreement exists concerning the role of the editor of an oral text (Allen 1982, 33-35). Should the editor seek a "clean" text, similar to that of most written materials, or should the researcher "resist the editorial ego" (Allen 1982), and make only those changes which would "enhance the reader's awareness of what was actually said" (Allen 1982, 35)? More succinctly, should the researcher "edit a lot or edit a little" (Allen 1982, 39)?

Despite this diversity of opinion regarding the editing of oral materials, there is a general consensus that the objective of the editor of an oral text should be accuracy and not grammatical or literary cleanliness (Allen 1982). The aim is to introduce "the least possible tampering with the primary source" (Yow 1994, 238), and the editor must simply seek to enhance the clarity and accuracy of the text, and not over-edit by introducing unwarranted changes (Hoopes 1979, 115). In short, the editor must recognize that oral materials

> ...exist within an oral mode of thought which, regardless of how irrational it may appear to us, is rational and coherent when understood on its own terms. The task of the historian is not to prune away what we see as irrational, leaving what we judge to be rational, but to accept the whole as rational within a mode of thought that is different from ours, and then try to translate the rationality of that mode into the rationality of ours (Spear 1981, 177).

More specifically, then, the objectives governing the editing of the *Johera Narrative* are the same as those already noted for the three other transmissive processes: accuracy and authenticity. These concerns required further editing of the *Johera Narrative*, yet I have been careful not to jeopardize these objectives through over-editing. Accordingly, the editorial changes reflected in the version of the *Johera Narrative* used in this study (Appendix 1) were those believed to be necessary to preserve the accuracy and authenticity of the text, yet also produce the requisite clarity.

Methods

In order to implement the concern for accuracy and not cleanliness of the *Johera Narrative*, the following editorial procedures were followed:

1. For the sake of clarity and flow, certain words were inserted; these insertions are enclosed in brackets.

2. Punctuation was kept to a minimum, and was used only to "clarify the sense of the narration" (Allen 1982, 37).

3. Obscure passages, that is, passages that seemed unclear in both the recorded and written versions, were underlined, yet otherwise left unchanged. Even though this produces a certain awkwardness, it

preserves the text's authenticity and accuracy. These passages are happily few.

4. As much as possible, whenever it did not hinder understanding, the Kenyan dialect of English which lacks the articles and makes extensive use of participles was preserved for the sake of authenticity. The applied editorial method was to accept what Ajuoga passed to me, making textual changes only when necessary for basic comprehension. Consequently, parts of the text are in more standard English, either because Ajuoga narrated them this way or because he made the editorial changes himself. The more idiomatic use of English was preserved where it originally appeared in the transcription to indicate the desire for authenticity rather than cleanliness.

Problems

In addition to the editorial difficulties already noted, two problems were encountered which fundamentally influenced the version of the *Johera Narrative* used in this study. These problems elicited editorial decisions which will ultimately affect the wider reception, assessment, and interpretation of Ajuoga's narrative.

The first difficulty relates to the title of Ajuoga's text. Although this problem, at first glance, may appear inconsequential, upon further consideration its significance can be appreciated. Because a title can, and perhaps should, convey the primary focus of the data concerned, it consequently requires an interpretation. Entitlement is especially problematic if the title is imposed externally, yet because Matthew Ajuoga failed to produce a title for his narration, it was left for me to provide one. A title was believed to be necessary for easy references, nevertheless I desired to entitle Ajuoga's text in as generic and objective way as possible, so minimizing the transference of my biases to future researchers. After struggling with several titles, the present appellation of *Johera Narrative* was chosen. It is sufficiently general, yet accurate; it offers minimal interpretation of the intents and contents of the text, yet it conveys that the text is a "narrative," meant to tell the story of "Johera."[23]

The second crucial editorial decision regarded the organization of the *Johera Narrative* into smaller units. Ajuoga did not recount his narrative in any of the basic units of written literature, such as chapters or even paragraphs, yet it was believed that such organizational structures were necessary for facilitating the examination of the text. On the other hand, it was realized that "even paragraphing changes the nature of the medium," because "it shoves material onto mental shelves where something may be missed" (Allen 1982, 45).

Even so, convinced that there was no better way to address the concern for facility and accuracy, Ajuoga's text was divided into 297 units, numbered consecutively. The units follow, as much as possible, clear shifts or pauses in Ajuoga's original narration. By employing numbers to designate these units the text can more easily be examined and referencing is facilitated, yet the over-interpretation resulting from the introduction of chapters with headings was avoided.[24]

A third editorial problem related to Ajuoga's mixture of the vernacular with standard and idiomatic English. As noted above, the concern for authenticity required that the idiomatic style of English be preserved where it was present in the original text. However, this produces a lack of grammatical cleanliness in certain paragraphs, and this could be interpreted negatively. Yet, these idiomatic sections are actually one of the text's greatest strengths, because they communicate the narrative's orality, conveying common Kenyan spoken English. Ajuoga's mixture of the vernacular and pidgin reflects the common practice of his time and place, thus by preserving these sections as they were narrated or edited by Ajuoga himself, the text is presented as close to its original form as possible.

The version of the *Johera Narrative* presented and examined in this study, therefore, evolved through the gestational stages and transmissive procedures described in this chapter. Additionally, the text is the product of the labors of four partners: Matthew Ajuoga, John Okoth Okelo, Keta Peterson Midida, and myself. We, with varying degrees of input, cooperated to transform Matthew Ajuoga's vernacular oral account into a readable yet accurate English version, suitable for presentation to the wider community.[25]

With the understanding of the formation of the *Johera Narrative* provided by the above description of the text's gestation and transmission, we can now move to Part Two which focuses on issues related to the presentation of the text itself.

Chapter 5

The Kenyan Legacy

Matters of study and text formation were the focus of the previous part of this study. General perimeters, methodology, and sources were outlined, followed by a discussion of the development of the version of Matthew Ajuoga's *Johera Narrative* which forms the basis of this study.

Beginning with this chapter, Part Two will focus on the presentation of the *Johera Narrative* and its contexts. General characteristics and value of the text will be reviewed, then an index which will assist the reader/listener in approaching and interpreting Ajuoga's narrative will be offered.

However, before this closer scrutiny of the text can be undertaken with understanding, it is necessary to consider the general historical[1] and religious contexts from which the *Johera Narrative* has emerged, and this will be accomplished through the discussion found in the next three chapters. This focus on the broader contexts of the *Johera Narrative* is necessary for at least three reasons. First, within his text Ajuoga employs a multiplicity of terms that are directly linked to a particular time and place. If these are to be understood and appreciated, then a general understanding of the historical and religious backgrounds to the text must be attained. In order for the language of the text to be comprehended fully its fundamental historico-religious framework must be appreciated.

A second reason for the necessity of understanding the contexts of the *Johera Narrative* is because Matthew Ajuoga's text proceeds from a particular time and place, and like all reflections on experience, the *Johera Narrative* bears the marks of the environment which has formed it. Not only Ajuoga's choice of vocabulary, but also the issues discussed, the problems encountered, and the perspectives presented betray a particular historical and religious milieu. Consequently, any attempt to accurately understand, assess, and interpret Ajuoga's text can only follow a basic comprehension of the formative contexts which have given birth to Ajuoga's experiences related in his text.

This influence of time and place upon Christian reflection and proclamation has been recognized for centuries, and during the past several decades the relationship between context and theology has become one of the primary preoccupations of scholars of Christian Mission.[2] While modern scholars differ on almost all other areas of this complex debate, a general consensus exists on the central premise that context significantly influences all aspects of Christian theologizing. It is generally agreed that, following the example of our Lord Himself who became incarnate in a particular culture, all succeeding efforts to perpetuate His message must inevitably be understood and expressed according to a particular human context. If, then, the Christian message is essentially incarnational and is always, everywhere translated into the context of its immediate time and place,[3] then Matthew Ajuoga's "God-Talk" cannot be understood unless its historical and religious backgrounds are appreciated. Like all forms of theologizing, Ajuoga's reflections are also translations of his appropriation of the Christian message that are grounded in a particular environment.

Third, not only does a general understanding of the historical and religious contexts of the *Johera Narrative* allow an understanding and accurate interpretation of its contents, but an appropriate appreciation of the distinctive character of the text can also proceed only when its background is duly noted. In Chapter 8 below the more specific characteristics and contributions of Ajuoga's text will be discussed, yet from a more general perspective the *Johera Narrative* represents a distinctive type of literature born from a particular historico-religious contextual womb. Because the time and place narrated in the *Johera Narrative* was an environment of crises and resolutions, the text can rightly be understood as a theological document of crisis.[4] Ajuoga's text narrates one individual's Christian experiences arising from several dimensions of crisis present in late colonial and early independent Kenya, and so the *Johera Narrative* must be understood and interpreted bearing these crises in mind.

Beyond doubt, since his birth, Matthew Ajuoga's life has included numerous crises, and not only has the direction of his life been determined by these tension eruptions, but his life since the founding of Johera has been dedicated to the resolution of these crises.[5] Rather than involuntarily and aimlessly reacting to these crises, Ajuoga has attempted to manage intentionally and purposefully and resolve the crises of his time and place. This objective has been dominant in the formation of the Christian experiences of Matthew Ajuoga's life, and these experiences are narrated in his *Johera Narrative*. Accordingly, the crises of Ajuoga's experience must be discerned if his life's work is to be appreciated.

The literature related to the crises created by the coming of Europeans—settlers, colonial administrators, and missionaries—to Africa is vast and detailed enough to concede the point. Here, however, it is simply noted that within the scholarly community crisis/resolution is a widely accepted paradigm for understanding many of the events in colonial and post-colonial Africa. It is commonly held that, directly resulting from the introduction of the European colonial era, African individuals and societies were confronted with several forms of stress. These strains created individual and social crises, and consequently African efforts emerged to reduce and/or resolve these tension eruptions. This process has been noted and analyzed both in the economic and socio-political spheres, as well as in the religious.[6]

Crisis and its resolution is one of the most illuminating comprehensive paradigms for understanding and appreciating Matthew Ajuoga's experiences as related in the *Johera Narrative*, and, therefore, it is necessary to understand properly the crises to which he has responded throughout the course of his life since the 1950's. In order to appreciate properly these crises, it is necessary to understand the factors which formed them. It is, therefore, the purpose of this present chapter to provide an overview of the primary components of the broader historical stresses present in Matthew Ajuoga's time and place, and to describe the causes of these crises which have so influenced the *Johera Narrative*.

It is not our purpose here to detail or explain all the dimensions of the comprehensive historical developments which produced the crises which Matthew Ajuoga sought to resolve beginning in the 1950's. The limitations of this study do not permit such in-depth documentation. Moreover, the relevant general historical chronicle of these events has been the focus of numerous excellent studies; several have been utilized in the writing of this chapter, and these sources will be duly noted. Rather, it is the intent here to identify and clarify the most evident and significant historical influences on the *Johera Narrative*. These influences illuminate the components of the crises encountered by Matthew Ajuoga, and these influences will be concisely summarized below.

One final introductory comment regarding the historical context of the *Johera Narrative* is in order, and it relates to the relationship between religious developments and their broader contexts in the study of African Instituted Churches. The necessity of investigating the broader social and historical context when analyzing African Instituted Churches was emphasized almost twenty years ago by Harold Turner (1979, 74-75), and more recently H. L. Pretorius has echoed this concern by arguing that any study of African Instituted Churches must begin with an examination of their socio-historical milieu.

> The starting point of an appropriate approach which does justice to the religious movements [AICs] should be the concrete social and historical background in which they are embedded (Pretorius 1995, 99).

Even so, a temptation exists, indeed it is often fallen into by studies of African Instituted Churches, either to over-emphasize or under-emphasize the significance of social and historical context in the formation and development of these communities. On the one hand, AICs are often reduced to no more than "crisis cults," whose dynamics are viewed as solely a result of socio-historical factors, and whose theological concerns are either ignored or denigrated.[7] On the other hand, it is possible to focus on the religious life of an AIC with little regard for the broader historical environment in which the Christian theologizing takes place. This creates a myopic and simplistic image of African Instituted Churches.[8]

Our intention here is to avoid both extremes: to be aware fully of the general historical context which has formed Matthew Ajuoga's experiences related in the *Johera Narrative*, and to identify and appreciate the impact of these contextual influences. Yet, at the same time an effort will be made to avoid over-interpreting these environmental determinants, thus recognizing and appreciating the religious and theological dimensions of Matthew Ajuoga's responses that cannot be understood in solely social scientific terms. Therefore, while this present chapter will focus on the general historical context of the *Johera Narrative*, the two following chapters will focus on the religious influences and theological responses evident in Ajuoga's text.

This chapter, therefore, will proceed with a summary discussion of the major historical components of the crisis from which the *Johera Narrative* has emerged. These critical issues are products of the social and political dimensions of the Nyanza Luo colonial and post-independence experience. While this broader historical framework will be given serious attention, it will be examined in light of its influence on Matthew Ajuoga's Christian experiences as related in his *Johera Narrative*, and its subsequent ability to assist in the understanding and interpretation of Ajuoga's text.

CRISES AND RESPONSES IN NYANZA TO 1993[9]

In 1888 the East African Kingdom of Buganda and the land between it and the Indian Ocean, today known as Kenya, were officially designated a British sphere of influence to be exploited solely by the Imperial British East Africa Company. By 1894 an extremely reluctant yet desperate British Government was obliged to declare a protectorate over the kingdom of Buganda, and the next year, 1895, in order to protect the trade route between Buganda and the coast, the land that now comprises the nation of Kenya officially became a British Protectorate (Ogot 1963, 249). Thus the British, almost by default, became the sole European proprietor of Kenya, a vast area valued initially as a mercantile right of way.

However, soon this original British view of Kenya as simply a commercial afterthought was drastically altered. Partly resulting from the ramifications of the establishment of the separate East Africa Protectorate in 1895, and together with the decision of Sir Charles Eliot, Commissioner for the Protectorate (1901-4) to introduce white settlement, Kenya was to become an area of intense British administrative focus. Consequently, over the next few years, driven by the unsympathetic and ambiguous concerns of commerce and European politics, the British employed force to turn their Kenyan caravan route into a "conquest state." "In the ten years between 1895 and 1905, Kenya...was transformed from a footpath 600 miles long into a colonial administration" (Lonsdale 1989, 6).

One of the greatest challenges facing the British administration of their new Protectorate was the resistance to their control raised by most of the indigenous inhabitants. Between 1895 and 1900 C. W. Hobley, the Sub-Commissioner of the new Protectorate responsible for Kavirondo, as Nyanza Province was then called, was given the task of organizing punitive campaigns against most of the local tribes, of which the most powerful were the Nandi (Ogot 1963, 249). While diverse methods of pacification were used with varying degrees of success throughout Kavirondo, the ethnic group of particular concern for this study, the Luo, provide a rather unusual chapter in the story of initial African responses to British colonialism in Kenya.

In stark contrast to the violent resistance of most of the other local tribes in Kavirondo, the Luo, who today form the majority in Nyanza Province, offered no armed resistance to the British. The Luo's acquiescence, however, was not due to their lack of military prowess, but rather to their religious devotion. Luo diviners (*jobilo*) had foretold the coming of the "red strangers," the Europeans, and the Luo were warned against resistance. "Hence, the Luo people welcomed the Europeans cordially, cooperated with the administration in all possible ways, and generally expected great things of the white man" (Ogot 1963, 249).

Sadly for all concerned, however, this initial Luo confidence and acceptance all too soon dissipated, so that the Luo historian Bethwell Ogot asked, "What became of the Africans' great expectations" (1963, 250)? How and why was the initial trust in the Europeans extended by the Luo betrayed? The answer is the story of the creation of a crisis in Nyanza and throughout Kenya which ultimately erupted in the 1950's. This is the same crisis which would forever alter the life of Matthew Ajuoga and form his later reflections recorded in the *Johera Narrative*, and so it is a story of significance here.

Our summary of the formation and eruption of this crisis in Nyanza is here divided into four chronological periods, and within each period the major contributing events and personalities will be noted. The nature of the 1950's crisis in Nyanza will hopefully become clear, and hence a greater appreciation of Matthew Ajuoga's individual response as recounted in his narrative can be developed.

Roots of the Crisis in Nyanza, 1902-1921

The origins of the crisis among the Nyanza Luo go back at least to the time of the transfer of Western Kenya, including Kavirondo (Nyanza), from the Uganda to the East Africa Protectorate in 1902. This change in jurisdiction brought the initial, intensely concentrated efforts at direct British control over Kavirondo, and for the next decade the major challenge facing the British would be "the establishment of a sound system of administration" in Nyanza. "Positive administration" of Nyanza only became possible, however, after the pacification of the Nandi in 1906. Then, with "law and order" thus established in the region, all British resources could be concentrated on organizing effective government (Ogot 1963, 250).

Even so, from the beginning the British administration was hindered by two factors, the first being the inferior quality of many of the earliest British colonial administrators. "The type of administrator who was sent out to East Africa in the early days...was on the whole below standard." Most had little education, did not even claim to be members of the educated class, and at least one was on record as being illiterate. This lack of preparation for their posts in the colonial administration, coupled with the effective power these officials held over large numbers of Africans, caused many British administrators in this early period to behave like "little emperors" (Ogot 1963, 251). This perversion of power and position assisted in the creation of a climate of tension among the Nyanza Luo.

> As a result of the misuse of power by some of these officers, the original friendliness of the Africans in the District [Nyanza] towards the Europeans soon changed into suspicion and distrust of the white man's motives, and later still, into open hostility (Ogot 1963, 251).

As if this misuse of power was not enough, the situation was exacerbated by a second factor, a shortage of European administrators, and this predicament greatly magnified the negative impact of these ill-suited civil servants.

> The collectors and sub-collectors who had to administer the districts under a Sub-Commissioner, not only lived among strange peoples and in a hostile climate, but had also to be jacks-of-all-trades. Besides being administrators and tax-collectors, they were also builders, judges, policemen, engineers, doctors, etc. (Ogot 1963, 250).

Given normal work loads and expectations these incompetent agents would have been merely detrimental, but given the mammoth responsibilities and authority laid upon these earliest administrators, they were disastrous. Even so, while these under-qualified, yet over-stretched and over-empowered civil servants were partially responsible for the creation of Luo tension in Nyanza during this period, they were not solely responsible.

Because of this shortage of Europeans to man the British colonial administration in Nyanza, the government was originally hopeful of employing indigenous civil servants. Yet, unlike Uganda where

Baganda agents served effectively, in Nyanza a pool of suited locals did not yet exist. Therefore, the British were forced to resort to indirect administration in Nyanza, and in so doing, they were to employ traditional Luo leaders, but in an untraditional, and even anti-traditional, way (Ogot 1963, 251-253). This would also contribute to the frustration of the Nyanza Luo.

Before European contact the Nyanza Luo were divided into twelve or thirteen sub-tribes (*ogendini*), each consisting of between ten and seventy thousand persons. Each group (*oganda*) was divided even further into patrilineal clans, and each clan occupied and administered a particular territory. Thus, for the traditional Nyanza Luo a direct relationship existed between a particular clan and a distinct geographical area; land and authority were related (Ogot 1963, 252). This was one of the fundamental understandings of government among the Nyanza Luo.

Moreover, each oganda was an independent unit led by a chief (*Ruoth*), who often served as both religious and jural-political leader. The powers and authority of the *Ruoth*, however, were limited by a system of checks and balances. A council of local clan elders (*Buch Piny*) served as advisors and mitigators to the *Ruoth*, and also a hierarchy of sub-chiefs, each with their own councils (*Doho*) and authorities, was developed. The Nyanza Luo then developed not a central government, which would have better suited a sedentary society, but rather a series of local administrations to serve their migratory and semi-pastoral requirements (Ogot 1963, 252). This second element, that of multiple leaders each with greatly limited and balanced power, was also part of the Nyanza Luo's fundamental understanding of government.

Not surprisingly, given the presence of this traditional political framework and the shortage of European civil servants, the British sought to exploit Luo governmental structures for their own ends. However, in order to serve the needs of the colonial administration, and in violation of Luo fundamental understandings of administration, changes in the traditional Luo system of government had to be made. Whereas under the traditional understanding authority was always geographically based and confined, under the British collaborative Luo leaders could exercise authority over areas that did not correspond with the traditional boundaries. Additionally, even though traditional rulers were restricted by the checks and balances of Luo tradition, the Luo working for the colonial government were bound only by alien British law.

In all fairness, it should be pointed out that the British were not, then, fully aware of the workings and underlying philosophies of traditional Luo politics. They were not deliberately, in this case, sowing seeds of dissension or employing the tactic of "divide and conquer."

> Most of the overworked and ubiquitous collectors had no time to study African institutions, and the Kenya Government could not at that time afford the luxury of employing a sociologist to do this essential work. Hence, many administrative mistakes were made through sheer ignorance of this background of African societies (Ogot 1963, 251-252).

Even so, this situation set the stage for wide misuse of power and position by many Luo civil servants. Liberated from the old system of checks and balances, and with this traditional structure in question and disarray, "the new chiefs were prone to get power-drunk" (Ogot 1963, 253). Feeling thus betrayed by many of their own elite, and beginning to doubt the ability of their traditions to withstand the new colonial era, many Nyanza Luo became frustrated and disillusioned. This popular Luo vexation, therefore, formed another element in the foundation of the impending crisis in Nyanza.

Yet another root of the crisis among the Nyanza Luo in this period was related to white settlement in Kenya. As already noted, the decision to introduce white settlement into Kenya was a primary determinant for the future of the entire colony. However, whereas the policy of reserving traditional lands for whites would become the major point of contention in other parts of Kenya, this was not the problematic issue among the Luo. "In fact, the only alienated land claimed by the Luo was the Miwani-Muhoroni-Songhor area" (Ogot 1963, 254). Rather, among the Nyanza Luo the contention with white settlement was the related issue of African labour.

Accompanying the designation of Kenya as an area for white settlement were a series of legislative decisions which discouraged Africans from developing their own reserves. Between 1907 and 1911 several policies leading to the deliberate neglect of African lands were enacted, and these were designed to eliminate economic competition and to make the Africans more governable through creating economic dependencies. Furthermore, these measures would release a large and reliant work force to labour in colonial projects and on white farms. Within this context "Central Nyanza was regarded as a reservoir of cheap labour" (Ogot 1963, 255), and indeed throughout Nyanza labour camps were erected and many among the Luo were recruited for work throughout Kenya.

This policy initiated the disintegration of traditional Luo social and political structures, and so heightened popular stress. Added to the existing tensions already described, the cumulative effect was the alienation of the Luo from their established means of support and resolution. Not only had their traditional way of life been radically altered, but it appeared that it would never again be the same. With the traditional Nyanza Luo support structure in such a state of upheaval, it is not surprising that as the tensions mounted in the coming decades, radical measures were taken by many Luo to resolve this state of crisis.

One final root of the Nyanza crisis will be noted, and it relates to the Nyanza Luo experience during and immediately following the First World War (1914-1918). All of Nyanza sacrificed during the war, and increased tensions in part resulted from the burdens inflicted by British procurement of cattle and taxes. However, the major cause of Nyanza Luo anxiety resulted from British voracity for manpower, especially for the Carrier Corps. Approximately 165,000 African porters served with the British during the war, yet the Nyanza Luo were especially active. In one year alone, 1917-1918, about nine thousand men were recruited from only one district in Nyanza, and the Luo were so prominent in the Carrier Corps that one European contemporary stated that, "it can be said with truth that they [Nyanza Luo] helped win the war" (quoted in Ogot 1963, 258). Indeed, Nyanza Luo porters were so popular in the Carrier Corps that a common nickname, *Omera* (Dholuo for "brother"), was used to refer to the porters, and in tribute to the Luo carriers "numerous simple verses entitled *Omera* were composed during the war" (Ogot 1963, 258).[10]

Despite Luo readiness to sacrifice for an alien European war, this loyalty was not rewarded, but was rather abused. Not only did Africans serving in the Carrier Corps endure the usual hardships related to that particular form of service, but the African porters suffered numerous additional inhumanities. The carriers were generally mistreated through the lack of proper medical care, rations, and accommodation. This maltreatment is reflected in the staggering fact that of the 165,000 Africans serving in the Carrier Corps, over fifty thousand never returned (Ogot 1963, 258), and it was believed by the Nyanza Luo that as many, or more, porters died from deprivation than from enemy aggression. "This indifference to the suffering and hardships of the porters, coupled with the high mortality rate, became a major grievance of the Luo..." (Ogot 1963, 259).

A further effect of the war on the Nyanza Luo was the reversal of their image of Europeans. Before the war most Africans regarded the Europeans with a respect and awe which bordered on worship, and the initial willingness of the Nyanza Luo to serve in the war was largely due to this high regard. However, the war experiences drastically changed all this, because during the war many Africans were given their first close-up view of Europeans. In the East African theatre African and European soldiers ate, slept, bathed, and fought side by side, and warrant and non-commissioned African officers even instructed many European volunteers. This new familiarity revealed that Europeans were not omniscient or omnipotent, yet it also revealed another, even darker side of the Europeans. Europeans were shown to be just as willing to fight a tribal war as the Africans, they could also be barbaric, and consequently many Africans ceased to consider the Europeans to be morally superior. "In the eyes of the Africans, the experience transformed the Europeans from supermen to men—they were brought down to earth from the clouds" (Ogot 1963, 259).

So, when the war ended the Nyanza Luo were weary and disillusioned, acutely feeling the results of their ill- placed loyalty and respect. The returning soldiers and porters passed the news about the true character of Europeans, widespread anxiety was produced, and it was soon to increase. The end of the war brought a series of government capitulations to the white settlers in Kenya, all of which further alienated and restricted the rights of Africans throughout the colony. And to add insult to injury, the rains failed in Nyanza immediately following the war, famine resulted, and then an epidemic of Spanish influenza took a heavy toll on the population. Insufficient compensation from the colonial government was offered, and consequently by 1920 the Nyanza Luo were on the verge of crisis. Believing that their original trust in the Europeans was obviously misplaced, a popular sentiment grew that if the plight of the Nyanza Luo was to improve, they would themselves be required to act (Ogot 1963, 260).

Influences from this Period in the Johera Narrative

Influences from the events in Nyanza during this period are evident in Matthew Ajuoga's *Johera Narrative*. Ajuoga, who was not born until 1925, was not personally involved in this period, yet two references in his text betray events which occurred during these early days of tension creation. First, in paragraphs 17-22 Ajuoga refers to his father, Oguna, who was a Luo sub-chief, and who was also selected by the British to serve as an indigenous colonial administrator. In spite of the lack of detail in Ajuoga's text, the internal and external conflicts caused by this form of collaboration are evident. Oguna was ultimately arrested for failure to rightly serve the colonial administration (par. 20), and one can only imagine Oguna's feelings towards the radical alterations in his society and personal life. Without doubt, Oguna's individual conflicts were felt by his son, and, consequently, it can be assumed that Matthew Ajuoga was born and raised in this tense atmosphere. One can only wonder to what extent these childhood experiences of tension contributed, even unconsciously, to Matthew Ajuoga's own later struggles with crisis and resolution.

The second influence from this period evident in the *Johera Narrative* is Ajuoga's references to the Luo diaspora in various parts of Kenya and East Africa (pars. 203-206; 224-233). As a result of the recruitment of Luo labourers in Nyanza that began in this period, thousands of Luo were living outside Nyanza by the 1950's, and when Johera began it would spread to other areas primarily through this uprooted Nyanza Luo workforce. It can also be understood why the Luo diaspora, who in their own situations daily felt the tensions of displacement and de-tribalization, were often ready to seek solace and resolution in Johera. Johera's growth and spread, therefore, is partly a result of the British labour laws enacted during this earliest colonial period.

Initial Formation of Resolution Models in Nyanza, 1921-1939

When in 1920 Kenya was officially declared a British colony rather than a Protectorate, African opposition to colonial rule had already become overt and organized. In Central Kenya among the Gikuyu, the tribe most affected by land alienation to white settlers, a group of chiefs formed the Kikuyu Association in 1920. By 1921 a more militant pressure organization with a larger and younger membership, the Young Kikuyu Association, was established under the forceful leadership of Harry Thuku. The following year, after fruitless attempts to gain government concessions, a riot broke out in Nairobi resulting in the deaths of several Africans. Consequently, a crackdown was enforced, and Harry Thuku was imprisoned for eleven years (Ochieng' 1992, 113- 114).

Reactions to the rising tensions in Nyanza were just as organized and intense, if not as violent. In 1921 a political pressure group was also established among the Luo. With assistance from Harry Thuku the Young Kavirondo Association was formed and led by a group of young graduates of mission schools. This association in part assisted in the spreading of Western ideas and ways among the Luo, but it primarily was established to address the Luo grievances as outlined above. Specifically, the YKA sought government attention and redress for the laws relating to forced African labour, oppressive taxation, and the restrictions on travel imposed on all Africans (Ogot 1963, 261).

In contrast to the situation among the Gikuyu in this period, the efforts among the Luo were generally more fruitful and peaceful. The government at first tried to ignore the work of the Young Kavirondo Association, but considering the fact that by late 1921 the association was attracting as many as two thousand to its rallies, British officials soon recognized Luo seriousness. Beginning in 1922 a series of meetings between leaders of the Young Kavirondo Association and government officials was held throughout Nyanza. After initial attempts by the government to superficially placate the Luo, in July 1922 then governor of Kenya, Sir Edward Northey, met leaders of the YKA in Nyanza. His presence, attention, explanations, and minor concessions served to allay Luo anxiety and for a time restore Luo confidence in the colonial administration. It was largely due to the nature of Luo concern and activism as well as British serious attention, that the situation in Nyanza never became violent as it did in Gikuyuland (Ogot 1963, 261-263).

Even so, in the presence of government "get tough" measures against African resistance in the wake of the Thuku riot, government attention and flexibility in Nyanza were also to a large degree a result of the efforts of one champion of the Luo and African cause, Walter Edwin Owen (1878-1945). Walter Owen served with the Church Missionary Society for twenty-six years as the Archdeacon of Nyanza (1918-1944), yet when Owen was first posted to Nyanza the Luo raised a petition to have him sent back to Uganda because of his inability to speak Dholuo (Ogot 1963, 263).[11] However, during the 1919 epidemic in Nyanza Owen almost single-handedly inoculated eleven thousand people. Moving about on his motorcycle Owen "won their [the Luo] hearts by...helping their women folk and children, who were dying of plague in great numbers" (Ogot 1963, 263).

Owen soon developed a reputation as a "staunch champion of social justice."

> From the earliest, Owen concerned himself with making Africans men in a genuine sense. Paternalism and spoonfeeding were to him a great mistake. Africans, he maintained, were men, and had therefore to make their own future (Ogot 1963, 263).

This atypical and untimely broad-mindedness expressed itself through Owen's diverse interests and activities, which included medicine, geology, archaeology, and administration (Hewitt 1971, 140). Yet, it was Owen's political activism which not only earned him the name "Archdemon" from the white settlers (Strayer 1976, 11), but also drew attention and sympathy to the Luo and general African plight. "Owen's basic tactic was simple: to raise a ruckus" (Spencer 1983, 54), which he did through his wide travels and voluminous correspondence. His political agenda included promotion of Luo initiatives for African political participation and appreciation of African culture, and protest of forced labour and all unjust colonial legislation (Spencer 1983, 47). "It is an undeniable fact that Owen gave shape and direction to many political administrative issues affecting Africans in Kenya generally, and in Nyanza in particular" (Ogot 1963, 264).[12]

Perhaps Owen's greatest influence in the political arena on behalf of the Nyanza Luo was through his involvement with the Kavirondo Taxpayers Welfare Association. By 1923 Owen realized that the Young Kavirondo Association was too limited in both its base of support and agenda. Accordingly, Owen led the conversion of the parent organization into the broader Kavirondo Taxpayers Welfare Association, which was "at once a trade union, a welfare association and a political pressure group." Owen served as the first president of this new organization, which popularly became known as *Piny Owacho* (the Voice of the People) (Ogot 1963, 264).

Despite Owen's warnings against the dangers of division within the KTWA, by 1924 the organization had split into four smaller groups: Luo and Bantu factions, as well as Protestant and Catholic splinters. Yet, the consistent efforts of Owen and Luo leaders brought numerous, though limited, political successes. By 1932 the KTWA, still representing the majority of Nyanza Luo, won concessions from the governor on a whole range of issues, from land and tax reform, to African political representation (Ogot 1963, 265).

"It is difficult to exaggerate Owen's influence on the Luo people" (Ogot 1963, 263), yet it can be argued that his most impressionable legacy was not his political achievements. As laudable as it was, Owen's political activism merely served to temporarily alleviate the symptoms rather than solve the problem that was British colonialism. Rather, given the state of Luo anxiety and disillusionment which Owen encountered in 1918, his most effective and long-lasting contributions to the Luo situation were the organizational experiences and confidence he provided the Nyanza Luo.

Between 1918 and 1939 Owen's presence and serious attention helped direct the expression of Luo tension through organized and nonviolent means. These were at least tolerated by the government, and in this period they proved to be relatively successful. Thus, Owen helped to arrest the Luo's fast fading confidence in the British system and in their ability to cope with it. Additionally, his appreciation for Luo culture encouraged the Luo not only to guard and preserve their traditional way of life, but it also offered the Luo hope in the possibility of coexistence or even a synthesis of African and European ways.

Owen, therefore, provided a model of acceptable, effective, oppositional political activism and dialogue through which the Nyanza Luo could properly address and resolve their tensions within their modern colonial milieu. He legitimated their tensions and protest, and offered the Luo models for protest amplification and resolution through organizational creation and innovation. In a sense, Owen became a player/coach who modelled and encouraged mastery of the previously unfamiliar rules and techniques of a hitherto alien game.

During this period these new strategies and aptitudes would satisfactorily address Luo tensions, and would thus be accepted and applied basically as they were taught. However, as we will see by the 1950's these newly acquired abilities to play the European game by European rules would ultimately result in wider African and Luo activism which changed the very nature of the game. Africans would then employ European ways against the Europeans in the political realm, but for Matthew Ajuoga and others, new applications of European models would emerge in the religious world as well.

Influences from this Period in the Johera Narrative

The explicit references to this period in Matthew Ajuoga's text are few, primarily due to the fact that it was in this period that Matthew Ajuoga was born, grew, and began to attend primary school. As a very young man it cannot be expected that Ajuoga would retain profuse and detailed memories of the political events of this period. However, it can safely be assumed that Ajuoga, born in Nyanza in 1925 (par. 3) and attending primary school in Nyanza from 1936 to 1941 (par. 5), was affected by the increasing tensions and political activism in Nyanza during this period.

Two paragraphs in the *Johera Narrative*, both reflecting the retention of vivid memories, hint at Ajuoga's personal experiences of the political developments of this period. In paragraph 21 Ajuoga mentions the multitude of visitors who came to consult his father, Oguna, whom we already have seen was much involved in Luo colonial politics. Ajuoga remembers that many Luo regularly visited their home, seeking advice and physical assistance. These problems would not have been unrelated to the calamities and colonial legislation of this period, and one can assume that the advice that was sought also related to the Luo tensions of the time. Consequently, Matthew Ajuoga grew up in a home where the daily routine included leadership in times of need. Ajuoga thus was, from the beginning of his life, introduced to a model of his family providing aid and leadership for their people. The house of Oguna was a refuge, and the human model produced was that the sons of Oguna, likewise, were expected to be leaders in tension and crisis resolution.

The second explicit reference to this period, though not limited to it, in the *Johera Narrative* is paragraph 148. In four sentences Matthew Ajuoga pays his tribute to the political and social activism of Walter Owen, and it is clear that for Ajuoga, Owen continues to be remembered as the European hero of the Luo (Hewitt 1971, 140; Ogot 1963, 263- 264). Considering that the general context in which Ajuoga's praise for Owen appears is one of general criticism of missionaries, this acclamation is all the more significant. Because Walter Owen was active in Nyanza until 1944, the year Ajuoga turned nineteen, Ajuoga personally encountered this missionary hero on many occasions. The impression Owen made on Ajuoga is still remembered and described in this paragraph some fifty years later, and as already noted, Ajuoga's lasting memories of Owen reflect those popularly held even today.

At least three influences of Walter Owen's activism on Matthew Ajuoga can be deduced from paragraph 148, and all three suggest enduring opposition and resolution models which were produced. First, Ajuoga remembered that Owen "made a lot of noises" (par. 148), and indeed Matthew Ajuoga himself, in his adult life, has followed that example. Second, according to Ajuoga's memory Owen "really battled...to the extent that he even started some parties here in Nyanza" (par. 148). Owen's model was of tension resolution through the creation of new organizations, and this Matthew Ajuoga would emulate through the establishment of Johera. Third, Owen even appealed to England for redress (par. 148), and more than thirty years later Matthew Ajuoga would do the same.[13]

It is not being suggested here that Matthew Ajuoga's actions in establishing Johera were somehow, either consciously or unconsciously, mere imitations of Walter Owen. Not only would this be too simplistic an assessment which would fail to give proper credit to Matthew Ajuoga's personal innovations, but this view could also not be supported by the evidence. The implication is not that African attempts at crisis resolution simply mirrored those learned from the Europeans.

However, given the influential place Walter Owen is granted both in the scholarly literature and popular memories of this period, it can be argued that Owen's activities in the least encouraged and reinforced a model of acceptable and effective tension resolution for the Luo, one which continues to be impressionable almost sixty years later. Additionally, given the influence of missionary modeling and modus operandi on African observers, whereby often what is most impressionable is what is done rather than what is said, Owen's production of models cannot be discounted.[14]

To summarize the influence of this period on the life of Matthew Ajuoga as reflected in his *Johera Narrative*, this period created a situation in which mounting Luo tensions would be addressed and temporarily allayed through the creation of popular oppositional organizations. The high regard with which the Luo, including Matthew Ajuoga, held Walter Owen allowed his example to produce a model for crisis resolution. Moreover, from his domestic experience during his formative years, Matthew Ajuoga was presented with the model of leadership in crisis resolution. Consequently, when Matthew Ajuoga was confronted with tension and crisis in his adult life, two applicable and effective precedents were available from which he could extract motivation and direction in his quest for resolution.

Crisis Formation, Eruption, and Resolution, 1939-1963

It has been observed by one historian that "the decade between 1939 and 1950 was a very critical one in Kenya's history" (Zeleza 1989, 144), and if the focus is extended to 1963, these years can be seen as the most formative in the modern history of Kenya. During this period the latent tensions within the African communities would be exacerbated by the experience of the Second World War. Furthermore, the problems associated with the years immediately following the conflict would cause African tension to erupt into crisis by 1952, and during the next five years highlighted by the state of emergency, significant steps would be taken by both the British and Africans to resolve the crisis in Kenya. Hence, by 1957 when the state of emergency was lifted, Kenya would emerge radically altered: from a settler colony to an African nation well underway towards independence. Finally, in 1963 Kenya would gain its political independence, so resolving, not all crises, but the most urgent one of colonialism.[15]

Just when it seemed that Kenya's African population was beginning to alleviate some of the tensions created by their experience of the First World War, they were asked to participate and sacrifice in yet another European conflict. To an even broader extent than before, the entire colony was mobilized, and by the end of the Second World War over 97,000 Kenyans would serve in the allied military in diverse capacities and in far-off places like Burma and Palestine (Ochieng' 1992, 124). Again, the Nyanza Luo were called upon to sacrifice, tens of thousands would serve in the military or its auxiliaries, and those left in Nyanza would again bear the burdens of taxes, rationing, and procurement (Ogot 1963, 269).

At war's end the Africans in Kenya were once again proud of their heroic service and sacrifices, and they returned to the colony with great expectations. Had not they helped to fight, even win, a war against tyranny and racism? Were not freedom and justice for all two of the ideals for which the conflict was waged? Moreover, if the British were willing to fight to see these principles extended to foreign lands, certainly they would allow these rights to prosper within their own jurisdiction. Sadly, however, this was not the case; in fact, the opposite would be the harsh reality for Africans in the Kenya of 1945.

First, the post-war situation brought a severe economic crunch. Already subsistence level minimum wages were frozen, consumer goods were scarce, and those that were available were prohibitively expensive. The situation was further aggravated by increased alienation of land from the Africans and forced production of non-food crops like sisal, sugar, and pyrethrum. Consequently, many Africans could not afford to buy food, yet their ability to produce it for themselves was hindered or denied (Zeleza 1989, 146-148).[16]

A second element in crisis formation in post-war Kenya was continued African disaffection with the political process. Because of war-time exigencies, civil liberties for most residents of Kenya had been restricted between 1939 and 1945. However, those who forfeited most were among the African population, and those who actually increased their political standing were the European settlers.

> It is hard to escape the conclusion that during the war the hand of the settlers vis-a-vis the Kenyan government and that of the Kenyan government vis-a-vis the Colonial Office were undoubtedly strengthened" (Zeleza 1989, 146).

The Kenyan Legacy

While the settlers enjoyed virtual self-government, African coerced labour was broadened and increased, and many Africans were deceived into joining the military (Zeleza 1989, 147). Consequently, by the end of the war two of Kenya's major population segments had conflicting expectations. The white settlers expected their increased political powers to at least continue, while the Africans expected political compensation and balance.

While the European settlers would utilize their existing organizations and channels of influence to preserve and increase their political power after the war, the Africans would be required to create and revive pressure groups to channel their grievances. Immediately following the war several groups were formed in Nyanza to seek redress for the Luo. The Ramogi African Welfare Association and the Nyanza Ex-Soldiers Association were formed, and the defunct KTWA was revived. However, the Kenya Africa Union, formed in 1946 and a year later headed by the man who would become Kenya's first President, Jomo Kenyatta, would never be effective in Nyanza. Although the KAU was the most broad-based African political organization in post-war Kenya, and in spite of the fact that it would ultimately have the greatest influence in Kenya's struggle for independence, in Nyanza it was never popular or effective (Ogot 1963, 269- 270).[17]

The political organization which would have the greatest support and influence in post-war Nyanza was the Luo Union. Originally formed immediately following the war as a non-political organization, by 1950 the Luo Union had become the primary channel for addressing Luo political tensions. Its effectiveness resulted from its ability to reconcile groups of Luo that had previously been alienated from each other. Within the Luo Union rural and urban dwellers cooperated, the formally educated laboured alongside the illiterate, and the elders made a place for a new generation of leaders. The most popular among this younger generation of Luo leaders was Oginga Odinga, who became *Ker* (chief) of the Luo Union in 1954, and who later was to become independent Kenya's first Vice-President (Ogot 1963, 270-271).

However, in spite of its membership solidarity and charismatic leadership, the Luo Union was unable effectively to bring lasting resolution to the tensions of the Nyanza Luo during the post-war period. This was primarily because the attention of the colonial government and the Luo Union leadership became preoccupied with issues outside Nyanza during the period 1952-1957. Even though Luo tensions were mounting, they had not yet, by 1952 reached crisis proportions. However, by 1957, the Luo would be on the verge of crisis, primarily because of their marginalization in the political process and the indifference of the colonial administration towards Nyanza during the State of Emergency which was in effect between 1952 and 1957.

Among the Gikuyu in Central Kenya, political activism, agitation, intrigue, and violence had produced a full eruption of crisis by 1952, and the colonial government and indeed most of Kenya focused its full attention on resolving this situation. This state of crisis eruption within the Kenyan African community is widely referred to under the umbrella term of "Mau Mau" in modern Kenya historiography, and its comprehensive definition illustrates the breadth and depth of African desperation in post-war Kenya. Over the past forty years scholars have differed and radically revised their views of "Mau Mau," yet the movement resists simplification. "Whatever the Mau Mau uprising was, it was certainly not a simple historical event, for which there is any easy, single explanation" (Furley 1972, 105).

It is not within our purpose to provide an in-depth analysis of Mau Mau or even to chronicle its major events; these can be found in the relevant literature.[18] Rather, here it is sufficient to note that during the period many perceived Mau Mau to be demonstrative of the popular and critical African state of crisis produced by the colonial experience. Particularly for the white liberals of 1950's Kenyan society, Mau Mau was blamed "on the bewildering psychological effects of rapid social change and the collapse of orderly tribal values" (Lonsdale 1990, 421). Indeed, post-war Kenyan society was an environment of critical mental stress produced by widespread secrecy, mistrust, ignorance, imagination, and suspicion in the experience of both whites and Africans (Lonsdale 1990). It is not, therefore, surprising that violence erupted, resulting in the declaration of the State of Emergency in October 1952, and that intense political activism from both settlers and Africans followed.

The epicentre of Mau Mau was Central Province among the Gikuyu, geographically far from Nyanza, and the most crucial dimension of the eruption for the colonial government related to the presence and demands of the white settlers, an element not present in Nyanza. Accordingly, the Nyanza Luo did not experience the violence of Mau Mau, yet they were nevertheless directly affected by the crisis. The general strained climate described above dominated Nyanza, and local tensions were heightened by two additional factors. During this period more than 50,000 Nyanza Luo adult males worked outside Nyanza, and upon their return from Nairobi and Central Province they passed the news of violence and the abuse of Africans, so adding to

Luo fears and frustrations. Additionally, differing responses to the declaration of the State of Emergency also caused a split within the Luo political leadership, reducing Luo political clout and producing further grassroot frustration (Ogot 1963, 271).

Consequently, by 1957, weary of being on the Kenyan political periphery and of being ignored by the colonial administration, the Nyanza Luo were in a state of popular crisis and were desperate to amend their situation. This same African resolve was present throughout Kenya, and when the State of Emergency was lifted, it was clear to all Africans that they could and would struggle, even violently, to gain their full political independence. Recognizing this popular African resolve, London conceded that independence was inevitable, and it simply remained to work out the timetable and the personalities to be chosen to represent all Africans in the new independent government.

In spite of Luo political fragmentation during the State of Emergency, and because of their dedication to peaceful crisis resolution, numerical strength and charismatic leadership, the Luo would become actively involved in the post-1957 road to independence. Oginga Odinga, manager of the Luo Thrift and Trading Corporation and *Ker* of the Luo Union, not only used his political prowess to become leader of the most influential Luo political organization of the time, the African District Association in 1957, but his radical nationalist views and charisma would earn him the Vice-Presidency under Kenya's first Head of State, Jomo Kenyatta.[19] Within the independent Kenya of 1963 the Nyanza Luo were thus represented by one of their own at the highest levels of government, and as a result, the popular colonial crisis in Nyanza was generally alleviated by 1963.

Influences from this Period in the Johera *Narrative*

The historical period under consideration here, colonial Kenya from 1939 to 1963, has exerted more formative influence upon the experiences of Matthew Ajuoga as expressed in his *Johera Narrative* than any other. Moreover, central to this study's interpretation of the *Johera Narrative* as a theological document of crisis is the premise that the tensions and resolution arising from this period have been deterministic in the life and ministry of Matthew Ajuoga. The stresses of this period, mounting into crisis for Johera by 1957, were being addressed and alleviated by Johera's split with the Anglican Church in that year.[20]

Even so, Johera's emergence and activism within the religious realm, which will be discussed in the two succeeding chapters, cannot be divorced from the broader historical context of tension and African activism in this period. The general climate of strain and the African search for resolutions were the most critical aspects of Kenyan history during these years, and Ajuoga's reflections cannot be correctly interpreted without considering this tense and activistic milieu.[21]

The dominance of this period over Ajuoga's life and recollection is illustrated by the fact that 73% of the total paragraphs in the *Johera Narrative* contain Ajuoga's reflections upon this period.[22] On the one hand, this is not surprising, because this period was the one in which Ajuoga was educated and began his controversial public ministry. Yet, on the other hand Ajuoga could have been expected to focus primarily upon his more recent past, for example the last thirty years, in which the CCA has developed and gained wider credibility. Why should Ajuoga seek to excavate the distant and most controversial past, when he could have rather focused on the less disputed recent years of Johera's greater "respectability"? The answer is that Ajuoga's attention to this period reflects its formative dominance upon his subsequent life and ministry. Choices made in this period would forever change his life, and to a large extent determine his future.

Because of the sheer number of paragraphs devoted to events which occurred in this historical period, and given the purpose and limitations of this study, it will not be possible to closely scrutinize all of Ajuoga's reminiscences relevant to these years. However, Ajuoga himself summarizes his understanding of the significance of the late colonial period for his experience in two instructive paragraphs.

Paragraph 184, after referring to the general climate of political tension in the late 1950's, expresses Ajuoga's understanding of the reason for Johera's emphasis on love and unity. Given the hatred and dissensions of the period, Ajuoga relates that Johera's resolution was love, and so the popular name and even the *raison d'etre* of the church was partly formed in direct response to its social and historical context.

The second summary interpretive reference to this period made in Ajuoga's text is paragraph 187, and the literary context is Ajuoga's listing of reasons why Johera was so readily and widely supported. Again, Ajuoga refers to the environment as one characterized by "struggle" and "serious fighting," and within this milieu Ajuoga understands that Johera readily gained widespread support in Nyanza, in part because it was perceived to be another demonstration of the anti-colonial activism that characterized 1950's Nyanza. This reference then reveals that at least for many in Nyanza, the Anglican Church was fully recognized as the Church of *England*, that is, as representing colonialism, and any who "broke" from it were to be appreciated, lauded, and even supported.

Therefore, these two paragraphs support this study's contention that a proper understanding and appreciation of the *Johera Narrative* cannot be divorced from the climate of crisis/resolution of its time and place, because the tensions of 1950's Kenya were formative on the Christian community described in Ajuoga's text. Furthermore, Ajuoga here acknowledges that Johera was originally considered to be, in part, an indigenous oppositional and alleviatory response to popular tensions, and also that the very essence of Johera was a deliberate attempt at crisis resolution. Even though Johera is much more than a mere "crisis cult," this dimension is nevertheless unapologetically recognized by Ajuoga. Therefore, Matthew Ajuoga confirms that the origins of Johera are directly related to the popular tensions of 1950's Nyanza.

Tension Creation Among the Nyanza Luo in Independent Kenya, 1963-1993

The Nyanza Luo, like most Africans in Kenya, believed independence would be a panacea for their communal and individual tensions that were believed to have been caused by colonialism. With their own most charismatic leader Oginga Odinga as Vice-President, they believed they had good reason to be optimistic. Unfortunately, however, that was not the case. In fact, the thirty years of post-independent Kenya's history under examination here, 1963-1993, was dominated by still further tensions, primarily resulting from conflicting political ideologies and personalities among the African leadership. These difficulties would adversely affect all Nyanza Luo throughout this period, largely due to their loyalty to Oginga Odinga, but also because of widespread opposition to the administration of Kenya's second President, Daniel Arap Moi. Consequently, instead of permanently alleviating the tensions present in Nyanza Luo society, independence rather served to recreate and magnify those strains.

Almost as soon as the independence celebrations in Nairobi were concluded, fundamental ideological differences between the President, Jomo Kenyatta, and his Vice-President, Oginga Odinga, began to intensify. These personal political dissimilarities had been present before independence, for while Kenyatta had always been more moderate in his assessment of Western capitalism, Odinga was more influenced by Marxist ideology. At least in the initial rhetoric of the period, however, a fragile compromise had been struck, so that in his Independence Day address President Kenyatta "announced that his government would build a democratic African socialist state" (Ochieng' 1992, 147).

Even so, in the reality of governance this paper compromise failed to be practical. The locus of dispute between Kenyatta and Odinga concerned the ownership of land and the means of production. Initially, President Kenyatta appeared to appease Odinga and his more radical supporters by instructing the Minister for Economic Planning and Development, the Luo Tom Mboya, to draft a general blueprint for economic development. Yet, when this paper, entitled "African Socialism and its Application to Planning in Kenya" was published in 1965, it became clear that "apart from its rhetorical character, this blueprint clearly had no intention of altering the inherited colonial economic and social structures..." (Ochieng' 1992, 148).

This political smokescreen was immediately recognized and resented by Odinga, and he intensified his criticisms of Kenyatta's policies which he labelled "neo-colonial" (Ochieng' 1989a, 202). When his efforts for policy change within the government failed, in desperate protest Odinga and thirty other members of parliament resigned from the government and the ruling party, KANU (the Kenya African National Union), on 14 April, 1966. Odinga immediately led his colleagues into an opposition party, the Kenya's People's Union (KPU), which had been formed by Odinga just a month earlier. These newly organized opposition members were allowed to occupy their positions in parliament for only one day, however, for within 24 hours of the new party's registration the government introduced a constitutional amendment which required the opposition members to seek re-election (Ochieng' 1992, 154).

During the resultant by-election of late 1966, of the 39 seats being contested, KANU won twenty-nine and KPU only nine. Consequently, "for the next three years KANU and KPU called each other names..." (Ochieng' 1992, 154), and in 1969 the KPU was finally banned following the eruption of violence and bloodshed during a visit by President Kenyatta to Odinga's hometown, Kisumu.

This move by the government ushered in a period of one- party rule in Kenya which would officially last until December 1991. As Kenyatta's power was solidified and increased, Oginga Odinga became a political pariah and virtual *persona non grata*. Odinga would suffer house arrest, harassment, and ban, and this policy was continued and even intensified during the Presidency of Daniel Arap Moi, who became Kenya's second President upon Kenyatta's death in 1978. Odinga was to lead a politically alienated, low-profile, and even reclusive existence until 1990, when he led the formation of another opposition party, the Forum for the Restoration of Democracy (FORD), which would not be legalized until 1991. Odinga was FORD's candidate for the presidency of Kenya in the General Election of 1992, and after losing to Moi in a close race he continued to be a leader in opposition politics until his death in 1994.

Throughout this period, 1963-1993, most Nyanza Luo overwhelmingly maintained their support for Oginga Odinga. In spite of his split with KANU, or perhaps because of his opposition to the government, Odinga continued to be widely recognized as the most respected and influential spokesperson for the Luo in Kenya. However, the Luo would pay a tremendous price for their support of their *Ruoth* (chief), Oginga Odinga. Since 1966 many Luos believe that they have been generally marginalized by the KANU governments, and although it ranks third among Kenya's eight provinces in terms of population, it is widely believed that Nyanza has been politically and economically neglected.[23] Therefore, for many of the Nyanza Luo, Kenya's period of independence has brought not the fruition of tension resolution that they had hoped for in 1963, but rather an environment which has only served to increase the stresses of daily life.

Influences from this Period in the Johera *Narrative*

The historical period under scrutiny here, post-independent Kenya from 1963 to 1993, is given only minor attention in the *Johera Narrative*. Of the total paragraphs contained in Ajuoga's text only 67, or 23% of the total, relate to this period.[24] Nevertheless, these paragraphs are sufficient to reveal the influence the events of the first thirty years of Kenya's independence have had on the experience of Matthew Ajuoga and the development of Johera.

The political alienation of the Nyanza Luo is evident from Ajuoga's silence and reserved comments related to this period. For a person with very definite political views, it might seem unusual that Ajuoga does not refer or even allude to post-independence politics in his text. However, understood within the broader context of the political climate in Nyanza during these years, Ajuoga's silence is not surprising.

Ajuoga's silence regarding politics in post-independence Kenya could also be interpreted, as some have done for other AICs (e.g., Sparks 1990, 293ff), as illustrating a lack of engagement with his world. Yet, the paragraphs in the *Johera Narrative* that do relate to this period describe the CCA's aggressive involvement in a number of social welfare projects, and so it can be argued that instead of having no social conscience, Ajuoga and the CCA rather have a more broadly developed social agenda, one not confined to politics. Ajuoga's concern is not limited to freedom from political oppression, but rather it focuses on the more fundamental and prerequisite liberation from psychological, religious, and economic domination (Hexham 1994, xi).

Moreover, Ajuoga's description of the CCA in this period reflects that it is a community devoted, not to crisis creation through political confrontation, but rather to crisis resolution through grassroot empowerment. Just as it has been observed of other AICs, Matthew Ajuoga and the CCA have not become directly involved in politics, in part because the CCA is offered as an attractive "haven of security" in a milieu of fear and oppression (Oosthuizen and Hexham 1992, 6). Ajuoga's reflections, therefore, express not only the influence of this period on his life and ministry, but also his resolution of the tensions present in post-independent Nyanza in creating an alleviatory community.

This lengthy discussion of the creation, eruption, and resolution of crisis during the last one hundred years of Kenyan history is fundamental for this study, because an appreciation of this Kenyan legacy of crisis is a prerequisite for any balanced understanding and interpretation of Matthew Ajuoga's *Johera Narrative*. The assessment and interpretations of the text which follow in succeeding chapters, therefore, have been formed in view of this foundational historical context, and any additional and future analyses of Ajuoga's text must also give serious consideration to this critical background.

In summary, we have seen that as a theological document—like all chronicles of theologizing—the *Johera Narrative* has been influenced by its broader historical milieu. We have attempted to describe this context in four chronological stages, and the influences of each period evident in Ajuoga's text have been identified and interpreted. This exercise has provided at least three observations about the *Johera Narrative*: (1) that sufficient evidence exists from within the text to recognize the crucial interplay between historical context and theological development in Matthew Ajuoga's experience; (2) that the dominance of the cycle of crisis/resolution, present in broader Kenyan history during Ajuoga's lifetime, has also been preeminent in the formation of the experiences narrated in the *Johera Narrative*; and, more specifically, (3) that Johera's essence, origins, and later development have been fundamentally influenced by the Kenyan historical legacy of the recapitulation of this crisis/resolution cycle.

However, even as the foundational nature of the Kenyan historical context is appreciated, it must also be recognized that the *Johera Narrative*, though it bears the marks of its broader Kenyan legacy, is essentially a theological text that narrates religious experience.

Accordingly, Ajuoga's story must also be understood and interpreted with due consideration of its religious contexts. Because Matthew Ajuoga's story is, therefore, one which was formed from these "interrelated pressures" (Ogot 1963, 272) of history and religion, it is now time to focus upon the other two religious influences evident in the *Johera Narrative*.

Chapter 6

The Christian Legacy

The Kenyan legacy of crisis described and analyzed in the previous chapter provides the requisite general historical background within which the *Johera Narrative* is to be understood and appreciated. Now, however, with this foundational dimension of the historical context of Ajuoga's text in place, we must lay alongside it a second, equally crucial yet even more immediate element of the crisis from which the text has emerged. This component is the text's Christian legacy.

Concern for this broader Christian context of the *Johera Narrative* is consistent with this study's introductory statement that Matthew Ajuoga's *Johera Narrative* is essentially a theological text which narrates Christian experience. Likewise, it must be acknowledged that the individual and shared crisis related within the text was innately religious. More specifically, the Christian experiences expressed in Ajuoga's narrative reflect Johera's struggles to understand and manage the crisis of their time and place, and this shared stress essentially concerned the nature of Christian presence in Nyanza. Though significant, the wider political and social elements of the Kenyan crisis are not given paramount attention in Matthew Ajuoga's narrative. Rather, Ajuoga's text is the story of the management of a religious crisis in which the most crucial elements—the localized contentious climate, the debated issues, and the attempted resolutions—were all directly related to the character of Christianity most immediate and influential in Ajuoga's experience.

It is, therefore, the purpose of this chapter to describe and interpret the influence of this Christian legacy of crisis, produced by the nature of the adopted religion in Nyanza during the period narrated in the *Johera Narrative*. The purpose of this study does not permit nor require an exhaustive chronicle, so this chapter will summarize the major components and effects of the two major contributors to Matthew Ajuoga's Christian legacy of crisis: the work of the Church Missionary Society in Nyanza, and the effects of the East African Revival. The influences of both of these factors on the *Johera Narrative* will also be identified and assessed.

THE CHURCH MISSIONARY SOCIETY IN UGANDA AND NYANZA, 1877-1958[1]

The Church Missionary Society (CMS) was established in 1799 by a group of evangelicals within the Church of England who were discontented with the policies of the existing Anglican missionary societies.[2] The evangelical heritage of the CMS, particularly as expressed in the theological positions of its missionaries and its "low church" orientation, directed the society's policies and determined its methods (Murray 1985, 3-8; Stock 1899, 64-67). This heritage and its implications for future policy and methods were expressed in one of the "two essential and unchanging principles of the CMS," namely, that "spiritual work must be done by spiritual men" (Stock 1899, 65).

Even though at its founding the CMS was instituted to specifically initiate evangelical work in India and Africa,[3] the society did not establish itself in what is now Kenya until 1844. In that year a German Lutheran, Johann Krapf, who had been serving with the CMS in Abyssinia opened CMS work on the Indian Ocean coast at Mombasa. However, the CMS field geographically closest and most influential for its later work in Nyanza was not Kenya, but rather Uganda.

The CMS established its work in Uganda in 1877, finally responding to Henry Stanley's plea of 1875 for missionaries to be sent to the East African Kingdom of Buganda. In June of that year Shergold Smith and Charles Wilson, two of the four survivors of the original party of eight, reached the Bugandan Capital, Rubaga (Groves 1954, 326). Thereafter, officially until 1921 and practically throughout the period of colonialism, CMS efforts in Nyanza would be directly influenced by this older and more mature work in Uganda. In fact, the roots of the crisis within the Anglican Church in Nyanza during the 1950's are to be found in the precedents established by the CMS in

Uganda seventy-five years earlier. A summary, then, of the foundational work of the CMS in Uganda is required.

CMS Precedents in Buganda, 1884-1906

From its beginning CMS work in Buganda was robust. In spite of, or perhaps because of, the hardships and martyrdom suffered by some of the earliest CMS missionaries and African Christians, ten years after its beginning the Anglican Church had become numerically large and vigorous. The number of baptisms had increased from the first five in 1882 to almost seven thousand by 1890. This growth and vitality was reflected by the establishment of the Diocese of Eastern Equatorial Africa in 1884, an area which included all CMS work between Lake Victoria and the Indian Ocean. The first bishop of this new diocese, James Hannington, resided in Uganda where he and several Bugandan Christians were martyred a year later. Even so, their deaths and the associated events greatly influenced CMS work in Buganda, fuelling this rapid growth and maturity (Groves 1955, 90-97).

Hannington's successor, Alfred Tucker, managed and fostered the development of the Ugandan Church during the next thirty years.[4] Bishop Tucker, who first served as the second Bishop of the Diocese of Eastern Equatorial Africa (1884-1899), and then became the first Bishop of the newly formed Diocese of Uganda (1899-1912), was a rare missionary. In spite of the racism and paternalism of his time, Tucker was convinced of the abilities of Africans to govern and support their own church, and he consequently interpreted and implemented CMS policy on that basis. "The greatest service Bishop Tucker rendered the Ugandan church was to believe in it" (Taylor 1958a, 84).

In this regard Tucker was an heir and staunch advocate of the policies set forth by one of the most influential modern pioneers of mission method, Henry Venn. Henry Venn served as the Secretary of the Church Missionary Society for thirty-two years (1841-1873), and his "three-self" principle became, not only the official policy of the CMS, but also the accepted ideal of many other mission societies. Venn's policy, reaffirmed by the CMS repeatedly over the years, stated that "the desire of the CMS...[is] to see, one day, the formation of independent native churches, with their own bishops and clergy" (Stock 1916, 395).[5]

True to this spirit and policy "from the first, Bishop Tucker set himself to prepare the way for a self-supporting, self-governing, and self-extending church" in East Africa (Stock 1916, 98). From its beginning, because of this policy and local conditions, the CMS work in Buganda was not missionary-dependent. "For the first fourteen years of the church's life there had never been more than a handful of missionaries in Buganda, with virtually no power to impose their will" (Taylor 1958a, 71), and Tucker sought to preserve and strengthen this independence of the African church. To accomplish this Tucker initiated several policies aimed at invigorating African initiative.

First, in 1892 Tucker drafted a constitution for the church in East Africa which created greater equality between the power of the African clergy and the missionaries (Murray 1985, 132-133). He fostered the economic independence of the African church by declaring that the CMS would provide financial support only for the missionaries. The local churches would receive no European funds—except for emergencies—and would consequently have to support themselves (Oliver 1952, 220; Taylor 1958a, 87).

Second, Tucker made African leadership training a priority, yet he refused to ordain any clergy or commission any catechist not supported by the local congregations; he had no desire to impose locally unacceptable African leaders on the African church. By 1893 the first six African deacons were ordained, and these measures quickly produced the desired results. By 1894 eighty-five new stations led by 260 African evangelists had been established (Taylor 1958a, 64-68, 87). As a result, by the turn of the century the "three-selves" were already visible within the Ugandan church (Murray 1985, 247).

This legacy of Alfred Tucker to the East African church provided a model of mission policy and African initiative. "Compared with most mission fields Uganda was blessed with an enlightened policy directed towards the early autonomy of the African church" (Taylor 1958a, 88). In spite of widespread missionary opposition, by 1906 when the Ugandan mission established the CMS work in Nyanza, the deliberate effort to Africanize and "hand over" the church in Uganda was not only producing fruit, but in African minds was setting a precedent for CMS policy throughout East Africa (Taylor 1958a, 85-87).

Indications of this Period in the Johera Narrative

The period of the formation of CMS policy and method in Uganda established precedents which would continue to influence the development of Christianity in Nyanza for many years. Not only, as we will shortly see, was the CMS work in Nyanza a child and heir of the efforts in Uganda, but additionally this period established a precedent in the direction of the flow of Christian influence into Nyanza. For many years after, many Nyanza Luo Anglicans would continue to view the church in Uganda as their spiritual mother, and would persist in their practice of looking to Uganda for spiritual direction and nurture.

This abiding preeminence of the Ugandan church for Nyanza Luo Anglicans is illustrated by three passages in the *Johera Narrative*. In paragraphs 29-32 Matthew Ajuoga recounts that in the early days of Johera several members were sent to Uganda. There, in the Christian motherland, they expected to find a model spiritual community and also counsel for their own difficulties in Nyanza. Almost fifty years later, many Nyanza Luo Anglicans still recognized the Ugandan church as their Christian mother, a giver of spiritual sustenance.

Paragraphs 115 and 206 also reflect this view of the Ugandan church. The direction of the flow of Christian influence continued to be from Uganda into Nyanza even during the height of the East African Revival (par. 115), and when Johera became independent it sought to establish itself in the Ugandan motherland among the cousins of the Luo, the Padhola (par. 206). Not only was it natural to be drawn to their ethnic relatives, but Johera also desired to maintain its relationship with its Christian geographical and spiritual kin. Johera, the energetic child, could now offer the vitality of innovation to their aging mother.

The Establishment of CMS Tradition in Nyanza, 1906-1921

From a very early stage, because of its geographical proximity and ethnic similarity, the CMS-Uganda mission was concerned to establish itself across Lake Victoria in Nyanza. The man most responsible for the formation of the CMS mission to Nyanza, John Willis, initially visited there in 1900 on his way to his field of service in Uganda. Then, over the next five years he would return to Nyanza for brief, fact-finding tours five times (Omulokoli 1981, 47-65). As a result, when the Nyanza mission was established at Vihiga in 1905, Willis had already acquired a basic knowledge of the area and its people.

From the beginning, the CMS mission in Nyanza under Willis perpetuated the policies and methods of Bishop Tucker, who in 1899 had become Bishop of the newly formed Diocese of Uganda. Nyanza, or Kavirondo[6] as it was then known, was part of this new diocese, and with a smaller and more homogeneous area to administer Tucker had time and energy to carefully form and nourish the new efforts in Nyanza. Accordingly, in 1904 Tucker accompanied Willis on a visit to Nyanza, and he participated in the discussions with the local elders which culminated in the selection of a site for the Nyanza mission (Hewitt 1971, 138).

Tucker's legacy to Nyanza can be illustrated by two CMS methods initially employed there. First, the use and even reliance upon African evangelists was continued in Nyanza. Upon arrival in Nyanza Willis was accompanied by several Africans, Bugandans and at least two Luo. These African Christians served as language and culture tutors for Willis, they were crucial in establishing congenial relations with the local inhabitants, and because of the shortage of missionary staff and the challenges of the local conditions, these African assistants served "at the Mission Station in many other capacities" (Omulokoli 1981, 69).

> The work of the CMS at Maseno in particular, and in Nyanza in general in the years 1906-1912, was shouldered jointly by the Baganda agents, by the initiative of the indigenous Christians, and by the Society's European missionaries (Omulokoli 1981, 106).

CMS practice in Nyanza, therefore, was initially to rely as much as possible upon Africans, and not to develop an atmosphere of missionary-dependency.

Second, from the beginning CMS work in Nyanza encouraged African empowerment through academic education. When the centre of the CMS-Nyanza mission was transferred to Maseno in 1906, one of the first evangelistic methods employed was the establishment of a boys' school. Willis was convinced that the most effective way of evangelizing the local area was through the education of Luo boys, and in 1906 the Maseno boys' school opened with four students, all sons of local chiefs. The first CMS converts among the Luo were products of this venture, for in 1910 fifteen school boys were baptized. The school in Maseno continued to grow and gain local influence, and by 1911, just five years after its founding, it boasted 120 students. The policy was broadened to address the concern for female education, and in 1914 a girls' school was also established at Maseno (Hewitt 1971, 139).

The Maseno boys' school developed a wide reputation, and came to be regarded as "one of the outstanding schools of East Africa" (Hewitt 1971, 139). In Kenya, the school became influential because of its rigid academic preparation of some of the earliest leaders in Luo and Kenyan society; Matthew Ajuoga and Oginga Odinga are two examples. In spite of its shortcomings and later deceleration, this initial CMS policy of providing academic education and empowerment to Africans was popularly attractive, appreciated, and effective.[7] Another crucial element of the early Nyanza mission consistent with CMS tradition in Uganda concerned the theological orientation of the missionaries. Since the CMS was the most conservative missionary society of the Church of England, it is not surprising that those sent out would be evangelicals. However, even within the CMS the early missionaries to Kenya were regarded as lesser educated and more theologically conservative than their colleagues who served in Asia.[8] "Within the CMS, Kenya remained a stronghold of an orthodox theological position" (Strayer 1978, 87), whereby "most of the missionaries were conservative evangelicals or fundamentalists" (Church of the Province of Kenya 1994, 3). Perhaps surprisingly, while this missionary conservatism often clashed with local customs like naming and dress (Temu 1972, 107), it could nevertheless be tolerant with other traditions like polygamy (Strayer 1978, 79). This conservative yet practical orientation was attractive to many African traditionalists, and it formed their first and lasting impressions of Christianity.

Throughout this period, these foundational policies and methods remained in force. As the CMS-Nyanza mission grew and expanded, these initial precedent and tradition-forming methods maintained their influence over many Luo in Nyanza, and all future CMS efforts would be evaluated by these pristine criteria.

Indications of this Period in the Johera Narrative

Popular and pristine Luo perceptions of CMS policy and methods in this foundational period are indicated in a number of references in Ajuoga's text. Remembering the earliest days of the CMS-Nyanza mission almost ninety years later, Ajuoga highlights the elements of early CMS methods that were still active in forming his Christian experiences.

The first indication of the influence of this period on Ajuoga's text and experience is in paragraph twelve, where Ajuoga refers to the "unscriptural teachings" of the Wahamaji. These questionable practices are outlined in one of Ajuoga's letters (1955), and are frequently referred to throughout the *Johera Narrative*. The hermeneutic Ajuoga employs both to identify and "correct" these "unscriptural teachings" betrays the theological conservatism of the earliest CMS missionaries to Nyanza. As we have noted, this religious traditionalism was attractive to many Africans, and consequently it would serve as the standard, functional interpretive paradigm in the Christian experiences of Johera.

A second vestige of this period formative in Ajuoga's experience concerns the early missionaries and the nature of their interaction with the Luo. Ajuoga praises the efforts of the earliest CMS missionaries, specifically lauding their offer of academic education (pars. 65-66). In paragraph sixty-two Ajuoga fondly remembers J. J. Willis, and expresses his honoured position in popular Luo CMS folklore.[9] Both references reflect the deep respect for and even romanticization of the first generation of CMS missionaries in Nyanza, with whom all successors were compared.

This veneration of the earliest CMS missionaries was due, in part, because of their perceived partnership with the Luo. In paragraph twenty-two Ajuoga expresses the popular recollection that the Luo elders permitted the presence of the missionaries. It is remembered that the Luo first extended hospitality, yet they retained control of their landscape; consequently the hosts and not the missionaries were initially understood by the Luo to be dominant. This perception of a partnership slanted in favour of the Luo persisted, and formed the popular criterion for appropriate missionary-African relationships.

This understanding of the retention of Luo power is indicated by a third set of references to this period. As already noted, Ajuoga praises the missionaries for their educational pursuits (pars. 65-66), and confesses that it was personally important that he attend the "schools valued by people" (par. 23). This was primarily because missionary education was popularly believed to offer empowerment within the new colonial reality. Even so, paragraph fifty-nine reveals the ambivalence of the older generation to missionary education. Ajuoga recounts that, while some Luo adults permitted their children to be educated in the missionary schools, they did not desire it for themselves. The chiefs and adult Luo were aware of the social tensions being produced by the introduction of the missionary schools, and although they were attracted to certain elements of this new form of education, they were nevertheless ambivalent. This reluctance, however, allowed the chiefs and adult Luo to retain power over the situation by deciding which of their children—if any—could be so educated. The popular perception was that the missionaries were present to serve on Luo terms, not to be served on CMS terms.

Another crucial influence from this period was also formative in the experience of Matthew Ajuoga and Johera. The place where the CMS-Nyanza mission was established among the Luo, Maseno, was recognized by the Luo Anglicans as a centre of Christian influence, even as a holy place. Through several references (pars. 58, 73, 77, 158) Ajuoga remembers that Maseno became a popular meeting site for Anglicans from all over Nyanza. In the development of Johera, however, Maseno came to symbolize the pristine form of Anglicanism which was first introduced in Nyanza. Consequently, Maseno would be selected as the headquarters of Johera and the CCA, and this decision was meant to claim and communicate that they were heirs of the Anglicanism originally brought to Nyanza.[10]

Portents of Crisis in the CMS-Nyanza Mission, 1921-1952

The future of the CMS-Nyanza mission was radically altered in 1921 as a result of the decision to transfer Nyanza from the Uganda Diocese to the Diocese of Mombasa. This change was initiated to allow the entire newly established colony of Kenya to be administered under the same Anglican purview. The Bishop of Mombasa at the time, R. S. Heywood (serving 1918-1936), consequently was given the oversight of all Anglican efforts in the whole of Kenya, an expanse roughly the size of Spain and Portugal combined (Hewitt 1971, 121).

This reorganization was the subject of a prolonged ecclesiastical controversy "negotiated" over a period of nine years, from 1912 to 1921 (Hewitt 1971, 119, 126). The primary reason for the debate was the dissimilarities between the African peoples and missionaries involved, the unmatched maturity of the local churches, and the disparate CMS policies and methods in force.

> The two dioceses [Uganda and Mombasa] were at very different stages of development, and it required nice judgment to decide when the gain to the Diocese of Mombasa of the vigorous church life of Kavirondo would outweigh the advantage Kavirondo received from the continued association with the Diocese of Uganda...(Hewitt 1971, 126).

A compromise was finally reached, one which called for the Diocese of Mombasa to be divided into three "spheres": the Coast, the Central Highlands and Nairobi, and Nyanza. Each area was to be permitted a degree of independence, and in that way preserve and nurture the existing heterogeneity of each region (Hewitt 1971, 126-127; Murray 1985, 133). Even so, in practice this decision only increased tensions between Nyanza and the rest of the Diocese, especially for many Anglican Luo in Nyanza.

This placement of Nyanza under the jurisdiction of Mombasa only served to emphasize and aggravate the differences between the CMS-Nyanza mission and the other Kenyan fields. Within Kenya's three spheres of CMS work, Nyanza was unique, even an anomaly. The focus of CMS labours in Nyanza had always been on the evangelization of the local inhabitants and the expeditious development of the "three-self" church. This was possible, in part, because the CMS-Nyanza mission was not required to concern itself with two radically different and distractive factors of primary concern in the other CMS spheres in Kenya.

The oldest CMS field in Kenya was on the Indian Ocean coast, yet here the focus had been on work among freed slaves and the expatriate population until the early decades of the 1900's. Additionally, the dominance of Islam created a delicate diplomatic element which determined CMS policies and practice. Likewise, in Kenya's Central Highlands and Nairobi extenuating conditions also existed. There, the presence of white settlers and the proximity of the centres of colonial economic and political power influenced the nature of CMS efforts (Oliver 1952, 245ff; Temu 1972, 11, 32). Given these political and perilous dimensions of the other two CMS spheres, by comparison the work in Nyanza was an oddity.

This mismatch produced a second consequence for many Anglicans in Nyanza. Because of their linkage with such dissimilar partners, many associated with the CMS-Nyanza mission became even more aware of their peerless condition in Kenya, and this self-revelation reinforced the existing custom of "praying towards Uganda." The differences between the other Kenyan CMS spheres and Nyanza caused many Luo Anglicans, and to a lesser extent some of the missionaries, to see a continued practical connection with Uganda desirable and even necessary. Not only was Nyanza much closer geographically to Kampala than to Mombasa,[11] but also in terms of Christian appropriation and the essential nature of the local church, Luo Nyanza Anglicans were more closely related to their Ugandan mother than to their Kenyan stepbrothers. Just as imposed physical boundaries have not often been practically recognized by many ethnic groups throughout Africa, so this forced ecclesiastical separation was often not honoured at the grassroots. In fact, rather than ending their relationship with the mother church, this unwelcome adoption by the alien Diocese of Mombasa produced an even greater desire for many Luo Anglicans to remain united to their spiritual Ugandan kin.

A third consequence of the CMS-Nyanza transfer to the Diocese of Mombasa followed the two already mentioned. As a result of the practical alienation of Luo Anglicans from the other CMS spheres in Kenya, and even though it was officially administered from Mombasa, because of the geographical and ideological distance involved the Luo within the CMS-Nyanza mission received only limited and cursory hierarchical attention. Consequently, during this period the CMS-Nyanza mission would be ill-equipped to wrestle with two major challenges encountered by the Luo.

The first test was the rapid growth and consequent demands of the church in Nyanza. By the late 1930's the Anglican Church in Nyanza boasted over fifty thousand baptized members (Hewitt 1971, 142). Writing in 1934, one CMS missionary in Nyanza characterized the Anglican Church there as "an immense baptizing machine" (quoted in Hewitt 1971, 142). This hasty increase was primarily due to the nature of the establishment of the CMS mission, the publication of the New Testament in Dholuo in 1926, and the effectiveness of the African clergy and lay evangelists (Oliver 1952, 240-243). However, this mass entrance into the Anglican Church was as much a burden as blessing, because it created more converts at a greater rate than could be effectively pastored. In 1936 the same CMS missionary in Nyanza observed that "the Church holds up no challenge, no higher ideal; [it] has its Church Council, divides its collections, condemns the polygamists and goes on in the same old way" (quoted in Hewitt 1971, 142).

This Christian superficiality was largely a result of the lack of sufficiently trained leaders in Nyanza, African and missionary. Due to conditions in Britain, mission contributions drastically declined between 1914 and 1949, and consequently the number of missionaries sent out also decreased (Hewitt 1971, 231-232). Additionally, the advanced training of African clergy lagged. Because of the perilous and more urgent situation in Central Kenya, specifically related to the vision of Kenya as a white reserve, the CMS policy for the theological education of Africans was altered and decelerated (Hewitt 1971, 155-160). This revision mirrored the 1949 assessment of general African education in Kenya as expressed in the controversial "Beecher Report."[12] As a result, the large yet immature church in Nyanza received insufficient and inappropriate assistance from Mombasa.

The otherwise preoccupied and understaffed Diocese of Mombasa would also provide inadequate direction for a second crucial challenge faced by Luo Anglicans in this period. The early 1900's brought not only the beginning of CMS efforts in Nyanza, but also the establishment of no less than seven additional Christian missions there.[13] In the domain of the Luo, the area most significant for Johera, this proliferation was particularly intense. By 1908 at least six Protestant societies were at work in Kisumu alone, and the same number were at work in the immediate area of Maseno (Hewitt 1971, 142; Mojola 1993, 131). Consequently, "within a radius of ten miles from Maseno by the first quarter of this century, white missionaries had already introduced the religious tensions and conflicts of Christian denominationalism" (Mojola 1993, 130-131).

Despite early efforts by J. J. Willis to form one "native" church, attempts which were primarily focused on the Central Highlands and Nairobi, this vision was never realized (Hewitt 1971, 142-147). Once again, the more delicate and high-priority environments of the other CMS spheres would receive the bulk of Mombasa's ministration, and the Luo Anglicans would again suffer neglect.

This environment of Christian non-cooperation and mercantilism was not only confusing but divisive for the Nyanza Luo. Luo traditional society, already weakened by colonial policy, was further undermined by this religious competition as families and clans were divided by conflicting Christian loyalties. Rather than healing the wounds and resolving the tensions of the Nyanza Luo, a popular perception arose that missionary Christianity only contributed to these inflictions. Furthermore, Luo disillusionment was increased because of the Anglican hierarchy's perceived unwillingness or inability to produce a remedy.

Indications of this Period in the Johera Narrative

The tensions for many Luo Anglicans that arose during this period are evident in the *Johera Narrative*. For Matthew Ajuoga personally, these years were most formative because they included his birth, early education, conversion, call, and initial training for the Anglican priesthood. Considering, then, that this period represents the one in which Ajuoga's engagement with the CMS mission in Kenya intensified, it is not surprising that he should express his personal frustrations with the difficulties summarized above.

Perceptions, impressions, and expectations formed in this period remained with Ajuoga and many other Luo Anglicans, and these precedents can be understood as portents of the crisis which came to the CMS-Nyanza mission in the 1950's. The persistence of the custom of seeking spiritual direction from Uganda was previously mentioned, and this practice can be appreciated when the increased alienation from Mombasa is considered.

Matthew Ajuoga's perception of a lack of serious attention from the Anglican hierarchy is woven throughout his text, and in paragraph 139 he records and summarizes his frustrations. If Ajuoga's desperate reminder that "the Bishop of Maseno is also the Bishop of Mombasa" (par. 139) would have or could have been more seriously regarded, many of the tensions rooted in this period and indicated in the *Johera Narrative* might have been resolved otherwise. Four such potentially relievable irritations are narrated by Ajuoga.

The Christian Legacy

First, major portions of Ajuoga's text record his disappointment with the inaction or inappropriate action in Nyanza of the Anglican hierarchy when faced with volatile situations. The doctrinal controversies which attained crisis proportions during the height of the East African Revival in Nyanza were, according to Ajuoga, insufficiently addressed by Mombasa. In several places (pars. 27-43; 61; 89-99) Ajuoga regrets the perceived excesses of many Nyanza Anglicans, and this all the more because of Mombasa's inaction. Yet, these controversies are not surprising when understood within the context of the rapid growth of Anglicanism in Nyanza during this period. Additionally, given the decrease in trained leaders during these years, it is no wonder that many looked to more appropriate and immediately accessible agents for spiritual direction.

Second, Matthew Ajuoga's disillusionment with Anglican theological training for Africans is recorded in several paragraphs (131-141), and his attention to detail reflects serious consideration arising from long-standing and widespread discontent. The popular disdain for the "Beecher Report," the document which epitomized the general paternalism and racism which undergirded all African education in Kenya, is expressed in two paragraphs. Ajuoga recalls that it was the "Beecher Report that messed up education here" (par. 147), and a consequent negative image of the Anglican Church in Nyanza later attracted many to Johera (par. 188).

Third, indications of the growing polarization between African and White which erupted during Mau Mau surfaced in this period. Even in Nyanza, originally far removed from the "white highlands" of Central Kenya both in terms of geography and in the nature of race relations, racial disharmony intensified during these years. Ajuoga records in several places his personal discomfort and anger over this growing paternalism and racism (pars. 56, 73-74, 81, 144-146, 166). He summarizes popular Luo feelings when he recalls that it was commonly believed that "a white man is holding the Bible on the right hand and on the left he was holding his own Bible, because few of them were good but many of them were against the blacks." This was all the more surprising and painful, for "despite this they were saying that they were Christians, [and] these things were troubling one's mind" (par. 149). This racial tension, therefore, aggravated by CMS policies in education and hierarchical inattention, contributed to Johera's crisis in the 1950's.

An additional factor which contributed to Johera's crisis was the presence of numerous Christian denominations in Nyanza, and the divisions they encouraged are noted and criticized. Luo land, once the possession of all, was partitioned by alien merchants of religion (par.

63); Luo marriage customs, which were intended to solidify and preserve the unity of the larger group, became a source of social fragmentation (par. 64); and, the Bible and education became instruments for the creation of new and inappropriate inequalities (par. 66). A novel tribalism was therefore introduced, a type that was foreign and bewildering. Religion, normally a unifying force among the Luo, became a basis for disunity, and rather than ethnicity remaining as the primary source of identity, new self-definitions based upon denominationalism were recommended.

These emerging frustrations and disillusionments among many Luo Anglicans increased in the mid-1950's, and largely due to the nature of CMS responses, a religious crisis erupted for Johera.

The CMS and the Crisis in Nyanza, 1952-1958

By the early 1950's "Kenya was a divided country," in which a "de facto apartheid system" existed (Murray 1985, 236). This racial division was demonstrated by the differing visions of the colony's future, and in the disparate roles expected of the various races. As discussed in the previous chapter these tensions erupted in the form of Mau Mau, and in 1952 the colonial government responded with the declaration of a state of emergency. Even though the epicentre of the crisis was far removed from Nyanza and the government officially considered the contested issues to be non-religious, the tensions would nevertheless directly affect the CMS-Nyanza mission.

The State of Emergency created a delicate dilemma for the CMS. As the representative of the State Church, the settlers generally expected the CMS to take their side, and because of the power of the white community the Anglican Church had to give it serious consideration. The popular settlers' interpretation of Mau Mau, shared by many CMS missionaries, was that it represented "an anti-Christian movement, a reversion to tribal atavism, paganism, and cultural barbarism." Leonard Beecher, Assistant Bishop of Mombasa from 1950 and the Bishop of Mombasa from 1953, believed the target of Mau Mau was actually the Church (Furley 1972, 106, 114). Even if they did not share Beecher's interpretation of the essential anti-Christian nature of the rebellion, most Europeans—missionaries and settlers—regarded Mau Mau as "anti-European...whose leaders planned to turn Kenya into a land of 'darkness and death'" (Rosberg and Nottingham 1966, xvi).

Even so, a few CMS missionaries working at the grassroots recognized that this interpretation was simplistic, and that for many African Christians another issue was paramount. Within the church, even among many of the most devoted Anglicans, "all the time the urge of the Africans to be free of British rule was becoming stronger" (Olang' 1991, 29). At large within the Kenyan Church was an African campaign to reclaim the initiative over their religious lives, and to reassert their power over their religious communities. For many Africans the crucial issue was not the acceptability of Christianity, but rather who was to administer that Faith in Kenya. Rather than violent "resisters," Mau Mau revealed many African Christians to be "disappointed collaborators" who were frustrated by their lack of effective control over their own Christian destinies (Strayer 1978, 70).[14]

Even missionary advocacy of Africans and their causes, for example the work of Walter Owen discussed in the previous chapter, betrayed latent paternalism and consequently aggravated many. "However genuine the missionaries may have been in desiring to represent natives, they were representing native interests as they themselves understood them, rather than as the Africans knew them" (Githige 1982, 123). Despite rhetoric to the contrary "the mission taught and demanded submission and total obedience, neither of which could be reconciled with the rising nationalism of the Africans" (Temu 1972, 9). Acknowledging this, a few sensitive missionaries recognized that Mau Mau "was as much directed against the missions [not necessarily Christianity] as it was against the British colonial administration" (Temu 1972, 2).

This popular campaign for increased African Christian self-determination was forming among many Luo Anglicans in Nyanza, and principal among them was Matthew Ajuoga. Ajuoga repeatedly sought CMS attention during this period, but given CMS's reaction to Mau Mau, an appropriate response was never realized.

Bishop Beecher was "bewildered and embarrassed" by the State of Emergency (Church of the Province of Kenya 1994, 89), and in view of this ambiguous and violent environment, the official CMS response to Mau Mau was to keep a low profile. Beecher warned against public outcries, both initiated by or even associated with the Anglican Church. The CMS, then, "officially refrained from public protests" and deliberately distanced itself from any public involvement. The CMS did not impede the efforts of the colonial authorities in dealing with the crisis; it did not desire to aggravate the situation (Murray 1985, 246).

In addition to questions concerning the morality of such silence in the midst of the appalling human rights abuses inflicted on Africans during Mau Mau, official CMS acquiescence produced two grassroot consequences for Johera. First, the popular image of the Anglican Church suffered (Murray 1985, 251-252). Even for the most dedicated

African Anglicans like Matthew Ajuoga, dismay and bewildering questions were produced. How could the agents of Christ and the alleged friends of Africans tacitly agree with the abuses, African or European, of Mau Mau? The obvious answer produced widespread disillusionment, because many Africans believed that for most Europeans colour was indeed thicker than theology!

A second consequence of the CMS policy of disengagement during Mau Mau was the increased estrangement of the church in Nyanza, particularly as it concerned Johera. For a Diocese that had always devoted primary attention to areas and issues outside Nyanza, the nature of Mau Mau and the CMS policy towards it only increased the Anglican hierarchy's preoccupation. Given the immediacy and volatility of the situation in the Central Highlands and Nairobi, the difficulties being experienced by a group of Nyanza Luo so far removed from the epicentre both in terms of geography and magnitude were relatively insignificant. A former CMS missionary in Kenya has acknowledged this Diocesan preoccupation, conceding that

> one realises why the Archdeacon in Nairobi, overworked and with the problems of the Kikuyu church during the Emergency on his doorstep, did not take it [Johera's difficulty] as seriously as he should have (Murray 1994).

The tension and activism of Mau Mau, and the nature of the CMS response increased the marginalization and frustrations of Johera. Because Johera's difficulties were not given proper attention by the Anglican hierarchy, increased disillusionment and feelings of abandonment and insignificance resulted. Accordingly, Matthew Ajuoga's numerous pleas for attention did not as much fall on deaf ears as on distracted ears. The Kenyan situation and the CMS determination to remain aloof prohibited Johera's distress from receiving proper attention, and Ajuoga's community was consequently left to fend for themselves. This tacit rejection from the Anglican hierarchy communicated that Johera was obliged to solve their own problems in their own ways; no sympathetic assistance would be forthcoming.

References to this Period in Ajuoga's Writings
The above summary of the crucial period 1952-1958 has highlighted the three most critical elements of Johera's predicament

during these years. By the beginning of the decade Matthew Ajuoga and his companions were suffering from perceived alienation and marginalization from the Anglican hierarchy in faraway Nairobi and Mombasa, and as these feelings increased during the middle of the decade, intense disillusionment and exasperation with the Anglican Church emerged. Matthew Ajuoga's repeated appeals for assistance were not given the attention he expected, and therefore by the end of the 1950's the second and third elements of Johera's condition appeared: a perception of abandonment and the necessity of self-determination.

These perceptions resound from Ajuoga's correspondence from the period, all pleas for attention. Ajuoga's first written petition offered to the Anglican hierarchy was his letter to Reverend R. Peaston, Missionary Advisor for Nyanza. Using two pages Ajuoga records his regrets of the contentions arising from various Revival-related meetings in Nyanza, and recollecting the disastrous historical record of such situations among Anglicans, he "humbly and respectfully" called upon Reverend Peaston "to take this matter really - [sic] deep into your heart and threat [sic] it honestly and sincerely" (Ajuoga 1955).

This same humble yet sincere concern for the Luo's growing perception of alienation is communicated by Ajuoga's three letters the following year.[15] In his letter to Bishop Beecher (Ajuoga 1956a) Ajuoga offers grassroots perspectives concerning the controversial suspension of a popular Luo clergyman in Nyanza. In yet another correspondence to Reverend R. Peaston (Ajuoga 1956b), he responds to Peaston's request for a list of the alleged "doctrinal errors" of the Wahamaji. However, Ajuoga's most detailed plea is offered in his fifteen page pamphlet, "The Light." From his perspective as a Rural Dean Ajuoga says that he was "very much burdened and concerned about the division existing in the church" in Nyanza, and he then sincerely and respectfully presents his detailed analysis of the problems and possible solutions (Ajuoga 1956c).

Within the *Johera Narrative* Matthew Ajuoga mentions two of these communiques, undoubtedly the ones he recalls as most significant. Ajuoga offers his commentary from a distance of almost forty years (pars. 83-86) on his letter to Reverend Peaston (Ajuoga 1956b), noting that he only wrote it after "things became bad" (par. 83). Likewise, in a lengthy commentary (pars. 87-151) Ajuoga reflects upon "The Light" (Ajuoga 1956c), which he wrote to illuminate the widespread frustrations among the Nyanza Luo (par. 87). Ajuoga's mention of these documents confirms, at least in his mind, the validity of his positions even after many years of reflection. Ajuoga's humility, sincere concern, and apprehension for the difficulties within the Luo Anglican community, as well as his persistent bewilderment, are clearly expressed. He regarded the problems of the 1950's as more of the same, perpetuated and aggravated by the continued lack of the Anglican hierarchy's resolve and appropriate action.

In one final act of desperation, and in his desire to remain united with the Anglican communion, Ajuoga sought redress from the Archbishop of Canterbury (pars. 241-245). In his petition (Ajuoga 1958a) Ajuoga reviews his interpretation of the difficulties in Nyanza, and then requests action which would allow the newly registered CCA to be officially recognized by Canterbury and so remain within the Anglican communion. After receipt of the Archbishop's reply, which was also perceived to be inattentive (Fisher 1958), Ajuoga writes a final, somewhat sarcastic letter to Canterbury (Ajuoga 1958b), which forever sealed the destiny of CCA to develop without Canterbury's blessing. With all attempts for serious attention exhausted, Johera's abandonment was complete and official!

While Matthew Ajuoga's fruitless attempts to attract attention to Johera's plight and his subsequent disillusionment is explicitly mentioned in several other places within the *Johera Narrative* (pars. 72-74; 78, 81), these impressions are implicit throughout the text. For the purposes of this study, in which a movement towards an interpretation of Ajuoga's perceptions is attempted, it is necessary to focus on the sources and impact of these perceptions rather than upon their actual basis in fact. Regardless of whether Ajuoga had reason to feel as he did begs the point; of significance here is that he did perceive neglect and abandonment, and he could, then, only act accordingly.

Consequently, two results of these impressions emerged, and both are crucial for the establishment of Johera. This perceived inattention and abandonment communicated not only administrative ineptitude, but blatant paternalism and racism. Were not Rural Deans, like Ajuoga, permitted such concerns and cries for attention? Should they not be deeply concerned for the welfare of their flock? Yet, the lack of serious attention to the sincere and respectfully presented concerns of a grassroots pastor suggested not only administrative clumsiness and inadequacy, but it also communicated a paternalism which esteemed silence and conformity and presumed to dictate what were valid and invalid concerns.[16]

Such treatment was offensive. Moreover, given the racially charged environment of 1950's Kenya, when Ajuoga perceived he was treated in such a condescending fashion by the Bishop himself (pars. 73-74), his dismay, anger, and desperation can be appreciated. The people of love (Johera), consequently, emerge to heal this hatred that was perceived even within the highest levels of the church (pars. 49-56).

A second consequence of Ajuoga's frustrated attempts at resolution within the Anglican Church relates to his own self-understanding. In order to encourage himself and Johera and justify his actions, Ajuoga recalls that he was not the first Christian leader to speak out against perceived abuses, nor to be disregarded and abandoned by the ecclesiastical establishment (pars. 84, 123-125). Calling upon a tradition that a more sensitive hierarchy might have anticipated and averted, Ajuoga invokes the names of Athanasius, Luther, Cranmer, Ridley, and Latimer in support of his cause and method. Indeed, from the very appearance of the abuses of the Revival in Nyanza, Ajuoga understood himself as a reformer, and decidedly accepted this mission for himself (pars. 43-45). Matthew Ajuoga sensed a call to be a reformer, and as a result, Johera emerges as a reform movement which understood itself to be an heir of this broader Protestant tradition of jilted definders.[17]

This section has provided a summation of Matthew Ajuoga's interpretation of Johera's difficulties with the Anglican Church in Kenya, and it is a story of mounting tension resulting from perceived misunderstanding, disregard, and abandonment. This component of their Christian legacy contributed to the formation of Johera's emergence and nature. In the mind of Matthew Ajuoga, Johera's formation was both inevitable and justified, given the demise of the administrative effectiveness and persistent inattention to local problems that characterized Nyanza Anglicanism as perceived by many Luo.

From Ajuoga's letters and his *Johera Narrative*, and from an understanding of CMS history in Uganda and Kenya from the 1880's to 1958, Johera's disillusionment with the Anglican Church was a result of two primary factors. The first was the conflict of missionary and Luo expectations arising from the transfer of Nyanza from the Uganda Diocese to Mombasa in 1921. The Nyanza Luo had come to expect the more liberal policies and methods established by the CMS-Uganda mission, their spiritual mother. However, these precedents clashed with the policies and methods that were dominant within the Mombasa Diocese, and consequently many Nyanza Luo were frustrated by their adopted Christian overseers.

Second, Johera's disillusionment with Anglicanism resulted from their increased perception of disregard and eventual abandonment. Given the drastic differences between Nyanza and the other spheres within the Mombasa Diocese, considering the more pressing issues in the Central Highlands and Nairobi during this period, and in the presence of the shortage of trained leaders and the official CMS reaction to Mau Mau, many Luo Anglicans became marginalized and alienated from the faraway centres of authority.

Consequently, by late 1957 Johera separated from the Anglican Church, and in the first month of 1958 it was officially recognized as the Church of Christ in Africa-Maseno. While this new community preserved much of its Anglican legacy in its faith and practice, in order to appreciate more fully Johera's choice of independency as narrated within the *Johera Narrative*, a second element of its Christian inheritance must also be understood. This component of Johera's Christian legacy emerged from the impact of the East African Revival in Kenya.

THE EAST AFRICAN REVIVAL IN KENYA, 1938-1958[18]

The East African Revival, also known as the Balokole (saved ones) Revival, was a mass movement of Christian evangelicalism which significantly affected the nature and future of Christianity in that region. Indeed, "for over a century the Balokole Revival has had a deep impact on many of the Protestant Churches of Eastern Africa" (Ward 1991a, 113), begetting "a tremendous effect on patterns of churchmanship throughout East Africa" (Church of the Province of Kenya 1994, 81). This manifestation of African Christian activism, because of its popular appeal and momentous impact, can rightly be included among the most significant events in the history of African Christianity.

More specifically for this study, the East African Revival is significant because the flames of the Revival were particularly intense in Matthew Ajuoga's 1950's Nyanza. The Awakening created contention and confusion throughout the region, and it provided the fuel for radical Christian zealotry parallel to the more socio-political activism of Mau Mau. Consequently, the Revival forms the second element in Matthew Ajuoga's Christian legacy, a spiritual heirloom which was crucial in the development of Johera, and one which is given paramount attention in the *Johera Narrative*.

Given this significance of the Revival for Matthew Ajuoga and his text, yet in view of the purposes and limitations of this study, this section will select those components of the Revival which were most crucial for Ajuoga's experiences as related in his narrative. First, a brief sketch of the East African Revival as it developed in Kenya will be offered. Then, a summary description of the major characteristics of the Awakening will be presented, and finally, this section will close with an examination of Matthew Ajuoga's recorded reflections of the Revival and their significance for his Christian experience.

Revival Comes to Kenya

The roots of the East African Revival have usually been located in the evangelical fervour of CMS missionary Joe Church and his colleagues in late 1920's and early 1930's Rwanda (Church 1981; Hastings 1979, 52), yet some find its origins in late nineteenth century CMS efforts in Uganda (Stanley 1978, 188-189; Ward 1991a, 113-114). Regardless however, of its exact time or place of beginning, by 1937 the Revival arrived in full force in Kenya (Murray 1985, 193). In that year the most popular proponent of the Revival, Dr. Joe Church, led a spiritual renewal convention in Kenya's Central Highlands, a one-week gathering attended daily by two thousand devotees (Hewitt 1971, 138). Also in 1937-38 the Revival came to Nyanza, when several teams carried the flames from the Anglican motherland of Uganda to the Luo and Abaluyia (Olang' 1991, 13).

These successful initial conventions generated sparks which were fanned by succeeding revival-related gatherings. Near Nairobi where he was serving as a CMS missionary, numerous meetings were organized by Joe Church's brother, Howard (Murray 1985, 193), and over the next twenty years local revivalistic assemblies were regularly held throughout Kenya.

Three colony-wide gatherings were also organized by the broad-based East African Revival Fellowship. The first was held in 1937 at Kabete near Nairobi, and the popularity of the Revival was demonstrated by the more than fifteen thousand who attended from all over the colony. The next two conventions were held at Maseno in Nyanza, the site of initial CMS labours among the Luo, and a place popularly regarded as holy. In 1951 the Maseno Convention attracted over six thousand revivalists, and in 1956 more than twelve thousand of the faithful were in attendance. This immense crowd of revivalists reflected the Awakening's persistent popularity over a span of twenty years (Barrett 1973, 113).

These assemblies also illustrate the mass appeal of the Revival, "so that during the '50's and '60's it was almost impossible for a[n] [Anglican] candidate to be accepted by his parish for clergy training if he was not deeply involved in the [Revival] fellowship" (Church of the Province of Kenya 1994, 82). This popularity and influence were a result of the Revival's attractive dominant characteristics.

Major Characteristics of the East African Revival

Even though the East African Revival occurred on the soil of that continent, and despite several distinctives directly related to African culture, a balanced understanding of the Awakening cannot be grasped without considering its broader historical context. The East African Revival must be interpreted within the tradition of recapitulating awakenings within the general history of Christianity, an approach which begs more intense scholarly attention. Even so, a few students of this East African version have understood this, at least superficially in principle (e.g., Stanley 1978; Warren 1954). Many of the dominant characteristics of the East African Revival, therefore, are common to all such movements throughout Christian history, and the local variants are primarily ones of chronology, geography, vocabulary, and impact. Four such local yet universal characteristics of the Revival will be summarized here.

A Movement Perceived to be "of the Spirit"

Alongside the sociological interpretations of the East African Revival (e.g., Welbourn 1961) must be laid the perceptions of those who actually shared its religious fervour. Indeed, the overwhelming conviction of the Revival's participants was that it represented a "movement of the Spirit within the Church" (Langford-Smith 1954, 77). One of the Revival's earliest sympathetic interpreters argued that the movement was a gift from God, a working of the Holy Spirit that was "uncoordinated by men" (Warren 1954, 13, 41). More specifically, another sympathizer believed that the Spirit was at work to convert and purge the Church in East Africa.

> It [the Revival] was, of course, primarily an answer to the unconverted state of a great part of the Church, and of some of the clergy. It was a revulsion from the hypocrisy of long-concealed sins, expressed in the release of open confession and restitution (Taylor 1958b, 15).

This intense movement of the Spirit was believed to be responsible for the revival and spread of Christianity across East Africa. Hundreds of thousands of Church affiliates became more active, myriads of non-Christians were converted, and thousands of new Christian communities were established. All these signs were affirmed and interpreted through the giving of public testimony, the Revival distinctive most commonly employed to proclaim the Spirit's movement (Warren 1954, 67-74).

Ecumenism Through an Individualistic Hermeneutic

A second distinctive of the East African Revival is a product of this intense movement of the Spirit perceived to be occurring in that time and place. The Spirit was understood to be no respecter of race or Christian tradition. Virtually all denominations were involved in the Revival to some degree, and all Protestants and to a lesser extent Catholics either actively participated or were directly affected by the Awakening. The Revival, therefore, brought together individuals and groups who had been divided by denomination and confession since the proliferation of Christian missions in Kenya at the turn of the century (Olang' 1991, 31).

This new common participation was not modern-day ecumenism, whereby formal ecclesiastical mergers are completed through the alteration of administrative structures and polity. Rather, while denominational and confessional distinctions were officially perpetuated during the Revival, in daily practice a common grassroots approach to Christianity emerged. Because all revivalists were expected to have a personal religious experience, Christianity came to be understood as an essentially individualistic faith, which by design and necessity was molded to meet the needs of each person's unique situation. Therefore, the commonality that arose was an expectation of intense, direct, and highly personalized participation in Christianity. Regardless of formal Christian affiliation, all revivalists thus shared a common set of spiritual expectations, and spoke a common Christian language. This oneness was illustrated by the standardized program used with little variation by all Revival fellowships, regardless of the denominational or confessional affiliations of their members (Warren 1954, 118-121).

This grassroots ecumenical effect produced two consequences of significance here. First, this emphasis on individual participation in the Revival denigrated the importance of individual involvement in the established churches, and indeed the Revival tended to withdraw people from their previous Christian affiliations. The newly established Revival communities, because of their commonalties and exclusiveness, often attracted more attention and resources from individuals than did the churches in which they held official membership. Consequently, the Revival fellowships were not only para-church, but were often anti-church (Hastings 1979, 53).[19]

A second consequence of the individualistic ecumenical effect of the Revival was its promotion of a form of ecclesiastical relativism. Many revivalists came to believe that of crucial importance for the individual was not denominational or confessional affiliation, but rather the possession of a personal faith experience; what was required was not church membership but a valid testimony. For many, this belief relativized traditional ecclesiastical structures, not only making one virtually as acceptable as another, but also tending to denigrate them all. Because the Revival was more concerned with the spirit of the Church than its form (Warren 1954, 19), it produced an ecumenical effect through spiritual individualism and ecclesiastical relativism.

The Mobilization and Empowerment of African Christians

A third distinctive of the East African Revival follows this popular understanding of Christianity as an essentially individualistic religion which could operate and even flourish outside the inherited, traditional ecclesiastical structures. This populistic and activistic environment created by the Revival mobilized and empowered masses of African Christians. Indeed, while many clergy and missionaries were actively involved in the Revival, especially in the beginning, the fervour and initiative quickly spread to the masses of grassroot Africans, and the Awakening "remained a very unclericalised movement" (Hastings 1979, 53).

The Revival was intensified and perpetuated through the small prayer and fellowship groups formed across East Africa by the laity, and that group is credited with most of the evangelism which resulted, even into "unevangelized" areas (Langford-Smith 1954, 79). The opportunity and effectiveness of this laity-led movement convinced grassroot Africans of two certainties: that "untrained" Africans could ably form, administer, and even advance their own Christian communities; and, that this could be accomplished without missionary assistance or agreement.

> Thus it [the Revival] enabled Africans in churches dominated by Europeans to exercise leadership and to show that they could set and maintain higher standards than the rank and file of their European counterparts (King 1968, 160).

One historian of African Christianity has argued that the East African Revival was, "from one point of view...the solidest proof of 'Africanisation,' something which missionaries could assuredly not control..." (Hastings 1979, 53). Accordingly, the East African Revival must be interpreted within the broader context of African activism which emerged across the Continent during the post-War period. Just as Mau Mau in Kenya demonstrated the intention of Africans to regain control over their landscape, so the Awakening expressed popular initiative for Christian self-determination. Without recognizing this element of the East African Revival, its final major distinctive cannot be appreciated.

Schismatic Effect

The more romanticized interpretations aside, the evidence confirms that the East African Revival created an environment in which schisms took root, grew, and blossomed. Numerous contentions were created by the Revival's legalistic zealotry, and while many disputes were contained and managed within the traditional ecclesiastical structures, many were not. Several African Instituted Churches were formed as a result of the Revival's schismatic effect—both within and without Kenya—because for many participants the "Revival was divisive" (Hastings 1979, 53). Indeed, because of the effects of the East African Revival, within Kenya "the seeds of separation were sown..." (Church of the Province of Kenya 1994, 86).

Most observers recognize the presence of Revival-related divisions, and it has been acknowledged that even missionaries could not agree over the validity and nature of the Awakening (Murray 1985, 191-192). Even so, this element of the Revival has yet to be given serious and in-depth scholarly attention.[20] To date, most interpreters have been content with the shallow and romantic versions of the type promoted by some of the earliest writers. These interpretations do not take the Revival's schismatic tendency seriously, either by failing to identify it (e.g., Langford-Smith 1954), or by denigrating its effect (e.g., Warren 1954).

However, soon after the embers of the Revival had cooled, F. B. Welbourn identified the schismatic effect of the East African Revival and attempted to assess its significance. In so doing, he sought to understand these Revival-related dissensions within the broader Protestant tradition of such tendencies (1961, 168-177). The highly individualistic, para-Church and even anti-Church element within the East African Revival, therefore, can be understood as part of the European Protestant legacy begot to Africa. This heritage was vigourously appropriated during the 1950's in Matthew Ajuoga's Nyanza, and it was crucially formative for Johera. The significance of this impact of the Revival for Ajuoga and his companions is given prominence within the *Johera Narrative*, and we now turn our attention to these references.

The East African Revival within the Johera Narrative

The significance of the East African Revival in the Christian experiences of Matthew Ajuoga and Johera is illustrated by the Awakening's saliency within the *Johera Narrative*. Forty-two percent of the paragraphs in text directly relate to the East African Revival, and consequently Ajuoga's narrative is in part a reflection on a personal experience of that Awakening. [21]

Given this prominence of the East African Revival within the *Johera Narrative*, yet in view of this study's limitations, an examination of Ajuoga's reflections on the impact of the Awakening in Nyanza must be comprehensive yet general. Therefore, two major themes of Ajuoga's Revival experience, both vital features of this element of his Christian legacy, will be identified and summarized.

An Encounter with Excesses

One of Matthew Ajuoga's most potent memories of the East African Revival is of an environment of excesses. The spiritual zealotry of this time and place created both legalism and license; it produced both doctrinal and moral abuses which heightened tensions and created dissensions (par. 12).

First, Ajuoga recounts the anti-Church tendencies of the Wahamaji (pars. 36, 52-57), a position produced by an individualistic legalism, and this in turn resulted in several doctrinal errors (pars. 83-86; 93; 103). Ajuoga understands these abuses to be the result of a diluted understanding of the work of Christ on the one hand, and on the other a faulty appropriation of religious rituals. The separatists in Nyanza were consequently dubbed *Joremo* (people of the blood [of Jesus]), because of their belief in salvation by merely claiming and confessing the efficacy of Christ's sacrifice. This ritualism was all the more shameful, according to Ajuoga, because many were not sincere (par. 28).

Second, this often insincere ritualism created a perception of moral license which in turn produced widespread immorality. This involved various forms of licentiousness (pars. 27, 39, 100), which often resulted in the disintegration of stable family units (par. 37) and the arrangement of invalid marriages (par. 35). Not only was such behaviour contrary to traditional Christian teachings, it further weakened already beleaguered Luo society.

The response of Matthew Ajuoga and his colleagues was to proclaim love in the midst of such extremism. Because of the tensions and divisions produced by these revival-induced excesses, Ajuoga and others became convinced of the need for love: both brotherly love and the love for God that Jesus taught. Only such love, according to those dubbed *Johera* for this position, could reconcile and heal the wounds of revival- stressed Nyanza (pars. 49-57; 157).

These reflections of the Revival's excesses and Johera's response provide two significant insights into Matthew Ajuoga's Christian experience. First, these paragraphs confirm that 1950's Nyanza was indeed a locale of crisis. The previous chapter described the general historical elements of the crisis of this time and place, and these references from Ajuoga's text affix another dimension. The East African Revival, directly related in both cause and effect to the wider tensions in 1950's Kenya, aggravated an already edgy environment by adding religious extremism. Consequently, Matthew Ajuoga was besieged by crisis from within and without the Anglican Church.

These references offer a second insight into Matthew Ajuoga's Christian experience, in that they portray Johera's own appropriation of certain components of the Revival's excesses. In order to counter the Christian reductionism and legalism of their opponents, Johera reverts to the same. Instead of confessing the sufficiency of "the blood," the adequacy of "love" was propounded. Likewise, while Joremo could be rigid in declaring their spiritual authority, Johera could be just as legalistic in questioning their opponents' orthodoxy. Even though the Wahamaji were openly and boldly anti-Church, Johera could be just as exclusivistic and ultimately even more schismatic in their rigid promotion of the "true" Church.[22] Consequently yet not surprisingly, Matthew Ajuoga and Johera were not unaffected by the excesses of the Revival. While they rejected the dominant beliefs and practices of Joremo, they nevertheless accepted the same spirit and methods.

A Movement that Betrayed Tradition

This revival-induced crisis was acute for Matthew Ajuoga, not only because it produced these excesses, but also because of what Ajuoga perceived this particular brand of zealotry represented. In Ajuoga's understanding the Wahamaji were indeed immoral and heretical, but they were also un-traditional and even anti-traditional. What the Wahamaji believed and practiced did not perpetuate the form of Anglicanism they had received, yet their beliefs and rituals had the further bane of being directly opposed to the fundamentals of the Anglican Church as understood by Johera.

These perceptions are expressed in several paragraphs within the *Johera Narrative*. Ajuoga's understanding of "unscriptural" and "biblical faith" (par. 12) was in relation to his notion of the Anglicanism he had received; "unscriptural" meant un-Anglican, and "biblical" meant consistent with Anglican tradition. Operating from this point of reference, Johera "tried to correct things biblically within the Church of England..." (par. 13), which reflects their original intention to preserve the unity and purity of the Anglican Church as they understood it.

This interpretation of the Wahamaji's excesses being un-Anglican is traced to the efforts of their spiritual ancestor, Ishmael Noo. Ajuoga remembers that in 1948 Noo and his followers had opposed "the church's doctrine" and subsequently left the Anglican Church; they were both un-Anglican and anti-Anglican (par. 27). On the other hand, the faithful were considered such because they "did not have any quarrel with the [Anglican] church," and remained faithful in the beliefs and practices of the Anglicanism they had received (par. 30).

In the presence of such anti-Anglicanism, when many "were separating [and] leaving the Anglican Church," Matthew Ajuoga concluded that he was the only "church leader who opposed that idea, who stood and said that that is not so" (par. 43). Instead, Ajuoga records deep appreciation for his Anglican heritage, yet by 1951 he perceived a massive betrayal of that tradition. He remembers that even the bishops, rural deans, and padres approved the false teachings (par. 44). Consequently, Ajuoga and several colleagues were then determined to "complete school [theological college] and come back to correct those false teachings in the church" (par. 45).

Ajuoga's contention that the Revival had produced an un-Anglican and even anti-Anglican variation of Christianity is the theme of his treatise "The Light" (Ajuoga 1956c). He begins by establishing his own Anglican orthodoxy, then throughout the next fourteen pages Ajuoga identifies the numerous aspects of Nyanza Anglicanism that he considered to be inconsistent with the traditions he had received. After offering his suggestions on how to return the church to its pristine state, he concludes with a prayer that "our church functions well along the proper line" (Ajuoga 1956c, 15).

This narration indicates the depth of Matthew Ajuoga's Anglican traditionalism, his personal theology that was dominated by ecclesiology, and his increasing frustration with those whom he considered to have betrayed this heritage. The appeal of religious traditionalism for Matthew Ajuoga will be discussed further in the next chapter, yet here it must be noted that one of Ajuoga's most cogent memories of the Revival was of a movement which betrayed his notion of Anglican tradition.

These references within the *Johera Narrative* express Matthew Ajuoga's impressions of the impact of the East African Revival on his experience. When these are coupled with his personal perception of the policies and methods at work within the CMS in Nyanza, a clearer understanding of the nature of Matthew Ajuoga's frustration emerges. Despite the contentions of those who would resign all leaders of African Instituted Churches to the categories of heretics, resisters, and rebels, Matthew Ajuoga constructs a radically different image of himself and Johera.

Ajuoga recalls that it was Johera who were first abandoned by the Anglican Church, rather than the reverse. He also perceives that in the face of widespread un-Anglican and anti-Anglican activities in Nyanza during the heat of the Revival, those involved in such were ultimately received warmly back into the Anglican fold, while Johera's faithfulness was not honoured, but repudiated. Among others, this communicated to Johera that organizational tidiness was more important than doctrinal and moral purity. Matthew Ajuoga's experience was thus not dissimilar to that of the older son in Jesus's parable (Luke 15:25-30), whose anger burned because of the notion that his loyalty was not appreciated as much as his brother's infidelity.

Consequently, Matthew Ajuoga can best be understood within the category of "disappointed collaborator" rather than "frustrated resister" (Strayer 1978, 70). His cooperation and faithfulness to the pristine Anglican tradition he had first received—his loyal collaboration—was not only disregarded, but punished. His disappointment quickly degenerated into disillusionment, and the establishment of Johera as an independent church became a reality.

This chapter has described the nature and significance of the two elements of Matthew Ajuoga's Christian legacy—the work of the CMS in Kenya-Uganda and the East African Revival—which not only contributed to his crisis in 1957, but which also provided patterns for his resolution. Moreover, Matthew Ajuoga's Christian legacy enlightens a paradox representative of African Christianity: the missionary religion's bequest of spiritual attraction and satisfaction, yet its bestowal of tension and crisis. This paradox would be managed, however, through the appropriation of the third context of Matthew Ajuoga's *Johera Narrative*, his primal heritage, and we turn now to a discussion of this element of Ajuoga's religious legacy.

Chapter 7

The Luo Legacy

As we have seen from the previous two chapters, Matthew Ajuoga's theological reflections have not developed in an historical vacuum, nor have they emerged from a context void of Christian tradition. Even so, the *Johera Narrative's* most immediate context is Ajuoga's primal heritage. Matthew Ajuoga was born into the rich religious tradition of the Luo, and this inherited "religious world" (Paden 1988) was not only the first religious system into which he was initiated, but additionally it was this "primal imagination" or the "abiding presence of the primal worldview" (Bediako 1995b, 93), which managed Ajuoga's later appropriation of Christianity, his adopted religion.[1] It was also this primal legacy which directed his innovative resolution to the crises already described, an experience recounted in his *Johera Narrative*.

In order to enlighten this presence and influence of the Luo primal imagination in Matthew Ajuoga's text, this chapter will seek to describe the nature, content, and significance of this inherited, Luo primal religious world. The discussion will proceed as follows: first, in order to provide a basic interpretative framework, a brief review of selected scholarship related to the relationship of primal religion and Christian appropriation will be presented; second, the Luo primal religious worldview will be summarized within its universal primal religious context; third, influences of this primal imagination evident in the *Johera Narrative* will be identified and interpreted; and finally, the tradition of religious innovation contained within the Luo primal imagination will be described, and its influence on Ajuoga's text will be examined.

THE INTERACTION OF PRIMAL RELIGIONS AND CHRISTIANITY

Twenty years ago John B. Taylor provided a now classic definition of "primal" as it relates to religion.

> "Primal" is used in the sense of "basic" or "fundamental," and to refer to those forms of society or religion, or those forms of comprehensive reference- systems, which are associated with what are commonly called tribal peoples or cultures. It is not meant to suggest that these are more fundamental, authentic or "true" than other religious systems, but simply that in historical fact they have been widely distributed across all continents and have preceded and contributed to all other known religious systems of mankind. In this purely factual sense they have been the most basic forms in the overall religious history of mankind; they also continue to reveal many of the basic or primary features of religion (1976, 3).

A year later Harold Turner summarized and re-phrased this definition, by stating that "primal religions"

> conveys two ideas: that these religious systems are in fact the most basic or fundamental religious forms in the overall religious history of mankind and that they have preceded and contributed to the other great religious systems. In other words, there are important senses in which they are both primary and prior; they represent a common religious heritage of humanity (1977, 28).

A further clarification of the meaning and nature of the primal religions came ten years later, when Andrew Walls argued that these religious systems reflected a "basic, elemental status in human experience," and consequently they held "historical anteriority" over all other subsequent religions (1987, 252).

The use of the term "primal" as it relates to religion, however, has not been universally accepted. In a recent article James C. Cox (1996) surveys this opposition and concludes that, because of the term's interpretive presuppositions, it should not be used in the more empirical or "scientific" study of the history of religions. Nevertheless, Cox affirms that the concept of "primal religion" does hold significance for theological studies, especially through illuminating the nature of Christian appropriation.

Indeed, it is because of this missiological significance of the primal religions that the scholars quoted above—Taylor, Turner, and Walls—devoted their attention to a study of these systems. More recently, Andrew Walls (1990b, 1995) has further developed his understanding of the significance of the primal religions for the appropriation of Christianity, and based upon the foundational studies of these pioneers, other scholars have also focused attention on this subject (Bediako 1995a, 1995b, 91-126; Cox 1996). From the writings of these scholars three basic insights have been gleaned which are relevant to this present study.

Primal Religions as "Receptor Language"[2]

The first fundamental assertion concerns the essential nature of the primal religions, and is drawn from the writings of John B. Taylor and Andrew Walls. Taylor's concern for studying the primal worldviews was related to inter-religious dialogue, and within this context he argued that an understanding of these primal religious systems was a prerequisite for understanding all other types of religious expression, and, hence, inter-religious communication. This was because he believed that, as the primordial and basic human religious experience, the primal religious world "can survive along with modern secular or humanist faiths and ideologies," and that

> their [primal religions] characteristic outlooks and experiences form part of the inescapable religious inheritance of all mankind—operative at varying depths and in varying degrees in all of us.... Even within those who do not practise one of the primal faiths, these views may continue to exist as unconscious values, outlooks, patterns of thought or longings which lie behind the more evident tensions, or the unexplained beliefs, aspirations, inhibitions and behaviour of individuals in any of the successor cultures (1976, 2).

Andrew Walls not only later agreed with this presentation, offering that "primal religions underlie all the other faiths, and often exist in symbiosis with them" (1987, 250), but he was also more blunt, arguing that "all other believers, and for that matter non-believers, are primalists" (1987, 252). Taylor and Walls, therefore, introduce the innate resilient and reincarnate nature of primal religious systems.

Consequently, when an individual undergoes religious change, the appropriation of the new religion is conditioned, either consciously or unconsciously, by the primordial religious worldview.

Furthermore, Andrew Walls clarifies this association of the primal religious world and Christianity to be a relationship in which "much of the configuration of primal religions" is incorporated "into Christian...communities," which produces "overlapping worlds of spiritual perception" (1987, 269-270). This process "is not about substitution, the replacement of something old by something new, but about transformation; the turning of the already existing to new account" (1990b, 25-26). Walls argues that instead of the primal religious world merely giving way to the universal religions, the primal imagination is carried over and "absorbed" into the new religious world.

The specific nature of this interaction between the primal religion and Christianity has been given various names, yet the most widely used term in the literature presently being discussed is "translation."[3] Within this interpretive framework, it is understood that "conversion...directly parallels the process of translation" (Cox 1996, 68), and therefore, the two processes of conversion and translation are actually two dimensions of the same experience of religious modification.

> Primal religions represent the base language, the already existing, into which the translation of the incarnate Christ occurs. The primal religions will be transformed by the process, but they will not simply substitute the new for the old. They will continue to live in the new but in such a changed condition that to speak of them as primal any longer is really inappropriate. They are Christians who have used the primal religions as a kind of receptor language into which the translation of the message has been received (Cox 1996, 68-69).

Based upon this understanding that the primal religious world forms the basic, interpretive paradigm for Christian appropriation, one can expect that Matthew Ajuoga's Christian experiences related in his *Johera Narrative* have also been managed by the primal religious worldview he inherited. Hence, in order to understand Ajuoga's appropriation of Christianity as it is expressed in his text, one must understand his primal imagination. Without understanding Ajuoga's primal "receptor language," it will be impossible to appreciate his

Christian "translation" (Cox 1996, 69) recorded in his *Johera Narrative*.

Primal Religions and Crisis Response

A second gleaning from recent scholarship on the primal religions basic for this study is again based upon the work of Andrew Walls.[4] Because of the local and ethnic nature of primal religions, and because the modern world is characterized by an accelerated trend towards universality, Walls argues that the primal religions of the world have undergone "disturbances of focus" in recent history. According to Walls, the omni-dimensional forces of modernity, paramount of which is the spread of the universal religions of Christianity and Islam, have issued "certain threats to primal religions" (1987, 266-267). Consequently, these local religious systems have been required to accommodate this new reality, which Walls interprets in terms of eight different responses (1987, 266-277).

Significant here is Walls's paradigm of "disturbances of focus" or crisis in understanding the appropriation of Christianity by the myriads of converts who have come to the Church directly from their primal religions in the last two hundred years. Walls acknowledges that the spread of the universal religions into the primal strongholds has resulted in religious clash and tension; that the resilient and reincarnate nature of the primal religions has been revealed through their survival responses to this challenge; and additionally, that this environment of crisis has formed and even determined the nature of Christian appropriation.

However, Andrew Walls is not the first scholar to identify and examine the role of crisis in the religious responses of primal religions. Forty years ago Anthony Wallace developed a now classic study of "revitalization movements," which he understood to be "deliberate, organized, conscious effort[s] by members of a society to construct a more satisfying culture" (1956, 265). Wallace's argument attempts to describe and explain organized religious responses to three "states" of social and cultural stress,[5] and it is relevant here simply to note that Wallace also understood the fundamental correlation between social crisis and primal religious innovation. In fact, Wallace argued that these religious responses to social tensions "are recurrent features in human history" (1956, 267), and therefore are to be expected in all situations of crisis.[6]

This declaration of the fundamental relationship between crisis and primal religious response is consistent with this study's paradigm for understanding the contexts of the *Johera Narrative*. We have already noted that Matthew Ajuoga's time and place was one of broad historical crises, and these perspectives of Andrew Walls and Anthony Wallace enlighten the religious dimensions of this crisis also previously discussed. Indeed, resulting from the environment of crisis in Nyanza, and compounded by the introduction and spread of Christianity, Matthew Ajuoga's primal religious world was confronted with novel challenges. According to the views of Walls and Wallace we can expect, then, that Ajuoga's religious response—the formation of Johera—was managed by his primal imagination. Consequently, Matthew Ajuoga's experiences with religious clash must be approached as a case study in the interaction between the primal imagination and Christianity within an environment of "interrelated pressures" (Ogot 1963, 273) or "disturbances of focus" (Walls 1987, 266).

Primal Religions as Theological Indicators

Before we proceed to describe the primal imagination which managed Matthew Ajuoga's religious crisis response, a final basic insight, this one from the recent writings of Kwame Bediako, must be noted. Using the above framework for understanding the interaction of primal religions and Christianity, Bediako offers that, not only can an understanding of the primal imagination enlighten our awareness of the translation process involved in the appropriation of Christianity, but it can also illuminate our appreciation for the nature of the newly adopted religion.

> If there is only a minimal "paradigm shift" as we pass from the spiritual universe of primal religions into the spiritual environment of the Christian faith ("this is what we have been waiting for"), then one would want to pursue the matter by asking how the primal imagination might bring its own peculiar gifts to the shaping of Christian affirmation (Bediako 1995b, 96).

For Bediako, an appreciation for the primal imagination will assist in the clarification and interpretation of the Christian theology of those whose theologizing is "moulded" by the primal worldview (Bediako 1995b, 96). Any theological innovations reflected in this fresh appropriation of Christianity can be indicated by an understanding of the primal religious background.

This assertion, therefore, instructs us to approach Ajuoga's text being alert to the primal "gifts" offered and revealed in his reflections on his Christian experience. If an understanding and appreciation of Matthew Ajuoga's Christian appropriation is to be attained, instead of carrying out a theological scan of the *Johera Narrative* in terms and standards alien to Ajuoga's inherited religious past, we must search for the primal indicators within the text, then from these begin to interpret his theologizing.

The recent arguments summarized above now require us to examine the specific content of Matthew Ajuoga's primal imagination, because it is this primal religious heritage which has managed his appropriation of Christianity, and it is this inherited religious world which offers a clear "window" through which to view and understand Ajuoga's Christian experiences related in his *Johera Narrative*.

THE LUO PRIMAL IMAGINATION

A number of scholars have attempted to describe and summarize the primal religious world,[7] yet for our purposes the general "six feature analysis" developed by Harold Turner (1977, 30-32) has been most helpful and will be used as the basic shell for our reconstruction of the Luo primal imagination. In addition, three classic studies have been used to form a basic contextual understanding of the primal religions of Africa,[8] and for describing the specific content of Luo primal religion, several additional sources have been utilized.[9] Together these studies permit an appreciation of the complexity and richness of Matthew Ajuoga's inherited Luo primal imagination within its universal context of primal religious traditions.

Kinship with Nature

Turner's first general feature of the primal religious world is "kinship with nature," by which he describes the innate sense that "man is akin to nature, a child of Mother Earth and brother to the plants and animals which have their own spiritual existence and place in the universe" (1977, 30). In Africa this understanding has been described as the belief that "man, who lives on the earth, is the centre of the universe. He is also like the priest of the universe, linking the universe with God its creator" (Mbiti 1981, 33). This belief results in all of nature being regarded as sacred and sacramental, and therefore, a person "endeavours to live in harmony with it" (Mbiti 1981, 39).

Specifically for the Luo, their entire religious system was based on this belief, and is reflected in their understanding that all creation possessed *Juok* (spiritual power or reality) (Ocholla-Ayayo 1976, 170). Two specific components of the Luo primal imagination, however, more vividly express this belief.

First, like all primal peoples the Luo had a deep reverence for their land, a veneration which cannot be understood in terms of the Western idea of land ownership and exploitation. "The Luo regarded the land as their mother, and the tribe as a whole was the proprietor of all the land in its area," and thus the Luo did not practice individual land ownership, but rather communal land appropriation (Odinga 1992, 13). The Luo understood that their land was a precious resource to be conserved: it had been secured for the use and enjoyment of all succeeding generations of Luo by their ancestors,[10] and it was additionally the source of their very survival as a people. This sacred perception of land produced a communal Luo identity, an understanding of a Luo nation that was inseparably linked with their ancestral land; to be Luo was to reside in, use, yet conserve a particular place.[11] Accordingly, it has been argued that, rather than speaking of Luo "land," it is more accurate to speak of a primal Luo "landscape," where the Luo did not merely reside and make a living, but where "the whole expanse of their experience" was commemorated (Cohen and Odhiambo 1989, 9).

Second, this sacramental understanding of landscape caused the Luo to select and revere many places as being especially sacred. These sites were chosen because of their affiliation with a particular holy event or person, and in these places shrines were built or identified to commemorate this natural sanctity. "Each [Luo] chiefdom had a shrine on a hill, in a dark forest or by a riverside. Some of the larger chiefdoms had more than one shrine" (P'bitek 1971, 59). These shrines were not temples, but usually trees (*libaga*) which were venerated (Hauge 1974, 105) because the *Jok* (spirits) of the universe were believed to reside there. These holy places reminded the Luo that they lived within a wider sacred community.

Human Weakness

Harold Turner's second feature of the primal imagination is "the deep sense that man is finite, weak and impure or sinful and stands in need of a power not his own" (1977, 31). The primal condition, in which humans were struggling to gain even elementary control over their environment, encouraged this belief. Whenever a situation arrived over which people had little or no control, humans were reminded of their finite and therefore vulnerable plight.

John Mbiti has recognized this belief as foundational for the primal religions of Africa, illustrated by the various creation myths present on the continent. In spite of the differences in specifics, most peoples in Africa believed that the original, perfect relationship between humans and God was severed to the detriment of humankind. Therefore, people live in alienation from God, and hence they are morally and physically weak and vulnerable (Mbiti 1989, 92-99). This belief in the fragility of the human condition is also an explicit basis for the felt need for sacrifices and mediators in African primal religions (Mbiti 1989, 58-91).

The Luo primal belief in the compromised condition of humanity is expressed in the Luo proverb, "In man two personalities exist: a positive and a negative" (Ocholla-Ayayo 1976, 42). Within Luo primal society two types of people were believed to be present: those possessed by good *juogi* (spirits), and those controlled by bad *juogi*. Not only did people's weakened moral condition make them susceptible to possession by evil forces, but even a good person lived in fear of attacks by evil *juogi* and their human agents (Ocholla-Ayayo 1976, 155-165). Consequently, the Luo recognized, honoured, and sought the assistance of those believed to be possessed by the good *juogi*, among whom were the "diviners, prophets, or priests." Conversely, those believed to be possessed by bad juogi, among them the witches, wizards and evil-eyed ones, were avoided and punished (Ocholla-Ayayo 1976, 160). The presence of these specialists were constant reminders of the insufficiency and vulnerability of humankind.

Humankind is Not Alone

Directly resulting from this primal belief in human weakness is the perception "that man is not alone in the universe for there is a spiritual world of powers or beings more powerful and ultimate than himself" (Turner 1977, 31). Not only did Turner understand this belief to be reflected in the universal primal recognition of the existence and activities of a multitude of lesser spirits, as noted above, but perhaps more significantly, most primal peoples are acutely aware of the presence of "God" or a Supreme Being.

In partnership with most primal peoples, yet employing a diversity of names with a myriad of meanings, "African peoples believe in God. They take this belief for granted. It is at the centre of African Religion and dominates all its other beliefs" (Mbiti 1981, 40). Indeed, through his study (1969) of nearly three hundred different primal groups in Africa, John Mbiti found "without a single exception, people have a notion of God as the Supreme Being" (Mbiti 1989, 29).

"In every African language and people, there is at least one personal name for God," and Mbiti offers that these African ideas about God fall into four broad categories: "what God does, human pictures of God, the nature of God, and people's relationship with God" (Mbiti 1981, 43).

A rich understanding of the presence and nature of a Supreme Being is also present in Luo primal religion. The primal Luo possess a central belief in a creator and sustainer God, *Nyasaye*, whose name comes from the verb "to adore," and means "He who is beseeched" or adored (Dirven 1970, 30). The Luo are, therefore, strongly monotheistic, they believe that *Nyasaye* is approachable, that He daily intervenes in human affairs, and that He "still creates, heals, and provides people with good harvests, cattle and many children" (Hauge 1974, 105).

Resulting from this popular belief in a personal and benevolent God, the Luo regularly offer prayers and sacrifices to *Nyasaye*, and His protection and good will are continually sought.[12] Especially significant here, however, is the Luo belief in a God who is deeply concerned for the plight of individuals as well as the group, whose assistance and will is to be sought by each individual, and who is ready and able to come to the aid of His people to save them from personal and communal tragedies. *Nyasaye* was understood to act as, in an unequivocal if not Christian sense, a personal saviour, who comes to the aid of the Luo in times of crisis.

Relations with Transcendent Powers

Implicit in this widespread primal belief in a Supreme Being is the understanding that humans are able to dialogue with and even manipulate the Transcendent. Harold Turner described this feature as the primal "belief that men can enter into relationship with this benevolent spirit world and so share in its powers and blessings and receive protection from evil forces" (1977, 31). To facilitate and channel this human relationship with the transcendent world, most primal peoples believe that "the gods have given men religious specialists...and special powerful rituals and correct sacrifices and proper customs" (Turner 1977, 32).

The rituals and religious specialists which direct primal people's communication with the spirit world are richly diverse throughout Africa (Parrinder 1969, 67-77), where this endeavour to relate to the Transcendent

> generally takes on the form of worship which is eternalized in different acts and sayings. These acts may be formal or informal, regular or extempore, communal or individual, ritual or unceremonial, through word or deed (Mbiti 1989, 58).

While the concept of worship is universally present in the primal religions of Africa, there is great diversity and flexibility in its specific expressions across the continent.

We have already noted that among the Luo relationships with the spirit world were fostered by the offering of sacrifices and through the veneration of sacred places. In addition, we have seen that within their primal religious system the Luo incorporated beliefs and rituals which permitted them to manipulate both the good and bad spirits. However, an additional element of this Luo primal dialogue with the Transcendent is particularly relevant here.

Preeminent among the many channels for primal Luo communication with the spirit world were the various types of charismatic human leaders that were popularly recognized, communally sanctioned, and highly honoured. Within Luo primal religion at least twenty distinct types of "mantics" were recognized,[13] and these can be divided into three broad categories.

The most powerful mantics were the *jabilos*, "those who possess magic." These leaders presided over public, communal and formal religious rituals and sacrifices, and consequently their functions were primarily ceremonial. A second type of mantic, considered to be the least powerful, was the *jakor*, or prophet. His duty primarily involved foretelling the future, and usually did not include the conduct of formal religious rituals, public or private (Hauge 1974, 49, 54; Ocholla-Ayayo 1976, 159).

Most significant for this study is the third type of traditional Luo mantic, the one perceived to possess the second greatest amount of spiritual power, yet who exerted the greatest degree of popular influence. This mantic was *ajuoga*, short for *ajuoga nyaka iondo*, "one who knows all." The *ajuoga* was believed to be possessed by a good *juok* (spirit), and was a religious general practitioner. He usually functioned as a diviner, priest, and prophet, and would conduct private and informal consultations and sacrifices (Hauge 1974, 49, 54). The *ajuoga*, though less powerful than the *jabilos*, was usually more influential because he was perceived to be more accessible and approachable. Accordingly, the *ajuoga* was most commonly called upon to settle personal disputes, to cure individual illnesses, and to manage personal oaths and ordeals (Ocholla-Ayayo 1976, 162-164). The *ajuoga* was the leader the Luo most frequently turned to for stress management and relief.

Afterlife

The fifth feature of Harold Turner's description of the primal imagination is the belief in an afterlife. "Man's relationship with the gods, his kinship with them indeed, is such that he shares their life and power not only in this world but also beyond death, which is not the end." Reflective of this belief is the widespread primal veneration of the ancestors, "the 'living dead,' [who] remain united in affection and in mutual obligations with the 'living living.'" In many primal religions the perception of the role of the ancestors as mediators between humans and the higher spirits is so prominent that an ancestral cult is created, in which this preoccupation with the ancestors "obscure[s] the spirit beings before whom they otherwise serve as mediators" (Turner 1977, 32).

Likewise, most of the primal religions of Africa contain a rich belief in the afterlife, also most prominently expressed through a focus on a particular individual or group's ancestors. "The ancestors are some of the most powerful spiritual forces in African belief, and in many places they take the place of the gods" (Parrinder 1969, 69). This is because the ancestors represent, not only the existence of an afterlife, but also the coexistence and interdependence of this life and the next.

Prayers and sacrifices are offered to the ancestors, who "are believed to show their power through the welfare or misfortunes of their family, in sending children and blessing the crops, or the reverse." The ancestors are so venerated because "they know all the intimate family concerns and will pass on to God the most pressing needs" (Parrinder 1969, 69). Usually, therefore, the significance of the ancestors arises from their potential benevolence and immanence, as opposed to the extreme apathy and transcendence of the higher spirits in many systems.[14]

Among the primal Luo, a fundamental belief in the afterlife was present, and the immanent reality of this spirit world was also expressed through a veneration of the ancestors.[15] For the Luo the ancestors were the focus of unity (Dirven 1970, 30), the source of their existence as a people and as a nation. They were also believed to have power over the daily lives of the people, and consequently various rituals involving prayers and sacrifices to the ancestors were practiced.

For our purposes, the most significant point here concerns the role of the ancestors in the Luo understanding of history. Because life in the present was believed to be lived in full view of, under the oversight of, and even with the aid of the ancestors who were vestiges of the past active in the present, all individual and communal actions were to be tested against the precedence and will of the ancestors. This deliberate linkage of the past and present was meant to produce a continuity between what is and what was, so expressing that "for the Luo, history is an active force shaping the present" (Dietler and Herbich 1993, 252). More specifically, "the Luo believe that the present is a result of past action and events" (Dietler and Herbich 1993, 256). As representatives of the past the Luo ancestors were an immanent bridge between the past and the present, and were considered to be the overseers of all history: past, present, and future.[16]

The Luo primal worldview can, accordingly, be characterized as deliberately conservative, one which prefers and seeks the preservation of the existing order, and one in which change takes place only with the sanction and guidance of the ancestors. Within such a traditionalistic religious system the present must always be managed and authorized by the past.

The Physical as Sacramental of the Spiritual
The sixth and final feature of Harold Turner's general description of the primal religious world is

> the conviction that the 'physical' acts as the vehicle for 'spiritual' power, in other words, that men live in a sacramental universe where there is no sharp dichotomy between the physical and the spiritual (Turner 1977, 32).

This belief produces a monistic view of life in which a mental or existential separation is not perceived between the secular and the sacred, or between religion and the rest of life. This perception gives rise to "the development and importance of the whole range of ritual and cult paraphernalia, healing objects and materials, and...the fetishes and charms used in magic" (Turner 1977, 32). These material objects are believed to symbolize and even channel the presence of the spiritual realm into the physical world.

John Mbiti has expressed this belief in the sacramental linkage between the physical and spiritual worlds in African primal religions as the perception of the universe as "religious," possessing "mystical" powers (1981, 33, 37). Consequently, because they believe they inhabit a sacred and sacramental universe, in African primal religions "people feel that many objects...have a religious significance. Some of these are natural objects..., and others are made by people themselves" (Mbiti 1981, 141). All these objects—charms, fetishes, masks, etc.—are understood to represent the presence and power of the spiritual in the midst of the physical.[17]

Within the Luo primal imagination this sacred connection between this world and the other is expressed, most commonly and obviously, through the giving of sacramental names to children. The Luo commemorate the time of day or night when a child is born by giving a related name that has religious significance. This practice reflects the Luo understanding of ritualized time, and practically means that all people live a life-cycle initiated and largely determined by the time they were born. An individual's life is believed to be directed by the nature of the spirit world's intervention at the time of birth.[18]

The Luo also commemorate the interdependence of the physical and spiritual worlds through the use of certain animals as totems or religious symbols. These totemic animals are venerated but not worshipped. Rather, these sacred creatures are used as symbols to teach and remind people of this sacramental relationship with all creation (P'bitek 1971, 91-92).

INDICATIONS OF THE LUO PRIMAL IMAGINATION IN THE *JOHERA NARRATIVE*

Our basic reconstruction of the Luo primal imagination offered above is requisite to a proper appreciation and understanding of the *Johera Narrative*. This preceding overview has been necessary because, according to the argument of those scholars mentioned in the first part of this chapter, the primal religion acts as the "base" or "receptor" language (Cox 1996, 69) into which Christian appropriation is translated. Therefore, Matthew Ajuoga's Christian reflections recorded in his *Johera Narrative* have been managed by the Luo primal imagination, and accordingly, indicators or vestiges of this primal religious world should be discernible within the text. The purpose of this section is to identify and interpret those influential and formative components of the Luo primal religious tradition that are most evident in the *Johera Narrative*.

However, a cursory reading of the *Johera Narrative* suggests that Matthew Ajuoga's primal imagination has had little if any influence on the text, because within Ajuoga's narrative the Luo primal religious heritage is not explicitly mentioned. Perhaps surprisingly, nowhere does Matthew Ajuoga expressly refer to his inherited religion, even in a negative sense. Why this silence on a religious heritage that, according to conventional scholarship, is so significant? If, as the scholars mentioned above argue, the primal imagination is indeed fundamentally formative on Christian appropriation, then why is this crucial factor not clearly addressed by Matthew Ajuoga? Three possible answers will be examined. First, it could be argued that the answer is related to

Ajuoga's intention for the *Johera Narrative*. Perhaps, because Matthew Ajuoga has narrated his text primarily for an external audience for reasons of positive image creation, he therefore deliberately avoids the subject of his primal past which could be easily criticized. To be sure, AICs are often attacked for alleged syncretistic tendencies, and perhaps Ajuoga is simply trying to avoid and even invalidate such negative impressions by refusing to mention his primal religious heritage.

Yet, this possible solution is not convincing, because it assumes that Matthew Ajuoga is attempting to exclude something from his text that he flaunts in other contexts; it suggests he is being deceptive or hypocritical. To those who know Matthew Ajuoga and the CCA, it is clear that Ajuoga is, and always has been, openly critical of much of his primal religious past. His sermons, lessons, and personal conversations are replete with critiques of parts of the Luo primal imagination, and Ajuoga's sincere and outspoken Christian conservatism is evident throughout his *Johera Narrative*. Indeed, Ajuoga's inflexible Christian conservatism is at the root of his disagreements with the Wahamaji.[19] This strict and critical attitude is not the exception but the rule among CCA leaders and members; it is the official CCA position. In fact, the CCA has always been known as one of the "least syncretistic" AICs, and this is evident from the CCA's beliefs and practices. Rather, the reality is that Ajuoga and the CCA have often been criticized by other AICs for being too "Western," for not reflecting their African primal heritage more visibly.[20]

A second possible explanation is to argue that Matthew Ajuoga represents the same category of African theologian as Byang Kato (Bediako 1992, 386-425). According to this interpretation, Kato, who was known for his unbending and hyper-critical attitude towards the African religious past, understood that

> the relationship between the African heritage in religion and the Christian faith...constituted quite distinct and discontinuous entities, different religious systems with little or no common ground between them (Bediako 1992, 389-390).

This argument would offer that, like Kato, Ajuoga has not referred to his inherited religion because he has become so thoroughly "Westernized" that he can see no possible use for his primal heritage, and thus his life is dedicated to a deliberate, conscious crusade to escape and repudiate his religious past.

Once again, this solution is not convincing. Unlike Byang Kato, Matthew Ajuoga not only founded an AIC because of his unease with Western Christianity, but he has spent his life promoting the rights and even the preeminence of Africans within the Christian enterprise. Ajuoga's efforts within the CCA and the OAIC reflect, rather than a repudiation of his primal imagination, a celebration of God's revelation among Africans, in African ways.[21] Additionally, those who know Matthew Ajuoga understand that he is extremely proud of much of his Luo heritage, and in many ways he lives and functions as a traditional Luo patriarch. Over the years Ajuoga has even suffered for his advocacy of Luo traditions and opinions.[22]

A third reason why Matthew Ajuoga does not expressly mention his primal imagination in the *Johera Narrative* is the most convincing. This solution is based upon the thinking of Kwame Bediako (1995a, 55-56), who argues that the African theologians who are the most vocal advocates of the primal past are not the only ones who value that heritage. Rather, it can be argued that those who are not preoccupied with the primal imagination are those who have in a sense "made peace" with their religious past, and then with this resolution in force, have progressed in their theologizing. Those who have been able to reconcile the tensions between the two religions—the inherited and the adopted—are, therefore, among the most mature, and consequently are among those who can teach the most about the interaction of these dual religious traditions.

This insight offers the most satisfying solution to the problem of Matthew Ajuoga's silence, because it allows us to reconcile on the one hand his staunch Christian conservatism, with his sincere appreciation of much of his primal heritage on the other. Moreover, this answer also is the one which best explains the reality of Ajuoga's life and ministry, in which he daily moves between and incorporates components of both religious worlds.

This argument, then, permits us to view Matthew Ajuoga's silence as symbolic of his theological maturity, as a sign that he has "made peace" with his primal imagination and has moved on in his thinking. Rather than evidence that his primal past is of no consequence, Ajuoga's silence is reflective of the fruition, vigour, and potency of his religious translation. His unconscious and automatic intellectual movement between his two religious traditions has become so natural and unpretentious, that he sees no need to mention it; it is obvious to him, yet unaffected. Ajuoga's silence, then, indicates the complete and completed integration of his two religious worlds.

Any examination of the *Johera Narrative*, therefore, must consider this reality and significance of Matthew Ajuoga's reconciliation between his inherited and adopted religions. However, in the absence of explicit statements from Matthew Ajuoga relevant to this relationship between his primal imagination and his Christian appropriation, the interpreter of Ajuoga's narrative is required to approach the text with an awareness of the particular nature of the primal indicators that are offered. Because the *Johera Narrative* is not intended to be a treatise on the role of the Luo primal imagination within Matthew Ajuoga's Christian experience, but rather a narration, explanation, and defense of his personal African Christian experience, the influence of Ajuoga's primal heritage is implicit rather than explicit.

Consequently, the *Johera Narrative* contains a "between the lines" exposition of Matthew Ajuoga's personal Christian translation from his primal "base" language, and so what must be anticipated within the text are vestiges or subtle, general indicators of the Luo primal imagination. Instead of including a "first line," or word-for-word explanation of religious translation, what Ajuoga offers is rather a "third line," or tight paraphrase of religious transformation, in which the frame of his primal heritage is preserved, but the specific expressions are modified. Ajuoga's resolution represents a "free" religious translation, in which the content is genuinely Christian, yet one in which the basic religious structure is incorporated from his primal imagination.

What is to be anticipated, therefore, is to locate within the *Johera Narrative* not analogues between Ajuoga's two religious traditions, but rather motifs of the presence and function of his primal religious heritage within his Christian experience. Even though such exact matches or direct translations could be identified and discussed, for example Ajuoga's concern for sacred places and wholistic ministry,[23] what is believed to be most significant here are the fundamental components of the primal grid employed by Matthew Ajuoga in his appropriation of Christianity.

The nature of this indication of Matthew Ajuoga's primal imagination requires that, in order to understand the role of the primal heritage in Ajuoga's Christian appropriation, his text cannot be best approached through content analysis. Instead, an approach more closely resembling structural analysis must be adopted, in which the most formative features of Ajuoga's primal religious framework can be identified. Below, because of the limits of this study, we identify and interpret only the two most crucial components of Ajuoga's primal grid which have formed and managed his Christian experience.

The Luo and East African Prophetic Tradition

One of the most obvious and formative components of Matthew Ajuoga's primal imagination, indicated from and in his text, is the Luo and East African prophetic tradition. Throughout his narrative Ajuoga portrays himself as a mantic, providing leadership and innovation during a crisis. Indeed, the very fact that he has narrated his experiences reflects his consistency with the Luo and broader East African prophetic tradition. As a prophet, Ajuoga is obligated to relate his experiences because of his mantic responsibility to explain and instruct. It is, therefore, within this context of the Luo and East African prophetic tradition that the actions of Matthew Ajuoga can be enlightened.

A fascinating publication (Anderson and Johnson 1995b) illuminates the existence, richness, diversity, and significance of the prophetic tradition among the peoples of East Africa. More specifically, throughout Kenya and among the Luo and all their neighbours, an ancient mantic tradition is present and active. These beliefs and practices overlap and have produced a trans-ethnic or "shared and syncretic prophetic tradition" across East Africa (Waller 1995, 55).[24] This common prophetic tradition

> refers to a community's perception and apprehension of a prophet and prophetic activity, the confirmation of forms of prophetic behaviour through the expectations of the community (Anderson and Johnson 1995a, 16).

Two aspects of this shared mantic tradition are particularly significant for our purposes.

The Prophet as Crisis Manager

Within the East African prophetic tradition, a prophet is understood to be "a charismatic leader" who emerges and is crucial "at times of stress" (Anderson and Johnson 1995a, 4). Indeed, "the stimulus to the rise of charismatic authority is usually found in a crisis involving conflict and suffering," and consequently the prophet in East African tradition is primarily a "crisis leader" (Anderson and Johnson 1995a, 11- 12). During times of internal or external stress, the prophet is believed to possess special knowledge which can assist the community. Through his direct communication with the spirit world, the prophet is able to instruct and guide the community in crisis resolution.

Given this historical function of the prophet as crisis manager, it is not surprising that during the period of greatest crisis in modern

African history—the last two hundred years—a proliferation of prophets was realized.[25] Across East Africa, beginning in the nineteenth century and continuing to the present day, the presence and importance of prophets has been widely recorded. "The stories of the colonial conquest of Kenya tell of many prophets" (D. Anderson 1995, 164), and indeed a common and collective Kenyan response to colonialism and the spread of Christian missions was the rise of myriads of African prophets, each providing direction for managing this new European crisis.[26]

The presence of this tradition of crisis management through prophets was still present and strong in 1960's Kenya (Ambler 1995, 233). Additionally, as we have seen above, a rich prophetic tradition exists among the Luo, in which three types of mantics are especially influential. We have noted that two of the three, *jakor* and *ajuoga*, function as prophets. These specialists act, in part, as mediators between the community and the spirit world providing knowledge, direction, and instruction for daily living. The influence of these mantics, however, is greatly increased during times of individual or communal crisis. Because crisis situations include little if any historical precedent, specific direction for handling these novel situations is sought directly from the spirit world through the mantic.

It is not surprising, therefore, that this abiding primal prophetic heritage influenced Matthew Ajuoga's experience as recorded in his *Johera Narrative*. Living in a time and place that valued and even expected prophetic activity, growing up in a family of crisis managers, and, in fact, bearing the very name ajuoga and believing he was called by God,[27] when Matthew Ajuoga is confronted by crisis in 1950's Kenya, he could not be expected to act in a manner inconsistent with this heritage. Indeed, the *Johera Narrative* records that many looked to Matthew Ajuoga for leadership in crisis management, and his personal experiences in that role are narrated. Ajuoga's text, then, cannot be fully appreciated without understanding it within the broader context of this prophetic tradition of crisis management in East Africa

The Prophet as Innovator

A second aspect of the shared East African prophetic tradition is also significant here. As crisis managers often confronted by novel situations, East African prophets were required to be innovators, and this aspect of their function was not only popularly appreciated, but expected. The prophet is sought and respected, to a large degree, because he is believed to be able to "offer a new order, a new vision of society" (Anderson and Johnson 1995a, 4).

Indeed, the "fundamental basis" of the East African prophetic tradition has been defined as "the notion that at times of need God guides a community by speaking directly to particular women or men" who possess and communicate a hitherto concealed solution to a crisis (Ambler 1995, 234). Usually, this solution represents an innovation, in which the prophet introduces new beliefs or actions, or fresh interpretations of the past or present. The prophet is not, then, always valued for his predictions, but often he is expected to pronounce innovative "commentary upon the past" or offer novel "guidance on the regulation of social and political practice in the present" (Anderson and Johnson 1995a, 18-19).

Within this heritage of anticipated prophetic innovation, an understanding and appreciation of both the dilemma and actions of Matthew Ajuoga can be formed. Living in an atmosphere of crisis, people looked to Ajuoga for resolution, but a resolution that required innovation; the new crisis was popularly expected to produce a novel response. Therefore, Matthew Ajuoga's choice for African Christian independency, and more significantly, his own innovative form of independency,[28] was widely supported because it was anticipated and popularly believed to be required. The Luo and East African prophetic tradition demanded that Matthew Ajuoga take the lead in crisis resolution, and the mantic heritage necessitated that this resolution be innovative.

Luo Primal Traditionalism

The second most formative aspect of the primal grid through which Matthew Ajuoga makes his Christian translation concerns the traditionalistic nature of Luo religion. While within the Luo and East African prophetic tradition the prophet is expected to provide crisis resolution through innovation, he is also required to act within the constraints of the primal religion's traditionalism. Even though the prophet is permitted a degree of flexibility, he nevertheless is required to explain and justify his innovation within the basic traditions of society (Anderson and Johnson 1995a, 16-19).

Above, we have noted that the Luo primal religion is traditionalistic, in that it teaches that the past is present, and that, therefore, the present must be lived and explained in relationship to the past. "Indeed, a desire to remain faithful to a pattern of life laid down in the past by ancestors, gods, heroes or kings is a dominant characteristic of all simple societies" (Turner 1971, 50). Given the fundamental nature of this traditionalistic orientation of primal religions, it can be expected that primal conservatism would influence Christian appropriation.

In an enlightening article Philip Turner (1971) argues that instead of the "conservative, legalistic and pragmatic" theology of most African Christians being reflective of their Westernization, they rather "describe a form of Christianity which fits easily with many (though not all) aspects of traditional cultures of Africa and which can with justice be called adapted or even indigenous" (Turner 1971, 45). Given the traditionalistic nature of most primal religions in Africa, the conservative forms of Christianity frequently offered by missionaries were the most comprehensible and attractive. Consequently, this shared primal traditionalism has produced a reality in which "the essential elements of the belief and practice of the majority of Protestants in East Africa are identical" (Turner 1971, 46).

It is within this context of primal religious traditionalism and its widespread influence on Christian appropriation in East Africa that Matthew Ajuoga's staunch Christian conservatism must be interpreted. As was noted in the previous chapter, within his *Johera Narrative* Matthew Ajuoga describes his frustrations with the perceived liberalism of both the Wahamaji and the Anglican hierarchy, and this frustration was in part produced because of its inconsistency with the traditionalism of his primal imagination. Additionally, Ajuoga would claim and perpetuate the "original," more conservative form of Anglicanism, because this type of Christianity was most consistent with his primal religious heritage. Therefore, the conservative and traditionalistic nature of Matthew Ajuoga's Christian innovation is reflective of his primal imagination.[29]

The above discussion of the East African prophetic tradition and the primal religion's traditionalistic orientation has provided the background for an appreciation of a final crucial element in Matthew Ajuoga's primal legacy. The primal religions of East Africa, confronted by the novel realities of colonialism and missionary presence in Matthew Ajuoga's time and place, responded by managing numerous religious innovations. Indeed, the vigour and resilience of the primal imagination is reflected in the rich religious responses to the coming of Christianity that emerged, and this component of his primal religious world was formative for Matthew Ajuoga's experiences as related in his text.

EAST AFRICAN RESPONSES TO CHRISTIANITY

Despite more traditional approaches to the History of Christianity in Africa, which propound the heroic initiatives of missionaries and portray the virtual helplessness of Africans in grabbing all that was on offer as it was offered, it is now widely acknowledged that Africans were not passive in this encounter.[30] On the contrary, it is now recognized that across the continent Africans were active, not only in the proclamation and reception of Christianity, but also in producing new forms of the missionary religion. Consequently, an appreciation of African religious innovations is expanding.

For this study, the most significant African innovative response to Christianity is the nineteenth century movement which produced thousands of African Instituted Churches (AICs).

> It is in fact the case that on a scale unparalleled in the entire history of the expansion of Christianity, schisms from foreign mission bodies in Africa have been taking place for the last one hundred years (Barrett 1971, 148).

From the first appearance of these communities in Sierra Leone in 1819, AICs had by 1985 proliferated to an estimated 7170 separate denominations in forty-three countries, and had grown to include an estimated thirty-three million adherents. Ten years ago the growth rate of these groups was estimated to be 850,000 new members per year, and there is no evidence that this figure has radically declined (Barrett and Padwick 1989, ii).

The significance of these movements in African Christianity is reflected by the scholarly attention they have received: in 1989 an estimated three thousand books and articles had been written on studies of AICs (Barrett and Padwick 1989, 2). Not surprisingly, this volume of material represents diverse—even opposing—approaches and attitudes, and numerous theories have been proposed to explain the origins and significance of these communities. Since we cannot survey this vast amount of literature here, it is sufficient to note that regardless of the specific details of the arguments propounded by each scholar, virtually all observers of AICs agree that their appearance and proliferation "were the spontaneous result of the impact of the white man's presence on native society..." (Lanternari 1963, 4). AICs are thus recognized as a crucial element of the total African religious response to the coming of Christianity south of the Sahara.

Within this wider emergence of AICs, African responses to Christianity were especially potent in East Africa. In Uganda and Kenya, the two areas most influential for the experiences of Matthew Ajuoga, AICs began to appear soon after the turn of this century, and by 1985 more than 250 had been registered with the Kenyan government alone (Barrett and Padwick 1989, 18).

Our purpose here is not to survey each case of African Christian innovation in Kenya and Uganda, but rather to acknowledge their presence and assess their impact within the *Johera Narrative*. More specifically, the vitality of AICs and other religious responses among the Nyanza Luo must be recognized, and the significance of this potent precedent of local Christian innovation in the experience of Matthew Ajuoga must be appreciated.

African Religious Innovations in Nyanza

The first African Instituted Church to appear in Nyanza was the Nomiya Luo Mission, which was established by the Roman Catholic catechist John Owalo in 1907. During the next decade more than thirty independent bodies would be formed from the Anglican Church alone, and most of these were in Western Kenya and Uganda, both influential areas for Matthew Ajuoga's experience (Barrett 1973, 59). This tendency continued, and during the forty years between 1920 and 1960 approximately one hundred AICs would be established in this region alone.[31]

The propensity towards Christian independency was particularly acute among the Nyanza Luo. Within a year of the coming of the first Christian missionaries to Nyanza, the first Independent Church among the Luo, the Nomiya Luo Mission, was established. A proliferation of Luo AICs began, so that by 1966 at least thirty-one distinct Luo AICs had registered with the Kenyan government (Barrett 1968, 14). This tradition was especially intense in the heartland of Matthew Ajuoga's Christian experience, for in addition to his CCA, no fewer than eight AICs appeared in the immediate vicinity of Maseno alone (Mojola 1993, 140). From this group of African religious innovations present in Matthew Ajuoga's landscape, two examples will be highlighted to illustrate the impact of this tendency among the Luo.

The Mumbo Cult

In 1913 the Luo prophet, Onyango Dunde, began to proclaim that he had been swallowed by a serpent in Lake Victoria. According to Dunde, upon spitting him out onto dry land the creature gave him this prophecy:

> I am the God Mumbo whose two homes are in the sun and in the lake. I have chosen you to be my mouthpiece. Go and tell all the Africans...that from henceforth I am their

God. Those whom I choose personally and also those who acknowledge me, will live forever in plenty.... The Christian religion is rotten.... All Europeans are your enemies, but the time is shortly coming when they will all disappear from the country (quoted in Ochieng' 1992, 97).

Faithful to this calling, Dunde immediately began to preach the religion of Mumbo and against Christianity and all things European. He criticized wearing European clothes, the cutting of hair, and pronounced that both the European invaders and their religion would soon be gone. He also prophesied that the European exodus would usher in an African "golden age" (Ochieng' 1992, 97).

From its beginning Mumboism was popular in South Nyanza where it attracted a large following among the Luo and Abagusii (Ochieng' 1992, 96). The movement eventually became influential throughout the entire region, however, even among those Luo who were not officially affiliated with the group. Indeed, Mumboism became so popular, and its anti-European message so alarmed the colonial administration, that in 1921 the Luo leaders of the movement were arrested and exiled on the holy Islamic island of Lamu in the Indian Ocean (Maxon 1989, 83). The cult was ultimately banned in 1954 (Wipper 1977, 73).

Understood within the rich Luo prophetic tradition especially vital around Lake Victoria, the appearance and appeal of Mumboism is not surprising. Additionally, given the tensions of the time—products of the introduction of colonial administration and Christianity into Nyanza—Mumbo's nativistic and millenarian message offered security and resolve for thousands of Luo. Even so, to be noted here is the presence and appeal of this movement, both of which would contribute to the eventual formation of a tradition of Luo responses to Christianity.

Dini ya Msambwa

Even though it was an early and influential religious innovation among the Nyanza Luo, Mumboism did not profess to be Christian. However, one of the most influential religious innovations in Nyanza was an African Christian movement, *Dini ya Msambwa*, the "Religion of the Ancestral Spirits." Founded in 1943 in Nyanza by the Luhyia prophet, Elijah Masinde, Msambwa was "an attempt to return to the teachings of the Bible in its literal sense." Accordingly, the church particularly emphasized many Old Testament teachings and practices like the offering of animal sacrifices and a strict legalism. Msambwa was decidedly anti-political, and was understood to be an African

Christian innovation in which Africans could enjoy a form of Christianity "of their own," and one in which many of their most valued customs and traditions were preserved (Were 1972, 87).

Dini ya Msambwa became extremely popular among Nyanza's major peoples, the Abaluyia and Luo. In part because it was involved in several acts of violence during the mid-1940's, and partly because of its increasing popularity and influence, the movement was eventually perceived as a threat to the region's stability and the success of Christian missions in Nyanza. Accordingly, in 1948 Msambwa was proscribed and Masinde was arrested and deported to Lamu. This eventually led to an eruption of violence in Nyanza in 1950, in which over fifty Msambwa members were wounded and four policemen were killed (Rosberg and Nottingham 1966, 328-329). However, instead of destroying the church, this persecution served only to strengthen it, and *Dini ya Msambwa* continues to be popular today in parts of Nyanza and Western Provinces.

Just as the Cult of Mumbo established the resilience of Luo primal religion and the readiness and ability of the Luo to formulate and accept religious innovations, so Msambwa reflected the willingness of many Christians in Nyanza to accept local Christian innovations. In both groups the prophetic tradition was accepted and active, and Nyanza consequently proved itself to be a receptive environment for African religious—even Christian—innovations.

Several scholars (Barrett 1968, Rosberg and Nottingham 1966, Wipper 1977) have noted this Luo tradition of innovative response, in which they generally reacted to the strains of European contact "through accommodation rather than opposition." "The Luo...did not attack the source of strain...but cooperated...and utilized instead a 'coping' mechanism" which allowed them to perpetuate the old ways while accepting the new (Wipper 1977, 51).

The tradition of Christian innovation among the Luo must be interpreted within this particular pattern of response. Likewise, as a product of this time and place, Matthew Ajuoga's Christian experience was greatly influenced by this tradition of Luo Christian innovation, particularly by Luo Christian independency. The significance of this element of Ajuoga's Christian legacy is illuminated within his *Johera Narrative*.

References to this Tradition within the Johera Narrative

The presence and significance of this tradition of African Christian innovation is noted in several references in Ajuoga's text. First, Ajuoga specifically mentions the ministry of Alfayo Odongo (pars. 89-90).

Commenting on his treatise "The Light" (Ajuoga 1956c), Ajuoga remembers that in 1934 Odongo believed he was called to establish a new church, and indeed he formed *Dini ya Roho* (Religion of the Holy Spirit) in that year. Odongo had started his "Holy Spirit Movement" almost twenty years earlier, but it had remained within the Anglican Church, partly because of the greater tolerance and informality of early Nyanza Anglicanism. He also remembers the related violence which eventually erupted.

Ajuoga also refers to the innovations of Ishmael Noo (pars. 27, 92), who in 1948 formed the "Christian Universal Evangelical Union" (Barrett 1968, 11). Ajuoga recalls the immoral and unscriptural teachings of Noo and his followers, and the accompanying social breakdown (see Welbourn and Ogot 1966, 29ff).

A brief mention is also made of three other African Instituted Churches which Ajuoga identified as being influential in Nyanza during the 1950's. First, he mentions the Gikuyu, Bildad Kaggia (par. 94), who in 1946 left the Anglican Church and formed the AIC, *Arata a Roho Mutheru* (Friends of the Holy Spirit) (Murray 1994; Welbourn and Ogot 1966, 30ff).[32] Ajuoga then recalls two AICs formed in 1948: Reuben Kihito's *Dini ya Jesu Kristo* (Religion of Jesus Christ) (par. 96), and Elijah Masinde's *Dini ya Msambwa* (par. 97). As before, Ajuoga recalls the groups' excesses which destabilized both the Anglican Church and the relevant African societies (see Welbourn and Ogot 1966, 49ff).

Ajuoga's interpretation of these innovations, as well as his reason for mentioning them in "The Light," is expressed in paragraph ninety-eight. There he states his opinion that these occurred because "things were not good...when the Anglican Church did not become careful and seriously teach to put people in the right direction." This paragraph, taken within its broader context, illuminates the significance for Matthew Ajuoga of the African tradition of Christian innovation active in Nyanza during the 1950's.

Ajuoga was aware of the existence of this tradition; he acknowledged its wide appropriation, its popular appeal, and its potent influence. He also recognized its potential for disharmony, both within Anglicanism and African society. However, it is interesting that Ajuoga blamed the Anglican Church for these schisms (par. 98). While he criticized the excesses of the schismatics and their betrayal of Anglican traditions, Ajuoga perceived that the Anglican Church was ultimately responsible. Because of its inattention and laxity, the tradition of African Christian innovation had been resorted to repeatedly, and taken within the context of Johera's strains, these observations can be understood as a warning of Ajuoga's temptation to appropriate the same tradition of Christian independency.

Issued in 1956, Ajuoga's veiled threat to appropriate this tradition of Christian innovation himself suggests two elements of his initial perception of African Christian independency. First, this tradition was popularly regarded as a legitimate African response to a novel situation and an alien faith. When Ajuoga later understood this tradition of local responses within its broader historical context (pars. 211-220), he was able to argue that innovations based upon culture have been a perennial element of the universal Christian story. Second, Ajuoga perceived that a choice for independency was not therefore innately wrong; it had historical precedent, and especially when the local situation left no other choice (pars. 123-125), local Christian innovations could actually be positive developments.

These paragraphs, therefore, confirm that a tradition of Christian innovation was both present and active in Matthew Ajuoga's time and place. Ajuoga himself was aware of this legacy, both in its negative forms and in its historically and locally legitimated manifestations. This Nyanza legacy of African Christian innovation consequently wielded influence—both consciously and sub-consciously—and held out the possibility of resolution in the midst of Johera's crisis. Vigourously appropriated in his time and place, the formation of innovative responses to Christianity was a crucial element of Matthew Ajuoga's primal legacy.

In summary, an understanding of the Luo primal imagination can enlighten both the process and content of Matthew Ajuoga's Christian appropriation indicated in his *Johera Narrative*. Most formative, however, are three features of Ajuoga's primal heritage: the prophetic tradition which required that Ajuoga direct crisis resolution through innovation; his primal traditionalism which, coupled with his sincere grasp of Christian evangelicalism, required that his resolution follow a direction perceived by Ajuoga and the Luo to be traditionalistic: historically justifiable and conservative; and, finally, the precedent of Christian innovations which offered models, encouragement, and legitimation for the formation of the CCA.

Chapter 8

A Literary Survey

The three preceding chapters have described the specific historical and religious contexts from which the *Johera Narrative* has emerged, and the influences of these formative environments on the text have been interpreted. Now, with this contextual understanding of the narrative in place, the next three chapters will focus on the text itself. Our purpose will be to gain an understanding of the essential characteristics of Ajuoga's narrative, its value as a theological text, and to offer concomitant interpretive guidelines.

Accordingly, the purpose of this chapter is to examine the singular nature of the *Johera Narrative*. This will be accomplished through an overview of the text from three literary perspectives. First, the text's forms will be examined, a topical review of the narrative's contents will then be presented, and finally a discussion of the text's two primary genres will be offered. The intent is to establish a general foundation of textual understanding, in order that, in the succeeding chapters more specific and accurate assessments and interpretative paradigms can be presented.

THREE PERSPECTIVES ON FORM

An appreciation of the form of Matthew Ajuoga's *Johera Narrative* must precede any assessment and interpretation of the text. This is because "form is content" (Denzin 1989, 9), that is to say, all evaluations of *what* Matthew Ajuoga says in his text must be interpreted with due consideration of *the way* he says it; the substance of Ajuoga's text is inseparable from the way he has structured his message. Moreover, the form of the *Johera Narrative* is significant for assessing the value of the text, because the form utilized by Ajuoga directly relates his message to various fields of study, each offering their respective insights into Ajuoga's contributions. Accordingly, Ajuoga's narrative will here be viewed from three literary perspectives.

Oral Historical Studies

An understanding of the form of the *Johera Narrative* can be assisted by using categories employed in the study of oral history. Even though, as already noted, the orality of the *Johera Narrative* should not be over-emphasized, still the original message was transmitted orally, and consequently Ajuoga's text bears certain marks of oral literature. Two oral forms are clearly evident.

Oral History

The form of the *Johera Narrative* is that of oral history as opposed to oral tradition. Jan Vansina has established that "oral traditions are no longer contemporary," but rather "have passed from mouth to mouth, for a period beyond the lifetime of the informants" (1985, 12-13). However, oral history refers to "events and situations which are contemporary, that is, which occurred during the lifetime of the informants" (Vansina 1985, 12). What Matthew Ajuoga offers in his text, therefore, is oral history, for he recounts events of which he was an eyewitness, happenings and experiences in which he was directly and actively involved.

It is necessary to make this distinction between oral tradition and oral history because both types of messages present different challenges to the researcher. Oral traditions are "the collective memory of a society which is explaining itself to itself." This is done via "key utterances," such as proverbs, riddles, and legends, which are "a means of preserving the wisdom of the ancestors" (Vansina 1981, 142).[1] Oral traditions are more official and communal, and usually reflect a degree of standardization of form. Their strength is the information they provide about the facts of the institutions of a given people (Vansina 1981, 149).

On the other hand, oral history provides a less formal and communal message, and consequently the narrator of oral history exercises more freedom and innovation in narrating events that are contemporary. The sources of oral history are "reminiscences, hearsay, or eyewitness accounts" (Vansina 1985, 12), which communicate private interpretations rather than public tradition. In oral history the form the message takes is less influenced by tradition than by the intentions of the messenger.

In approaching the *Johera Narrative* these distinctions must be recognized. While the limits of this study do not permit a fuller discussion of the significance of these differences, it must be noted that, in the case of the *Johera Narrative* because Ajuoga is recounting oral history, the form of his text says more about himself and his intentions than it does about Johera. Because the *Johera Narrative* is oral history, it primarily communicates the private perceptions of Matthew Ajuoga, and so the text should be viewed as a private rather than a communal account.[2]

Reminiscence

While the form of the *Johera Narrative* is that of oral history, such accounts can be expressed in various forms, such as hearsay or eyewitness accounts (Vansina 1985, 12). Even though Ajuoga's account bears some of the marks of these types of oral historical messages, the *Johera Narrative* primarily takes the form of reminiscence. According to Jan Vansina, reminiscences are

> the recollections of past events or situations given by participants long after the events...; they are bits of life history...; they are the image of oneself one cares to transmit to others (1985, 8).

Because reminiscences are personal, they allow a great degree of innovation in regards to form. Ajuoga's choice of narrative prose, as well as his decision to use a primarily chronological format, reflect his personal intentions for the message, and his intentions relate primarily to issues of legitimization and identity. Through the medium of personal reminiscence, Ajuoga's text reflects his construction of Christian identity and his attempts to legitimate his actions and Johera's existence. By using the form of reminiscence, Ajuoga conveys his primary intentions, and this understanding must be considered when interpreting his text.[3]

Studies of "Documents of Life"

A second helpful perspective for understanding the form of the *Johera Narrative* comes from the study of "life documents" in the social sciences.[4] In this context, "life documents" refer to materials such as oral accounts, letters, diaries, photos, or even dreams, which provide insights into the subjective reality of the informant (Plummer 1983, 105). "Life documents are an immensely valuable and vastly under- rated source" for the study of human experience. Their value is their ability to reveal life as experienced, rather than life as it actually occurred (Plummer 1983, 11). Three types of life documents are represented by Matthew Ajuoga's text.

Life History

First, Ajuoga's text is essentially a "life history," for it is "a spoken autobiography in which the informant is asked to relate at some length those parts of his life that seem to him most interesting and important" (Henige 1982, 106).[5] To be even more precise, Ajuoga's message is a "biographical life history," because it reveals the development of Ajuoga's life over a thirty-six year period (Plummer 1983, 105).

Like all life histories, Ajuoga's relates three levels of experience: his life as actually lived (reality); his life as he experienced it (experience); and, his life as he remembers and tells it (expression) (Bruner 1986a, 6). Therefore, consistent with the values of life stories, Ajuoga's text is full of insights into the phenomenology of his life, and the text's contributions are primarily a result of these rare glimpses of subjective reality within an African Instituted Church.

A "Self Story"

A second perspective regarding the form of the *Johera Narrative* emerging from the study of life documents reveals that Ajuoga's text can also be regarded as a "self story." A "self story" is a particular type of life history comprised of four major components: the self of the narrator is at the centre of the story; the story relates a number of "turning point" experiences; the story is not necessarily linear; and, though the primary focus of the story is the actions and experiences of the narrator, still a group dimension is expressed (Denzin 1989, 43-44). All of these elements are found in the *Johera Narrative*, and this perspective of the form of Ajuoga's text highlights yet again that the story is intended to relate more the private experiences of Ajuoga than the communal experiences of Johera.

A "Personal Experience Story"

Even so, there is a very strong communal dimension in the *Johera Narrative*, and Ajuoga has made it clear that he intends to tell the story of all Johera, for all Johera. Consequently, a third perspective of the text's form from the study of life documents discloses that the text can also be viewed as a "personal experience story." This is a life history that evidences a strong sense of community. Three elements are present in "personal experience stories": a description of communal experiences; interpretations of experience that relate to an entire community; and, the narrator communicates that his or her experiences were also those of a larger group (Denzin 1989, 43-44). These insights are helpful in understanding Ajuoga's desire to tell a story of a larger group, but they also reveal how the personal and communal dimensions in most life histories are intertwined; they cannot easily be separated without compromising the meaning of the text. Ajuoga's text is accordingly both about himself and about Johera; it relates private experiences in community.

Narrative Studies

A third and final perspective from which to view the form of Ajuoga's text comes from the study of narratives as a unique method of communication. The pertinent perspectives for this study have come from the study of narratives in both literature and theology,[6] and the "general assumption of narrative analysis is that telling stories is one of the significant ways individuals construct and express meanings" (Mishler 1986, 67). Narratives are regarded as "the first and oldest intellectual tool of the human species" (Mays 1983, 339), and one scholar has even theorized "that the formal quality of experience through time is inherently narrative" (Crites 1971, 291).

A narrative is recognized by two simple characteristics: a story and a story-teller. "For writing to be narrative no more and no less than a teller and a tale are required" (Scholes and Kellogg 1981, 4), yet at least five components are found in all narratives: meaning, characterization, plot, point of view, and the perspectives of an eyewitness (Scholes and Kellogg 1981, 17-56).

Because Ajuoga's text contains all these elements, and because the term "narrative" is broad and interpretatively neutral, I have chosen to refer to Ajuoga's story as a "narrative." As such, one particular value of the *Johera Narrative* emerges, and this is the text's ability to speak clearly in the language and forms chosen by Matthew Ajuoga himself.

> By focusing on narratives...we leave the definition of the unit of investigation up to the people, rather than imposing categories derived from our own ever-shifting theoretical frames. [Narrative] expressions are the people's articulations, formulations, and representations of their own experience (Bruner 1986a, 9).

Because Ajuoga's text is a narrative, it communicates an "inside" understanding of religious experience within an African Instituted Church, employing categories and emphasizing themes deemed important by Ajuoga himself.

In summary, our overview from three perspectives of the form of the *Johera Narrative* has provided an understanding of its following characteristics:

1. Ajuoga's text relates more a private rather than a communal account. Insights from the study of oral history require that the *Johera Narrative* be interpreted as the personal reminiscences of a Christian patriarch, not the corporate story of a Christian community.

2. Viewed from the perspectives of the social scientific study of "life documents" Ajuoga's text is understood to relate more to subjectivity than objectivity. His purpose was to narrate more his experiences of what occurred than what actually took place. The value, then, of the *Johera Narrative* is primarily in its ability to communicate phenomenology.

3. From the studies of narratives in literature and theology Ajuoga's story is viewed as a "narrative," which offers an "inside" understanding of an experience of African Christian independency. Because it is a "narrative," Ajuoga's text is truly *Ajuoga's* story: told in his way, employing his categories and themes; these are not imposed by an outsider. Consequently, the *Johera Narrative* offers a rare glimpse into the internal life of an African Instituted Church.

A TOPICAL PERSPECTIVE ON THE TEXT'S CONTENTS

With these insights into the form of the *Johera Narrative*, we are now able to turn to an overview of the text's contents, noting its major topics.

Six Major Topics

As noted earlier, the version of the *Johera Narrative* used in this study has been divided into 297 paragraphs (Appendix 1), and in an attempt to summarize the contents of the text and so understand its singular nature, six major topics developed by Ajuoga in these paragraphs have been identified.

Autobiography

Not surprisingly, Matthew Ajuoga opens his narrative with details of his private life. In these twenty-three paragraphs he narrates his birth, his education through seminary in Kenya and the US, briefly mentioning his first wife and his eleven children.[7] He recounts his Christian conversion and call to the ministry, and summarizes his extensive international travels. In six paragraphs he commemorates his father, Oguna, a Luo sub-chief who often cooperated with British missionaries and colonial authorities.[8] Even so, Ajuoga notes with pride that his father always acted independently, and was not a British "puppet."

In these paragraphs Ajuoga portrays himself as someone who greatly values his Luo heritage, yet at the same time who is proud of his pursuits in the wider world. Ajuoga is therefore not unconscious that he has chosen to live between two worlds: the Luo world of his inherited past, and the Christian world of his adopted past (Walls 1980). Ajuoga presents himself as an African, yet an African Christian. This topic, therefore, reveals one of the dominant themes of Ajuoga's text: his production of an African Christian identity, a theme which will be taken up further in Chapter 10.

Origins of the Church of Christ in Africa

Using forty-six paragraphs, Ajuoga gives his perspectives on the origins of the CCA.[9] This is one of the most developed topics in the *Johera Narrative*, and in these paragraphs Ajuoga describes his experiences, already discussed in Chapters 6 and 7, in overcoming a multitude of obstacles to establish an independent yet viable African Christian community. This topic is especially significant for understanding one of the text's dominant characteristics. Through it Matthew Ajuoga seeks to legitimate the past, and in a sense heal his wounded pride and seek wider acceptance for his actions.[10]

The Development of the Church of Christ in Africa

The second largest number of paragraphs are devoted to the development of the CCA from its inception to 1993. In seventy-five paragraphs Ajuoga recounts how the CCA grew in number and spread from its rural Nyanza base to several other Kenyan provinces and African nations.[11] Ajuoga gives three reasons for this growth and spread: the cultural sensitivity of the CCA, especially in regards to polygamy; the unpopularity of the Anglican Church in Nyanza; and, the enthusiastic support given to the CCA by colonial officials and influential white settlers.

In these paragraphs Ajuoga also emphasizes the diverse ministries of the CCA. Education, community development, medicine, and the advancement of women are all areas in which Ajuoga boasts involvement for his church. Here is evidence of the CCA's perpetuation of the traditional religion's wholistic understanding of life. Moreover, this topic also underscores Ajuoga's construction of the identity of the CCA as a large, diverse, socially engaged community, assisting its members to live amidst the everyday struggles of daily life in Kenya.

Challenges and Conflicts

Even though Ajuoga constructs an enhanced image of the CCA, still it is not idyllic. He devotes fifty-one paragraphs to a detailed account of the challenges and conflicts encountered by the CCA during its history.[12] Ajuoga understands these threats to the very existence of Johera to have come from four primary sources, two external and two internal. The external challenges came from the Anglican Church (CMS) and the National Council of Churches in Kenya (NCCK), and the internal conflicts resulted from a 1960 schism led by Ajuoga's deputy, Meshack Owira, and the CCA's popularly perceived lack of Christian legitimacy.

"God Loves Africa!"

A fifth topic, directly related to Ajuoga's concerns for legitimacy, is developed in a seventeen paragraph sermonette on the topic "God Loves Africa!"[13] Here Ajuoga reflects upon Africa's unique role in salvation history, and his texts are taken from the Scriptures and from the annals of Church history. He observes that Christian communities in all times and places have been formed according to racial and ethnic groupings, and is this regard he specifically mentions the Roman Catholic Church, the Greek Orthodox Church, and the Church of England. He therefore argues that, if God has a special role for Africans (and He does), and if there is Christian historical precedent for churches to represent specific human communities (and there is), then why can't Africans have their own churches if they so desire?

Commentary

The final major topic in the *Johera Narrative*, and the one to which Ajuoga devotes the greatest attention, is commentary on four of his writings. In eighty-five paragraphs Ajuoga explains and justifies three of his letters and one pamphlet written between early June 1956 and late October 1958, the period when Ajuoga's frustrations and disillusionment with the Anglican Church climaxed.[14] Ajuoga's commentary not only indicates a continuity in his thinking over a period of more than thirty years, but it also exposes the nature of his discontent with the Anglican hierarchy in Nyanza.

The above review of the *Johera Narrative* has introduced six major topics developed by Matthew Ajuoga, and each is worthy of further, more detailed analysis. However, given the purposes and limitations of this study which focus on the text's presentation, it is necessary to more broadly understand these topics as highlighting three dominant modes of expression employed by Matthew Ajuoga. Ajuoga's commentaries, and his focus on the origins, struggles, and development of the CCA suggest the first two. These topics relate to the internal dynamics of Johera over time, and reveal the literary and theological modes of expression related to crisis and legitimation. The topics of autobiography and Ajuoga's defense of African Christianity suggest Ajuoga's concerns for Christian identity, historical continuity, and restitutionism. These topics underscore the third basic idiom employed by Matthew Ajuoga: identity formation through a present appropriation of the past. These three basic literary and theological idioms will be further examined in Chapter 10.

TWO PERSPECTIVES ON GENRE

A final fruitful and necessary perspective from which to gain insight into the singular nature of Ajuoga's text results from an examination of the genres of the *Johera Narrative*. In noting the importance of understanding genre in the study of oral materials Vansina has stated,

> It is necessary to go further and to determine to which genre the message belongs. Genre is a concept that includes notions of form and specifications of content. A message is expressed in a given genre when it is put in a given form and internal structure, and when its subject matter corresponds to the rules prescribed (1985, 79).

Genres "are recognized in every culture" (Vansina 1985, 79), and in sub-Saharan Africa at least one attempt has been made to compile and classify various generic genres (Finnegan 1970, 55-76). Even so, variations on the specific types and purposes of genre are found from culture to culture, and this is due to the fact that genres are "concepts that are culture bound" (Vansina 1985, 81). A proper understanding of an oral text's genre, therefore, will follow only after identifying the genres that are recognized in the culture from which the text emerged.[15]

The primary genres of Matthew Ajuoga's *Johera Narrative* arise from the two traditions between which Matthew Ajuoga lives: his inherited Luo past, and his adopted Christian past (Walls 1980). These dominant genres will be summarized below, and the insights into the nature of Ajuoga's text which emerge will be presented.

The Luo Genre of Pakruok

Matthew Ajuoga is very proud of his Luo heritage, a point that comes across quite clearly in the early paragraphs of his *Johera Narrative*. Even though he has spent most of his adult life in a multi-ethnic environment, it is clear that Ajuoga has been, and continues to be, formed by his inherited Luo culture; this point has been highlighted in the preceding chapter. Moreover, this fact is of crucial importance for understanding the *Johera Narrative*, but in no area is it more significant than in understanding one of the primary genres represented by the text.

Among the Luo, one of the most common literary genres is *pakruok*, a Dholuo noun which is often translated as "praising oneself," "praise poetry," or "a praise story." This genre of literature, which praises the mighty deeds of past and present heroes, dominates both traditional and more recent Luo literature.[16]

While *pakruok* as a literary genre resists "reduction to easy definitions" (Amuka 1992, 95), all such literature has at least two characteristics in common. First, *pakruok* is literature which always contains praise, often lauding the great deeds of the ancestors, but also expressing the self-praise of the messenger. In addition, *pakruok* always contains several layers of meaning. The literal meaning is not necessarily the most important or even the intended meaning of the messenger. Thus, this genre lends itself to the praise of the quality of life and individual experience, more than a mere recounting of the quantity of heroic deeds (Amuka 1992, 76-96).

Even though *pakruok* is most often represented in brief, terse forms of literature, nevertheless the tradition of creating messages for the purpose of individual praise is not limited to riddles, proverbs, personal names, etc. This genre is also used to compose what is closely akin to what Vansina calls "great man" accounts, where personalities are at the fore, people control events rather than vice versa, and where events are never perceived as impersonal, but either good or bad. Such an account expresses the dominant role of the "great man" in *making* history (1985, 108).

The abiding use and significance of this genre can be illustrated by two modern examples of *pakruok*. The Luo political leader, Oginga Odinga, has employed the use of this traditional genre in writing his autobiography (1992). Perhaps more than most such accounts, Odinga's narrative is full of self-praise, recounting his victory over numerous struggles and forming a portrait of himself as an able leader. Likewise, *pakruok* is commonly used today by political leaders in Kenya who desire to impress their constituents. The genre is used to convince others of a leader's qualifications and experiences, and Matthew Ajuoga's use of *pakruok* is not dissimilar.

A second modern example of the use of this genre is recorded in Cohen and Odhiambo (1989). In this volume the authors have collected the personal stories of numerous Luo, and each account focuses on the individual's encounter with modernity. Poverty, unemployment, de-tribalization, and sexual discrimination are among the themes addressed, but throughout the individuals recount and praise their ultimate resolution of various problems. These stories highlight the persistent, grassroot influence of this genre, which is naturally and even unconsciously employed by the Luo when asked to relate personal experience.

Matthew Ajuoga's *Johera Narrative* should be understood within this *pakruok* tradition. As a Luo leader Ajuoga is well aware of the literary and historic traditions of his people, and he often refers to these traditions in his preaching and teaching.[17] Yet, while Ajuoga would not be considered a "tribalist" in the terms of modern Kenya, he is nevertheless a Luo activist. Ajuoga has definite opinions about the identity and role of the Luo in modern Kenya, and he is widely respected as a Luo spokesman, especially by the poorer Christian classes.[18]

This abiding appreciation for his Luo heritage is articulated in Ajuoga's explicit remarks in the opening paragraphs of the *Johera Narrative* (pars. 1-23). However, the enduring influence of Luo paradigms upon Ajuoga is also evident in his implicit use of the genre of *pakruok* throughout his story. From the opening paragraph Ajuoga introduces his *Johera Narrative* as one about "its founder and leader," and he expresses his understanding that the story of the group, Johera, can only be understood by comprehending the testimony of an individual: its founder and leader, Matthew Ajuoga (pars. 1, 2). As his story unfolds, Ajuoga's focus is on himself and his experiences, and he develops his narrative, therefore, by focusing on the two dominant themes of *pakruok*: self-praise and the quality of experience.

In keeping with the *pakruok* tradition Ajuoga's story recounts his experiences as a "great man." The purpose is to describe his deeds, and in a very real sense to "praise" himself for the actions and beliefs he narrates. Even so, the choice of this genre should not be interpreted as vanity on the part of Ajuoga, and this for at least four reasons. First, Ajuoga appropriates a tradition of self-praise which is both understood and appreciated by the majority of his audience, and it is simply effective communication to use this genre. Second, his use of *pakruok* is expected as the appropriate genre to be employed by someone of his social and religious standing. Third, praising oneself is not considered to be unattractive or haughty in Luo culture, and finally, the writing of memoirs by a public figure, most of which usually contain self-praise, is universally accepted and even expected; even non-Luos should understand Ajuoga's use of this particular genre.

Even so, it is also observed that nowhere in his *Johera Narrative* does Matthew Ajuoga refer, even implicitly, to his mistakes, uncertainties, miscalculations, or sins. Unlike many memoirs, in which confessions and regrets are often expressed, Ajuoga makes no intimation of wrongdoing. Once again, this lack of transparency reflects Ajuoga's use of the genre of *pakruok*, in which such admissions are not appropriate. The purpose of his narrative is not to relate the personal side of the man, Matthew Ajuoga, but rather to recount the public experiences of the founder and leader of Johera. This intention, then, reflects Ajuoga's use of the second theme of *pakruok*: the expression of the positive quality and nature of one's experiences, rather than a comprehensive description of the totality of one's life. *Pakruok* is used to describe the elements of one's experiences which one desires to be remembered, as well as those which have had the greatest impact on the group (in this case, Johera).

Therefore, by noting the major characteristics of the genre of *pakruok*, and by examining Ajuoga's use of this genre, a greater appreciation for the *Johera Narrative* can be realized. In addition to continuing one of the most prominent literary traditions of his people, in recounting his story Matthew Ajuoga is also offering insight into the experiences of the "great man" of Johera. From this perspective, it is again noted that Ajuoga's story is about what he experienced, and not about what actually happened; accordingly, he is continuing the rich Luo tradition of *pakruok*.

The East African Revival Genre of Testimony

A second perspective on the genres used by Matthew Ajuoga in his *Johera Narrative* comes from the literary traditions of his adopted Christian heritage. In general terms, the genre of Ajuoga's text conforms, in varying degrees, to at least two genres widely used in Christian history. Ajuoga's concern to explain, defend, and justify his faith (evidenced in his actions) reflects continuity with the ancient tradition of *apologia*,[19] and Ajuoga's detailed revelation of his personal Christian beliefs expressed in the context of his particular spiritual pilgrimage relates closely to the tradition of confession.[20]

However, even though Matthew Ajuoga is conversant with general Christian history[21] and is aware of these two literary traditions, still his

Johera Narrative employs a Christian genre that is much closer to his context both in terms of geography and chronology. This dominant Christian genre appropriated by Matthew Ajuoga is that of testimony as it was employed in the East African Revival.

A summary of the events of the East African Revival and its influence on the contents of the *Johera Narrative* was discussed in Chapter 6. It was noted that among others, the Revival was characterized by an individualistic approach to Christianity. Within that context, individuals were invited not merely to join the various revival fellowships, but they were especially encouraged to make public confession and testimony of their new faith. Thus, "meetings for public testimony and confession became one of the most marked and most controversial features of the Revival" (Stanley 1978, 199).

While public confession of personal sins was often encouraged to controversial extremes (Warren 1954, 67-74), the practice of public testimony was generally viewed with less suspicion. The "singing and dancing" of the revivalists' gatherings "was always interspersed with spoken testimony." One revivalist made the following observation on the practice of testimony.

> Some of the spoken testimony outside Church is designed to reinforce what was said in the sermon, or— more in earlier days than now—to make up for the Gospel not having been adequately preached in the sermon. Now I notice more often in the fellowship meetings people mentioning things which have helped them in the sermon, even when not preached by a Mulokole [saved one] (quoted in Warren 1954, 66).

> The significance of 'testimony' in the Revival is precisely this: that it represents an attempt...to speak in the name of the Lord, to bear witness to His grace, and to persuade men to receive it (Warren 1954, 108-9).

In their personal testimonies individual revivalists were, therefore, expressing their personal experiences of the Faith: how they understood the Scriptures, the nature of their spiritual struggles, and the victories God had accomplished in their lives.

This Revival tradition of testimony remains, and in modern Kenya it is a popular and fundamental characteristic of evangelical Christianity. Across the denominational spectrum testimonies are still widely solicited in the context of regular worship services, and regardless of one's denominational affiliation, a common Christian greeting in Kenya is, "I'm a Christian and I'm saved." By this is meant that the individual not only holds church membership, but that they also have had a personal salvation experience. In other words, they have a testimony, and will freely offer to share this testimony, usually in its most elaborate and detailed version.[22]

Matthew Ajuoga has appropriated this East African Christian tradition of offering a personal testimony in his *Johera Narrative*, and by using this genre Ajuoga is once again employing a type of message with which his audience is well acquainted. Additionally, he employs a genre of Christian communication that is widely considered, not only appropriate for a pastor or bishop, but necessary for the patriarch of an African Instituted Church. Such a Christian leader is expected and required to "have a testimony," and consequently the most detailed public version of Matthew Ajuoga's testimony to date is offered in his *Johera Narrative*.

Before we leave our examination of the genres of the *Johera Narrative*, it is instructive to note the significance of Matthew Ajuoga's use of both the Luo genre of *pakruok* and the Christian genre of testimony. In so doing, Matthew Ajuoga is once again demonstrating his appropriation of his two religious pasts. The "inherited" genre of *pakruok* identifies him as a Luo leader, and this genre clearly communicates to those who share his Luo past. Likewise, Ajuoga's use of the "adopted" genre of testimony identifies him with the mainstream of evangelical Christianity in Kenya, and so communicates in a mode which is understood and respected by even those Christians outside AIC circles.

To conclude our examination of the primary genres utilized by Matthew Ajuoga, it is helpful to note again the formative role of culture on message creation and expression.

> All messages are part of a culture. They are expressed in the language of a culture and conceived, as well as understood, in the substantive cognitive terms of a culture. Hence, culture shapes all messages and we must take this into account when we interpret them (Vansina 1985, 124).

Therefore, before we proceed to our assessment of the *Johera Narrative*, it must be recognized that the text has been shaped by the two cultures from which it has emerged: the Kenyan Luo and the East African Revival traditions. This formative role of culture is especially acute in the genres employed by Matthew Ajuoga, and by understanding the dominant culturally determined genres represented by the *Johera Narrative* we have observed the following about the general nature of the text:

1. It presents the self-praise of a Christian patriarch ("great man"), who through his narrative intends to recount the quality of his experiences as well as his role in the making of the history of Johera. This is consistent with the Luo tradition of *pakruok*.

2. It offers the story of the Christian pilgrimage of an evangelical leader who "has a testimony." The purpose is to recount the great acts of God in and through the life of Matthew Ajuoga, as they are understood by him. This is consistent with the East African Revival tradition of offering personal testimony.

The purpose of this chapter was to provide an overview of the singular nature of the forms, contents, and genres of Matthew Ajuoga's *Johera Narrative*, for without this broad understanding of the nature of the text accurate assessments and interpretations would be impossible. Hence, this general description of the essential characteristics of the text presented in this chapter must necessarily precede the more specific assessment of the text which now follows.

Chapter 9

A Theological Assessment

Having presented a general overview of the essential contexts and singular nature of Matthew Ajuoga's *Johera Narrative* in the preceding chapters, we are now ready to examine more closely the relationship of the text to broader theological scholarship. Towards this end, this chapter offers a discussion of the specific contributions Ajuoga's testimony provides for several fields of theological studies in Africa. Then, to conclude this chapter, Ajuoga's text will be used to explore and demonstrate one theological approach originating in the West, yet holding promise for understanding current African theologizing.

However, before we embark upon our assessment of the *Johera Narrative* in relation to broader theological studies, it should be noted that Ajuoga's text also holds potential value for scholarship quite apart from theology. Oral historians and historians of Kenya and East Africa will find information of interest in the *Johera Narrative*, and sociologists and anthropologists might also mine this field with benefit, especially for understanding religious change. Additionally, scholars of African literature, particularly those interested in Luo verbal art, could add helpful insights by examining the text from the perspectives of their academic discipline. But perhaps most importantly for a deeper and more precise appreciation of the *Johera Narrative*, linguistic scholars who are native speakers of Dholuo could analyze the original language of the text and provide an understanding of the text not possible within the confines of this study.[1]

In spite of this potential value of the *Johera Narrative* for several fields of scholarly enquiry, here we must limit the scope of our assessment. Since this study makes the initial presentation of Ajuoga's *Johera Narrative*, the evaluations which are offered are therefore understood to be preliminary. It is hoped that this text will be examined in the future by many scholars, from many disciplines; yet, given the limitations of this present study, our concern here is the text's relationship to theological studies in Africa. More specifically, five sub-fields within theological studies in Africa have been identified as obvious beneficiaries of Matthew Ajuoga's narrative, and the potential value of the text for each area will now be described.

ORAL THEOLOGY

The more traditional study of theology as it has developed in the West is based almost exclusively upon written sources, and consequently theological studies after the Western mold have tended to take seriously only those theologies that are written. However, this theological myopia often disregards the fact that, "in the first fifteen to twenty years after the death and resurrection of our Lord, the early Christians circulated stories of his life and teaching largely through oral communication" (Mbiti 1986, 54). It must, therefore, be recognized that large parts of the major text for the West's written theology, the Bible, were used as theological source materials long before they were written down. Oral theology thus has a rich and time-honoured, if not oft-remembered, tradition within Christianity.

Even so, the denigration of oral theological materials continues despite its lack of historical and practical rationale.

> To restrict the theological process to what is written and thereby to exclude from it the oral dimension is arbitrary and incorrect. While it is true that analytical and speculative theology finds its ideal medium in the written word, it is wrong to suppose that that sort of theology is the only one in which faith seeks understanding and expression (Molyneux 1993, 152).

These observations by a Western theologian suggest that, at least for some trained in and of the West, oral theology is finally beginning to be viewed as valid and worthy of serious scholarly attention.

Moreover, it must also be recognized that for many Christians in the modern world, oral theology is more authentic and powerful than written forms.

A Theological Assessment

> Among every non-western people where a popular church...exists, there is a developed dialogue carried on in the oral culture between the Gospel and Tradition. And if we do not get this fact recognized in its breadth and depth, the very existence of this basic, rich and potentially very exciting inculturation will be endangered...(quoted in Jenkins 1988, 141).

Because of this significance of oral theology for a great number of the world's Christians, this same missiologist makes a very persuasive case for the formal recognition, collection, and study of oral theologies.

> I simply want to make the point that oral theology and oral tradition *exist*. And on the day of judgement we shall hold our heads in shame, we academics, if we do not shift our...priorities...so that the task of getting oral tradition and oral theology on tape gets taken much more seriously than it is at the moment (Jenkins 1988, 143).

Thankfully, such strong words were not in vain, for in the same year the International Association of Mission Studies recommended that "IAMS take seriously oral tradition and oral theology in the pursuit of missiology." Accordingly, the IAMS Network for Documentation, Archives and Bibliography declared,

> We emphasize, in particular, the importance of oral records. It is a problem in many Christian communities that the literate culture...does not correspond well with what people communicate in the oral culture.... To neglect one or the other record is to truncate Christian witness, to distort—through neglect—inspiration from and knowledge of the past, and so to make it difficult for a church to explain what she is, and how she came to be so (Jenkins 1988, 142).

These changing attitudes and methodologies are especially welcome for the study of theology in Africa, because oral theology is recognized as one of the three main components of African Christian theology (Mbiti 1986, 46). This arises from the fact that "much of the theological activity in Christian Africa today is being done as oral theology" (Mbiti 1986, 229). This oral theology in Africa is produced in the fields by the masses, in African languages, through song, sermon, teaching, prayer, conversation, and the like. It is theology in the open air, often unrecorded, often heard only by small groups and audiences, and is generally lost as far as libraries and seminaries are concerned (Mbiti 1986, 46-47).

This significance of, yet limited access to, oral theology in Africa is especially problematic for the study of African Christian independency, where oral theologies have dominated. This fact, perhaps more than any other, has perpetuated the theological misunderstandings and alienation of most African Instituted Churches. For example, after noting the general lack of theological seriousness reflected in most studies of African Instituted Churches, one scholar has commented that "the overall impression one has from the literature in the field is that these groups [AICs] can be seen as struggling to learn the ABC's of Christian theology" (Nussbaum 1985, 5). This caricature directly results from misunderstandings of the unique challenges of oral theology.

> We are rather slow to recognize them because we expect theology to come in explicit, written, propositional form and the force of their [AICs] implicit, spoken, acted-out theology is lost on us (Nussbaum 1985, 5).

Source Creation
It is within the context of these misunderstandings of African Instituted Churches due to their production and use of enigmatic oral theologies, that one of the contributions to the field by Matthew Ajuoga's *Johera Narrative* can be recognized. Oral theologies are widely unappreciated in part because so few are available for wider analysis. However, from the obscure reserves of oral theology Matthew Ajuoga has handed over his text, now in written form, yet still bearing the essential characteristics of the oral original.[2] Hence, the *Johera Narrative* records and presents the oral theology of its author, with the intention to communicate his hitherto arcane oral theology to a wider and more diverse audience. This then is the first potential contribution to oral theology made by the *Johera Narrative*: it is now widely accessible for a field of study where such source materials are extremely rare, and little understood.[3] Ajuoga's text has been offered, preserved, and presented as a theological droplet from a previously concealed oral theological wellspring.

Oral Theology in Translation

A second potential contribution of the *Johera Narrative* to the study of oral theology arises from the text's capacity to bridge the gap between oral, more grassroot theologies, and written, more specialized presentations. Because Matthew Ajuoga has himself been initiated to both approaches to theology, and because he lives between and appropriates these dual theological traditions, his text bears the marks of both types of theologizing. The *Johera Narrative*, because it was intended to eventually be written down, is more analytic, premeditated, and doctrinal than most strictly oral theologies, yet it also preserves crucial aspects of oral theology. This quality also reflects the desire that the text be used and appreciated by those outside Johera, and therefore the text can be more readily understood by those more familiar with the intricacies of written rather than oral theology. Ajuoga's text, therefore, contains oral theology, but oral theology in translation; it has been partially translated into the dialect of written theology for the sake of those who are novices in the "language" of oral theological reflection.

Demonstration of the Essential Nature of Oral Theology

Yet, at the same time and as already noted, crucial aspects of Ajuoga's oral theology are preserved in the text, and these reveal a third potential contribution to the field. The components of oral theology that survive and are retained in Matthew Ajuoga's theological translation demonstrate the essential nature of oral theological reflection, at least in Africa. Three such fundamental components of oral theology are obvious after a close examination of the *Johera Narrative*.

Origins in Praxis

First, like other non-western theologies, Matthew Ajuoga's oral theology in translation proceeds from praxis. Similar to Latin American Liberation Theology, in which "concrete, everyday prayerful action and reflection, their response to their own oppressive situation—in short, their praxis—...produces theology" (Ferm 1988, 18), Ajuoga's theology emerges from his struggles as an African Christian pilgrim in the midst of oppression, theological and otherwise. The text reveals that Ajuoga's theology is produced in response to his experiences, that his theologizing is intended to describe, explain, and even legitimate his experiences rather than the reverse, in which his concrete actions would be formed by his theology.[4] This insight is requisite for understanding the theology of the *Johera Narrative*.

Primarily Descriptive

Directly resulting from Ajuoga's commencement with praxis is a second fundamental component of oral theology, another which is preserved in his oral theology in translation. Because Ajuoga's theology is formed by his experiences, his theological purpose is more about detailing those experiences than about his personal cognition of them. While it is true that one must attain a certain cognitive appreciation of one's experiences before they can be offered in testimony, nevertheless Ajuoga's theology highlights his description rather than his analysis of his religious experiences.[5] From Ajuoga we learn that oral theology is more descriptive than cognitive.

Emphasizes "Coming to Belief"

Third and finally, Ajuoga's oral theology in translation suggests that oral theology is more about the process of belief than the beliefs themselves; it is more concerned with "coming to belief" than the statement of or argument for those beliefs (TeSelle 1975b). Certain sections of the *Johera Narrative* do, however, contain Ajuoga's defense of certain beliefs (e.g., pars. 83-86), and doctrinal disputes were significant in the formation of Johera. Yet, more of Ajuoga's text is devoted to describing the religious processes which formed himself and Johera than about the polemics involved; polemics are a part of the text, but they play a limited and secondary role, that of illustrating the nature of his theological pilgrimage. So then, from Ajuoga's theological translation we learn that oral theology is primarily a pilgrim theology, done and appropriated by those "coming to belief" rather than by those who have arrived at belief.

To summarize this discussion of the insights into oral theology offered by the *Johera Narrative*, we have seen that Ajuoga's contributions are in three areas: source creation, translation of oral theology, and demonstration of three fundamental components of oral theology.

WRITTEN AFRICAN THEOLOGY

Oral Theology, as noted above, is but one of three widely recognized main components of African Theology. According to John Mbiti, a second constituent and the one which has received the most attention in the scholarly world, is "African written theology" (Mbiti 1986, 46). This sub-field within African Theology is significant here, because even though Matthew Ajuoga's *Johera Narrative* makes contributions to the study of oral theology due to its essential orality, because it was intended to be written it also has value for the study of written theology in Africa. According to John Mbiti,

> written African theology is the privilege of a few Christians who have had considerable education and who generally articulate their theological reflections in articles and books, mostly in English, French, German or other European languages (1986, 46).

This particular representation of African theologizing traces its modern roots to the late 1950's, and its "flowering" (Bediako 1989, 59) corresponds to the climax in the quest for political independence by most African peoples.

Nevertheless, in spite of the common features of modern Africa's independence struggles and subsequent developments in Written African Theology, it must be noted that even though the widely accepted term "African Theology" is used here, it is more accurate to speak rather of "African Theologies."

> The sheer size and range of the Christian churches in Africa today, not to speak of their vitality, can hardly not require the emergence of a whole range of theologies.... Africa has after all not for centuries been linguistically, culturally, politically or religiously homogeneous, though people— Africans as well as non-Africans— often carelessly speak as if it had been. A Christianity straddling so many traditions is hardly likely to produce a homogeneous theology (Hastings 1984, 363).

Consequently, written theology in Africa is not homogeneous. Rather, it reflects the diversities of the Christian communities on the continent, where cultural variations, linguistic distinctions, and differences in Christian traditions all contribute to the formation of a multiplicity of local theologies.

Nevertheless, over the years common themes have emerged in the pursuit of Written African Theology, and they all focus, more of less, on the relationship between the traditional religious heritage and Christianity. "The real significance of modern African theological writing lies in the attitude that is taken towards the African religious past" (Bediako 1992, 2). The nature of the relationship between Africa's primal religions and the continent's mass reception of Christianity has formed the fundamental arguments in the field for a least a generation. Kwame Bediako, one of the most innovative current

African theologians, has argued that this discussion has provided a necessary foundation for the further study of theology in Africa,[6] yet this issue should not continue to monopolize the attention of scholars. He contends that it is now time to focus on issues which will produce "greater depth" in the study of African Theology (Bediako 1995a, 56), and two of these issues introduce contributions to Written African Theology by the *Johera Narrative*.

"Actual Life" Theology

The first contribution of Matthew Ajuoga's *Johera Narrative* to the study of Written African Theology directly relates to Kwame Bediako's call for more "scholarly penetration" (1995a, 55) and "interpretive depth" (1995a, 58) in African Christian scholarship. Bediako contends that what is missing in the study of African Theology is sufficient serious attention to the theologies emerging from the experiences of the burgeoning African Christian communities themselves. This not only relates to allowing the members to tell their own stories, but also to the analysis of these theologies by the wider scholarly community, allowing these local expressions to influence more academic theological representations. These "actual life" (Bediako 1995a, 58) reflections must be allowed to inform, instigate, and even correct more scholarly and academic articulations. Bediako believes that this scholarly appropriation of grassroots African theologies constitutes "one of the most important tasks of the future" (1995a, 55) for students in the field.

This task "will require that due stress be placed on the observation and study of the actual life of African Christian communities" (Bediako 1995a, 58), for it is from these stories that written theology will be enlightened and made more authentic and relevant.[7] Bediako does not intend to imply that the study of traditional written theological source materials is no longer important, but he does argue that

> the phenomenon studied cannot be fully circumscribed within the literature on it, [and] that one needs to pay particular attention to the more `informal' expressions of the Christian presence in the African scene (1995a, 58).

This indispensable role of "actual life" theologies is due to the observation that "the more helpful contributions" to Written African Theology have been made by "writers, who, on the whole, have maintained a close contact with and involvement in African church-life" (Bediako 1995a, 59),[8] and if Written African Theology is to maintain and increase its relevance and depth such sources must be created and analyzed. Matthew Ajuoga's *Johera Narrative* is one such source, for it relates the story of "actual life" within Johera, a large and dynamic African Christian community attuned to the grassroot struggles and needs of its constituents.

As such, the *Johera Narrative* illustrates, more specifically, why "actual life" theologies are essential for achieving the "greater depth" of Written African Theology called for by Bediako. Because written theology in Africa has been primarily the pursuit of a very small elite within the African Church, it has by and large concerned itself with the issues this elite deem important. Yet, in the *Johera Narrative* the issues central to "actual life" in an African Christian community are narrated, and so its use as a theological source can assist in producing a more authentic Written African Theology, one which speaks for a wider constituency.[9] As "actual life" theology Ajuoga's narrative speaks with legitimacy for thousands of grassroot Christians, expressing their concerns rather than the preoccupations of a small elite.

For example, Written African Theology has been largely polemical, carrying out a dispute vis-a-vis traditional Western theologies over the value and role of Africa's pre-Christian heritage. Likewise, much effort has been exerted in the discussion of discovering and/or forming African Christologies,[10] yet these two much discussed issues in Written African Theology are not explicitly highlighted in the *Johera Narrative*. Not only has Matthew Ajuoga obviously made peace with his pre-Christian African heritage and has moved on in his theologizing, but his Christology reflects solid orthodoxy which he has refused to alter.[11]

These two issues, then, illustrate not only how far removed formal theology can be from grassroot experience, but they also point to the potential value of Ajuoga's "actual life" theology. If disputes about the role of pre-Christian tradition and Christology are not "actual life" issues, at least for Ajuoga, then what are? Here we introduce two issues which appear as central themes in Ajuoga's "actual life" theology.

African Christian Identity

The first "actual life" theological motif which emerges from the *Johera Narrative* is that of African Christian identity, an issue which has recently been analyzed in Written African Theology.[12] Andrew Walls observed that for African theologians "no question is more claimant than the African Christian identity crisis" (1980, 218), and likewise Kwame Bediako notes that now African theology is faced with "an essentially intellectual problem—how African Christianity...may set about mending the torn fabric of African identity" (1995b, 5). The significance of this issue results from the experience of living between the two worlds of African Christianity: the more distant pre-Christian past and the more immediate past and present of Christianity. The nature of this crisis and the many ways it is being confronted and resolved by African Christians is now recognized as a fundamental concern of Written African Theology.

In the context of this search for an African Christian identity, Matthew Ajuoga's *Johera Narrative* provides rare insights into the formation of Christian identity within an African Instituted Church. Indeed, Ajuoga's testimony describes his self-perception as an African Christian, and the components and processes he employs to construct this African Christian identity are articulated. His experience thus makes significant contributions to the current discussion of the role and nature of the quest for an African Christian identity within African Theology, and this motif is further examined in Chapter 10.

Synthesis of Two Religious Worlds[13]

A second motif of the *Johera Narrative's* "actual life" theology has already been introduced in Chapter 7, yet it can be further illuminated by the recent writings of Kwame Bediako. Within the context of the African struggle for Christian identity, Bediako recognizes the formative roles of the two worlds of African Christianity mentioned above. However, Bediako observes that a synthesis of these two religious traditions, the pre-Christian and the Christian, is being determinedly formed by members of African Instituted Churches, and consequently the problems of spiritual duality are not as marked among them as among members of the mission churches.

> The phenomenon of "living in two worlds," half-traditional and half-Christian, and not belonging fully to either, can be said to be more characteristic of members of the historic, so-called "orthodox" churches than those of the "spiritual" churches. Whilst the latter appear to be attempting to work out their salvation in Christ within the traditional religious milieu, the former, on the whole, are failing to do so (1995b, 68).

It is in this arena of the formation of such a religious synthesis that another contribution of the *Johera Narrative* can be seen, for in it we are given a road map or guide to the religious synthesis that has been forged over the years by Matthew Ajuoga. Ajuoga narrates his life-long struggle to incorporate the two religious worlds of which he is a part, and moreover, he describes the components of each tradition which he uses to "work out his salvation" as an African Christian. He also reveals the ultimate nature of this synthesis as a product of primal traditionalism and Christian restitutionism, issues which will be further discussed in the following chapter. Ajuoga's experience, then, relates a story of religious synthesis which is all too rare, and by examining this dimension of the *Johera Narrative* the African Christian experience of straddling two religious worlds can be more accurately mapped and understood.

Theology-in-Community

The final contribution of the *Johera Narrative* to Written African Theology to be introduced here concerns the essential nature of African theologizing itself. As noted above, Matthew Ajuoga's theology proceeds from praxis, and his narrative describes the nature and details the contents of many of his religious experiences. However, even though Ajuoga's narrative is about his personal experiences, his were experiences-in-community, merging from a specific chapter of African Church history. His testimony can thus be viewed as a theological source arising from his ecclesiastical experiences, and this insight raises questions concerning the very nature of African Christian theology: is it best understood within the more individualistic, often anti-ecclesiastical Protestant tradition of the West, or might it be better comprehended as theology growing out of shared ecclesiastical experiences? Does African theology essentially employ the personal reflections of its theologians—formally trained or otherwise—as its primary source, or does it principally draw upon the historic experiences of the local Christian community? To be more succinct, is African theology basically individualistic and original or more communal and historical in nature?

This discussion is informed by contributions from Adrian Hastings, who has noted that African Theology has three "sparring partners" from which it derives stimulation, direction, and content (1984, 365). Two of these theological sources are widely recognized and heavily used; these are African primal religion and the contemporary political/social situation (Hastings 1984, 365-367). Yet, it is the third stimulus for theologizing in Africa which is most relevant here, "less talked of but not necessarily less influential: recent Christian and ecclesiastical experience" (Hastings 1984, 369).

After a reminder that "the life and experience of the Church herself has in the West been traditionally the principal sparring partner of the Bible in the evolution of theology" (1984, 369), Hastings argues that African theology proceeds from the continent's unique brand of ecclesiastical experiences, rooted in Africa's distinct ecclesiastical history.

> In a similar way much recent African theological thinking has grown out of explicitly African Christian experiences.... The worship and ministry of the local church may well be in practice the most powerful and consistent source in the shaping not, perhaps, of the rather limited field of academic theology but of popular and preached theology in Africa today (Hastings 1984, 369- 70).

Here Hastings has highlighted the essential communal nature of African theology, over against the more individualistic forms influenced by the traditional Protestant models.

Likewise, Kwame Bediako has argued that all theologies emerging from the Two Thirds World proceed from ecclesiastical experiences. He contends that the struggles of Christians in the South have revealed that theologizing there is "fundamentally the experience of community" which produces a theology "borne of community and spiritual experience" (Bediako 1995b, 160).

> Because of the strong element of 'the experience of community' in the theologies of the South, these theologies have a distinct inclination to being `ecclesial' theologies, which is not to say that they are confessional or denominational. Rather, this simply expresses the way in which the theologies of the South are rooted in the churches, and are produced from within the churches, to the extent that they proceed on the basis of seeking to understand and articulate the longings and aspirations of the communities they represent (Bediako 1995b, 162).

Matthew Ajuoga's theologizing as revealed in the *Johera Narrative* both supports and enlightens this observation concerning the ecclesial essence of African theology. Because Ajuoga's testimony is the story, not merely of himself but also of his Christian community, his theology is consequently founded on and formed by the historical experiences of this church. Accordingly, Ajuoga's narrative lends credence to the argument that African Theology is fundamentally a theology-in-community. Because Matthew Ajuoga is the Patriarch of Johera and not a theologian in ecclesiastical exile or isolation, it could be nothing else. Even so, Ajuoga's is both a personal theological reflection and a theology-in-community. This construct is not only potentially tensional but also seemingly contradictory. Such theological stress between the individualistic and communalistic elements, however, highlights one of the primary problems in current African theologizing, and this then is an additional value of Ajuoga's narrative to the study of Written African Theology.

Nevertheless, Ajuoga's narrative provides specific detail concerning the exact nature and intention of this theology-in-community. Just as Ajuoga provides a road map for his individual quest for an African Christian identity, so his *Johera Narrative* also reveals that two of the primary issues of communal theology within an African Instituted Church involves forging an ecclesiastical identity and legitimacy. These concerns are necessary for an AIC like Johera, due to their alienation from the mainstream. Consequently, Ajuoga's ecclesial theology reflects the historical development of Johera, as well as their perceptions of this shared story as the basis for the formation of Johera identity. These issues are also re-examined in the following chapter. According to Ajuoga, then, theology is communal: it emerges from the shared historical experiences of the group, and focuses on the community's fundamental need for a shared identity.

To summarize this section, the *Johera Narrative* offers contributions related to the most fruitful sources, the more pressing issues, and the essential nature of Written African Theology. It reveals that the more academic forms of African theologizing must learn to appropriate "actual life" accounts like Ajuoga's, and from these rich theological sources "actual life" theological concerns will emerge. For Ajuoga, the two dominant issues are Christian identity and theological synthesis, and these motifs are articulated in the midst of an ecclesial story, confirming that—at least for Ajuoga—African theology is essentially theology-in-community.

AFRICAN CHURCH HISTORY

Directly related to the insights of the *Johera Narrative* into the study of Written African Theology are the text's contributions to the study of African Church History. Because Christian theology in Africa proceeds from the historical experiences of the people of God, the study of African history in general is essential for a balanced understanding of African theology. Indeed, it has been argued that "one of the more helpful academic disciplines which...will prove useful to African Christian scholarship will be African History" (Bediako 1995a, 56). Moreover, because African theologizing is essentially ecclesial, then the study of African Church History in particular is fundamental to understanding the historical contexts of the continent's theological articulations.

In the story of the Church this symbiosis of theology and history has been a constant reality, for representations of the Faith have always been conditioned by history. Yet, this alliance is particularly significant in modern Africa, where recent Christian history and accompanying theological developments have produced the latest of the "three real turning points in church history...when the whole balance of the church...has altered" (Walls 1980, 214). Consequently, in the modern world the African Christian story is not peripheral, but rather central to the understanding of the nature of the universal Faith in our time.

The crucial significance of modern Africa's chapter in Christian History was heralded almost twenty years ago by Andrew Walls, who by then realized that "the shape of the church, the theology that later church historians have to write about, is likely to be determined by what happens in Africa over the next few generations" (Walls 1980, 214). This was because of the shift in the centre of Christianity that occurred late in this century, resulting from "the most substantial accession to the Christian faith for at least a millennium; ...[one which] has taken place in the southern continents, especially Africa, Latin America, and the Pacific" (Walls 1995, 7). In Africa this acceptance of Christianity is especially phenomenal, for while in the Africa of 1900 there were only approximately ten million professing Christians, today an educated estimate places that number at well over 250 million (Walls 1995, 6).

This recent rise of Africa to the ranks of the world's most Christianized continents means, among other things, that "Christianity in Africa is set to play a crucial role in the future shape of the faith and its impact in the world at large" (Bediako 1995a, 64), so that "Africa...may thus become, for a period in the foreseeable future, the privileged Christian laboratory for the world" (Bediako 1995a, 62). Within this context the study of African Church History takes on renewed importance; the sheer size of the African Church, to say nothing of its vitality and influence, merits the serious attention of those who would chronicle and assess its history. For, if a broader and deeper understanding and appreciation of this monumental story of African Christianity is to be approached, more attention must be given to the study of African Church History, particularly to its most recent chapters.

Even so, the problem concerning the most fruitful approach to African Church History arises, so that some have understood African Church History to be the history of missionaries in Africa (Walls 1972, 169), while others have pursued the study of African Church History by focusing on the story of the ecclesiastical institutions that have been formed on the continent (Kalu 1993, 173). While these two perspectives have certain—though greatly limited—degrees of merit, a call has been made to approach African Church History with the intention to strike a balance between the local and inward and the more general and outward. The contention is that an understanding of the great diversity and complexity of African Church History is not possible without complementing the breadth arising from general studies with the depth of local investigations (Kalu 1993, 173ff).

This call, however, is simply the latest in an on-going campaign, for others have also noted the relationship between the general and the local in the study of African Church History (e.g., Shenk 1996, 56; Sundkler 1987, 78). In the context of this appeal two volumes of a general nature are especially significant (Hastings 1994; Isichei 1995). Nevertheless, if this balanced approach is to become a reality more local studies in African Church History are required, for these localized examinations continue to be of insufficient number and quality to attain the necessary historical equilibrium (Ayandele and Ajayi 1979; Bediako 1995a, 56ff; Jenkins 1986). "Rethinking African church history...indicates that we cannot have too much documentation of grassroots Christian belief and practice in Africa" (Jenkins 1986, 70).

An understanding of the immediacy and significance of the modern story of African Christianity, as well as the need for greater quantity and quality in the examinations of grassroot Christian experiences, leads to an appreciation of the contributions of the *Johera Narrative* to African Church History. For, in its pages we read the chronicle of one local and dynamic component of the burgeoning African Church; simply one chapter in the crucial African Christian story, yet one full of rare detail which contributes to a more enlightened understanding of African Church History. Three specific contributions of the *Johera Narrative* will be noted.

Reflects a Requisite Methodology: "Going to the People"
The first contribution of the *Johera Narrative* to the study of African Church History follows from the recognition that the text is the product of a particular approach to the study of Church History in

Africa. Rather than seeking to understand the story of the African Church by drawing primarily upon fragmentary and one-sided missionary sources, this "bane of African church history" (Kalu 1993, 175) has been counterbalanced by accessing a local story of African Christian experience. The *Johera Narrative* is the result of a methodology which seeks to uncover, preserve, and examine an indigenous Christian story, that is, a localized African account that expresses local faith concerns, faith struggles, and faith experiences.

This method of "going to the people" (Jenkins 1986, 70) in the quest for historical building materials allows African Church History to become what it should be, "the story of the pilgrim people of God and their experiences of God's redeeming grace" (Kalu 1993, 173). This methodology has stimulated and formed Matthew Ajuoga's story, which is a crucial chapter in the history of African Christianity, and one which might never have been offered to a wider audience in the absence of this approach towards doing African Church History.

The people of God possess their own stories which are shared, examined, and even revised among themselves. These recitals recount the dynamics and motifs which produce the vitality of modern African Christianity, and consequently these stories are requisite for an enriched and balanced understanding of African Church History. The only way to access these local faith-tales for use by the wider Church, however, is by "going to the people" who tell the stories, and it is this approach that has produced the *Johera Narrative*.

Transmits a Requisite Voice: The "God Talk" of the People

A second contribution of the *Johera Narrative* for the study of Christian history in Africa proceeds from the approach of "going to the people," for in so doing, one is permitted to overhear the "God talk" of the people, in their words (Kalu 1993, 176). This "God talk" is the faith-focused conversation which takes place among the members of all Christian communities, and it narrates how Christian history is being lived and experienced. By listening to this internal exchange an historical understanding emerges which is grounded in the real-life, dynamic stories of the primary players, rather than in the static, distant observations of the analysts.

This historical eavesdroping produces what Terence Ranger has called an "inward-looking" history, a necessary perspective for the balanced historical understandings of religion in Africa (Ranger 1975, 3-6). According to Ranger, "inward-looking" history focuses on the events and concerns that dominate the shared experiences of religious communities, as opposed to an "outward-looking" history which highlights external factors. While the study of African Christianity often contains and has benefited from the "inside" views of missionaries, such studies have usually remained "one-sided" due to their exclusion of an "inward" focus on the African responses to the missionaries' messages (Ranger 1975, 4).

A valid "inward" history of Christianity in Africa—again according to Ranger—must possess at least two characteristics. It must be "particularistic," that is the historical story of African Christianity must be based on particular case studies, and this because of the diversity and individual nature of Christian experience (Ranger 1975, 5). Because of the different types of "God talk," more general studies must be founded on more localized analyses. Second, only by focusing on the dynamics of the religious encounter can a genuine "inward" African Church History be constructed. Developments in the on-going encounters between the message and contexts of the messengers and the responses and contexts of the receivers must be traced. Such focus will highlight the dynamic nature of both the Faith and the ways it is appropriated (Ranger 1975, 5).

Both of Ranger's characteristics of an "inward" Christian history of Africa are present in Matthew Ajuoga's *Johera Narrative*. It narrates the faith experiences of one specific individual-in-community, and it narrates the dynamics of these experiences over time. By relating both a particularistic and dynamic faith-history, the *Johera Narrative* makes a significant contribution to the study of African Church History.

Includes a Requisite Focus: The Indigenization of Christianity

The final contribution of the *Johera Narrative* to the study of African Church History to be presented here arises from the text's narration of the process of indigenization. According to one historian of the African Church,

> The major need in African church history is for it to play its proper role in the discussion of indigenization. It should take as its analytical starting point not the beginning of the local churches, but the nature of present-day religious belief and practice, and concern itself with how this has evolved as an interaction between tradition and Christian impulses (Jenkins 1986, 68).

Indigenization, a rather slippery term which focuses on the adaptation of the Christian message to the local situation, has been at least the officially stated goal of virtually all Western missions to

Africa in recent times. Not surprisingly, different agencies have endeavored towards this goal with fluctuating degrees of resolve and continuity, employing diverse methods, with varying degrees of success. These processes, all primarily focusing on the missions' understandings of and experiences in the indigenization process, have been the traditional foci of African Church History. Yet, an established and enlarging group of scholars has highlighted the importance of the other end of the indigenization process, namely the understandings and struggles of African Christians to make their faith relevant and meaningful to their contexts.[14]

African Church History must focus on the process of indigenization because it is only through describing and examining this development that the local essence and contents of Christianity can be uncovered. As local Christian communities wrestle with appropriating the Faith in their specific contexts Christianity at the "centre" is formed, and a particular adaptation of the universal message emerges (Jenkins 1986, 68). The significance of this faith from the "centre" is that it communicates the concerns, questions, answers, continuities, and discontinuities of the indigenized form over against more universal forms of Christianity. The indigenization process utilizes all the ingredients, both locally grown and imported, which interact to prepare African Christianity in all its rich diversity. Consequently, only by focusing on the process of indigenization can the central issues which shape the history of the African Church be uncovered.

Matthew Ajuoga's personal blend of indigenized Christianity is described in his *Johera Narrative*, and not only are the major ingredients disclosed, but the most formative historical determinants can also be identified (cf. Chapters 5-7). In short, the process of indigenization highlighted in Ajuoga's text is both proactive and reactive. Johera's innovation in adapting imported Christianity includes a widespread popular initiative to take charge of the indigenization process, and evidence of Johera's determinism is their choice for religious independence that produced freedom to construct a Christian community along the lines of their choosing.

The reactive element in Johera's indigenization process is evident in their decision to distinguish themselves over against the Wahamaji and in their reaction against certain practices of the CMS in Nyanza.[15] Accordingly, in the *Johera Narrative* sufficient attention is given to Johera's experience with the indigenization of Christianity to make a significant contribution to this necessary focus in African Church History.

To conclude this section it is noted that the contributions of the *Johera Narrative* to the study of African Church History all relate to its narration of one significant yet local chapter of the story of African Christianity. If

> a concern with local church history in Africa is...a wish to see the grassroots engagement with, and experience of, the Christian faith and its institutions given the central place it deserves in African church history (Jenkins 1986, 70),

then the significance of Ajuoga's text, which communicates this perspective, can be appreciated.

AFRICAN INSTITUTED CHURCHES

Indeed, Matthew Ajuoga's *Johera Narrative* recounts a local chapter of African Christianity, yet more specifically, it must be recognized that his testimony relates a story from within an African Instituted Church. Even though the text makes contributions to the study of African Church History in general, its most immediate insights and intentions relate to a personal experience of African Christian independency. Consequently, the academic study of African Instituted Churches is another obvious beneficiary of Ajuoga's text.

For more than a generation now, mostly because of their phenomenal growth, African Instituted Churches have been the focus of sustained and intense scholarly attention.[16] Most early studies concerned themselves primarily—almost to the point of preoccupation—with issues related to the origins of these communities, and various factors were put forward to explain the reasons for their existence. Among others, some blamed the appearance and growth of the AICs on the measured readiness of Africans to comprehend a "higher" religion, others regarded the insensitive and authoritarian policies of missionaries as the root cause, while yet another group focused on various non-religious factors, such as politics, economics, and cultural crisis.[17]

Regardless of the diversity of reasons given for the appearance of AICs, however, most of the early literature tended to see these communities as an aberration, as a sure indicator that something, somewhere was seriously amiss.

> By and large these churches...have been presented as unorthodox aberrations and bastards, beyond the pale of redemption and absolutely unqualified to be considered legitimate branches of the Church universal. Their history,

it has been contended, has been one of unmitigated sinfulness. Their origins were sinful: the founders were either rabid power-hungry rebels against 'constituted authority,' or hyper-erotic individuals who wished to debase Christianity by flooding the Church with polygamists, or pagan-at-heart rebels who aimed at heathenizing Christianity (Ayandele 1979, 211).

While these observations are, perhaps, an extreme and unfair generalization which disregards the numerous exceptions, still they convey the perceptions of many within the AICs themselves of the typical premature and lopsided approach to African Instituted Churches.

Thankfully, with time these early prejudices and biases against AICs have become less common, and currently there exists a widespread scholarly recognition that these communities are, rather than a symptom of the malaise of the African Church, an indicator of her vigour. Many concede that the AICs are, among the myriad of Christian denominations on the continent, those "which have most authentically Africanized Christianity" (Hastings 1976, 53). Subsequently, they are now broadly considered to be making significant contributions to the development of Christianity in Africa, and so they deserve continued and expanded scholarly attention.

For example, it has been recognized by one African scholar that these groups have

> all the time looked upon themselves as rightful professors, practitioners, and propagators of Christianity in Africa, as builders of the authentic African Church in which Africans feel and find themselves completely at home, fulfilling untrammelled their spiritual nature to optimum advantage, without in any way compromising the verities of the Christian religion (Ayandele 1979, 212).

Accordingly, yet another has argued that "no study of Christianity as it is developing in Africa would be complete without serious account being taken of the life and thought of the Independent Churches" (Dickson 1984, 114), because "these churches are on the front-line of the indigenization process of Christianity in Africa" (Oosthuizen and Hexham 1992, 1). Moreover, instead of these communities now being widely regarded as aberrations of only peripheral significance, they are "on the whole [considered] to be integral to the mainstream of Christianity" (Daneel 1993, 143).

Given this growing recognition of the importance of African Instituted Churches for the study of Christianity in Africa, and realizing that Matthew Ajuoga's *Johera Narrative* is essentially about African Christian independency, the presentation and contributions of this text are significant. More specifically, Ajuoga's text promises to provide further insights into the nature of AICs themselves, and three major contributions of the text in this regard will now be highlighted.

An Accessible and Inside Source

In all fairness, the above mentioned bias of some scholars against African Instituted Churches was partly the fault of the AICs themselves. Because of the understandable skepticism and even paranoia of most AICs towards outsiders, especially researchers coming from or of the West, many AICs were initially reluctant to cooperate in projects aimed at analyzing their communities. This common AIC orientation then resulted in their further marginalization and isolation, and consequently much research focusing on AICs suffered from a lack of inside sources and cooperation, virtually ensuring misrepresentation.

Moreover, this reluctance of many AICs to share of themselves permitted the establishment of an unfortunate yet inevitable cycle. Due to their suspicions and disinclinations to cooperate with the efforts of outsiders to understand them, these AIC attitudes, in turn, allowed for the creation and perpetuation of biases against these communities, which created even more AIC mistrust, etc. Accordingly, it is not surprising that some of the early and most influential studies of AICs were based entirely upon the observations of outsiders, whose conclusions resulted from minimal contact with AIC materials and members.[18] However, others would make use of different attitudes and approaches from both AIC insiders and outsiders, and this produced a second type of literature about these communities, one which resulted from the observations of outsiders, yet with greater access to inside cooperation and sources.[19]

Still, the most fruitful approach to the study of AICs, unfortunately, remains insufficiently explored. For, even though this second type of literature resulted from greater quantity and quality of contact with AIC materials and members, it nevertheless continued the observations of outsiders *about* these communities, rather than an examination of what these communities *said* about themselves. Instead of discovering and examining the historical and theological categories the AICs themselves deemed crucial, they continued to be analyzed in terms of the agenda of outsiders.[20] Unfortunately, only rarely have AICs been allowed to speak for themselves, using their own categories and paradigms, with the ability to attract the widespread and serious attention of outside scholars.[21]

For example, after surveying twenty-five years of missiological research in South Africa, and despite lauding the growing interest in AIC research, it was noted that "too often it [AIC research] has remained a study of secondary sources, lacking empirical field work" (Kritzinger 1994, 158). In effect, "the 'story' of the AICs from their point of view has not yet been told" (Oosthuizen and Hexham 1992, 13), often because the AICs are not offering their stories for wider use, yet also because the scholarly community is often unwilling or unable to listen. Consequently, AIC research is being cheated of its most fruitful source materials.

It is within this context of the rarity of inside AIC source materials that the first contribution of the *Johera Narrative* can be appreciated. Matthew Ajuoga's story is evidence that he and Johera "have become conscious of themselves" (Kitshoff 1992, 49), and have subsequently desired to share their internal reflections with a wider audience. With the presentation of Ajuoga's text a significant source has been added to the inadequate existing corpus of materials for the study of AICs, making possible the hearing of an infrequent, inside voice. In a field of study where such materials are a rarity, the *Johera Narrative* is especially welcomed; with the addition of Ajuoga's story, more accurate and current understandings of AICs become possible.

A Fresh and Diachronic Source

Another crucial contribution of the *Johera Narrative* for the study of AICs, one which illustrates the text's promise to provide greater understanding of African Christian independency, is the text's fresh communication of a timely story. Many of the most respected studies in the field, though significant for their time and place in the literature, are now seriously dated; their opinions and methodologies have become like antiques: still revered yet stale from lack of up-to-date and rigorous handling. Their foci and conclusions, though still of fundamental importance, are based upon necessary yet merely inceptive examinations. Therefore, these pioneering investigations should not be considered as the final word; they remain required reading, yet their dated sources and analyses must be supplemented and revised with more current examinations, utilizing up-dated approaches and materials. Even so, it is surprising how the foci and conclusions of these studies of almost a generation ago are still often considered to be, not only timely, but even the final word on issues relating to AICs.[22]

Sadly, however, and as noted above, this is often due to the lack of fresh AIC inside materials which could communicate the current state of African Christian independency.

Furthermore, this current common approach to the early literature also betrays an implied disregard or failure to recognize the dynamic nature of African Instituted Churches. Dated studies are often considered to remain conclusive, in part because the development of AICs is not given serious consideration. What was true or at least persuasively argued a generation ago is often left unexamined, unrevised, and allowed to stand more or less as originally articulated. This absence of critical revision is all the more regrettable given the current AIC climate which promises greater access to fresh, inside information.

In addition, this academic stagnation in the study of AICs results because diachronic approaches, which alone can unveil the development of the lives of these communities, are not sufficiently utilized. While there is no shortage of studies which view these communities from various synchronic approaches, still these tend to reduce dynamic AICs into "still-life" snapshots, and consequently leave many questions unanswered. What remains to be sufficiently investigated are issues related to the "real-life" motion pictures of AIC experience.

For example, how have AICs developed over time; what factors—historical, theological, social, and otherwise—are most significant in determining the nature of AIC development? How have AICs weathered the generational changes in their leadership and constituencies; how have these communities responded to the challenges of an independent yet increasingly secular Africa? Are the AIC concerns and motifs of a generation ago still relevant and formative for their communities today? Accurate answers will be forthcoming only when the dynamics of AICs are given the attention they deserve, and therefore, instead of being content to overly rely upon dated materials utilizing primarily synchronic methodologies, fresh sources approached diachronically should be emphasized.

Matthew Ajuoga's *Johera Narrative* makes a crucial contribution precisely at this point, for it is not only a more recent testimony that represents many years of reflection, but it additionally relates a fresh perspective on religious experiences within an AIC. Moreover, the text narrates a story which concerns personal and communal developments within an AIC over a generation, and consequently insights into the specific nature of Johera dynamics are revealed. Individually, within the text can be identified the shifts in Matthew Ajuoga's central religious concerns, and the continuity and fruition of the direction of his theologizing can be traced over time. For the larger group, Johera, the developments in the dominant and formative communal motifs can also be observed, and innovations within the community to confront the more modern challenges of Kenyan society are also described. These diachronic revelations promise greater understanding and emphasis of the dynamic nature of AICs, providing fresh material with which to re-examine and supplement more dated and synchronic studies.[23]

A Source Indicative of Trends in AIC Theology

As noted above, a general scholarly agreement now exists regarding the significance of AICs for the present and future of African Christianity. Likewise, even though there are differences of opinion concerning the value and exact nature of AIC contributions, it has been recently observed that

> The significance of the independents, therefore, has been that they pointed to the direction in which broad sections of African Christianity were moving, and so they testified to the existence of some generalized trends in the response to the Christian faith in African terms (Bediako 1995b, 66).

However, "commendable as these observations are, they are but pointers to a task yet to be undertaken," for still lacking is "a scrutiny in depth of the specific contribution of the Independent Churches towards a *theologia africana*" (Daneel 1984, 64). While the realization that AIC theological contributions are significant is treated as a given by most scholars, very little in the way of specifics has been offered.

Indeed, AICs are grassroot communities that are currently, regularly, and relevantly doing African theology, but what exactly are the contents, trends, and directions of their theological labours? What does their theology look like; what materials—historical, scriptural, cultural—are used as their primary theological building blocks; and, what are the central motifs of their theologizing? And the theology that is being forged, how is it similar and/or dissimilar from that fashioned by the previous generation; how does it relate to the pre-Christian past in Africa, and what is its relationship with more historical and universal expressions? In short, from whence has AIC theology come, where is it going, and what concerns are determining the direction and nature of its development?

These questions beg answers, and the *Johera Narrative* responds. First, as to the current centre of AIC theology, Ajuoga's text confirms the contentions of scholars like Andrew Walls (1980) and Kwame Bediako (1992), that African Christian identity is a central and contemporary focus. In addition, the *Johera Narrative* reveals other theological motifs which are directly related to the issue of identity formation. For Matthew Ajuoga these are the issues of ecclesiastical and theological legitimacy, produced primarily through the support of Christian history. These are coupled with his own innovations in restitutionism, again bolstered by a selective use of Church History. African Christian identity forged through a discriminating recall and production of Christian historicity are, according to Ajuoga's text, the current focal imperatives of AIC theology; these issues are further examined in the following chapter.

Second, the *Johera Narrative* offers a clearer and more specific understanding of the formative trends and directions of AIC theology, two of which are immediately obvious. Ajuoga's reflections, first, suggest that AICs are now, in varying degrees, desiring to end their isolation and enter into sincere dialogue with those outside, and this gesture is significant for both AIC self-understanding and more accurate AIC understanding by those outside. As AICs enter into dialogue, they must first examine themselves, and both processes— dialogue and self-examination—promise enlightenment for all involved.

From the text it is also clear that a second general direction—one resulting from the first—is that Matthew Ajuoga's theology moves away from the primarily local and novel, and towards the more universal and historical. Ajuoga's testimony, perhaps not surprisingly for a text intended to be used in forging better relations with those outside AIC networks, devotes little attention to local, primal issues; in fact, Ajuoga's theology is more explicitly oriented towards his Christian past and present than to his pre-Christian heritage. His major concern, rather than attempting to bridge his inherited and adopted religious traditions—which he nevertheless implicitly accomplishes—is to synthesize his Anglican and broader Christian heritage with his choice for African Christian independency. Consequently, the *Johera Narrative* supports the prophecies of those who foresaw that the dominant direction of AIC development would be away from their isolationist local preoccupations, and towards more ecumenical concerns.[24]

In spite of the more open approach of most scholars to AICs and the succeeding literature, much still remains to be accomplished to end the isolation and misunderstanding of these communities. This unfinished agenda points to the need for AICs themselves to take more initiative in communicating their stories, yet it also raises a challenge for those outside the AICs to listen and learn, even if this means slowly, carefully, and humbly learning a new theological "language." The need, therefore, is for a continued dialogue in which both parties—AICs and those outside—speak and listen. AICs have, in the past, been short on addressing those outside, and theirs is now a challenge to share more freely and openly of their theological treasures. And, for those outside these younger churches who have more often spoken than listened, the test is for them now to learn to attend sincerely to what the AICs are saying.

In the midst of this on-going dialogue Matthew Ajuoga has made his contribution in the form of his *Johera Narrative*, through which he has offered a significant source for the study of AICs, and from which can be extracted fresh indications about the current state of AIC reflections upon their past and present. The challenge now is for those receiving his text to "have the ears to hear," and a guide for approaching this listening and learning is the focus of the following chapter.

NARRATIVE THEOLOGY

This chapter has so far focused on the specific contributions of the *Johera Narrative* to four fields of theological studies in Africa. However, in this final section an additional purpose is at work, in which Ajuoga's text will be used to illustrate the potential of one area of theology—the approaches of the theology of stories—for understanding African theologizing. This value will be demonstrated by exploring how Narrative Theology is able to assist in forming answers to three crucial questions currently being asked of African Theology, illustrated from the vantage point provided by the *Johera Narrative*.

The particular theological orientation at the fore here is termed Narrative Theology, because it seeks to understand, form, and articulate Christian theology by utilizing stories. In the literature, however, a distinction is usually made between Narrative Theology proper, which has a more general focus including the narratives within the biblical text, and Biographical Theology, which is limited to an examination of the faith stories of individuals. However, for our purposes here both approaches will be combined under the broader term Narrative Theology.

Rooted in the 1940's yet gaining prominence in North America only in the 1970's, Narrative Theology is a broad term used to designate that school which examines and evaluates the theological usefulness of stories.[25] Generally, Narrative Theology is expressed in three major forms, each focusing on a particular type of source material: canonical, which examines biblical narratives; human life, which focuses on more recent stories of individual faith experiences; and, classic communal, which mines stories of shared faith recorded in the history of Christianity (Fackre 1984, 6).

George W. Stroup (1975) has offered an excellent bibliographical critique of Narrative Theology's early and most influential literature, and while he examines the serious deficiencies and dangers of utilizing stories as primary theological source materials, in another place Stroup nevertheless concludes that "the use of narrative theology provides rich possibilities for understanding and interpreting the content of Christian Faith" (Stroup 1981, 6). Among the many reasons given for this optimistic assessment is the contention "that the theme [of narrative theology] opens up new vistas to old and tired questions" (Stroup 1975, 142). Three such crucial and lingering theological questions in Africa are presented below, and these are meant to illustrate the value of this approach for unlocking the riches of African theologizing as demonstrated by their application to Matthew Ajuoga's *Johera Narrative*.

How is the Bible used in African Theologizing?

The first crucial question in African theology which can be enlightened with the assistance of Narrative Theology regards the relationship of the Bible to Christian experience. Because Christian experience is guided and formed by—in varying degrees—the Bible, textual analysis assists in understanding the relevance of Scripture for affecting individual lives. Yet in the reverse, by examining particular cases of Christian experience, the value and use of the Bible can also be enlightened.

It is at this point that Narrative Theology becomes helpful, for it has been argued that one of the most significant values of a theological examination of narratives is their ability to describe and map individual appropriations of the biblical text (Stroup 1975, 142). This observation stems from the fact that biographies and autobiographies, in particular, have an innate ability to communicate the "grammar of religious convictions" (Hauerwas, Bondi, and Burrell 1977, 8), and also from the contention that all convictions—religious and otherwise—are rooted in some narrative (Goldberg 1982, 36). Because life stories are so adept in communicating convictions and the process of their formation, and given the importance of the Scriptures in Christian belief, these narratives can then reveal the ways in which the Bible is employed in the personal faith formation.

This general observation is especially relevant for Africa, where given the prominence of the Bible in African Christianity (Mbiti 1986), Christian experience and its succeeding theologies necessarily wrestle with the place of the Scriptures in forming individual and communal faith. Consequently, by examining the personal and corporate faith stories of African Christians clear indications of the role of the Bible in doing theology in Africa will emerge.

Moreover, by accessing faith stories some of the more crucial and pointed questions concerning the function of the Bible in African theology can be addressed. For example, how is the Bible approached by Africans: is it understood as authoritative, and if so, why, and in what sense? What parts of the Bible are most often used and most obviously relevant for current African theologizing; what books appear to be less heavily relied upon, and why? In addition, how are these segments of Scripture utilized: are they employed specifically to perpetuate or even legitimate some pre-existing theological propensity, and/or are they used to bring about theological change and development; in short, does the Bible contribute to the continuity or discontinuity of the pre-Christian African past, and how?

The answers to these questions, most certainly, will vary with the contexts, yet in spite of dated and general attempts to answer these questions (e.g., Turner 1965; Mbiti 1986), at present insufficient specific data exists to begin to form up-to-date answers. Moreover, rather than limiting the investigation into the function of the Bible in African Christianity to the more traditional theological sources of sermons, hymns, sacraments and rituals, or systematic compositions, personal testimonies should also be mined. For, not only do these faith narratives reflect a mode of communication which allows a greater number and variety of Christians to speak for themselves, but they alone hold the key for unlocking a mysterious dimension of this theme: how the Bible functions in individual spiritual development. Consequently, through collecting and analyzing local stories of Christian experience, and by examining what these narratives reveal about the ways the Bible is used in forming Christian belief and action, the crucial question of the role of the Bible in African Christianity can begin to be answered.

The insights of Narrative Theology as they relate to role of the Bible in forming personal faith stories has been valuable for this study's understanding of the *Johera Narrative*. Even from a cursory reading of the text, it is clear that the Bible is considered to be authoritative by

A Theological Assessment

Matthew Ajuoga, for his narrative is replete with scriptural references which he uses to both guide and justify his actions. Ajuoga's general orientation towards the Bible, as well as his understanding of the text's role in faith formation, are certainly in part derived from his evangelical heritage (cf. Chapter 6), yet his narrative also suggests significant personal innovations (cf. Chapter 10). Without the tools borrowed from the school of Narrative Theology, these mysteries would be less clear, and this same value of Narrative Theology for understanding the function of the Bible in Matthew Ajuoga's theology can also be realized through a similar approach to other personal faith stories.[26]

How can the Voices of the African Christian Majority be Heard?

A second value of Narrative Theology for the understanding of theology in Africa, again illustrated by its application to the *Johera Narrative*, concerns the lack of a suitable medium for the majority of African Christians to theologize for wider audiences. Even though the voices of Africa's academic theologians are heard by ever increasing audiences and have been for many years, still these voices from the academy represent a very small minority of African Christians, an elite whose concerns and conclusions often reflect their own extraneous preoccupations.

On the other hand, the voices of grassroot Christians in Africa, who together constitute the majority of believers on the continent and whose concerns are more representative of the heart of African Christianity, are rarely heard. In spite of the fact that grassroot believers are daily doing relevant and vital theology, and regardless of the certainty that insights into the time-honoured questions of African theology are embodied by this Christian majority, still they remain, in effect, voiceless.

Reasons for the African Christian majority being largely unheard are many, yet they relate either to the challenges encountered by the grassroot believers themselves, or to the biases of the methods traditionally employed to access theological source materials. In order for their faith stories to be heard by a wider audience, the African Christian majority faces the formidable obstacle of literacy, usually in a European language. As well, they must possess the confidence and desire to relate their testimonies, and perhaps most challenging of all, they must be granted the luxury of leisure to reflect and record their faith experiences. Additionally, even if they are able to surmount all the above barriers, they face the challenge of being unheard or misunderstood unless they are willing and capable of expressing themselves in categories and vocabulary that the theological elite readily recognize and respect.

This points to a further reason for the continuing silence of the African Christian majority: the inability or unwillingness of the theological establishment to encourage, access, and amplify the myriad of voices that are being heard at the local level. Rather than insisting that the African majority speak in traditional theological mediums, like systematic presentations, sermons, or hymns in order to be given a theological ear, and because these categories are unable to contain the full stories of the majority, it will require the patient acquisition of a new theological approach. Learning to recognize and handle non-traditional theological categories, vocabularies, and materials are required, and paramount among these atypical theological texts are the faith stories of the African Christian majority.

While there are obvious restrictions on the number and variety of African Christians who are capable of expressing their personal faith in sermons, hymns, or other more systematic presentations, the medium of story is potentially accessible to all. The propensity of African Instituted Churches to utilize stories rather than more traditional theological forms of communication has been widely observed (e.g., Becken 1992, 29; Pobee 1989, 88-89), and because AICs are primarily grassroot communities it can be conceded that the form of narrative holds great potential for giving a theological voice to the voiceless among AICs and other grassroot Christian communities.

Within this context of the unique aptitude of stories to transmit and amplify the voices of the African Christian majority, yet another promising function of Narrative Theology can be recognized. Indeed, one widely recognized value of story is its ability to provide a verbal forum for the hitherto voiceless. "Narrative...is a way of giving voice to the voiceless," and as such, stories are often used as "a weapon of the marginalized in the struggle against their cultural captors or a preserve of identity in a world of uniformity." Consequently, "there is a strong activist strain in this kind of narrative theology: personal growth, moral claim, [and] social change" (Fackre 1983, 347), and these are the very issues which are necessary yet rare components for a fuller picture of current African theologizing. Personal faith stories are hence an attractive, available, and effective means for the theological dispossessed to express their religious struggles, and to contribute to the wider theological discourse from which they are often excluded.

This particular dimension of Narrative Theology provides deeper insight into Matthew Ajuoga's intentions for his *Johera Narrative*. As the patriarch of an AIC Ajuoga has lived a theologically marginalized life. His religious beliefs and those of Johera were not considered significant by most, and despite the rich theological life within Johera, in the opinions of outsiders Ajuoga's voice was unimportant. Consequently, Ajuoga was himself relegated to live among the theological voiceless. This condition was to be corrected by the presentation of the *Johera Narrative*, and it is significant that in attempting to overcome his voiceless condition Ajuoga chose the medium of story, and particularly the telling of his story rather than the recounting of another's (Fackre 1983, 347). Here again Narrative Theology provides methods for approaching and understanding such activist theologizing, and should be used more widely to encourage and amplify the faith stories of the African Christian majority.

How is Theology in Africa to be Universally Understood?

Finally, Narrative Theology holds potential for replying to yet another crucial question for African Theology, one which relates to the obstacles of theological discourse between Africa and the rest of the Christian world. Indeed, perhaps the greatest challenge facing African theologizing are the problems related to its expression in terms that can be understood by those outside Africa. Essentially, the challenge involves the difficulties of articulating and explaining the nature and central concerns of a theology emerging from societies still close to their primal heritage, to those in the World Church who are further removed—at least chronologically—from their primeval religious and cultural traditions.

In the past at least two approaches have been followed to bridge this barrier in the theological discourse between Africa and the rest of the Church. The first involves attempts to fit African theologies into a more universally understood theological mold, and usually this has meant the translation of African theological expressions into those categories and concerns which are dominant in the Christian heritage of the West. Illustrative of this approach are those theological articulations intent on expressing African reflections on the person of Christ within the broader understanding of "Christology" as it has developed within the Western Church.[27]

A second attempt at a more universal expression of African Theology has been made by those who would emphasize the uniqueness or otherness of theology in Africa, and would thus attempt to explain the nature and rationale for its essential dissimilarities to the uninitiated. This approach basically seeks to teach the language of African theologizing to outsiders, and is reflected in the efforts of those who try to explain Africa's appropriation of Christianity within the context of the continent's pre-Christian religious heritage.[28]

In spite of the benefits of both these approaches to the problem of African theological expression, difficulties remain. However, given the significance of African Christianity within the modern Church, in which Africa has become "for a period in the foreseeable future the privileged Christian laboratory for the world" (Bediako 1995a, 62), it is paramount that the Church outside Africa develop the ability to communicate with and subsequently learn from the African Church. It is at this point that another benefit of Narrative Theology arises, for instead of either the African or non-African Church being required to translate its theologizing into expressions understood by the other, Narrative Theology holds out the promise of a common and universal theological language—that of story.

Narrative Theology's usefulness as a universal theological language arises from two characteristics of stories. First, it has been argued "that the formal quality of experience through time is inherently narrative" (Crites 1971, 291). Even across time and cultures, the premise is that all human experiences, religious and otherwise, are always and by everyone expressed in a narrative way, because the category of story is universally understood. All humans tell stories, because "there is no other way we can articulate the richness of intentional activity" (Hauerwas, Bondi, and Burrell 1977, 76).[29]

Consequently, a second observation emerges, which maintains that the use of narratives is the answer to the problem of translating knowing into telling, even across cultures. Because narratives make use of this universal form of understanding human experience—story— and because they provide a universal means for expressing experiences, narratives are not as "culture-specific" as most other forms of human communication (White 1980, 5-6). "While our story is shaped by the traditions in which we live, there is a unity that underlies all our separate paths" (Fackre 1983, 348), and that commonality is the human predilection for stories as a mode of expression.

For Christian communication there is yet another value of narratives for theological expression: historical precedent. A generation ago it was observed that Christian theology throughout history has been based on story, and that the Church could not do otherwise (Niebuhr 1960, 35). Later another eminent theologian noted that "our faith...did not initially come to us as 'theology,' and particularly not as 'systematic theology.' It came as story" (Brown 1980, 547). These scholars have highlighted the use of narratives as modes of theological expression throughout Christian history, and by examining both the narratives found in Scripture and the faith stories of contemporary believers Christian theology can reclaim its most time-honoured and universal communicative vehicle.

A case in point which illustrates the potential of Narrative Theology for expressing theology in Africa is Matthew Ajuoga's *Johera Narrative*. It is again noted that, of all the possible modes for the communication of his Christian experiences, Matthew Ajuoga chose to employ a narrative, and this supports the contention that story is a universally understood and attractive mode of expression. Ajuoga's story was also intended to communicate to outsiders—even Westerners—and this study demonstrates the possibility that exists for a wider audience to understand the *Johera Narrative*. Had Ajuoga chosen another, more culture-specific medium, greater obstacles would have been encountered in cross-cultural communication. However, by telling a story Ajuoga speaks the universal theological language of narrative, and built upon the rich Christian tradition of story-telling, his testimony is both understandable and historically compatible.

Given the potential of narratives to bridge the cultural gaps existent in African theological expression, more research utilizing this approach is needed. Additional narratives must be recorded and examined, and by using the methods of Narrative Theology the hitherto best-kept secrets of African Theology will become more widely accessible.

The purpose of this chapter has been to demonstrate the value of Matthew Ajuoga's *Johera Narrative* as a text for theological studies in Africa. Since this study provides the initial, wider presentation of Ajuoga's text, it was preferred to present a more general consideration of the text's theological benefits than to offer a more detailed yet limited discussion. Therefore, it is hoped that future researchers will explore each of the above theological beneficiaries in-depth, so providing even greater insight into the theological riches of both Ajuoga's text and mode of theological expression.

Chapter 10

A Listener's Guide

In the preceding chapters the formation of Matthew Ajuoga's *Johera Narrative* has been described, and a presentation of the text has been offered through an examination of its major contexts and their influences, an overview of its essential nature and contents, and through an assessment of its value as a scholarly source. Throughout we have attempted to move "inside" the text and its contexts, to avoid mishandling by seeking an understanding consistent with Matthew Ajuoga's intentions. We have recognized that an African Christian is offering his "God-Talk" through the text to a wider audience, and we have exhibited our desire to listen and learn.

However, appreciating and appropriating the *Johera Narrative* is no easy task. Given the nature of Ajuoga's text—its oral and subjective characteristics, as well as its provenance outside the centre of established theological circles—it cannot be approached using most conventional methods, attitudes, and perspectives. Indeed, it is now widely acknowledged that the oral theological language of the younger churches is significantly different from the literary and conceptual theologizing of the older churches (Hollenweger 1989, 10). New patterns of engagement, therefore, must be formed if Ajuoga's text—and others like it emerging from the younger churches—are to be properly appreciated and utilized in the worldwide Christian community. Hence, many would-be readers/listeners must be instructed in both the attitudes and idioms central to listening to Matthew Ajuoga's "God-Talk."

It is, therefore, the purpose of this chapter to offer such instruction, to provide a "listener's guide" to Ajuoga's "God-Talk," so facilitating its understanding, appreciation, and application. Toward this end, an index to Matthew Ajuoga's parlance is presented in this chapter, a reference tool which will aid the listener. First, three attitudes or postures essential for approaching the *Johera Narrative* will be highlighted. Then, in order to chart a course for a journey towards appreciating Matthew Ajuoga's narrative and to provide signposts to guide the listener's understanding, this chapter will conclude with a list of three, basic theological idioms Matthew Ajuoga employs in his story of African Christian experience.

Accordingly, this chapter will in part serve as a recollective summary, recapitulating crucial issues introduced in previous chapters. However, as these scattered subjects are reassembled, they will be given a new sense of purpose and immediacy, as their significance for understanding and appreciating Ajuoga's text is underscored.

REQUISITE POSTURES FOR HEARING MATTHEW AJUOGA'S "GOD-TALK"

In view of the singular characteristics of the *Johera Narrative* described throughout this study, three attitudes and perspectives necessary if the text is to be engaged and appropriated properly will be highlighted in this section. While Ajuoga's text is the most immediate application for these postures, these attitudes of approach are also necessary for understanding other texts of the same genre emerging from the younger churches.

Extend Sincere Regard

Our above examination of the *Johera Narrative* has illuminated one of Matthew Ajuoga's most regrettable yet potent memories of his Christian experiences—that of personal disregard. The text narrates Ajuoga's perception that his concerns and those of Johera were not given serious attention by the relevant ecclesiastical authorities, and indeed Ajuoga interpreted this as at least personally degrading. His sincere concern for the state of Anglicanism among the Luo was disregarded, and as a result, his most valued possession—his dignity—was peeled away. A personal and communal crisis consequently emerged.

Unfortunately, Ajuoga's experience is not atypical among the modern hosts of Western missionaries. This perception of missionary and broader Western disregard of indigenous peoples forms a major component of cross-cultural relationships in the modern missionary era, and its effect has been devastating. T. Jack Thompson refers to this widespread experience as "dismemberment." He argues that

> ...this Euro-centrism is a legacy of paternalism which has tended to create in Third World Christians, not so much an inferiority complex, as a feeling of being regarded as inferior by Westerners (1996, 133).

Consequently, due to this "anonymous" regard or complete disregard, many peoples have suffered "...one of the most serious forms of dismemberment—the stripping away of human dignity" (Thompson 1996, 129, 133).

This common posture of the past unfortunately lingers, albeit in modified forms. Today, while Third World peoples may be given more public regard as individuals, communities, Christians, or scholars, this same attitude often persists towards their spiritual resources. The difficulties in gaining scholarly regard for oral theological materials has been noted in Chapter 9, yet even when these materials are given attention, often it is condescending. The posture of disregard persists, therefore, when sources emerging from the Christian experiences of the younger churches—like Ajuoga's text—are at the least treated as inferior. Either they are not considered "accurate" or "balanced," or else they are approached irresponsibly because they are allegedly not complex. In either case, these materials and their Christian creators are not given serious regard but are instead patronized.

This attitude also remains towards the Christian experiences of the younger churches. Matthew Ajuoga has identified this patronizing posture and inconsistency in many from the older churches, and refers to it in his text (pars. 211-218). He recalls that many breaks with established Christian communities have occurred throughout Christian history; indeed this represents a major motif of the Christian story. Even though most of these historical separations have been culturally based, they are still regarded as genuine expressions of the Faith and a legitimate focus of serious consideration. Ajuoga argues, however, that when Africans attempt to appropriate this tradition of Christian translation for themselves, they are challenged, distrusted, criticized, investigated, and even excommunicated by Christian communities whose very existence can be traced to the same historical process.

During my research for this study I often contacted would-be informers affiliated with the older churches, who asked why I wanted to devote my time and stake my academic career on the mad ramblings of a schismatic heretic (my paraphrase of common descriptions). Such failure to regard seriously the resources of the younger churches, let alone the refusal to accept their Christian legitimacy, perpetuates into the present the indignities of the past. Yet, if Ajuoga's text—and others of its genre—are to be engaged and appropriated, such postures must dissipate. Instead of the stories of the Christian experiences related by Matthew Ajuoga—and others among the younger churches—being considered as proof of the dementia of the heretics, they must be regarded as the rich narratives of the genuine spirituality of vital Christian communities.

Likewise, if one of the deepest wounds of Matthew Ajuoga's Christian experience has been personal disregard, then the first and most important posture for approaching his *Johera Narrative* is sincere and total regard. Hypocritical, hypercritical, and patronizing attitudes, as well as those postures which formulate assumptions based upon condescension, must be cast off and replaced with a humble and genuine willingness to consider the story of this African Christian patriarch. Only such complete regard can unlock the treasures of Ajuoga's narrative and sooth his spiritual wounds.

This attitude of serious regard for the *Johera Narrative* and the experiences it relates also requires a humble re-reading and even revision of Church History. Most of the older churches must acknowledge their own origins and traditions in Christian translation which has usually produced dissension, and their culturally-bound appropriations of the Faith must be conceded. Then, without historical arrogance, the experiences of the younger churches cannot only be seriously regarded, but a movement towards appreciating the diversity and even divergence of Christian experience can be initiated.

Appreciate Divergent Christian Experiences

A major obstacle in the appropriation of Christian resources like the *Johera Narrative* is the failure to appreciate divergent Christian experiences and their expressions. Because the Christian experiences emanating from the younger churches are usually vividly dissimilar from those in the older churches, they are often not valued. Accounts of visions, calls, prophets, and healings—not to mention tales of the "dark side" of revered denominations, missions, movements, and personalities—not only dismay but often dissuade.

Part of the reason for this lack of appreciation for the spirituality of the younger churches is because their Christian experiences often diverge from Western-based expectations and norms. A common impression pervades the older churches that there are certain fixed patterns for Christian experience, ones established, administered, and monopolized by or of the West. Whenever these expectations are transcended or seemingly contradicted, especially by those bold enough to practice their faith outside these Western-instituted molds, the resulting Christian stories are denigrated. The divergent Christian experiences of many within the younger churches are consequently not understood or even tolerated.

A critique of this posture is expressed in the *Johera Narrative*. Because Johera's experiences were radically divergent from the "established" and "official" interpretations of the events and personalities of their locale, their story was not then, and is still not, widely regarded. In Ajuoga's time and place, the expected, myopic, and rigid pattern for African Christian experience, which refused to address the dangers but rather focused on the advantages of CMS efforts and the East African Revival in Nyanza, was fixed and perpetuated by the Western-dominated ecclesiastical hierarchy. Those whose experiences were contradictory to this established grid of perception were disregarded, because no allowance was made for the legitimacy of a divergent Christian experience outside these Western-drawn boundaries.

A degree of diversity *was* allowed only as long as it acceded to Western control and acknowledged the right of these instituted authorities to manipulate the expectations of Christian experience. The Wahamaji, though guilty of many abuses, were ultimately counted among the faithful because of their acquiescence to Western dominion, and because of the hierarchy's consequent willingness to alter the expected patterns of experience in their favour. Johera, however, despite their loyalty to most Anglican beliefs and practices, were disregarded because of their disavowal of Western manipulation and the ecclesiastical authorities' resultant refusal to modify the boundaries of Christian experience on their behalf. Johera's story is thus that of a group whose Christian experiences not only diverged from Western-instituted expectations, but who also failed to secure official recognition of this dissimilarity and the concomitant shift in Christian expectations.

This is not an uncommon experience within Christian history. Since the founding of the Church divergence of experience and expression have formed perennial and crucial chapters of the Christian story. Often those whose experiences diverged from or even superseded the established patterns were revered and even granted sainthood (e.g., Hermas, St. Anthony). Allowances were made, boundaries were altered, and consequently vital movements often emerged (e.g., monasticism, the Reformation, the Counter-Reformation). On the other hand, others were criticized and even branded heretics (e.g., Tertullian, John Wycliffe, the Anabaptists). In such cases expectations of experience were not modified, and the "guilty" consequently suffered.

The difference was, in part, the individual or group's relationship with those in a position to establish and alter the norms of Christian experience. It has been acknowledged that in Christian history heresy is as much about falling foul of those in power as it is about orthodoxy. It can be argued that heresy is often revealed to be "...an opinion [or experience] held by a minority...which the majority declares unacceptable and is powerful enough to punish" (Christie-Murray 1990, 1). This was Johera's ordeal, and the unfortunate experience of myriads among the younger churches. Their Christian experiences are often regarded as heretical simply because of their failure to coincide with Western-established standards of orthodoxy.

The movement towards forming an appreciation for divergent Christian experiences, however, can be fostered by recalling and appropriating lessons from the history of Christian mission. Andrew Walls (1982) has interpreted the history of Christian expansion in terms of the crossing of cultural and geographical frontiers. When crossed, these frontiers usually produced a shift in the centre of Christian influence, control, and effective paradigms of theology (Bosch 1991). The existing cultural hegemony was also challenged and modified or superseded (Sanneh 1989). A product of this process was the assimilation of diverse and even divergent Christian experiences, as the standard shifted from the Jewish to the Hellenistic, to the Latin, then to the English, etc. Today such a shift in the centre of Christianity has also occurred (Walls 1980, 1995), but the concomitant appreciation of divergence in Christian experience is yet to become widespread in the lands that previously held hegemony.

It is conceded that standards for belief and practice must be instituted and enforced within any viable Christian community. However, in view of the present composition of world Christianity, these expectations should not be established on behalf of the entire Church by or of the West, and these more balanced and representative standards must be consistently managed without hypocrisy; the older churches should not impose on the younger churches expectations which they are unable to bear themselves. Moreover, the previous understanding of Western-based Christian boundaries must be challenged, and previous postures must be modified to allow greater appreciation of many of the Christian experiences emerging from the younger churches which diverge from established norms.

By way of illustration, the labels usually attached to those, like Johera, whose experiences reflect vivid divergence must be removed from usage by the older churches. Terms like "separatists" and "rebels," although expressing a degree of accuracy, are offensive. Such labels betray condescension and the propensity to identify and understand these experiences from foreign and imposed perspectives rather than from internal standards. In such a context, these divergent experiences may be recognized, but only when their mysteries entertain the curiosity of the older churches. Radical dissimilarity is thus appreciated, but only if it can serve the patronizing purposes of those intent on examining perceived exotic artifacts of Christian mutation. Instead, the nature of these experiences must be approached on their own terms, and efforts must be forthcoming to transcend labelling and implement genuine appreciation.

Therefore, the second posture required to unlock the spiritual records produced in the younger churches like the *Johera Narrative* is recognition of the legitimacy and significance of divergent Christian experiences. Without this posture which precludes labelling, the riches of these dynamic experiences will be lost to those who arguably need their vigor the most: the older churches and those in the lands of the present-day Christian minority.

Adjust to the Shifting Margins of World Christianity

The inability or reluctance of the older churches to hear and appreciate the divergent experiences of the younger churches is, in part, a vestige of the hegemony the northern lands have enjoyed within world Christianity for so long. During the past centuries, when the Christian resources of the northern lands formed Christendom, a dominant relationship with the minority of southern Christians was understandable (although not necessarily excusable). However, recent massive accessions to the Church from the southern continents have radically altered the composition of Christianity (Walls 1980, 1995, 1996). Consequently, Christians residing in the North are now in the minority and must accordingly adjust to this shift in the margins of world Christianity.

This southern shift of the centre of Christianity has produced a Faith that it is now most commonly practiced by a "non-white" majority, most of whom have come to Christianity directly from the primal religions. The resultant inversion of the status of northern Christians in world Christianity, from majority to minority, has subsequently produced shifts in the margins of common Christian experience. No longer do the majority of the world's Christians experience their Faith in deference to northern patterns or expectations; instead, new theological sources, methods, languages, and centres of influence are being established. Many among the new Christian majority now express their Faith outside the previously established margins for Christian experience, thus confusing many within the Christian minority. This inversion, therefore for many, is painful and bewildering.

This predicament of the newly-formed Christian minority requires first, that this new status be acknowledged; and second, that the minority adjust to these new realities of world Christianity. Instead of stubbornly guarding the previous boundaries of Christian experience, the minority must recognize, and learn to live with and even appreciate, their inverted status. They must embrace the shifting margins of the Christian experiences of the majority, and this requires at least three intellectual movements.

From Eurocentrism to Polycentrism

Despite the actual southward shift of Christian numbers and initiative, many Christians in and of Europe continue as if nothing has changed. While the Christian minority may concede that the bulk of Christians now reside outside the North, still many persist in perceiving Christianity as legitimately Euro-focused. Not only popular beliefs and practices, but even academic theology is often still expected to reflect established European patterns and methods. Not only are local congregations in the South expected to mirror Euro-centred margins of Christianity, but the same is assumed within the academy as well. Theology, Church History, and History of Christian Mission are often still approached as not only originating, but also concluding in and of Europe. The story is presumed to begin, develop, and end with a focus on European hegemony.

This Eurocentrism, however, must shift to reflect the new Christian reality. What is now required is "poly-centrism" (Thompson 1996, 137), in which Christian experience is seen "...from a variety of different perspectives" (Thompson 1996, 138).

> In looking at the story of world Christianity, those of us in the west must be prepared to learn new ways of seeing

things. We must be prepared generously and joyfully to accept poly-centrism which affirms that the story doesn't just revolve around Europe (Thompson 1996, 136).

Such a perspective will not only permit Matthew Ajuoga's narrative of Christian experience—and others like it—to be understood properly, but it will also create a posture which recognizes that these experiences are valid and even normative for many. Rather than perceived as aberrant, Ajuoga's Christian experience should be acknowledged as typical for many in the younger churches, whose admission into the Church has been accompanied by crisis, pain, and suffering. From the comfortable geographical and existential distance of Eurocentrism, these might appear to be questionable themes for Christian spirituality. Yet, they are validated by the witnesses of Scripture and history, and today constitute crucial themes in the experiences among the Christian majority.[1]

Such experiences among the new Christian majority highlight one of the most crucial areas in which a move from a Eurocentric to a more polycentric perspective of Christian experience is required. One of the most restrictive legacies of Eurocentric Christianity is a rigid ecclesiology which tends to equate the visible, usually Northern-looking church with the invisible Church; one which takes seriously only those expressions of the Faith which are contained within the "historic" Christian communities. Hence, any Christian experience which refuses to defer to these existing institutional structures, or those which form their own communities, are suspect.

This tendency results from a particular definition of the Church, which—though perhaps not invalid—is not the only ecclesiology at work in world Christianity today. Myriads of believers in the lands of the new Christian majority express their faith within Christian communities which are chronologically new, yet which nevertheless are historic in the sense that their formation reflects the continuation of an historical process, which are consistent with precedents within Christian history. These communities do not consider leaving an already established church as a negative development. On the contrary, their understanding of the Faith requires them to translate Christianity into their contexts, and this often evolves into the formation of new Christian communities.

> To start a new cell of born-again believers is not seen as severing communion with any church, but as a step towards fulfilling the great commission, an act of great virtue, and

regarded as such even by those with whom one used to worship (Gifford 1993, 198).

Accordingly, an issue which the Christian minority considers to be a sign of immaturity or heresy—separation—many among the new Christian majority consider a sign of spiritual maturity and vitality.

Such an inversion of ecclesiology is part of Matthew Ajuoga's experience, and this study has intended to reflect the shifts in methods and perspectives necessary to engage this upside-down appropriation of Christianity. However, this issue illustrates merely one among many adjustments the new Christian minority must make to engage and appreciate the experiences among the Christian majority. Rather than continuing to grasp a one-sided perspective of Christianity, a move must be initiated to incorporate other understandings, even inverted ones.

From Domination to Partnership

Following the movement towards polycentrism is a second requisite mental adjustment to the shifting margins of world Christianity. Because of the minority status of northern Christians and the general decline of both the numbers and vitality of their churches, a move from Christian domination to a spirit and practice of partnership must be undertaken. Not only are northern Christians no longer in a position— either numerically or dynamically—to "lord it over" their southern brothers and sisters, but the conditions of the southern churches also necessitate a fraternal relationship. The era of northern imposition has past, and the time for mutual North-South ministry has arrived.

This Christian partnership will ideally draw upon the strengths of both the majority South and the minority North. The younger churches will be called upon to inject the theological and experiential vitality of their youth into the stagnant or declining life of the older churches. On the other hand, the older churches can offer (not impose) the lessons and fruits of their greater age. The younger churches can assist in the revival of the "indigenizing" principle within the older churches, thus equipping them to be more sensitive and relevant to the shifting needs of their societies. Likewise, the older churches can share of their "pilgrim" experiences, which can equip the southern churches to engage better the universal Church by overcoming an unhealthy fixation on their own locales (Walls 1982).

Within such a new, more balanced relationship a crucial role remains for northern Christians, but it is a radically different part from the one played in the past. Rather than dominating the theological arena, playing the leading role by establishing methods and determining the agenda for the entire Church, the new Christian minority will now be called upon to take a supportive part and encourage the younger churches in their own theological quests. Instead of the minority writing the story of world Christianity as if they still dominated by imposing their stories on the majority, they must now allow and assist the younger churches to write their own stories for themselves, thus forming their own Christian identities.

A number of scholars of Christian mission have long identified this role as the most legitimate part for missionaries from the North to play. Twenty years ago, H. W. Gensichen advocated collaboration between North and South in the "doing" of Church History in the Two Thirds World (1976, 258-261), and specifically in regards to Africa, M. R. Spindler has more recently argued that "the role of the western research-worker...is to act vicariously in the place of or to assist at the discovery by the African Christians themselves of their own history" (1990, 80). Even more recently this sentiment has been echoed and clarified by T. Jack Thompson, who offers that Westerners "...must become facilitators, rather than directors. At best we should merely be encouraging people to tell their own story, and assuring them that it is a story worth telling" (1996, 139).

This study intends to demonstrate such a North-South Christian collaboration. In Chapter 2 partnership was identified as one of the fundamentals of the methodology for moving towards an "inside" understanding of the *Johera Narrative*, and from the initial planning stages of this project, it has been intended that Matthew Ajuoga would tell his own story, in his own way. The role of this writer has merely been to offer encouragement, affirmation, and external stimulation. Additionally, through this study which presents Ajuoga's narrative within the broader context of scholarly discourse, it is intended that others—particularly in the older churches of the North—will benefit from the *Johera Narrative*, and that Matthew Ajuoga and Johera will themselves be stimulated to engage their story and further clarify their identity.

This study then stands as a demonstration of the type of cooperation that can be produced when the new Christian minority moves from an attitude of domination to one of partnership. When this occurs, a third, concomitant shift emerges, one particularly significant for members of the older churches.

From Teacher to Pupil

Ideally, the movement towards greater balance in the relationship between Christians of the North and South will benefit both groups. As noted above, much attention has been given to the ways in which the older churches can now serve the younger, and to how the lands of the new Christian majority can best utilize the resources of the minority. What has not been so well established, however, are the contributions of the younger churches to the older. In what ways can the Christian minority benefit from their partnership with the southern majority? To be more precise, what do the younger churches have to offer their older and more established brothers and sisters? Do not the minority churches still possess the majority of Christianity's material and "trained" human resources? What then can the younger churches provide that is needed by the better endowed Christian minority?

These questions betray an arrogance which must be surrendered, and to begin to formulate an answer, the Christians of the North must move from their self-understanding as Christianity's teachers, and shift to become pupils; from a posture of educating they must humble themselves to be educated. Then, possessing this teachable spirit, the older churches will be in a position to receive what the more youthful churches have to offer. Two areas of Christian experience, both highlighted in this study, illustrate what the older churches can learn from the younger.

The first concerns the younger churches' engagement with their primal religious heritages. Our discussion of the primal imagination in Chapter 7 demonstrated that Matthew Ajuoga's Christian experiences were managed by his primal religious heritage. Yet, while Ajuoga's experience in synthesizing his two "pasts"—Luo primal religion and Christianity—is individual and singular, there are nevertheless universal implications. Ajuoga's story, as it relates to the broader translation of Christianity from a primal base, is significant for all believers.

The universal implications of this African encounter with the primal heritage have recently been underscored by Kwame Bediako.

> ...Africa has played a major role in bringing about the realisation which we may now take for granted...that the Primal Religions of the world have provided the religious background of the faith of the majority of Christians everywhere in Christian history to the present (1995a, 57).

The experiences of African Christians in seeking to understand the role of their primal heritages in their appropriation of Christianity have highlighted this same influence of the primal religions for all believers. What was once "taken for granted" by northern Christians, who assumed that they were far too sophisticated and their primal pasts were too far removed to exert pressure on their theologizing, is now being revealed as still formative in their Christian experiences. African Christian experiences can thus help to explain our own theological agendas and histories.

One example from Matthew Ajuoga's narrative illustrates this point. From our illumination of Ajuoga's Luo primal heritage in Chapter 7, it was noted that one of the most influential components of that inherited religious past was its traditionalism, which equipped the Luo to confront the present and future by engaging the past. It can be argued that a similar primal concern has revealed itself in the perennial motifs of primitivism, restitutionism, and restorationism in the history of Christianity. The Christian theme of returning to the past to assist in the living of the present has been formative in shaping the story of Christianity in the West, and an examination of this concern against the backdrop of its primal heritage can enlighten the theme, the process, and even our own fascination with it.[2]

According to Bediako, there is also a missiological contribution from the African Christian reflection on its primal past. Not only can a study of the primal heritage enlighten Africa's recent mass accession to Christianity, but it can also equip the older churches to engage their societies in which a resurgence of the primal religions is emerging (1995a, 59-61). As northern Christians increasingly find themselves confronting neo-pagan societies, they can be instructed to meet this challenge by recalling their pre-Christian pasts. Skills and insights thus gained from an engagement with the primal heritage can revive the older churches' ability to confront and reverse their declining influence at home.[3]

A second, more personal, example of what the younger churches can teach the older is taken from my own experience in conducting this study. Matthew Ajuoga's story of Christian faith resulting from and responding to crisis, as well as his subsequent choice for Christian independency, has provoked renewed yet re-directed reflection upon my own Christian heritage.

From my college and seminary days I have been taught the history of my particular Christian tradition, the Stone-Campbell movement (Christian Churches/Churches of Christ), and I have long recognized that our roots were in religious conflict on the nineteenth century

US-American frontier. Even so, through my attention to Matthew Ajuoga's story of an African Instituted Church, I have come to view my own denomination as a US-American Instituted Church (are not even the names—Church of Christ—the same?). The stories of revival excesses, resulting doctrinal controversies, perceptions of hierarchical disregard, desire for religious self-determination, and eventual schism from the mother church are parts of both our Christian stories. Ajuoga's story has, therefore, stimulated a renewed desire to revise my perception of my own Christian heritage, and I have consequently been able to identify more closely with his struggles; in a sense, they are also mine and those of my spiritual ancestors.

Accordingly, while their stories are unique in many ways, nevertheless the faith experiences of the younger churches contain universal implications, and if the older churches will humble themselves to become pupils, their own faith-stories can be enriched by hearing the dynamic testimonies of the Christian majority. Despite our many differences, such Christian story-sharing can highlight the many similarities between churches North and South.

This section has introduced three requisite postures for approaching Matthew Ajuoga's *Johera Narrative* and other texts of its genre. These attitudes represent radical shifts in the ways Western Christians have traditionally engaged non-Western Christians and their faith expressions. However, unless these new postures are formed, the dynamic Christian experiences of the younger churches will continue to be misunderstood and mishandled by those who most desperately need to hear them: the Christians in the older churches.

BASIC THEOLOGICAL IDIOMS IN MATTHEW AJUOGA'S "GOD-TALK"

The previous section of this chapter has presented requisite postures for approaching the *Johera Narrative*, anticipating understanding and appreciation. Coupled with the previous chapters of this study, all these have been offered to prepare the reader/listener to hear Matthew Ajuoga's "God-Talk"; to provide the appropriate background information necessary for a fruitful listening process to begin.

Additionally, throughout this study we have actually listened to Ajuoga's "God-Talk" and interpreted its contents. First, we have interpreted the influences of the historical and religious contexts upon what is narrated by Ajuoga, then we have assessed the contents' value for theological studies in Africa. This exercise has introduced several modes or patterns of expression which emerge as basic to Matthew Ajuoga's narration of Christian experience. It is now our purpose to recollect these basic theological idioms and to highlight their significance for understanding the *Johera Narrative*.

Yet, this endeavour is replete with dangers. Even interpretations of established texts, for example the Christian Scriptures, are always limited and often controversial. However, this is even more the case when the object of interpretation—like Ajuoga's text—is a virgin, non-standard, oral text emerging from a culture other than that of the interpreter. Ideally, such a text should be interpreted by someone who shares the culture and who possesses "mother tongue" fluency in the text's original language. Neither, however, is the case for this study's presentation of the *Johera Narrative*.

Consequently, because this study is offered by a cultural and linguistic "outsider," a serious hazard is present. This is the danger of the Christian external examiner of religious experience in Africa, who "too easily finds...just that which he is looking for" (Hastings 1976, 52). To use the imagery more appropriate to this study, it is all too easy for the listener to hear what s/he wishes to hear from Ajuoga's "God-Talk." It is possible for the outsider who approaches texts such as Ajuoga's with questions and concerns arising from a radically different context, to locate evidence that is really not there, but was rather planted by his/her own presuppositions and expectations.

As noted in Chapter 2, according to Sundkler this was the specific short-coming of Oosthuizen's (1967) critique of Nazaretha hymns.

> Shembe's "Hymns of the Nazarites" is religious poetry of great beauty. It was born, not at the dogmaticians's writing-desk.... We suggest that Shembe's Hymn-book should be understood *not* from the outside, from a Western standpoint, measuring its contents according to the standards and ideas of a European catechism, but rather from its own presuppositions (Sundkler 1976, 186).

Then, in offering a more specific alternative methodology for interpretation, Sundkler suggests "that one should discard such heavy and learned Western panoply and let Shembe walk along as he used to and loved to: moving light, barefoot" (1976, 190).[4]

Once again to take Sundkler's advice so as to minimize our mishandling or mis-hearing of the *Johera Narrative*, and to be consistent with this study's general methodology as described in Chapter 2, we will here attempt to "move light, barefoot" upon Ajuoga's text. The most responsible and fruitful way to accomplish this at this stage in the text's development is to choose to err on the side of simplicity, to risk under-interpreting and superficiality rather than commit the greater crimes of over-interpretation and textual distortion. Especially since this study is primarily concerned to describe the formation of the *Johera Narrative*, and then to present it for consideration to the wider academic community, the summary interpretation of the text's contents here must be preliminary: accurate, revealing, and stimulating, yet uncluttered and open. "Any theological reflection that is done in this type of study should be made with extreme caution and tentativeness; it can never be definitive..." (A. Anderson 1995, 293).

So, to engage this mammoth challenge, instead of a conclusive interpretation an index will be offered of three theological idioms or three forms of expression which emerge as basic from the *Johera Narrative*. By identifying and explaining Ajuoga's basic theological expressions or characteristic narrative styles within their broader contexts, this index will serve as a reference tool to guide the reader/listener in understanding Ajuoga's "God-Talk" without establishing unnecessary interpretive restrictions.

The three theological idioms identified here have been selected because of their prominence and dominance within the text itself. Not only are these styles of expression given highest priority by the large numbers of paragraphs Matthew Ajuoga devotes to them, but these idioms are also clearly those which have emerged as most influential upon the development of the Christian experiences of both Ajuoga and Johera. Thus, the significance of these theological idioms arises from internal evidence rather than from external imposition. Because of this basic influence, therefore, any subsequent yet more detailed interpretation of the contents of the *Johera Narrative* must engage these modes of expression. This index, then, is of prerequisite significance.

The Idiom of Crisis

Upon our attentive hearing of Matthew Ajuoga's "God-Talk," the first and most striking mode of expression perceived is that of crisis. Throughout our study this theme has emerged time and again, and it is necessary to recognize that Ajuoga's tale is essentially one of crisis, recounting a painful personal and communal experience of faith-struggle against formidable opponents. It is a grievous story for many in the older churches to hear—hence the reluctance of many to listen—because Ajuoga recounts that his crisis largely resulted from Western domination and disregard. Yet, at the same time, it is an encouraging story for the younger churches, because it narrates the ability of personal faith and local Christian innovation to resolve faith-crises; it affirms the translatability of Christianity.

Broadly speaking, Matthew Ajuoga speaks the language of crisis, as he recounts his personal tensions directly related to the more impersonal elements of stress of his time and place. Chapter 5 has shown that historical clashes present in Nyanza exacerbated Ajuoga's individual crisis, and they therefore cannot be passed over lightly. However, we have been told that at the heart of Ajuoga's personal dissonance were religious issues, concerns which were also obviously shared by thousands of Johera. Thus, a reassembling of the religious dimensions of Ajuoga's crisis will be most helpful in understanding one of the basic idioms of his "God-Talk."

Our examination of the text and its contexts reveals three stages in the development of Matthew Ajuoga's religious crisis. The first was the least serious, and it involved the initial introduction of Christianity among the Luo. As was discussed in Chapter 6, the Luo at first warmly received the first CMS missionaries, and after initial role adjustments and the establishment of relational patterns, at least certain elements of the Faith—primarily education—were welcomed and seemingly easily accommodated.

It was, however, the second element of the Luo encounter with Christianity which would be more challenging, and it was this dimension which was personally frustrating for Matthew Ajuoga. Chapter 6 recounted Ajuoga's personal struggle with his perception of the lack of continuity in CMS policies and relations with the Luo; this perceived inconsistency created the greatest personal crisis for Matthew Ajuoga. He was personally quite willing to accept the initial Gospel as proclaimed by the CMS, and particularly within the liberal policies established by the early Anglican missionaries, the introduction of the Gospel was not the problem. Rather, Ajuoga's difficulty arose when he perceived that this pristine pattern which promoted African initiative was being violated, and this constituted the second element in his religious crisis.

This perception of the CMS's betrayal of history led Ajuoga to initiate a personal campaign to draw the attention of the Anglican hierarchy to the consequent tensions among many Luo. However, these attempts were met with disregard and even the harsh treatment of Ajuoga himself, and these formed the final component of Ajuoga and Johera's religious crisis. Their feelings of alienation and abandonment were so intense that they believed they had no choice but religious self-determination, which ultimately lead to Christian independency.

These three elements—initial social and relational adjustments, the betrayal of history and mutually agreed upon relational patterns, and personal disregard—are related by Ajuoga to be the cause of his shared religious crisis. Based upon these details of Matthew Ajuoga's faith-struggle, below we offer two implications this idiom of crisis has for understanding the *Johera Narrative* in particular and texts like it in general.

First, Ajuoga's story confirms the thesis of many scholars—theologians and social scientists alike—that the efforts of Christian missions initiated mass tensions among their African hosts. As recognized by many of these scholars the crisis Ajuoga narrates is multi-dimensional (e.g., Wipper 1977, 79ff), and consequently an interdisciplinary approach is the most fruitful for understanding the experiences of Johera and the wider phenomena of Christian dissent in Africa (cf. Barrett 1971). Not only, then, is the paradigm of complex crisis enlightening for understanding the story of Christianity in Africa, it is necessary.

More specifically, romanticized versions and good intentions notwithstanding, according to the *Johera Narrative* the story of African Christianity is an account of intense mass crisis primarily related to religious clash. Consequently, studies which not only take this element seriously but which also recognize the religious element as dominant (e.g., Welbourn 1961), are extremely valuable when directed by inside versions of such crises.

It is also significant that Ajuoga's crisis emerged from a revival context, for as we have seen in Chapter 6, the tensions of the East African Revival produced widespread dissensions and these were formative for Johera. The *Johera Narrative* thus suggests that illumination of many of the AICs whose origins can be traced to the East African Revival and other such awakenings, can be gained by adopting and modifying the existing paradigms for the study of such revivals throughout Christian history (e.g., McLoughlin 1978). This approach has potential for enlightening AICs by comparing them with other such groups which have perennially appeared in the Christian story. Such a comparative study would assist in moving closer to the experiences of the AICs by removing their exotic and stigmatic veils, and demonstrating their innate similarities with many of today's "more respectable" denominations.

A second implication of Ajuoga's idiom of crisis is perhaps more surprising. According to Ajuoga, his greatest struggle was not over the essence of Christianity, that is, the *message* that was preached. His narrative of conversion suggests that he welcomed the basic ideas of

Christianity. Instead, Ajuoga's major difficulty arose from the *messengers* of the Faith and their *methods*; the policies and postures of the missionaries who were agents of the message were far less appealing than the basic belief system.

According to Ajuoga's account, this same struggle was at the root of the crises of thousands of Nyanza Luo Anglicans during the 1950's, so Ajuoga's personal difficulties cannot be explained as a simple case of personality clash or desire for ascendancy. While myriads of Ajuoga's tribesmen were generally receptive to the message of Christianity, in part because in many ways it was consistent with their pre-Christian heritage (see Chapter 7), among them also crisis arose and persisted from the insensitive methods and attitudes perceived of the missionaries. Accordingly, for many Luo the problem was not about religion or even culture, but about personalities (cf. Strayer 1978, 158).

This revelation validates those rare studies which have identified this source of crisis (e.g., Strayer 1978). Yet perhaps more significantly, it also brings into question the preoccupation of many scholars of Christian mission with the debate about the need to contextualize the Christian message so as to minimize the clash of its initial introduction. Ajuoga's story suggests that the initial reception of the alien Faith is not the area most in need of our attention; this was not the focus of the most intense battle for the Nyanza Luo. Despite the past and present contextualization debate, according to Ajuoga the Luo were seemingly able to understand and appropriate the Faith with few major obstacles.

Rather, what is more worthy of immediate attention, if we are to understand the faith-story of Johera, is missionary methodology: not *what* is proclaimed but *how* it is presented and modelled. Ajuoga's story thus implies that modern mission studies, in attempting to comprehend the Christian experiences of many among the younger churches, should include an evaluation of past and present mission methods. While concern for the message and its "fit" into different local contexts remains important, the significance of the methods and postures of the agents of the message should not be neglected. The old adage, according to Matthew Ajuoga, is of utmost importance for the experiences of many African Christians: "I would rather see a sermon than hear one any day."

Those who would hear Matthew Ajuoga's "God-Talk," then, must recognize that he speaks the idiom of multi-dimensional crisis in which the religious element is dominant. Additionally, Ajuoga's mode of expression focuses, not primarily on the doctrines or rituals of Christianity, but rather on the practices and personalities of the missionaries who were agents of that message. To understand better this particular idiomatic style, the listener will be aided by consulting those studies which highlight the religious dimension within AICs, but also those which address Christian developments within environments of revival or awakening. Likewise, an understanding of the methods and personalities of the CMS in Nyanza will also illuminate Matthew Ajuoga's *Johera Narrative*.

The Idiom of Legitimization

Matthew Ajuoga's shared crisis eventually led to the establishment of the Church of Christ in Africa. To be sure this decision resolved several of Johera's more pressing dilemmas. In the realm of doctrine, their choice for independency permitted them to honour and elevate the beliefs they had been taught to cherish from the beginning of their Christian experiences. As for ritual and practice, within the CCA they were able to prohibit the abusive conduct of the Wahamaji, and at the same time perpetuate the foundational practices of the Anglican Church they had received. Their move for Christian self-determination also allowed them to create a community and hierarchy which would be more sensitive to local issues: the Christian maturity of individuals, the need for local development, and certain problematic aspects of culture like polygamy.

Even so, Johera's choice for Christian independency also created tensions, and according to Matthew Ajuoga's narrative, one of the most crucial was that of the need for legitimacy. As a sect that had split from the established and highly regarded Church of England, the CCA was suspect at best and despised at worst. Almost immediately, therefore, a need arose for Johera to legitimate its existence, and this need has continued throughout its history. In Chapter 2 we noted that one of Ajuoga's basic intentions for the *Johera Narrative* was to legitimate his life's work and the existence of the CCA, and here we return to this theme and identify it as one of the narrative's basic theological idioms. Within his text, Matthew Ajuoga is speaking the language of legitimization.

An understanding of this idiom, as well as Matthew Ajuoga's encounter with it, can be enlightened by studies of institutional legitimacy from the social sciences. According to conventional sociological theory, "unless an authority can successfully legitimate itself, its survival is unlikely" (Berger and Berger 1983, 287). Based upon this premise many theories of the legitimization process have been propounded, yet the most helpful for understanding Ajuoga's mode of expression has come from the American sociologist, Peter Berger and his colleagues. Expanding upon Max Weber's pioneering examination of institutional legitimacy, Berger and Berger (1983, 288-289) argue that, broadly speaking, institutions employ three major techniques to establish legitimacy. "Charismatic authority" is used when the initial legitimacy of a group is related to the mass appeal of its leader. This method of legitimization is particularly effective within an atmosphere of "intense excitement," yet is consequently short-lived. The other two methods for forming legitimacy usually develop later in the group's history. They arise from identifying the group with established and respected traditions ("traditional authority"), and from appealing to reason ("legal-rational authority").

According to the *Johera Narrative*, all three methods of establishing legitimacy have been used by Matthew Ajuoga. The mass appeal and widespread influence of Matthew Ajuoga himself demonstrates that he was popularly regarded as a charismatic leader. Especially when interpreted within the intensity of the East African Revival and Mau Mau, this source of legitimacy was clearly present and influential during the early days of Johera (See Chapter 5). Likewise, Ajuoga's use of more rational and even legalistic techniques to establish the legitimacy of his community's position is evident from his attack on the abuses of the Wahamaji (see Chapter 6 and Ajuoga 1956b).

However, as other charismatic leaders emerged and the intensity of the Revival and Mau Mau dissipated, and within a society that was not long impressed with Western-style rational arguments, another method to establish Johera's legitimacy had to be devised.[5] Moreover, according to Berger and Luckman (1975, 111), the need to establish lasting legitimacy becomes crucial during the second generation of an institution's life. It is thus significant that Matthew Ajuoga offers his latest attempt to formulate legitimacy—the *Johera Narrative* itself—in Johera's thirty-seventh year (during its second generation!). It is this particular method of legitimization employed by Matthew Ajuoga that is significant here and examined below.

To address this second generation demand for CCA legitimacy, and to respond to the changing times and concomitant developments within Johera, Matthew Ajuoga appeals to "traditional authority" (Berger and Berger 1983, 288). In using this method Ajuoga calls upon established and respected traditions to legitimate Johera. More specifically, Ajuoga constructs a "microcosm/macrocosm scheme of legitimacy" (Berger 1967, 34), in which he directly relates the smaller, more local

CCA with at least four, larger and more universal communities that are highly respected in his time and place. The development of this scheme of legitimacy can be traced through references within the *Johera Narrative*, many of which have already been presented in this study.

First, as noted in Chapter 6 Johera identified itself as the heirs of the pristine Anglican Church established in Uganda, and the same form of Anglicanism that was first offered to the Nyanza Luo. This variation of Anglicanism is still highly regarded by the older members of the CCA—chief among them is Matthew Ajuoga—and by establishing a direct link between Johera and the Church of J. J. Willis and Walter Owen, a powerful tool for forming legitimacy was produced among Ajuoga's age-mates.

The people of God as identified within the Bible is the second wider community to which Matthew Ajuoga relates Johera, and this appeal was especially attractive to those who were affiliated with denominations other than the Church of England. While Old Testament references are not as prominent within the *Johera Narrative* as mentions of the New Testament, the references that are included are potent. For example, in paragraph 156 it is clear that Johera was inspired by the example of Moses, and a link with Abraham and Sarah is established in paragraphs 207, 208, and 222. Ajuoga's references to Jesus, the early Church, and the disciples are more numerous (e.g., pars. 211-221), and the very name of the church—the Church of Christ in Africa (par. 182)—illustrates this attempt to establish a direct link between Johera and the New Testament people of God.

Third, Johera is also deliberately identified with African culture through its sensitivity to established local traditions. This method of legitimization is one of the most durable, appealing to both young and old who maintain respect for their primal pasts. In addition to those primal concerns already examined in Chapter 7, the CCA demonstrates a wholistic ministry (pars. 266-285) which is consistent with the primal view of humankind and their world (see Chapter 7). Likewise, from its beginning Johera has practiced patience, compassion, and cultural sensitivity regarding polygamy (technically polygyny). This practice, though currently diminishing in frequency and popularity in Nyanza, was previously a fundamental part of the stability of Luo society. While the CMS and most other missions rabidly opposed the slightest hint of concession to this hated custom (par. 61), Johera was more tolerant, even offering the sacraments to members of polygamous families (pars. 192-195).[6]

Within the *Johera Narrative* Matthew Ajuoga reveals a fourth source of legitimacy through identification. Johera is directly related to various ecumenical organizations, and this method of legitimization is meant to appeal primarily to those outside the CCA. This particular attempt to establish legitimacy is the most recent yet has been the most frustrating for Matthew Ajuoga and Johera. Ajuoga summarizes the CCA's general disappointment with ecumenism in paragraph 286, and Johera's failed attempt to join the National Council of Churches in Kenya (NCCK) is narrated in paragraphs 287-297. This experience of being blackballed by their own countrymen is unfortunately a common story among AICs. However, Ajuoga briefly recounts a more pleasant and successful relationship with the World Council of Churches (par. 294). Although they are not related within the *Johera Narrative*, under Matthew Ajuoga's leadership the CCA has been actively involved in further ecumenical efforts, ultimately leading in the formation of the largest council of AICs, the Organization of African Instituted Churches, in 1978.[7]

To illustrate the significance of Ajuoga's idiom of legitimacy, two related and crucial areas of religious experience within an AIC as revealed in the *Johera Narrative* will be highlighted. First, this idiom illuminates the development of the CCA over time, as different methods of legitimization are employed to counter changing times and social and religious needs. Second, this expressive style reflects Matthew Ajuoga's efforts in self-understanding. In the very act of identifying himself and Johera with certain macrocosmic groups, especially through the groups that he selects and the reasons he prefers them, Ajuoga reveals his understanding of his own Christian identity. Likewise, the method Ajuoga employs to construct this idea of his individual and communal Christian self is also implied. These efforts highlight the third basic theological idiom of Matthew Ajuoga's "God-Talk."

The Idiom of a Rearward-Looking Christian Identity

Since at least 1980 scholars have recognized what African Christians have always experienced: the identity crisis that is produced at conversion, when the African "inherited" past encounters the Christian "adopted" past (Walls 1980). The significance of this issue of African Christian identity and its background within African Christian theology was introduced in Chapter 9. Here, it is our purpose to return to the problem of African Christian identity, to identify it as a basic idiom within the *Johera Narrative*, and to examine Matthew Ajuoga's encounter with it.

Despite the scholarly attention the issue of African Christian identity has received in the past twenty years, gaps in the literature persist. The scholarly debate thus far has focused primarily on the identification and clarification of the problem. What is lacking is raw, inside evidence of the problem's encounter and resolution within actual African Christian experience. While a general agreement exists that most African Christians experience an identity crisis upon conversion, one that is both historically and culturally based, few insights have been offered on exactly how Christians on the Continent confront and resolve this dilemma; the synthesis and the method for its formation is still largely a mystery. To use the argument of Kwame Bediako referred to in our Introduction, what is needed is "...the necessary intellectual penetration for the establishment of a unified vision of identity and selfhood..." (1995a, 55). It is within this context that Matthew Ajuoga's third basic theological idiom is to be understood and appreciated.

One of the most prominent and dominant modes of expression reflected within the *Johera Narrative* is that of Christian identity formation. Throughout the text Matthew Ajuoga's construction of an African Christian identity can be traced, and this endeavour forms one of his basic modes of narration; Ajuoga speaks the language of Christian identity formation. This idiom is consistent with all Ajuoga's intentions for the text as listed in Chapter 2, and it is also a product of the two other basic idioms previously noted in this chapter. To move towards an understanding of Matthew Ajuoga's encounter and use of this idiom, here we will recollect the scattered elements of his identity formation already mentioned, and pinpoint Ajuoga's innovations and the general scholarly context for their further consideration.

In Chapters 5 and 6 we have described the crisis environment in which Matthew Ajuoga's construction of a Christian self has taken place, and his reactions to this cauldron in which Ajuoga's "stew" of African Christian identity was prepared was identified as one of his text's basic idioms. Also as noted above, Andrew Walls has named the raw materials available for the construction of an African Christian identity: elements from the "inherited" and "adopted" pasts (1980). In Chapter 7 we have pinpointed and interpreted the influence of the specific components of the Luo primal past which have been utilized by Matthew Ajuoga in his Christian appropriation. These are religious traditionalism and the prophetic tradition.

In this chapter our preceding discussion of legitimacy has introduced the materials and method Matthew Ajuoga has appropriated from his adopted Christian past to construct his African Christian identity. It is significant in this regard that two of the three adopted macrocosmic groups with which Johera is identified have their origins in the biblical and Christian past. The Old and New Testament people of God and pristine Nyanza Anglicanism are named within the *Johera Narrative* as groups from which Ajuoga and Johera derive their Christian identity. This method of forming a new identity by appropriating the Christian past is consistent with the rearward looking prophetic tradition and traditionalism of Ajuoga's primal imagination. However, more significantly, this particular construction of an African Christian identity illuminates Ajuoga's method by allowing us to compare it with other related endeavours throughout Christian history.

By constructing his present Christian identity through establishing relationships with past biblical and Christian communities, Matthew Ajuoga is appropriating a precedent and employing a method that is consistent with a rich heritage within the universal Christian story. This tradition has been referred to by many names, yet the most common in the current literature are "primitivism," "restitutionism," and "restorationism." This method of constructing Christian identity by attempting to re-institute or restore the primitive Church has been a perennial practice in Christian history, most common within Protestantism, yet its prominence within North American Christianity in the last two hundred years has been the subject of much study.[8]

The US-American historian of Christianity, Sidney Mead, noted "the tendency chronic in Christendom but perhaps more acute among Englishmen, to support every contemporary innovation by an appeal to 'primitive Christianity'" (1956, 211). Likewise, it has been argued that, although it has had many expressions, certain Christians in all places and ages have sought to form their Christian identity through an appeal to the Christian past (Hill 1976, 74-76). This practice was not only employed "to redress imbalances or reorder priorities or provide legitimacy," but it has also been used in Christian history "to inaugurate, [or] to create new forms which either correspond to a new revelation or [which] perfectly reproduced the old" (Hill 1976, 66). By calling upon this well-used and familiar method of legitimization, Matthew Ajuoga enlightens the nature of his own African Christian identity and that of Johera. Three components of this self-understanding and their implications will be noted.

First, despite the common practice of outsiders to refer to African Instituted Churches as New Religious Movements, Matthew Ajuoga does not perceive the CCA to be "new." While Johera obviously represents a recently established Christian community and a fresh phenomenon in *African* Christianity—and in those senses it could be considered "new"—Matthew Ajuoga prefers to view himself and the

CCA as representing "old" Christianity. Ajuoga's employment of a popular historical device—restitutionism or the attempt to re-institute an earlier form of the Faith—to construct the Christian identities of himself and Johera, confirms his desire to be understood within the wider (not just African) and older (not just twentieth century) story of universal Christianity. Thus, Ajuoga tells us that if we really desire to understand his Christian identity and experiences as well his Christian community, we must broaden our historical perspectives to consider his "newer" local chapter within the context of the "older" universal story.

Second, Matthew Ajuoga offers that his African Christian identity is innately traditionalistic. As already noted, this concern is carried over from the Luo primal imagination, yet applied in Christian terms. In relating Johera to the primitive and pristine Church—the Church of Christ—Ajuoga conveys that his Christian identity and experiences, including his theologizing, are rearward looking. His Christian present and future are deliberately directed by his understanding of the Christian past. So, if we really want to understand Ajuoga's Christian identity and his Christian community, his present and recent past experiences must be understood within the context of the Christian and Luo more distant pasts.

Finally, in addition to employing restitutionism and primitivism to construct his Christian identity, Matthew Ajuoga also adds an element of restorationism. From our discussion in Chapter 6 Johera's desire to restore the lost purity of early Nyanza Anglicanism emerged. This concern to restore the more perfect form of Christianity first preached at Maseno is demonstrated and summarized by Johera's determination to return to Maseno (par. 158). This suggests the abiding, even if it was romanticized, appeal of the Anglican Church as it was first presented. Consequently, as argued by at least two scholars (Ranger 1994; Strayer 1978, 159ff), the initial appeal of mission Christianity to many Africans might well have been under-estimated. The first form of Anglicanism introduced to Nyanza was so attractive, so efficacious, that Matthew Ajuoga and Johera partly derive their legitimacy and identity from efforts to restore it. Thus, if we really want to understand Matthew Ajuoga's Christian identity and his Christian community, we must search among the rubble of the early CMS mission in Uganda-Nyanza, to discover the source of its lasting appeal.

Given the nature of the *Johera Narrative* and this study, it has been the purpose of this chapter to provide a guide for interpreting Ajuoga's text. This has been accomplished by offering, rather than definitive conclusions, an index of requisite postures for approaching the text and basic theological idioms expressed in Ajuoga's "God-Talk." By highlighting approaches and basic modes of expression, and through pinpointing specific genres of literature that will most illuminate the text, this chapter has hopefully charted the course for future, more detailed—yet equally sensitive— interpretations.

Chapter 11

A Last Look

The purposes of this study were enumerated in the Introduction, and now this concluding chapter will review and summarize our progress towards these goals. Then, several areas for future research relevant to the *Johera Narrative* will be identified.

The general purpose of this study was to carry out the requisite tasks of the initial collector of oral materials. More specifically, our purpose was to describe the formation of the *Johera Narrative* and to demonstrate an effective presentation. This was accomplished through three, more focused processes: 1) a description and demonstration of the collection of the text; 2) a theological assessment of the contributions of the text in light of the relevant scholarly literature; and, 3) an offering of a thorough examination of the nature of the text, and sensitive interpretations in light of its contexts. Below we will summarize the development of these processes within this study.

Part One focused on the formation of this study and Ajuoga's text, thus addressing our first specific purpose noted above. In Chapter 2 the methodology that serves as the foundation of this study was described, yet this study design was also offered for consideration for others whose scholarly task is similar. Chapter 3 described the various types of sources utilized in this study, but it also highlighted a montage of the different types of materials available and necessary for studying texts of African Christian experience. Chapter 4 focused on the collection of the *Johera Narrative*: stages and methods of transmission were described, and concomitant problems were noted. Part Two focused on the various aspects of the text's presentation, thus addressing the second and third specific purposes noted above. First, in Chapters 5, 6, and 7 the most crucial contexts from which the *Johera Narrative* has emerged were identified, and their influences upon the contents of the text were interpreted. Then, Chapter 8 examined the singular nature of the text, noting its forms, contents, and genres. Although the extensive reference list appended to this study reflects the rigourous assessment of the *Johera Narrative* throughout this study in light of the scholarly literature of several academic disciplines, Chapter 9 was devoted entirely to this task. There, the *Johera Narrative's* contributions to five specific areas related to theological studies in Africa were discussed. To conclude the examination and interpretation of Ajuoga's text, Chapter 10 provided a "listener's guide," in which an index of basic interpretive postures and characteristics of the text's idiomatic language was offered.

The purposes of this study, then, were primarily descriptive and demonstrative. We did not intend to develop or examine a particular argument, nor did we attempt to test a specific theory. Our purpose was to present the "God-Talk" of an African Christian: to collect and relay, in a form more universally understandable, the narrative of an African Christian experience. Consequently, three conclusions arising from our study are offered:

1.) We have demonstrated the value of the *Johera Narrative* for theological studies in Africa. Additionally, texts of this genre have been identified as potential illuminators of several problems persisting in the study of African theology and African Instituted Churches.

2.) Even though Ajuoga's text and others like it hold great promise for enlightening several areas of African theology, we have also demonstrated that these texts must be approached with new attitudes and interpretive methods. If the treasures of the *Johera Narrative* and other such texts are to be uncovered, their "God-Talk" must be heard clearly, and this requires the academic theological establishment to learn their oral and narrative "language." This study has offered itself as a handbook or guide for such theological listening.

3.) Because of the value and singular nature of narratives of African Christian experience like the *Johera Narrative*, the need and urgency to collect more of these stories is acknowledged. If many dimensions of African Christian experience can only be known through such texts, then more efforts to preserve and examine these faith narratives must be forthcoming. This study also offers itself as a handbook or guide for the collection and presentation of such oral theological texts.

The value of African theological texts like the *Johera Narrative* highlights several areas of research that represent the logical "next steps" in the life of Ajuoga's text. Because this study made the initial presentation of the *Johera Narrative*, it had to concern itself with "first things," namely issues of text formation and presentation. Now, however, with this foundation laid, here we suggest two of the more pressing and promising future applications for the text:

1.) Because Matthew Ajuoga and Johera in a very real sense "own" the *Johera Narrative*, because it is first and foremost *their* story, the text must be rigourously examined by them. In this regard, plans are underway within the CCA to write the history of their church, and the *Johera Narrative* will serve as the basis for this project. Hopefully many within Johera will examine Ajuoga's text, and through this process many individual and communal reflections will be stimulated. Ajuoga's text, therefore, will hopefully encourage theological reflection within the CCA.

2.) Numerous topics for monographic studies of the *Johera Narrative* have been suggested by this study. For example, a native Dholuo speaker should carry out a linguistic analysis of the text, and its value as part of Luo traditional literature should be assessed. Second, Ajuoga's formation of Christian identity and his story of the development of the CCA over time both warrant further examination. These issues have suffered from the lack of "inside" source materials in the past, and Ajuoga's intramural contributions beg analysis. Also, this study has suggested a more comparative approach for the study of African Instituted Churches. For the most part, past studies of these communities have approached them as "other"; there is promise in also understanding them as "similar," through a comparison of other such movements within the universal and historical Christian story.

This study began by acknowledging that through the *Johera Narrative* an African Christian is offering his "God-Talk," and we confessed our desire to listen and learn. We have described and demonstrated how we have listened, what we have listened to, what we have heard, and what we have learned. However, the listening and learning have only just begun. It is our prayer that with Matthew Ajuoga continuing to lead, many more supporting voices may join in, and so transform Matthew Ajuoga's "God-Talk" from a solo into an ensemble.

Appendix 1

The *Johera Narrative*

As Recounted by Matthew Ajuoga

Transcribed, Translated, and Initially Edited by
Matthew Ajuoga, Keta Peterson Midida, John Okoth Okello,
and George F. Pickens

Present English Version Edited by
George F. Pickens

1   It would be difficult to understand fully the formation and the church unless you know a little bit about the Founder and his only begotten son, Jesus Christ [who was sent] to come and save the world. CCA walked in Anglican Church for over five years under the name of "Revival Movement in the Church". When it reached 1957 there was a complete separation from Church of England, and we began to organize ourselves, and in 1958 January 6th we were recognized and registered by the government.

2   This is the story of the Church of Christ in Africa, which is known in this part of the world as "Johera." It is difficult to understand the Church of Christ in Africa unless you know a little bit of its founder and leader. This is the history of the founder himself, [and] Abednego Matthew Ajuoga by the providence of God is the founder, the leader, and the Presiding Bishop of the Church of Christ in Africa since 1957.

3   I was born December 25th, 1925 at Kambare village in South Gem location, Siaya District in Nyanza Province of Kenya, East Africa.

4 My marriage: I was married to Jennifer Claris Ajuang' in the Anglican Church in Nairobi by the late Bishop Obadiah Kariuki on August 15, 1949. We had eleven children: eight boys and three girls.

5 Concerning my education: I went to Anglican Primary School, Kambare in 1936 to 1941. Then I joined CMS, which was Maseno Secondary School, as from 1942 through 1944, and then immediately I joined St. Mary's Yala Secondary School, which is a Catholic school, as from 1945 to 1946.

6 Teaching: I taught as an untrained teacher in 1947, then in 1948 [I was] at the Kenya-Uganda Railways and Habours training school in Nairobi. I trained as Assistant Station Master and a Train's Clerk.

7 My salvation: One Sunday morning in Nairobi when I entered our church for prayers (of course the Church of England) in the month of June 1948, the minister asked his people, "For how long will you hold between two opinions? If [you choose] the Lord, the God, then follow Him, but if Ba'al, then follow him." The word of God exposed me and found me of the same nature and character. When again I went to the other meetings after that it seemed as if all preachings were directed at me and against me. They preached I John 3:8, Revelation 21:7, 8 and Revelation 21:27. I felt that I am condemned to death unless I believe in the only Saviour of the world who is Jesus Christ. It took me more than a month to decide, then on July 3rd, 1948, I accepted Jesus Christ as my Lord and personal Saviour. I became new in my outlook and inward life: happy, assured of everlasting life through One who died on the cross for my sins [and those] of the whole world, Amen.

8 My call: After my salvation it was my rule of life to read the Holy Bible everyday. One day I came across these words, "Hereby perceive we the love of God because he laid down his life for us, and we ought to lay down our lives for the brethren" (I John 3:16). These words struck deep into my heart and the Holy Spirit of God led me and made me believe that God was calling me for full-time service. From that time I devoted myself [and] life to serve my Lord, Jesus Christ and His Church on this earth.

9 And while I was still battling with this matter within me my church also elected me to go to St. Paul United Theological College for theological training. This proved to me that the Lord was calling me to His service. We discussed with my wife, who also was saved before we got married, and [I] agreed wholeheartedly to leave my

The Johera Narrative

secular job so as to work for the Lord. I then resigned from Railways and Habours and went to Limuru college in 1950.

10 Theological Training: Anglican Church sent me for theological studies for four years at the St. Paul's United Theological College, Limuru, Kenya as from 1950 to 1952. I passed my examinations and was on top of my class, and was ordained Anglican Deacon. And again, [I attended] in 1953 to 1954 [and] I passed my examination second position in my class, and was ordained priest according to the Anglican Church order.

11 Then the World Council of Churches came in [and] I was given scholarship by the World Council of Churches in academic year 1964 to 1965 as an ecumenical student. I did my advance religious studies at the Union Theological Seminary in New York, USA. I had been external student of the International Bible Institute and Seminary in Florida, USA where I spent few days. I obtained both Bachelor of Ministry and Master of Ministry, [and was granted] a degree of Doctor of Divinity of the same institute.

12 In 1951 the unscriptural teachings, practices, and beliefs crept into the East Africa Revival movement of which I was a member. However, I was one of the few brethren who stood firm, opposing false teaching and called others back to the biblical faith. I represented the group in the church councils, after which we were recognized by the church and the government in 1952 to 1953 as "Revival Movement in the Church (Johera).

13 Apart from the old revival we emphasized love [for] one another (John 3:16; Romans 5:8; and John 13:34; Galatians 5:14, and I Corinthians 13). The Revival Movement in the Church entrusted me with the leadership of the group. We tried to correct things biblically within the Church of England, but eventually it was impossible. After all efforts for reconciliation failed the movement became the Church of Christ in Africa, [and] I am the founder and the Presiding Bishop since it was organized in June 1957. The Church of Christ in Africa is registered and recognized in Kenya, Uganda, Tanzania, Zambia, and Zaire. It received its registration here in Kenya in January 6th, 1958.

14 Experienced by travelling: I was longing and praying for opportunity to see how believers in other nations are serving the Lord in their own countries and as respective churches, [and] the Lord made it possible for me [to do so]; that [was] in 1962. I visited many countries and various denominations around the world and other religious bodies in other parts of Africa, in the United Kingdom, Europe, Near East, Middle East, Far East including

Malaysia, Indonesia, Japan, New Zealand, Australia, Hawaii, and the United States of America. Lastly, I visited Australia and other parts of Far Eastern countries.

15   I [have] here decided to speak in English and my mother tongue, Dholuo.

16   I have briefly spoken about how I was born and where I was born, and my primary education, up to secondary, up to college, up to university. Now I want to start this story right from its source when I begin from my father.

17   My father was called Oguna, the son of Ajuoga. This Oguna, the son of Ajuoga, some of his names known to his people were: Oguna Raten'g, Oguna Nyandiwa, Oguna Aloo. These were the names he was called by and he was distinguished with and he was being honoured with.

18   Oguna, my father, was not born from a rich family, but him, he was later better [economically]. He had more than ten wives, he had enough cattle, he had enough crop, and he was a humble man, and had a heart to help people with food or advice.

19   This my father, Oguna, was a leader of his people. He was a leader in fighting [for] he was a strong wrestler. He was a strong fighter, because he was born in the year 1800's (there before the coming of the white [men], [a] long time [ago]). After they had fought the war and they had wrestled, when the whites came [they] found him a grown up, and then the whites made him a leader, [because] they found [him] when he was already a leader of our people. He was given the name of "headman" [and] he was given security officers whom he was walking with. He was given his prison, he was given "baraza" court, and he was a judge who was coming to give judgement here in Kisumu, [where he was a] counsellor.

20   And one day in his life when the District Commissioner, who was a whiteman, wanted to employ somebody to become a chief he refused by getting hold of the DC's hand before the court (baraza), and then the DC ordered for his arrest. He was arrested, but after[ward] he came back and just went ahead by leading our people.

21   I, in my life right from my childhood, I [was] used to many visitors, for my father was advisor, and a man who fought for the nation, and he was loved by his people. I used to see many visitors. I used to see many people eating, and [I remember] when many needed things from my father, and when my father [was] also helping many people with advice when he was approached.

22   When it was so (as he was the leader of our village), [and] when the missionaries came in South Gem, they were the elders who welcomed the missionaries and he gave the CMS, which is called the Church Missionary Society, the land where they built up the Church. Therefore, he started attending the Sunday School when I was still very young. I went to Sunday School until I joined sector, which is these days [is] called primary, which was built there by the Anglican church because of the land which they were given by my father.

23   When I finished there, as I have told you, I again went to a CMS secondary school, which was Maseno, which was one of the schools which were respected here in Kenya, or [especially] in Western Kenya among Anglican churches. And again, [I attended] St. Mary's Yala [which] was also built in Gem. That was also a very important school, and was highly valued among the Roman Catholics. And, therefore, I went to all those schools because I wanted a strong education, and I wanted to learn at highly valued places--[at] the schools which were valued by people.

24   The East African Revival [began] in the year 1938 during the coming of the missionary, [and] that was called the "Church Revival" that emerged from Rwanda-Burundi. When this revival emerged people believed in Christ as the Saviour of their souls [who] forgave their sins, and they then praised Jesus. This revival spread in East Africa as a whole. This revival [came] when I was still a young school child, [and] I did not know what was happening.

25   In 1938 when I was with my brother in Nairobi I went to listen to the word of God, [and] then I got saved there. I confessed my sins there. I was still a young child, and I again backslid [for] I forgot the word of the Lord.

26   Then came the time I was in Maseno, [when] we were among those who were in the fellowship of revival. And when I went to Yala the Lord continued to reveal himself to me, and in most cases, I was the leader of all the Protestant students. I gathered them and sometimes I gathered them and we went to pray when there was prayer outside, or when there was Holy Communion among the Anglican Church outside. During that period those who were saved and were in the Revival were very few.

27   But during that period the leader of the Revival among us in the Anglican Church was the old man, Ishmael Noo. Many things were said about these revival people who were later called "the evangelists". Rumours spread and there was [a] split because many people liked to sleep on the mat with women, [because] they said that their bodies are dead, and they could not commit sin. That was

against many people's wish and this brought the split in the year 1948. Those who opposed that practice (I was following them just as a child), they went back to the Anglican Church because those revival people started to criticize and oppose the church's doctrine. They wanted fellowship only among themselves. They preached the gospel themselves, they had their own leaders, they walked [by] themselves, as they admired that first revival. Those whom they taught to leave their house, to go and preach the word of God outside, [they were the ones] which brought a lot of problems here in Luoland. They were those people who were wedded to their first wives. Later, a number of first wives ran away, leaving their houses [and] saying that they were out with Jesus.

28   First, an important thing that those who claimed to be revivalists were doing was confessing sins; they confessed serious sins. But when people saw [that] others were coming back to sin while others confess[ed] serious sins with their mouths, (but sometimes they were still in sin, and sometimes he comes back to sin), sometimes they left that revival and they became lukewarm.

29   This was later seen by those who had gathered, [and it was decided] that some brethren should be sent to Uganda. The brethren who were sent were three: Musa Amoke, who was from Seme (this happened when he had come from forces, but he was a revival man). Also sent was Peter Alaka, who was from Gem, and also John Onguko, who was from Bunyore. When these people went to Uganda they found William Nagenda and Yona Mondo, [and] they found many revival men from Uganda.

30   But these did not have any quarrel with the church. These people were working very peacefully in the church, [and] these people were paying their money in the church so well. These people were listening to the church leaders, these people were doing all the church duties, these people were partaking the Holy Communion, [and] these people were being baptized. These people were in church committees, these people were in the school committees, [and] these people were in the development committees of their nation or their village, or their church.

31   When Musa Amoke and his people told their brothers in Uganda how they had problems with the church, how people were struggling with the church, how people were criticizing the church, how people were leaving the church to join the revival, the brethren from Uganda told them that they were making a mistake, and that Satan was taking them astray. Then those people said that you are just confessing yours sins, but you are not yet saved [for] the plant

root is [still] in your heart. Then our brethren who were sent to Uganda continued to confess their sins and accept the Lord Jesus with all their hearts until they realized that they were forgiven their sins, and they found that they had renewed hearts and new thoughts.

32   Musa Amoke and his group, when they returned, they gathered brethren here and there. They told the church leaders here and there that the revival that they had found in Uganda was quite different with the revival here in Kenya. Therefore for them, they were saying that they were saved, [and] they were singing songs in Luganda that said, "Tuketendereza Yesu, Yesu mwana wandiga" (that means "I praise Jesus our Lord, Jesus is my Saviour").

33   Then people started to get healed, and people started to say that they were washed by the blood of Jesus Christ. People started to talk good about the blood of Jesus Christ [saying] that the blood of Jesus Christ was that which washes sins. People started accepting Jesus Christ and started talking good about the blood of Jesus Christ [which] was shed on the cross to wash away their sins.

34   So many people started to get saved. I got saved in the year 1948, and we were very few people who were young (or boys) who got saved. There were few girls who got saved like that, [but] those who always got saved were old people.

35   Getting saved went ahead like that until people started to talk about it. First, people started to say that when you want to marry you take the word to the brothers [fellow revivalists], and it's the brothers who tell you the lady you can marry, or it is the brothers who tell the man to marry you. But sometimes you could be shown somebody whom you didn't like. Sometimes you could be shown someone whose husband was dead or someone whose wife was dead whom you didn't love. If you wanted to marry the money was just taken to the brothers or the animals were just given to the brothers who took them for you to the lady's home (the woman whom the people from your family or the extended family had little concern about).

36   [Also] the word emerged from [among] us, the revival people, that the Holy Communion was sin, being a member of the school committee was sin, [and] paying church offerings was sin. You could not go and mourn the dead person where there was a dead body [for this] was a sin. Eating where somebody had died was a sin. Your chair could not be used anywhere someone had died, because your chair was also sacred. The padre who was not saved could not wed those who were saved. When somebody was praying in the

church, then someone who was saved could come up and preach or criticize him in the church where [while] he is still preaching.

37   Those who were the second wives, third wives, [or] fourth wives were taught that they had to leave their husbands. Many left their husbands and were given other husbands, or those marriages were broken just like that; many left their husbands. Some, when they had left their houses and their homes, they went and lived in somebody's home called "siro." "Siro" meant among the revival [that] they appointed somebody to stand for the revival in the church, [and] that [person] was "siro" for the church. They appointed somebody who stood for the revival in the pastorate or parish, [and] they appointed those men who stood for salvation in the diocese.

38   Then they arranged crusades for every month, crusades for Friday, [and] crusades for other months when people went and gathered at one place. Like here in western Kenya people were meeting at Butere, people were meeting at Kambare, [and] people were meeting at Ramba and other places which were there.

39   Places where these second, third, and fourth wives were taken, where they were living in the houses of those revival leaders, some of them got pregnant, and some got pregnant with those revival leaders. That made people criticize a lot those practices. I, as one of those who were young (who was there), I was one of those who criticized such practices, because I read the Bible, and I liked the Bible, and I loved God, and I liked his church, and I used to attend the Bible discussions.

40   Things became serious when there was a large convention for the whole [of] Kenya at Maranda School. At this convention were visitors of all kinds, even the missionaries were there. But it was led by those who led the convention [and who] were the revival leaders (that was Musa Amoke and other leaders).

41   That part that was read [to all who] were there was Genesis 10 and 12:1-3 that says, "Now the Lord told Abram, leave your country and among your kindred from your father's house and you go to that country that I will show you. And I will make you a great nation, and I will bless you, and I will make your name great, and you will be a blessing. I will bless those who bless you, and I will curse those who curse you, and by you all the families of the earth shall bless themselves." When this had been read, the leaders of the revival strongly encouraged before the church leaders that God said he [Abram] should leave, leave his country, leave his people, leave his neighbours, leave his garden or his house, leave his friends who he

The Johera Narrative 229

had been close to, leave and go to a foreign place where the Lord would show him. And it was there where the Lord would bless him.

42   This word was immediately translated, that when somebody is saved he must carry his tent just the same way Abraham carried his tent, [and] that he must leave the church [for] the church is sin. The church is [part of] the world, [and] the truly saved person, [the one] that is [in] the Lord must leave the church. [He] must leave his church work, must leave all that is done in the church, [and] must go out with the Lord. Jesus went out, [and] Jesus was persecuted outside in the world. That is the beginning of the word which we shall meet quite often, that is the "Wahamaji". The Wahamaji were those who were saved [yet who wanted to leave the church].

43   They were in the Anglican church and other churches, but more so in the Anglican Church. They were separating [and] leaving the Anglican Church, saying that the church is the world. I could see that there was only one church leader who opposed that idea, who stood and said that that is not so.

44   But us, during that period of 1951, we were in Limuru at St. Paul's Theological College. We left Limuru during that period, 1951, to attend that convention which was held at Ramba School (I together with some of my brothers with whom we were from Limuru, among who was the late Meshack Owira, who was a padre, and the late padre, Philip Okungu; we were all in Limuru). We left there [the convention] when we were greatly saddened. [We felt] that the church is empty, [that] there is no body leading the church, because it is here in the Anglican Church where they have Thirty-Nine Articles, they have the prayer book, the prayer group, [and] they have the Bible. [We had believed] that the Anglican [Church] that is here is the place for evangelical[s]. But if people are in all these, the old people are there, there are bishops, there are rural deans, there are padres, but they still approve these false teachings.

45   Us, we left that place when serious, [and we had decided] that we were going to complete school and come back to correct those false teachings in the church.

46   I knew as I was reading from the Bible, Matthew 16:17, 18, 19, [that] there Jesus Christ was telling Peter that, "Believe me, my rock, it is on that rock that I will build my church". It is Jesus who built the church. And we read when Paul the righteous says in I Corinthians 12ff, that the Lord had put some people in the church; it is the Lord that puts some people in the church. And we read in the book of Ephesians 5 where Paul tells the story of the wife and the husband, how he is supposed to love his wife as his own flesh just as

Christ also gave himself and loved his church (that is in Ephesians 5:27-31). But when somebody was saying that he was saved it is this same Jesus who saved him, it is this same Jesus who washed him with his blood, it is this same Jesus who shed blood--his blood--on the cross, and he again says that he leaves the church, that he gets out of the church, he does not want the church, he doesn't want to stay in the church, [this I disagreed with].

47   These words were bothering me. That is why from that time I knew that he who criticizes the church is criticizing Jesus himself, because Jesus is the Church. Jesus is the head of the church, [and] He said that he who isolates himself from him should be thrown away and can't bear fruit. That again split the Anglican Church into two. Some people got saved and ran away from the church, [and] they were called Wahamaji.

48   But when it reached 1952, that was when we had come from Limuru and I had been appointed deacon, the Lord revealed himself to me, and he also revealed himself to a number of brothers. He also revealed himself to sisters, [and He said] that [we] were saved people, and that if we were saved then we belong to the true Church of Jesus. Therefore, my brothers who were saved and criticized the church, I couldn't share with because Jesus is the head of the Church. This is the Church which is Jesus himself, [of] which Jesus Christ himself is the leader. There is the church which is seen, which is the building, [and] there is the church which is not seen, but Jesus is the head of the Church. Therefore the Lord revealed himself to us that when one is truly saved by the blood (that is the blood of Jesus), he is the true member of the Church.

49   But to us the Lord revealed himself so that we strongly encouraged one another with John 3:16 that says, "For God so loved the world that He gave His only begotten Son, that whoever believes in Him should not perish, but have eternal life." For this reason we started stressing the love of Jesus. We started loving the world [for] even when we were still sinners, he loved us. Even when we were still in sin he loved us. That is why [we told] those brethren [who were] being rebellious with those who are not saved [that] we must go out looking for those who are not saved so that they may also be saved. We must love those people who are not saved so that we [may] pull them away from sin.

50   The Lord encouraged us that we preach Revelation 2:2-5. Verse 3 says that, "Remember this [your] first love, remember when you have fallen, so that you change and stand". [In] the First Epistle of John 4:16 we read that, "God is love and he who abides in love

abides in God and God in him". Paul tells us in I Corinthians 13:13 that we [may] have hope and trust, but the most important is love. But all this chapter 13 tells us that even though you speak in tongues of angels or pray that you [can] remove mountains or give out your belongings, or you surrender your soul to be burnt but you don't have love, then you are like a brass or sounding bell that does not have meaning. In Exodus 25:5 Moses said that God said to those who love [that they] should give their wealth, that they give their gold, silver, and other things they have. Those who love (God was saying in the Old Testament) [are to] give, but those our brethren were saying that nothing should be given [to] the church. In Matthew 22 a man asked Jesus, "Which one is the great commandment?" In chapter 22:32-40 [it] says that the great commandment is love. [To] love your God with all your wealth, with all your strength, and with all your wisdom, and love your brother as you love yourself, that is the great commandment.

51   But us, as Anglican Church members, when I went ahead assessing the prayer book [I saw that] when one was to be baptized he was called "johera". When one was to be confirmed the first he was to read [was] "johera". When one was to wed "johera" [was used]. Love is the great commandment which was made by God, and that is the great pillar of the Anglican Church. But in such situations the leaders of the Anglican Church ran away from love.

52   Therefore, those brothers who separated [wahamaji] when we started to stress love, they started calling us secular people [and said] that we must just join the main revival for East Africa. But [they said that] we were not in that revival, that we are outside. Then [they said that our kind of love] is for Satan, [and] that [kind of] love is for the world. [They said] that [kind of] love is not with Jesus, that the original love was not Jesus'. [This is] where people were the first to call us the lovers (Johera).

53   We did not sit down and start calling ourselves "Johera". It was these people who started seeing how we were stressing love, how the Lord loved people, how Jesus loved people so that he gave his life, how the Apostles loved those who were in darkness, how John was teaching, how Peter was teaching, how Paul was teaching. Yes, how we read from Revelation, [it is true] that it was the people who started calling us (that we are) the lovers (Johera).

54   Because we started teaching and we started to love (we love those in sin, we love those who drink) we could see many of them getting saved. We loved those who committed adultery, we loved those who just roamed about, we loved those who were lost. We

were visiting them, preaching for them the word of God, and many of them were getting saved. We were visiting the witches, those who were medicine men we were visiting them and they were getting saved, and we were burning their witchcraft [charms] here and there. We destroyed their beer pots, [and] their pots for witchcraft here and there. And people started calling us the lovers (Johera), and that is our name to date, and that is how we are [still].

55   Jesus taught his disciples (in John 13:34) to love one another, and [He said] that is when other people or the unrighteous people will know that you are my disciples. But if you don't love one another, people will not know that you are my disciples.

56   When we started preaching the word of love, when we were watching the Anglican Church (we were watching the missionaries, we were watching those who say they were saved, we were watching the mediators) we found out that they did not have love. But that means that it was Jesus who was not there. Where there is no love it means there is no Jesus. Therefore, we started to preach love when we were in the Anglican Church.

57   During the time we started that word we were still padres who were working (three padres and the other three who had retired). But our secretary was Benson Otieno who was the CMS secretary at Maseno CMS Hospital. Then we decided that we were separated from other revival people who had separated and were criticizing the church. We called ourselves that we were the "Evangelical Revival Movement in the Church," because the other people were calling themselves the revivalists but were criticizing the church. That's why we resolved that we were the "Evangelical Revival [Movement]", which means those who preach here and there, who don't discriminate and who defend the Bible in the church, but don't leave the church.

58   Maseno was the centre of the Anglican [Church] here in Luoland. And the land at Maseno, it was chief Ogola (the son of Ayieko who was from Kisumu Karaten'g, [he] was the one who was found as the chief and was confirmed by the whites), he was the one who gave out that land so that the missionaries could live when they taught the children the word of God and academic knowledge. The word of God was first taught at Maseno, and that was the year 1906. And this is how it started:

59 ·   When the missionaries came they were humble people [and] they started to talk with the chiefs. They were visiting the chiefs, [but] they started teaching the children not the old people. They were asking the chiefs to take the children [to school], and the chiefs

were bringing the children. Some were the chiefs' children, but many chiefs refused to take their children to become students. Therefore, they were only taking other people's children, because these missionaries were teaching people how to dress, they were teaching people how to leave the knife, they were teaching people how to wash, they were teaching people how to read and write. Some people said that they did not want to learn how to read and write, because they were not hens to peck! Some people said that they did not want to wrap themselves with cloths which had [such a] bad smell that [it] could make him vomit. People were just being caught (the children were being caught) and taken to Maseno.

60 The whitemen also came with their fellow whitemen who were working in the government. They were bringing people black clothes, the clothes that were called "kanik". But people were just being forced with all these, [and] there was nobody who wanted to put on clothes. But when a few children who had gone there were being taught the word of God, they [the missionaries] were teaching them and they [the children] were going back home. They were being sent slowly to their rural homes to go and slowly teach the people all that they had been taught. When a few people had listened to the word of God, they were separating [and] leaving their homes. They were building themselves [new homes] and calling themselves Christians. That is [where] the home that they built was called "laini," because [they believed] that place should not be used for ritual practices or witchcraft, because people could not go there for witchcraft. That "laini" continued to exist when Christians isolated themselves from others.

61 The missionaries were teaching people to divorce especially among polygamous families. When you were a polygamist and you accepted to be a Christian, then you were told to send away some [wives] and remain with only the first wife. That is how it happened, and this brought quite a lot of problems in many homes. And then, later on, people started to talk bad about the "laini," and then people started to go back to their homes. People started to move back to where they had come from.

62 The Anglicans in Luoland are called "Jokogore." Ogore was a missionary whose real name was Willis, who used to greet people in the word "Ogore," and this is the reason why the Luos who are Anglican are called "Ogore" until today.

63 But during those days was when the Catholic missionaries started to arrive here in Luoland. The first arrived here at Ojola and when they became dissatisfied, they moved to Aluor in Gem. These

missionaries were competing [with] other missionaries (the SDA, many of them were in South Nyanza, African Inland Church had its centre and its large home at Nyakach and then [at] Kisumu here at Nyaera; we [are] also working here). Somewhere there these missionaries were dividing this our land [by saying] that here is for the Anglican, here is for the Catholic, here is for the SDA, and here is for the so and so. (That is why the Gikuyu land was taken by the Church of Scotland until today, [and] the land of Meru was taken by the Methodists of England). Then later the Salvation Army were running here and there, slowly here and there. The Anglicans were also scattered here and there, [and] the Catholics were also scattered here and there. And that was how this our land was divided during the missionary period.

64   During all that time the missionaries were teaching people that someone who is a member of one church should not marry from the other church. A man who is a member of one church should not marry a lady from the other church. And [then] the schools were built where the "Kogore" schools were called Anglican, and they were CMS schools. The Catholic schools were mainly for Catholics, [and] those AIM schools were mainly for the AIM [people]. And the schools were so classified that a school under one church became an enemy of another under the other church.

65   And [yet] we sometimes thank the missionaries for education. They were the first people to introduce education in this land, they were the first people to start hygiene in this land, they were the first people to start the health centres/hospitals in this land, and they were the first people to start hygiene, and they were the first people to start many development programs in this land.

66   The group of the Anglican Church that is called CMS was the group that brought quality education [here]. But the churches, like Catholics, thought that when people were taught they would be clever and then they would leave God. People were also prevented from reading the Bible. [They were told] that when you read the Bible you will have headache. (The father stands and just says some words verbally, and does not say from which Gospel the word has come). They used to educate people up to class two, three, [or] four, and then that was enough. And the African Inland Church also did not want to educate people, because they thought that when one becomes clever then he would leave God. When he becomes bright he would get job, then he gets money, then he begins to boast, [and] then he leaves the church and marries many wives. But when they saw the CMS people (which means the Anglican people) giving

people quality education, and [that] it was these people who got jobs, it was these people who became chiefs, and it was these people who became leaders, they became jealous and began providing education [too]. People also started asking what type of the church that was, where people don't learn like CMS? Then they started providing education, they started struggling for education and many people started to learn.

67   When we go back to where we left, in the year 1953 when the Rural Dean's Council had passed us, [and] when we wanted to take back the gospel where Bwana Ogore (Willis the missionary who first spread the gospel here on our land) [had come first], we again requested Archdeacon Stovold who officially opened for us the first convention at Maseno. And we were gathering every month there at Maseno. Johera were fellowshiping [there, at Maseno] but the Wahamaji were fellowshiping at Ramba in Asembo every month.

68   Then the Anglican Church revival or the saved were divided into two. Many Anglican padres remained on the fence, because many of them were still saved, but the padres who were saved were also divided into two. But a large number of the Anglican Church supported the Johera, because they stood on the word of God. The Johera were looking for those who were lost, [and] the Johera were encouraging standing and remaining firm in the church and giving in the church. When this happened jealousy started to emerge among the Wahamaji.

69   We who were leaders among the Johera, we were junior padres, [and] we were not so important. For this reason people started to run away from those who were fellowshiping at Ramba, which means the Wahamaji or the "blood people" (Joremo), when they were coming to us, the Johera. People started to get saved among the Johera when many were coming to us, the Johera. The Johera were loved everywhere (where there were [saved] people of the [Anglican] church) because we were attending people's funerals, we were preaching at people's funerals, we were encouraging education, we were supporting other church programs, [and] we were encouraging those who were lost so that they come back to Jesus. We were known here and there in the church, and it was this revival that did not separate people, but was the revival that united people, and it was an evangelical revival. It was a revival that was preaching here and there, here and there.

70   I can remember that during those days I could preach at two, three or four places in one day; in the morning at a place, in the afternoon at a place, in the evening at a place, and in the night at a

place. It was a serious campaign when we were moving on bicycles in a great convoy.

71   I can remember that those leaders of Wahamaji began to give some leaders of the Anglicans bribes by giving them clothes, giving them money, giving them other things so that they would become our enemies. But truly they started to become harsh on us and tried to punish us, so that we could not move here and there.

72   The Archdeacon for the Anglicans during those days was called Peter Hawse [sp.?]. This Peter Hawse (I cannot tell where he is now), after the fight between Johera and Wahamaji and also the Anglicans, Peter Hawse was removed and was taken back to England. I can remember one time [he] invited [me] and told me that he did not want me to go to any pastorate, that I [should] stick to my pastorate, [and] that if he finds me going to any [other] pastorate then he would punish me. I also told him that I have not seen anybody who was as primitive as he was, because I was called to preach the gospel and I have taken good care of my pastorate with everything. He [then] should tell me what was lacking. But when brothers wanted me to go and preach somewhere or people wanted me to go and preach somewhere, or if there was prayer somewhere which was not my pastorate or my parish, I had the privilege to go and fellowship with other people. Therefore, I could not accept what he was saying.

73   During those days the [now] retired Archbishop Olang' was a Rural Dean for Central Nyanza, and the word had reached Archbishop Beecher that we were stubborn children and were dividing the church. When Bishop Beecher came to Maseno, we were called to Maseno (myself, Owira, that is padre Owira, padre Okungu, and padre Silas Awuor). And when we went to Maseno, when we sat down the Archbishop said that I and Owira were still very young, [and] we should go back to Limuru for further training. But others, like Silas and like William Ogada, those people [we] should leave alone, because we were very young, but [we were] bringing problems in the church. Then I told Archbishop Beecher, that old man, that if it were us who separated like those who have separated, [then] you should have gone back to England long time ago. We are the people in the Anglican church. We are your people [and] we are those who have taken care of the church. Why can't you see this? Because what you tell us is what these people [Wahamaji] criticize, and what you want us to do, is what those people [Wahamaji] are criticizing, and if we are the ones who [you]

turn against saying that we are the bad people, then we don't know how you perceive of these things.

74   Then Archbishop Beecher told me that he was not the type of a person that could be replied to like that. He [said he] could get hold of me by the neck, break me, and throw me through the window. [He said he could] throw me out. He was not to be replied to as I did. When he talked to me he was that angry. Then padre Owira (with whom we were as my vice) told him that, old man, I can answer you. I can't say anything, because [if] whatever little you have been told by Ajuoga has angered you, then I don't have anything to tell now. Then he told us that we must follow the revival for East Africa, because there was where Rural Dean Olang' was, where canon Oywaya? was, [and] where other important members of the church were.

75   But us, we told him that God is love. Those people [whom] you are telling us to follow their suit have left the church and they are criticizing the church activities. They are criticizing all other things which have been planned by the Anglican Church. How then can we follow them? Besides that those people have left the teachings of the Bible and are teaching without a base. [They are] teaching what they have dreamed. They are abusing people, they are dividing people, they are discriminating others, [and] we cannot follow them! The old man left when he was furious with us. The old man, Beecher, went back to Nairobi.

76   When it reached the year 1955 Doctor Cogan came (who was the Archbishop of York). When he came we were collected, [that is] all the padres of Maseno. When we were collected Dr. Cogan really taught us how the church doctrine was, how the gospel was, how keeping the church was, [and] what the Bible says. He really taught about the love of God, [and] he really taught us that which Jesus left [us]. We all agreed that Dr. Cogan was a real evangelist, and that he was a real Archbishop who defended the Bible. Us, we followed all that Dr. Cogan had taught; we stressed and accepted it. But after a long while we realized that it was us who the church leaders were accusing before the Archbishop. [They were saying] that we were bad people. Then we wondered how come we were bad, yet we were the ones following Dr. Cogan's teachings?

77   We were fellowshiping every month at Maseno in padre Silas' house (which was near Maseno, that was where we were fellowshiping during the night), and in the morning we were going to CMS church in Maseno. We fellowshiped and after fellowshiping we left. Then, the church under Rural Dean Festo Olang' got

annoyed with Nathan Silas Awuor, and he was stopped. And during that time padre Omulo was also stopped, and it was me who took that thing seriously. When I took that serious I assessed that matter and found out that when the pastors were assessed (the constant review of the church), Silas' name was not there and also the name of Rev. Omulo. So what we thought about that matter (not really thinking but we knew) [was] that Silas was being punished for the reason that he allowed the Johera to fellowship in his house. [He was disciplined] because he allowed the Johera to camp in his house everyday, and [it was believed that] the Johera had divided the revival!

78   A missionary of the Anglican Church by then was called Rev. Peaston, [and] this Peaston was the missionary advisor. But things became difficult when there was a wrangle in forming the Maseno convention. When those Wahamaji wanted to control those matters (when the padres were not aware), I was one of the few padres who strongly opposed that idea, and also some of the things which were going on in the church I strongly opposed. When the padres gathered at Maseno, they did not allow Wahamaji to be the organizers of things in the church. But because at that time Rural Dean Olang' had become Bishop [and] he seemed to side with them (Wahamaji), we could do nothing.

79   But I wrote a letter of protest on 15th November 1955. I again wrote the letter to show how I was complaining on many issues, and I was reminding the leaders of the church that I was copying it to many people (the people who were there, many padres, and I distributed many copies here and there). Then I brought up many stories to show how the church had gone astray, and [I said that] we should take people back to the church. The elders of the church (for example Assistant Bishop Festo Olang' and the Rural Dean Evans Agola and such others like Archbishop Owuor) were not pleased by the words I spoke, [because] those [people] promoted the split. We proceeded like that with many people (and the greater part of the church) giving us support.

80   And when Rev. Nathan Silas Awuor was suspended I took the matter very seriously. I again wrote the letter on 13th February 1956, (and I complained when I wrote this letter) to Archbishop Beecher. I distributed copies to many places. I gave a copy to Assistant Bishop Festo Olang', [and] a copy to the missionary advisor, Peaston. I gave a copy to Vicar General Bostock, Nairobi, I gave a copy to Peter Mwan'gombe, [and] I gave a copy to the registrar, Mr. Olton in Nairobi. I took a copy to Lester who was the

provost for the cathedral, and I also gave a copy to the CMS regional secretary who was called Grimshow. I also gave a copy to the principal advisor, [and] I gave [a copy to] Mr. W. H. Carey who also represented the CMS. I also gave a copy to the principal of United Theological College, Limuru. I gave many people copies. I gave a copy to Archdeacon Stovold who was then in England. I also gave a copy to a missionary lady called Collins, and many of our padres. What I was complaining about [was] how the Johera padres were being mishandled and punished.

81   When I did that, [and] when Archbishop Beecher and Bostock (who was the secretary of the diocese) came to Maseno, they summoned me there. Bostock and Beecher took that letter from me and tore it in front of me, and threw it at me, demanding why I was revealing their secret to the public? Why was I saying many things that were spoiling the name of the church? But if those were dirty things, then why can't they be washed clean? Why am I just revealing them to people here and there? [They said] that I was doing bad. But I realized through my conscience that the way Bishop Beecher had torn my letter and threw it at me, [in] he same way the Kingdom of his Lord was finished. And that was how I knew he had torn apart the church! For me, I was never annoyed, but when I went and told our people that Beecher took that letter and tore it and threw it at me, we realized that the old man had gone astray and divided the church.

82   Then we went ahead like that knowing that the Archbishop and his assistant did not want us (and [nor did] his general secretary, Bostock). Then we went ahead spreading the gospel. [We decided] that whatever the case we shall continue to preach the word of God, [and] that we shall not stop fellowshiping at padre Silas' home, and that we shall not stop loving, and that we shall not stop our revival fellowships that always take place at Maseno. We shall not stop all these.

83   When things became bad, when division continued to occur and the church leaders continued to trouble us, and [after they] became our enemies thinking that we were the ones spoiling the church, I wrote [down] the doctrinal errors which I could trace. I wrote to the missionary in charge, or the advisor, who was called Rev. Peaston. And all that I wrote to him I wrote on July 5th, 1956. The doctrinal errors which I noted were like the ones below; I wrote them in English.

[He then reads the text of the letter.]

84   You can see the division that was there. We did not accept that daily confession of sin could make us walk with God. That is what the Catholics also do, and this was why Martin Luther opposed the idea of John Tetzel, when he, John, was buying penance and also talking about the daily confession and forgiving of sins.

85   But I believe that Jesus Christ came to save people from their own sins. He, Jesus, said that whoever believes in him, he has escaped death, and he is in life. He called Paul by telling him, "I am sending you to go and curse the powers of the devil and take them to God; [to] remove people from darkness and take them to light." That is the reason why there is no hell for whoever believes in Jesus. [He] has immediately come out of death and entered life. He does not have any more sin. That is the reason why, when the revival people (who were Wahamaji and [had] left the church) were teaching that people should confess their sins everyday, that was wrong doctrine; it was not biblical. But when somebody has been saved, he is under the power of Jesus Christ. It's not that he has to sin again, but in case he sins, he is the child of God. When he sins, he confesses his sin, and he is forgiven by God.

86   Preaching that Jesus has got two feet, one the revival and the other the church, that is unscriptural, because Jesus is only one. His church is also one, [and] his people whom he has saved are the true church; those were his true church. But not [did He say] that with his one foot he was the revival and with the other he was the church. That has been so difficult for the Anglican leaders to understand. That's why the Bible says that we are walking in faith, but not in confession, and not even in revealing our sins everyday. That is the stand of the Bible and that of the Johera.

87   In the year 1956, June 1st, I wrote a document called "The Light." The reason why I used "the Light" [was that] during that time we used to emphasize that one should walk in light, [and that] one should do things in light. [We know] what's light because Jesus is light. John emphasized so much this idea of light, [and] that is why in that year I wrote to Vicar General who was the Archbishop Bostock, and I wrote to him like this (I will read in English):

[He then reads the introduction (page 1) of his treatise, "The Light."]

[He next comments on the first major section of the treatise entitled, "Recollecting the Passed (sic)". This commentary follows and continues through paragraph 151.]

88   In this paper I went ahead remembering the previous events that had taken place in the Anglican Church, which people had taken

for granted, and the church did not take any action against until the bad separation occurred.

89   In the year about 1934 the late Rev. Alfayo Odongo, who was the minister for the Anglican Church, received a unique [call from the] Holy Spirit and left his church ministry, and people were just praying in his house and in other places. People were not going to work, people were not going to care for their children, [nor for] their houses. Both men and women [were doing this, and] that was in Ugenya where it is called Musanda Anglican Church in Mudhiero pastorate. Now when people went ahead with fellowship, this old man said that he had been told by the Holy Spirit that the confirmation he had received from the Anglican Church and those bishops was not good, and [that it] was not enough because those people did not have the Holy Spirit.

90   Then another lay reader who was called Levi Obonyo (even he was not a lay reader, he was just a layman) said that he had been full of the Holy Spirit, and that he had been confirmed [by the Holy Spirit]. He (Rev. Odongo) knelt down before Levi Obonyo and was then confirmed. People went ahead praying until they became hungry [and] until some people left for their homes. The food that was brought got finished, and some people left to go and steal cattle. They went and stole the cattle of somebody called Abuodha, a man from Kawango. When these cattle were repossessed, the owner of the cattle got annoyed together with the people of that area. Those people collected spears and simis to go and attack the old Alfayo Mango and those [with whom] he was fellowshiping in his house. There was a serious incidence, [and] those who came from there were showing us the scars that they received from spears when they were running away from the incident, [and] some people were being clubbed as they were running away. Those who remained in that house were full of the Holy Spirit, [and] they were lighting fire and going around the house. People got burnt there, [and] the padre got burnt there. There was an accident there, [and] very serious things happened there.

91   And all these I mentioned in that my letter, that the Anglican has again left people to go and fellowship [thus] getting lost. That is including the padres and those who were not the padres, both women and men and young girls. The boys and the Anglicans [missionaries] were just silent. That was why I reminded them of what had happened to the old Alfayo Mango Odongo at the village of Musanda. I encouraged them not to keep silent because the church

had gone astray, [and] very false teachings had emerged in the church.

92   I again went ahead remembering about that old man, Ishmael [Noo], who was a famous preacher, and he was the leader of a group called "the evangelists." I was also under them as a child, but later those who were fellowshiping, who were "the evangelists," were teaching that their bodies had become so weak and dead that even if they sleep on the mat together that would not cause anything. Ishmael was a man from Sakwa. He was at Akoko pastorate, and he was at the church called Bembei in Sakwa. There it was headed by the late padre Shadrack Osere. Earlier there was a wrangle between that Ishmael and Osere for leadership of the church or [over who was to be the] layleader. When the revival came, he [Ishmael] led the revival, and people say that this was why he was very [much] against the church, and he could not listen to the church. They could only fellowship in houses, and many of them had very tattered clothes, and the first wives who were wedded were leaving their homes and their husbands, and they were going to spread the gospel outside. That brought about fighting between the husbands of those women. The children of those women and the men who went out to spread the gospel, their families and their houses had a serious fighting. But the most important of all was that they were not emphasizing the church doctrines even that of going to church every day. They were saying that Jesus did not have the church, [but] that all those were men's churches.

93   The most important thing that brought about the division and the fighting [was] that they were teaching that their bodies were dead and they were not able to sin any more. [They taught] that when people had listened to the word of God until late in the night, then people can just lay down the mat, and they [can] just sleep together, both men and women on the same mat [for] they can no longer sin. But later, when it was found that some pregnancy cases emerged among them, there was a serious fighting there. People were divided in the year 1948, and the Wahamaji accepted to go back to the church and avoid sleeping on the mat. And [they agreed to] giving their gifts in the church, and [to] following church doctrines. I reminded the Anglican Church that Ishmael was someone who knew very well the word of God, and that he was a very good old man. But these petty words there at home, and the church leaders ignoring words just like that, brought about the division. [It] also brought about trouble in the church until today, to the extent that many followed those false teachings [and] many of them got lost.

94   I also reminded the church about Bildad Kaggia, who was later arrested with Jomo Kenyatta, as the organizers of Mau Mau. He started with the words of the soul (that I think was in the years 1945-48). Bildad Kaggia brought the church called "Kaggia." In this church of Kaggia, when he had got saved, he said that there was no going to the hospital; you just pray when you are sick and the Lord helps you. There was no taking of drugs of any kind or there was no seeking for treatment. You just pray because sickness came from sin, [and] that is why the Kaggias also confused many people, and many left the [Anglican] church. People prayed and they were just dying until people returned to their churches. Yes, this Bildad Kaggia was being assisted by somebody called Stanley Kagika. These people took many strong people and taught them very funny things. But they later ended up almost being members of the Mau Mau movement getting involved in political affairs, and they ended up that way. This teaching went like that until the Kaggias are about to disappear; they remained very few.

95   The people who don't allow [or who teach] that people should not take tablets or go to the hospital when they become sick, these people were long separated; they also left the church. [Among them] the Holy Communion was made of flour mixed with porridge and orange juice or soda or others. All these the [Anglican] church was witnessing, but the [Anglican] church did not take any stern measures against these, and this resulted in many troubles and many good people got lost.

96   After this I also reminded the church that in the year 1948 somebody followed the church called "Christians", which was led by Reuben Kihito. This Reuben Kihito was also a Gikuyu, [and] he also had many teachings (he was teaching politics).

97   In that same year was when the church called Musambwa also became very powerful, which was led by Elijah Masinde. These people were full of prophesying events, these people were full of jealousy for the white colonialists, and with many other things. They were very harsh with other tribes. Things became tough [when] many became political and the government got involved and arrested people. People were arrested, people were caned, and they were bleeding. Sometimes they were fighting, sometimes they were burning people's houses, [and] things became very serious and so many people got lost.

98   So I brought these issues to the Anglican Church that they may know that things were not good, [and] that [these things

happened] when the Anglican church did not become careful and seriously teach to put people in the right direction.

99   Those who were led by Ishmael explained the reason why they separated from him. One of them was opposing the church, (opposing the church and its leaders) and many [were] leaving his house and just wasting time [saying] that he is preaching the gospel. [Then] somebody becomes careless and puts on tattered clothes and takes women from their houses.

100 In 1951 those people (Wahamaji) who ignored evangelism, who were led by that Ishmael, confessed to us and were confessing in the church that they had returned to the church. They [said they] had been taught to ignore the church. They were so careless about their lives. Women had left their houses and did not bother about their husbands, [and they] didn't bother about their children. They became enemies of the church leaders, [because] they didn't want to give the church gifts. They didn't want to pray in the church which was built, but they were praying in their houses, and they were spreading the gospel. These people confessed how they were not willing to sleep on the mat with other people's wives (who were not theirs), and that they did not want to sleep on the mat with other people's daughters who were not their wives. They were saying that they had run away and were back to the church, and were willing to follow the church because Jesus was the Head of the Church.

101 When it reached 1951, when we were at the convention (or the revival meeting) at Akoko pastorate at Maranda School, there were very many missionaries [there], there were the Anglican church leaders [there], ([like) the padres, rural deans, teachers, lay readers), [and] those who led Luos in the revival here (like the old man, Musa Amoke, and others) were there. Those who came from Western Kenya Province, the Luhyias, were there, [and] people from other parts of the country were there, some from Mombasa, some from Nairobi.

102 I have already told you earlier that preaching [there] came from Genesis 12, and from the sermon the revival people said that Abram left, that God told him to leave and go to a strange land which he would be directed to by God. That illustrated how Abram left the world, [and] that is [just like] leaving the church and going out with Jesus to a place of refuge. That was what the revival people ought to do [they said]. That is [why] someone who is truly saved must leave the church, forget about the church leaders, forget about the church doctrines, forget about the church events, [and they] should not follow the prayer book of the church. [They said] he

should now go out and forget about the "dead" people in the church, that he should go out with Jesus to the place of refuge. I have already told you much about this in my previous talk, how the separation started. People were saying, "I have left! I have left! I have left! I have left with Jesus! I have left the church!" That was where the separation emerged from.

103   But those people were [also] emphasizing the blood. [They would say,] "The blood of Jesus has cleansed me! I have left the church! The blood of Jesus has cleansed me! I have left the church, the dead church of the padres who have clung to sin, the church of the lay readers who have held their teeth tight on sin!" Those who were the lay readers left, [and] many preachers also left. The padres who were weak and were not performing the work of God with sincerity also left. Some revival people were going to the church, but many of them did not go to the church.

104   There [they] started representation, [whereby] those who were saved in the church were represented by somebody called "siro" (a pillar). In each group whoever represented that revival was call "siro" of that given group. Also in the pastorate [they would choose] a saved person (a revivalist) who was also called "siro". [He] could criticize what has been said by the padre in the pastorate, and [he] had powers in the pastorate. This hierarchy continued through [to] the rural council, [and] the diocese each had their leaders who guided them, whom they feared, and [whom] they could listen to.

105   The money was collected and was taken to the revival [leader] when there was a collection in the church. Some places a little money was left to the church, while in other places there was not even a little.

106   During those days people were praying in the morning [at the Anglican church], but many were attending afternoon (two o'clock) prayers [which were held outside the church, because they believed] the church was not as pure. People were putting on funny clothes, the prayer book was thrown away, [and] people ignored partaking of the Holy Communion. They did not want to go for baptism, saying that baptism was useless.

107   There were so many problems that the church was spoiled. Many people who were saved were Anglicans, [but] other churches were also influenced, while others had experienced problems such as Catholics, AIM, and more. So many churches did not experience revival. Most of the revival was in the Anglican church.

108   Most of the things that happened during those days I tried to write about and verbally made them known everywhere. I was

preaching, and everywhere we were gathering for church fellowship meetings. Seemingly, I was their leader. I could say that [this was] through the mercy of God, and [because of] the little education I had received (slightly above others; I could read the constitution, the Bible and other words). Therefore during those days they could take me as their leader, [the leader] of those who wanted to have the revival in the church.

109   When things had passed I reminded the Anglican Church that things were going to be exactly the same as those in the past, as those I have listed above, [but] I wanted the church to remain firm. Then when it reached the year 1953, we presented the matter before the meeting of the canon council, Maseno. Then during that time, when we had presented the matter, we said that we could not follow those people who had backslid. We wanted the Jesus of the Church, we wanted the Jesus who was in the Church, and that was why we gathered as the "Revival Movement in the Church (the Evangelical Revival Movement in the Church)". Then we requested the council to allow us to be meeting at Maseno everyday, every month, because it was there at Maseno where the gospel of God started.

110   The one [who] was feeling alright [with these requests] was Canon R. A. Pittway, since he was the only one assisting us, and he was the only one understanding the doctrines as they were. In the biblical doctrines and the Anglican doctrines, he was the only one understanding these, and he was encouraging us a lot. Then the church also realized that we had taken the right course, because we were emphasizing love. We were then allowed to go back to our original place, which was Maseno CMS. And that church, which was at Maseno CMS, was where we were opened a meeting by the leader of the church, who was also the Rural Dean, Stovold. And it was there where we were gathering every month.

111   Now I go further to explain these things, the bad ones that happened in our Anglican Church, which were increasing. Some people started saying that they were saved, [and] some of them [were] women. Some were laying their hands on some padres like Julius Adoyo. And we were wondering how come these people were laying hands on these padres? This almost resembled what had been done by Odongo Mango. We cautioned that such kind of events should be checked for they were not the right thing.

112   I also said that the church had become materialistic, because the padres [in administration and missionaries] were spoiling the church by giving them [the African padres] sugar, giving them money, [and by] buying them shirts, while others were being built

The Johera Narrative

houses. These people were being lured so that they could allow the revivalists who were criticizing the church to just go ahead. All these I was strongly opposing in the pulpit or in the church meetings. We were opposing these very strongly and asking why people had turned the church into a robbery place. Because the padres, whoever gave them something (even if they were then spoiling the work of the church), it was them who were being praised. But it was such kind of things that gave way for evils in the Anglican Church.

113   Our old people (such as the Rural Deans, our old people), for example [those] who later became bishops, were being given some material things down here in Luoland. And when they had been given things by these people, then these people now spoiled the church, and we people who were trying to correct them, [we] were being seen as bad people.

114   Many people did not agree with these Wahamaji, these people who claimed to be separatists. People did not side with them, and many padres did not [want to] side with them, but they could not do otherwise. Many people were perplexed, and the church leaders (such as the Rural Deans and other leaders in that order) started to transfer the padres who were preaching love. They were transferred here and there, here and there, and they were looked at as bad people.

115   When things became this much worse, the Anglican church came to an agreement with the revival people (that was in the year 1955). The people of the Ugandan church [came to speak to us] when we were at Maseno. [One] who [spoke] was the meeting leader, Rev. Bishop Langsford Smith, who was also the Bishop of Nairobi. When we were there at the meeting, they really spoke. They taught two things which I clearly mastered. They said that when someone loves Christ he must also love his church. That was why they were trying to teach good things, and they did not agree with those who opposed the church, and those who had backslid. But people did not take this serious word.

116   After that the church leaders, the rural deans, the assistant bishops and important and senior padres, these people were not able to follow these clear teachings, and were only able to fight us (we the Revival Movement people in the church). They started to fight us when they wanted the revival to be one. And I was wondering what type of people these people were, who even after the good teachings of the meeting leaders, they still continued to mislead others, and they were not blamed? We really wondered about this, but we thought that those people were like Esau, who sold his

birthright, [who sold] his birthright for a little food. I realized that these people [and] their work was being bought by a little food just the same way Esau did. I tried to emphasize the teachings I had received, for people to hear, but none understood.

117   Now, when you look at the minutes for Central Nyanza Deanery Council, the minutes number 71/53, 1953, you will find that we were given freedom to go back to Maseno. When we had been granted permission by the council, we started the work strongly in Luoland. We started serious preaching when we were campaigning against these people called "sirni" (pillars). The "sirni" were people who had just appointed themselves in their positions so as to fight with the church leaders whom the church had appointed. They were people who had appointed themselves to make money outside the church. They were the people who had appointed themselves to these positions, but [they did] not have love. They hated those who had not been saved, [and] they hated those who followed the church. [They said] that they [the church leaders] were not sincerely saved, [and] they hated the church leaders.

118   We started serious campaigns here and there, and people started to realize that truly there were some revival people who truly loved the church. I made the Anglican Church realize that the government seemed to be better than the Mau Mau, but the two assisted each other, because it was the Mau Mau who knew where the letters were being kept, how they were moving, how they were hiding themselves away from people, how they were beating people, and how they were getting food. Those who were the old Mau Mau people helped the government to find out how to fight the Mau Mau. I told them to work in liaison with us who got saved [just like] those people (Mau Mau) [did], who talked together with those people [the Mau Mau]. [I said that the Anglican Church should] work in liaison with those returnees from the Wahamaji, those who returned from among the users of mats, those who returned from the backsliders' group. We were the ones who knew about these people and what they were doing. We were the ones who could assist the Anglican Church, but the Anglican Church did not agree; they disagreed with us.

119   I was using what Jesus was teaching in Luke 16:8, that the sons of this world are more shrewd than the sons of light because they are seeing. They read the signs, they read the images of things, [and] they forecast what may come in the future. They read symptoms and then they tell what is happening. I gave an illustration of what my Lord Jesus taught in Matthew, chapter 18:15,

that if your brother sins against you, go and tell him his fault, and if he does not listen, then take two elders along with you. If he remains adamant then tell the church, and if he refuses to listen to the church, then the church should leave him. And that was why I said that these people should be watched. Those who were completely changed [but had] left the true faith in Christ, they should be brought before the church council, and if they refused, they should be left as [outsiders]. But the Anglicans did not take that advice.

120   I gave an illustration from the Book of Acts 15, where when St. Paul went to Antioch, he found that some people were teaching Christ and circumcision, others were teaching false doctrines, [and] others wanted to force people to follow the Jews. Paul left teaching and went to Jerusalem. When he arrived he was welcomed, the apostles welcomed him, [and] the church people welcomed him. They forgot the teachings and fightings which had been there, and the apostles passed the resolution that this is the doctrine that you should go and teach people, and the elders were sent to go. Why could not the Anglicans do such things?

121   I went ahead to give an illustration from the book of Galatians 2, where Paul challenged and cautioned Peter, that he was walking in a manner of betrayal, because when he finds where people are being fired, he joins the group of Jews, and when he finds where there are no Jews, he joins the people. But Paul fired him point blank when telling him that he was not walking with the gospel truth. [Paul said] he should be straightforward in the gospel of Christ, being in unity with others, because the gospel of Christ does not have two phases; it has only one phase.

122   Here I also told them in writing how Paul wrote to Titus and Timothy pastoral letters, where he taught them how to treat heresy, how they could treat the wrong doctrines, and how they could deal with those people who were teaching false doctrines; how they could help them, how they could take them to church, how they could teach them in the way (it is required by the gospel), and how they could stand firm.

123   Then I wrote to the Anglican Church to recall the fourth century and the fifth century. Then, there was a serious false teaching. Athanasius, a young man, was called in Latin "Athanasius Contramudum," meaning that when the church elders were not upright and going here and there with false teaching, Athanasius even though he was young, he remained firm in the divinity of Christ, and he truly remained firm.

The Johera Narrative

124   I reminded them about the reforms. I reminded them about Martin Luther, how he was a junior man, but the pope was misleading the church, bringing different teachings: confessing sins, penance and others, buying penance, and other false teachings, [for example] people like padres were not allowed to marry. I taught them that Luther was a young man but he remained firm against the whole system that was misleading the church, and he rescued the church until today.

125   I again wrote to the Anglican Church and told them about the English Reformers: Cranmer, Ridley, Latimer and other people like that who remained firm against Rome and its false teachings. Again, all these people were not featuring anywhere in the history of the Church of England, and they could not do anything about it. That is why, when I presented these issues there was nobody to take up any action, and it was forcing me to repeat this twice.

126   After this I finished by saying in English, "We must sometimes allow other differences of thoughts or opinions, but it would be quite unwise and misleading to disregard the fundamental truths of the gospel and the fundamental principles of our Anglican Church."

127   Later, I arranged the doctrinal errors as I have earlier said. I clearly arranged five doctrinal errors, and as you will see later, you will find the things that I made clear for the Anglican Church, that there are doctrinal errors that the church should carefully watch out [for] according to the biblical standard [of] faith. But [in spite of] all those there was nobody who took them seriously. Therefore, we people who wanted to follow Christ and His Bible, Christ and His Church, it forced us to think of what to do at that particular time.

128   In August 21, 1952 I reminded them--I reminded the Archbishop and the Bishop of Mombasa, who was Bishop Beecher (he came with Bishop W. Carey and we worshipped at Maseno sunrise from 18th August to 21st August)--[of these things and] we discussed all the issues that were troubling the church. They taught us so well about the gospel, and they told us how laymen and the clergy should work in harmony. And we discussed so many things, how the church should grow and how the gospel should be preached. We also discussed at length about the issues concerning revival: how the church required revival and traditions of the church and such things. I reminded them, that we were very happy, a few of us together with the people from the Evangelical Movement in the church which was called Johera. We were really happy with the words which were discussed there, and we left there with joy. But

that group, the group of Wahamaji and many padres who were acting as their pillars, ([but] more so those who were leading them), left the place but they did not care.

129   Then I wrote to the Anglicans when I was reminding them about that meeting and all that was deliberated at that meeting. And I finished [by] saying that we Christians, we are built on the faith of the Apostles, and the evangelists, and Jesus Christ himself acts as the Head of that building. As we read from the book of Ephesians 2:20, that we can't accept all teachings that have no base, any teachings that don't come from the Bible, any teachings that come from no where, any teachings that one has thought of himself. Those don't make us Christians. More so, we people who are saved, we should think of the words from the Bible, and the saved man should be a clean man, who can preach. He should be a saved man and one who is firm on the Bible, not a person who is tossed here and there, just the same say the wind does to the grass.

130   And I told them that the meeting that was at sunrise was led by the Holy Spirit, [and] that if the Nyanza people and the Anglican padres could follow what was said there, [then] there could have not been any more trouble. I quoted for them from the writing that, "the Archbishop of Canterbury once said that it is an unreasonable church which changes its laws [and] regulations every hour and then."

131   After that I made the heading appear "General Views." That means I had to point out some general issues in the church which were not real, which made the church become weak. I said that St. Paul's Theological College should be improved and equipped, and that it should be seen that those who go there are well-trained to meet the standard required, because in this country people are now well-educated, [and] that if the padres are not well-trained, they will not be able to serve them, approach them, and preach to people in this country. Therefore, I told the board of governors and the leaders of the church to consider that issue of the United Theological College. Earlier it was a college for the Anglican Church in Kisanni in Mombasa, but us, [we were] the first people who were trained there together with other church members (we added three other churches: the Presbyterian Church of East Africa, the Methodist Church of England which is now the Methodist Church of East Africa, and the Anglican Church). We were the first three churches to meet there, the churches from England, until that place became ecumenical.

132   But I realized that there were so many drawbacks for that college to train competent leaders. I went ahead saying that the staff

should not be transferred every time, [for] that would make the students to not be well-trained. And I went ahead to say that the African tutors should be found there, and they should be well-trained people, because it seemed to me that the sick people or those who are being taken care of or those who are suspended and such kind of people were the ones being brought there. But the people who were being taken care of, who have other problems, and the sick and the old, that place should not be turned into a resting place like that. [Rather it should be] a place where people are trained who will later train other people. I therefore cautioned the Anglicans to be careful about that, that those who go there to teach should be big-hearted people, that they be people who are intellectually prepared, people who are academically prepared, people who are spiritually prepared, and it is these people who should become teachers there in such a theological college.

133   I went ahead to say that students should not just be collected and be brought there to be trained to become padres or other church leaders. They must look into their spiritual competence, they must look into their academic qualifications, and they must be the right people. It's these people who could be trained, and it is these people who could come back to correct the church as required. But [they should] not just bring people there because there is much work outside in the church. I saw that the church was just full of people like that, people who were half-baked, and the church was not going to be any better. The leadership should be carefully watched and qualified people [should] be appointed.

134   I went ahead saying that the syllabus and the doctrines were to be carefully prepared, [so] that which was in the right standard and that which would cover the areas that our padres would meet, [should be taught]. When the syllabus was just brought there and there was nobody to see that they are taught, [and] nobody to see that the syllabus was fully covered, that would bring a serious weakness in the church. I said that school inspectors should regularly inspect the schools, and the schools should be inspected by bishops, archdeacons, and other such kind of people in the church. They should also discuss other such issues with students there, and have prayers and fellowships with those who are learning there. And when they do that, they should also discuss issues with the teachers and the students. Then they will know and strengthen the school and bring it to the required standard.

135   I further said that the life of the students in the college was very poor. Something should be done to take care of the students'

lives, [and] that of their wives and their children, because during that period we were learning together with our wives and children, but we were facing difficulties since we were not taken good care of. Many people ran away because they could no longer bear that difficult situation, where sometimes there was no food, [and] they left the course. Therefore, I felt that the students who went there should have [been] taken good care of, and that their lives should not be subjected to sufferings (and yet they were people with their families there).

136 I also emphasized that the Bible colleges (such as St. Philip's Bible School and others which were elsewhere in the diocese), don't train padres well. But it is required that these small colleges (these small Bible schools in the villages) must see that the evangelists and the lay readers are well-trained in the villages so that they may know roughly what the church is and what the word of God is all about.

137 I went on to say that the word of God was being preached in the cities and in the surrounding districts, [and] I thanked the missionaries who had worked hard to teach the people and spread the gospel. They had done this when they were teaching people different things in places like Nairobi Detention Camp in Central Province, and in other places and now people have been preaching in prisons. We should work very hard to bring the true gospel [when] we see people in towns [and] people outside. The work of spreading the gospel should be thoroughly done, and that is when we can save the church.

138 I went on to suggest some items like how the church should be strong. [For example,] there should be refresher courses where the padres and the archdeacons in their deanery should regularly [be] held. I also went on to say that the contact between the archdeacons and rural deans and their padres in learning the administration work and the discussion in other available issues and prayer was seriously required. I again said that, [concerning] the mission and convention meetings, there should be convention meetings where people could come together from different parts, [from] the pastorates and the deaneries, where people could get renewed and become united and closer and should show people the route to follow.

139 I went on to say that we should know that the bishop of Maseno is [also] the bishop of Mombasa. We should know that he was a very busy man, but he should have regular visits with his padres and should also visit his churches, and should sometimes preach and teach and advise his people. [He] should not just

disappear, but should just be heard if the church has to grow stronger.

140   I went on to say that the clergymen should resemble a football team; the work of God should resemble a football team. In a football team there are eleven players. Everyone has his own position, but when one gets the ball, he passes it to his teammates. There is also the captain, there is a goalkeeper, [and] defenders are there, but all these people work as a team, where the work is not left to one player. That is why the padres, women, the layreaders, laymen, [and] all these people should be like a football team, where people understand one another, and that is when they can win the match.

141   I went on to speak [concerning] the training of the padres. We were seeing that the white padres were highly learned. They were coming [to Kenya] when one had come from college, [and] some had gone to the university. Then I said that even our padres at this time [should be trained at that level], because of the awareness that the people had acquired. [I also said that] competent people should be appointed to train them [(African padres)] well, because they may [even] go to teach how to preach the gospel in those colleges and universities. They should not be given only local practice [and] just local teaching. Then [when] they [(African padres)] are left, [they] may not be able [to] go in the pace of development of the world. I again said that there [were] recognized African chaplains who could teach in the intermediate schools and secondary schools, [and] who [could] teach at other centres where chaplains are required. There should be enough Africans, especially those who are fully trained, to join such places.

142   I went on to say that Sunday School was a very important thing in the work of the Lord, [and that] the church should stress the need for Sunday School. I again said that prayer group meetings or the women's meetings should [be] seriously stressed so that the women should pray in a group and they pray for their houses, and they pray for the church, and pray for their children. I said this because the Wahamaji had fully stopped the women's meetings; they did not want women's meetings. But this was the reason why the church had become weak, because the church just accepted that. That was the reason why I suggested that the women's meeting should be encouraged, because wherever I had been working, I did not allow that the women's meetings should die away, but I was really encouraging women's meetings.

143   Lastly, I suggested that there should be a commission of inquiry which had to arrange for a commission to investigate all

matters pertaining to the church: to investigate faith, [to] investigate the work, [to] investigate development, [to] investigate the missionaries, [to] investigate the padres, to investigate all matters pertaining to the church, because the church was facing a dangerous situation, and the church had become very hopeless. [I proposed] that the commission should appoint faithful people to investigate the things that were happening in the church, [for] this could save the situation.

144 I finished my twelfth point by saying this [about] racial relationships in the church. I finished by saying that the church is in the world, but it's always strange and hindering to see the world in the church. Outside the church people speak of racial discriminations and prejudices and other barriers between the races, [but] I think the Church of Christ is the only place where true human brotherhood could be practiced and encouraged. Let us do all we can to improve the situation, because the world is not only looking closely at us, but [it is] also waiting for us to give the lead in every way possible.

145 The reason why I touched the issue of racial relationships between the missionaries (who are Christians with their wives and their children) [and Africans], [is because] in many places (I can see even now) I saw that they [(the missionaries)] were not free with their fellow black brothers. The white padre and the black padre, it was being realized that there was differences between them. That was why I realized that if all these people were Christians and yet there was division, such that even if the non-Christian whitemen were discriminating us, the missionaries were then siding with them. [This happened] even when they [(the non- Christian whitemen)] were doing us wrong. They [(non- Christian whitemen)] were just being supported by these white missionaries. Even if we were struggling with other issues here and there in the colonial government, they [(non- Christian whitemen)] were just being supported by these missionaries.

146 But even in the church the white missionaries were not showing appealing faces to their black brothers. That was the reason why I touched the fact that it was [in] the church where unity should be found, the true unity among the races. But [if] it was again in the church where people were showing unappealing faces, then the world had failed. These people here just accepted the apartheid in South Africa. The farmers there in South Africa, who were also called the Boers, took the advantage of apartheid or discrimination to harass people. I could not hear any missionary who was against that.

147   There was also the Beecher report which turned out to [be] for the wish of the government. The government was thinking that since Beecher was a missionary, when he became the chairman then [the report] would be in its [the government] favour. But instead it was very much against the government's expectations. That was also the reason why, when this our church was to be started and the people heard that it was Beecher to lead the Anglican Church, then they were not so happy. They did not give us [Anglicans] support, because it was the Beecher report that messed up education here.

148   We really thank the Archdeacon Owen. Archdeacon Owen really made a lot of noises about the things that the people, the Boers or the colonial government, used to harass the people here. He really battled against [that] to the extent that he even started some parties here in Nyanza. Others he was going to appeal against when he went to England and that was so good.

149   There were a few missionaries who really penetrated into the black territories when they were spreading the gospel. They were eating with them [the rural Africans], sometimes they were drinking with them, [and] they were mixing up together with them. They did not fear the untidiness of the blackman, and they were taking good gospel here and there, here and there. That was the reason why the black Luo were saying that a whiteman is holding the Bible on the right hand and on the left he was holding his own Bible, because a few of them were good but many of them were against the blacks. Despite this they were saying that they were Christians, [and] these things were troubling one's mind.

150   That was in general, [nevertheless] I thanked the missionaries who gave themselves to preach to us the gospel. It was also required that these other missionaries who were following different paths should have also uplifted that standard of Christian love among all Christians.

151   I wrote "The Light" and I gave a copy to the Bishop of Mombasa, the Right Rev. Bishop Beecher. He was the one I wrote that letter to, [and I hoped he would] listen.

152   When it reached June 1957 at our usual meeting in the middle of that week, we had a refresher course [for] all padres of Maseno sunrise, [and] the meeting ended on a Friday. We went to where we were sleeping at Maseno, next to Maseno at Rev. Nathan Silas Awuor's, whom I had once fought for when he was excommunicated under Assistant Archbishop Festo Olang' (who was our Rural Dean during the inception of things, but became Assistant Bishop in 1955).

153   Now when it reached 1957 in the month of June, when we were assembling at Maseno church--listen very carefully to this word--we abruptly found (the [now] retired Archbishop) Olang' [there]. [He] came when he was still an Assistant Bishop. He came with his rural deans [and] with some of his padres to remove us from the church of God at Maseno-Kogore where the spread of the gospel originated. When he arrived he found when we were in the middle of our prayers, and he stopped us [by saying], "You Stop! Stop praying!" Some of our people wanted to refuse his order, but I told them that Olang' was our bishop. When he comes and orders us to stop praying, [it may be because] he may be having a word to pass to us. We should stop praying. When we stopped he stood and said that right from that moment (the time he was talking to us) the Evangelical Revival Movement in the church called "Johera" was finished. They must leave and go to Ramba, [for] it was there at Ramba where those Wahamaji were worshiping every month. [He said] that Johera must merge with the East African Revival. If not so, if they can't merge, then that marks the end of [our] worshiping and the end of our worship in that diocese in the Anglican Church!

154   Then some people among them wanted to start praying again but I told them to stop. And he [(Olang')] went on to preach those words which he was using to denounce us, which he had gotten from the Bible. He then made that announcement and later closed the prayer. We did not also refuse to leave the church; we left the church, but we again gathered behind the church. I am telling you what the people resolved to do: we started singing our song (it was number four in our hymnbook) which says "the prayer of Moses." We sang that song in a very loud voice [which says that] the prayer of Moses was heard by God, the prayer of Moses was heard by God.

155   In the year of 1957 when we were at our monthly meeting at CMS Maseno church, that found [us] when we had a seminar or refresher course for all the padres in Nyanza. We were at Maseno-Sunrise. When we had started prayer and we were in the middle, we suddenly found that Assistant Bishop Olang' [who] was being accompanied by some of his padres [was there]. They came when we were in the middle of our prayers. They came when they were already annoyed, and ordered us not to continue with our prayers. But they [(the group gathered there)] were trying to disregard their [(Olang' and the group with him)] order, [saying] that we should just go ahead with our prayers until the end of it, when they could tell us what they had to tell us. But when they [(Olang' and his group)] insisted that we had to stop so that they say their

word, I told them (my colleagues) to stop and listen to him because he was our elder. He was our bishop, [and] we should give him time to tell us the word he had. Then he told us that from that day onwards the meeting of Johera under the banner of the Evangelical Revival Movement in the church was finished there at Maseno. And [he also said] that we should go and meet ([if] we were the true revival people) with the revival of East Africa who were meeting at Ramba. [He said that] nobody should go back there [(Maseno)] next month, and that any other place there were Johera meeting in the church, [it now] was abolished. There was [to be] no more meeting there [(Maseno)]!

156   When the meeting was over we left and stood behind the church. We started to sing our song (in the CCA hymnbook, song number four), which says that the prayer of Moses was heard by God, [and that] the Lord heard the prayer of Moses which released the Israelites from the bondage they had in Egypt. We really sang very loudly there behind the church, so much that the people around and within Maseno said that it was a nice song, and that [it was that song] which was shaking people and the world, [and] that [song] which was shaking homes and the people's mind. They were thinking that something had happened in that song. And when we had sung that hymn to the end, I told the people three things:

157   First, I told them that God is love. Where do we go to leave love? John says it clearly in his letter, John 4:16, that God is love and he who abides in love abides in God. Us, we accept that we abide in God. How [then] can we go to those who criticize about the Church of God, those who criticize the Bible of God, and His word? St. Paul tells us very clearly in the book of I Corinthians chapter 13, that we have faith and hope and love, but the most important is love.

158   How can we leave love to go and roam about in the grassland? It was here at Maseno where the gospel originated [in Luoland]. This is Kogore, and it is where we have to return to. We came back to God, back to the place where the gospel started [in Luoland], where the gospel was first preached. Here in our village [is] where we want to come back to, but someone is telling us to leave. Where does he want to take us?

159   Jesus Christ is telling us in John chapter 13 that we have love amongst us so that people may realize that we are his disciples. But why [then] all these quarrels? How come the saved people became the enemies of the unsaved, and yet they were also preaching the gospel while they were still unsaved people? Us, we can't avoid love. When Paul was counting the fruits of love in Galatians 5 he

just began by [mentioning] love, and that is why we can't avoid love and follow those who have lost the direction, who are not in the church. That was why all Johera left that place confessing to continue with love. [They believed that] here in Maseno, as we have been sent away, we shall not come back!

160   Secondly, I told them that all the meetings that had been programmed for Johera here in Nyanza, we had to attend them all. And [I] warned them to come in large numbers, [and said that] nobody should miss them.

161   Thirdly, I told them that we were going to see Bishop Beecher in Nairobi, I together with our secretary, Benson Otieno, who was then the secretary for the CMS Maseno hospital.

162   And we left there and we went ahead with all our meetings as we had earlier programmed. But us, we went to see Bishop Beecher in Nairobi. When we told him that Olang' had fired us and [had said that] we could [not] go back to Maseno, [and] that he had banned all our revival meetings everywhere under him, [then] Beecher really quarrelled me and said that we [were] tough headed people. He heard what Olang' had said, [and] he said that he was hearing that we were the people who [were] causing trouble there in Nyanza. [He had heard] that other people were okay, but we were the bad people. But I told him that was wrong, that we were the ones following his rules. We were the ones who follow the Anglican rules, we were the ones supporting the church, we were the ones giving gifts in the church, and we were teaching our people to do so, but he registered the dispute with us.

163   Food was brought at about 12:30 noon, but that food stayed there on the table until around 3:00 PM. We later found the food already cold, and only tasted a little of it, and then we left the place. He chased us away. I clearly told him that we could not go to Ramba, [and that] we could not as well go to the revival because it was not the right one. Then we returned [home].

164   When we came back we went ahead with our meetings. Bishop Beecher left Nairobi, and was willing to go to the churches everywhere because people suddenly started to follow us. Very many churches, very many churches followed us. He then learned that there was a major division (we had almost twenty thousand at the start), and that [at] our meetings we had everywhere (we had the convention) people were turning up in large numbers.

165   This scared Bishop Beecher where he was in Nairobi, when he had [heard] the rumour. Then he came himself and went round visiting these churches to hear what these churches were saying.

Other churches chased him away, [because] the Anglican Church members did not want him where we were needed. Other places where the Anglican Church was not accepted, we were being invited to those places.

166 I can remember one day when we were at Kisumu location there was Peter Hawes, who was also an Archdeacon of the Church of England (he had not stayed here for a long time). He gathered people and told them that Ajuoga is just like a small rat, [and] he cannot play with whitemen! [Hawes said] Owira is also a small rat, but a whiteman is like a lion. He [(the whiteman)] will walk on people like Ajuoga and Owira, and then take them to detention where people like Kenyatta were taken. Those whom he had gathered, he was thinking that he had called them for the Anglican Church, but instead he annoyed them. People left there saying that if Ajuoga, who is our son and a brother, a blackman like ourselves, is the one being call a rat and the whiteman is the lion that will walk upon him, then we the rats are leaving. We have to follow our fellow rat. On that day the Archdeacon Peter Hawes really brought us many followers. All who attended that meeting, almost every one of them turned to join us!

167 Then later Archbishop Beecher came to witness the event. He started from the churches in Nyakach, [then he went to] the churches in Kano, the churches in Kisumu, the churches in Maseno, the churches in Seme, [and] he went to the churches Gem, and people were coming in large numbers to meet him. He was telling people that Ajuoga and Owira have left the church. [He said that] they have ran away from the church, [that] they are bad children, [and that] you should not follow them. But these people told him that these are the right people, [that] they are the ones taking people back to the church, and [that] those whom they [(Beecher and Olang')] think are good are the bad ones who take people away from the church. [The people told him that] they [(Wahamaji)] denounce the church, [and] they don't show love [for] they only meet among themselves and don't want the sinners. But it is people like Ajuoga who want the sinners and that is why people like them.

168 Then Beecher went ahead visiting places, but wherever he went he was being rejected. He even went to our homes, to our home churches, but he was really rejected. Others were asking him, "Are you the Beecher [that made the] report?" "Are you the Beecher who spoiled the education for our children?" "Are you the one?" "If so, then we don't want you!" Then that old man was faced with a lot of problems here in Luoland. He then went back to Nairobi, and

[he] later started to conspire with the policemen, the administration, the district commissioner, and the provincial commissioner so as to prevent us from holding meetings.

169   Then the police started chasing us with full force, and wherever we could go the police were there with us. Sometimes they were ordering people to disperse, and sometimes they were listening to what we were preaching. Most of their reports were good [for] they were saying that we were just preaching love. [They said] we were only preaching unity, we were only preaching goodness, [and] we were only preaching that the sinners should not sin any more, [and] that they (sinners) should come to God. Our report [was] good, and then instead of arresting us we were left to preach.

170   One day I can remember when the PC was still a whiteman, when the time for independence was not yet ready, (the PC was called Swann) [and] he called me and told me that he had heard that we were fighting here and there, and that we were demolishing Anglican churches. He said that he could arrest both Olang' and I, and warned me not to have any more problems there in the province. Then I told him, "Bwana PC, please listen to my plea. We are preaching love, that people should love God and they should love themselves, and that they should be saved from sin, theft, insults, drinking, adultery, [and] other forms of sin. [We encourage] people to work using their hands so that they may get something to feed on". [I continued to say] that [it is] some of the Anglican Church people who are saying we are the ones who have joined the group that has refused to join the right people. We don't want to join the Anglican Church people who don't want to support the church, [because] they teach people false doctrines that are [not] out of the Scriptures. I then told him some of the different things the Bible requires and those that are required by the Anglican Church. He then told me to go (leave his office), but [that I] should maintain peace. Then I left.

171   During those days the Anglican people were taking reports that we were fighting and demolishing churches everywhere. But when the government came out to investigate, they found that those were all lies. Later, when these police were here, the administration police realized that it was us who were saying the truth, that we were the true Christians, [and] that those other people were lying and even the Anglican Church was lying. Then we did not experience any more troubles in our meetings, because we were only preaching the gospel truth.

172 Then later the DC and PC sent so many district officers who were all whitemen [to investigate us]. But in other places the DC could go himself, when there was a meeting in a given church. Some people wanted the Anglican Church while others wanted Johera. This one forced the DC to physically go there, and call for a meeting where he could ask, "Whose church is this?" Most of the churches were saying that this church used to be the Anglican Church, [and] we used to be the Anglicans, but we now reject the Anglican Church because it has wrong dealings. We now support Johera, [and] therefore we the Christians who are here, we have returned to love. Sometimes the DC could ask people to raise their hand, and he could find that Johera were so many, and then [he] said that church belongs to Johera. And when he went to a place and found the Anglicans were more (the thing which was not so common), he could leave that church to the Anglicans, [and the] others [Johera] went to pray under a tree. When he found a place where there were many Johera he gave us that church, and the Anglicans [would] go and pray under a tree or in the school. He did this at so many places until very many people were now coming to join us.

173 There emerged a new story because it was the Anglicans who sponsored most of the schools. Many teachers who sympathized with "hera," some of them were fired from teaching while others were transferred. Some children, I can remember, were expelled from school because they had joined "hera." So many things happened at different places. Those who were members of the [school] committee and were members of Johera were removed from the school committees.

174 The Anglican Church tried all sorts of means, [and] they were being supported by the Catholics who were also the sponsors of some of these schools. Whoever was found to be a member of "hera" was to be excommunicated from the church or other church functions.

175 Things became difficult because every time we were reporting to the police, and many times the police were coming to us, at our homes, [and] where we were meeting, and in our churches. After discussing [about] us with the police, the government advised us that if we had refused to go back to the Anglican Church, [if] we continue[d] to hold meetings without license, and [if] we were not under the Anglican Church, then we would be arrested (because those were the days of Mau Mau movement). Some people were calling us "the passive Mau Mau," while others were calling us

"Wahamaji" and were misleading the people. Therefore, the government advised us to look for our registration, because they could not see anything wrong with us.

176 We then called our committee of four people. Earlier, before this committee was appointed, we had our meeting at Nyamninia in the Anglican church at Gem. The meeting deliberated upon many issues, and at that meeting people came from all corners of Luoland. That meeting was called to see that, if the Anglicans could not stop from all the bad things that had transpired, then we were to remain as a church. And these people [also] discussed [who] the leaders [should be].

177 The second meeting was held at Rabuor. This Rabnor was the Anglican church at the home of padre Mathayo Owino [and] it was in Kisumu location. There we also discussed about all that had happened, all that was happening, and about the current movement. We again agreed to stand on our own.

178 The third meeting was held at Masogo, which was in Kano Kobura. Masogo was also [where] the Anglican church [was located]. We met in the house of the late padre Eliakim Apunda. We met there because the people of both Masogo and Kano were the first to leave in greater numbers than the other locations, and therefore it became our very stronghold. And that is the reason why our diocese [today] is being called the Diocese of Masogo (Masogo is in Kabura location of Kano). Then, when we met there we confirmed to stand on our own. We [decided that we] were no longer fit to join other churches, and that our teachings were beyond those of other churches.

179 First, we elected the leaders, [and] there Johera who had gathered unanimously elected me to be the leader. They elected the secretary general, who was Benson Otieno, whom we had not yet confirmed, but later we confirmed him to be a padre. The treasurer was also appointed that day, who was Aguko, the son of Ag'ong'a. This Aguko was a man from Kano, Otieno was a man from Nyakach, and myself, I was born in Gem. When we had been elected that way, we again elected a committee of about five people who were going to construct the constitution. But since I had read the constitution while I was a padre of the Anglican Church, it did not pose any threat to me. I was on that committee, [as was] padre Owira, and padre Isaiah Ndisi, together with Mr. Phanuel Aguko, the treasurer. The layreader David Ochuodho also requested to join us in that committee, and we teamed up with him in that committee.

180   We met at Winam Hotel in Kisumu. We met on the upstairs where we had booked a room, and it was there where we were always meeting when we were constructing the constitution (that was north Kisumu). We clearly printed that constitution. And then our people agreed that we should be having collars, [that] we should be having the church robes (the minister's robes), [that] we should be strict on prayers (liturgical), and that our church will be resembling the Anglican Church in so many ways. We did not like the padres to walk without collars like those of the AIM and those other people. We wanted the padre to be well distinguished with his work as a padre. I then took responsibility of designing our robes and our style of dressing. I did this with a lot of ease, because I realized that the Lord was directing me and all that I was designing people were accepting without any quarrel.

181   Then we stopped after writing all those things, [and] we took them to Nairobi, and later on, we followed up the matter to meet the Registrar. During that period the Registrar General was called John Coward. When we met him, he was an old man whose health was declining. He asked if we people, who were fewer, could be right, and yet the Anglicans, who were nearly two million, could be wrong? But I, as a trained Anglican minister, I quoted for him some words. I told him some of the Anglican rules. I talked to him from the Bible [and] I talked to him about the 39 Articles. I talked to him about the Prayer Book, and I talked to him about what these people were doing. I told him that Anglicans in themselves, it is good, but the people who are working here (the missionaries who are now working here and some padres who are there, and other "saved people" who are here) were bad. They ignored the Bible, they ignored the word of God, and they have left the Anglican Church. And again I told him the difference between us and these people that fight with each other. And then he nodded his head but warned us not to fight each other, [and] not to bring troubles. He said that he had received our report, and we should then have peace and the government would assess and register our church. But truly speaking, there is no church whose registration has been so easy as that of the Church of Christ in Africa (CCA).

182   I was not happy with some of these churches although God had created me a happy man. I was not happy with churches like Church of England, Church of Scotland, [and] the Roman Catholic Church, [for it] was [from] Rome, a town and city of Italy. Now [I was not happy with] such [churches] as the Roman Catholic Church, Pentecostal Assembly of Canada, [and] Pentecostal [Church of]

Norway. I was not happy to see the Churches of Christ to be divided into such smaller groups according to how the countries were. Therefore, the thing that made me happy, that I had the feeling about, was that the Church must be the Church of Christ, just the same way we are reading in the Bible about the Church of Christ in Asia, the Church of Christ in Rome, the Church of Christ in Galatia. That was why when we met we wanted this name, but in this process there came two names. Somebody came up with the name of "National Church of Kenya," but I suggested the name "Church of Christ in Africa." Then the church unanimously voted [for] the name "Church of Christ in Africa (Johera)," and that is what we are today. And that was the name we used for registration which was done to us that much easier in the year 1958, January 6th.

183 There has not been any other registration that has been done to us in a cheaper and faster way like that. First, the recommendation that we got from the administration and the police was very clear. Secondly, our separation was also clear. Thirdly, our constitution was very clear. Fourthly, we remain firm that our sole pillar (which we were preaching) was love, and love is God. That is why our registration request was understood very fast by the government, and [they] immediately registered us, because during this same period the Mau Mau was fighting, and there was a lot of enmity and hatred amongst people. And since we were emphasizing love, then I think whoever had the right sense could see that we had taken the right course.

184 It was [in] this period when there was serious politics for the blacks were fighting for their independence, and that is why there was need for love amongst people. For instance amongst the blacks, amongst the whites, and even between the two themselves or the two and the government.

185 The Lord really helped us in getting our registration in a much faster way: The Church of Christ in Africa, registration number 886 dated January 6th, 1958.

186 Someone may ask me the reason why the Church of Christ started that much stronger. There are three main factors that show why the Church of Christ started stronger, and [why] many people were supporting its registration. First, the leadership of the Anglican Church had lost direction. A thing that made people feel disgusted [was] because many people were not properly buried when someone was dead. People were not properly attending his/her funeral. The Anglican Church also refused the use of a cross at the meeting where Christians would preach the gospel. People were disgusted with the

Anglican Church because the people could not tell its origin, and its end.

187 Secondly, it was the period of a serious political struggle. The Kenyans were seriously fighting the colonial government to leave, so that the whitemen should go back home and hand over rule. That is why people really gave us support, because we also broke from the Church of England. That made us receive a very strong support from our people, the young, the old, the learned, [and the] politicians, and that made our work easier.

188 Thirdly, the leader of the Anglican Church was Bishop Beecher. But this Beecher, as I have earlier said, [it was] his commission [which] spoiled African education. When they (Africans) heard that these people [Johera] had just come from Beecher, [and that] these people have rejected Beecher [and] the church that is led by Beecher, that also gave us a massive support. These three things made the Church of Christ (Johera) to receive support from many places.

189 After this the Church of England, Roman Catholic Church, AIM, Seventh Day Adventists, and those other denominations, when somebody had married more than one wife, then the second wife prevented him from partaking the Holy Communion. And, his children were not baptized, [and] he could not then be able to participate in other church activities. That is what all these churches that originated from abroad were doing. But us, when we read the Bible, we were finding that Jesus said to men, "Come ye all to me that are burdened so that I may relieve you from this." Therefore, we set out to look for all those who were burdened so that we could take them to Christ.

190 Jesus gave us an illustration from that old man who had organized the wedding, but those who were invited had [a] low opinion of him, and [they] were not willing to attend. He then told his servants to go out to the road junctions and bring all the blind, the crippled, the deaf, the wanderers, the poor, and bring them to his house so that his house could be full. That is why we (the followers of CCA) had heard that voice of the Lord Jesus Christ. We went out to bring all people: those who are burdened, those who have lost the way (all sorts of people), and take them to the Lord Jesus. Because during that wedding those who were sent out did not choose who to bring, even the bridegroom did not choose, but, it was the head of the wedding himself who came to select the people. Therefore, we take all those who are polygamists to Jesus, and when he gets saved, it is Jesus to tell him to divorce this wife and leave the others. [It is

for Jesus to say] do this and that, but us, we can't leave him. We call the drunkards to come with their drinks. When he receives Jesus, and Jesus tells him to go ahead drinking, then he may continue drinking. But when Jesus tells him to leave drinking, he should do just that. [Even] the wanderers, those who do wrong things, all [these] we were inviting.

191   Jesus compared this to a net which is out in water. [He said] that the Kingdom of God is like the net that is put in water. [He said] that the net is thrown into the water and it catches good fish [and] dead fish. It catches scorpions, it catches wood, [and] it catches snakes, but the owner does not select the good fish from the lake. He just has to first pull them all to the dry land offshore where he then selects them. We also leave and go out as the Church of Christ in Africa in the voice of Jesus. We go into the world to collect all that we come across, and we bring them to Jesus. Now, it is Jesus who will talk to them, and select them, and will know how to handle them.

192   When we turned to the doctrine of baptism as we read it from the book of Matthew chapter 28, in some verses [Jesus says to his disciples] that you go into all the world and preach the gospel, and whoever receives the word you baptize him in the name of the Father, and of the Son, and of the Holy Spirit with water. Therefore, whoever accepts baptism we do not ask him what he is [or] how he lives. If he accepts that Jesus Christ is the Son of God who died for all, then we baptize him. And that is why we had baptized polygamous families.

193   But when [it] comes to the work of St. Paul, he says that whoever accepts to take up the responsibility of the church or become a deacon, he should be a husband to one wife, or the vice versa as the Bible directs. Therefore, when we assign these people any church responsibilities, then we required only one wife and one man. And they wed as very healthy people and it's these people whom we assign any church responsibility. And all these other men we don't bother them, but instead leave them in the hands of Jesus.

194   Jesus Christ taught us that God is good, [and] when we greet or shake hands only with those who do the same to us, then where is the difference between us and the Pharisees? God is good and the Lord provides the rain to both the righteous people and the sinful man. If God can give rain to these sinners (he gives them the sun, he enables them to procreate, gives them food), then can I as a man denounce [these] fellowmen? That is why God is the God of love,

[and] we must also love the same way he does. We should leave the rest between God and the man.

195 [When] I was an Anglican and we were in the town of Eldoret where I was working, as it could be expected at any other Anglican churches elsewhere, we had some prostitutes. Their reports were coming to the church, but we were giving them the Holy Communion, [and] we were baptizing their children. These prostitutes were very free in the church, but as we know these prostitutes were people who were just roaming about and were selling their bodies. That woman who is bound in the Luo traditions or that of the world, and she is married to someone as the second or third wife, how then can I place this prostitute wife in the right place and leave the other one? That is why we were baptizing their children here in the Church of Christ in Africa (Johera). When people heard that we were baptizing those who had been rejected by those famous churches they were perplexed.

196 Starting from the year 1957 until 1958 we had very big baptisms where people could come up to more than five hundred. But one day when we had a big baptism at Ramula in Gem (the Anglicans called it the Ramula Pastorate, and that was where we again took people learning, only about two or three people), when we planned for a big baptism there (that was in 1957), people came in [such] a large number that the church was full and other people were forced to sit outside. This forced us to hold meetings outside under the tree because there were no sheds. Then the Anglicans got annoyed and reported us to the police [in] Maseno. [They said] that the Church of Christ in Africa are killing and beating people, and are forcing people to be baptized at Ramula. And [they said] that we were a very large group.

197 When the police heard that, they called for reinforcements from Kisumu. The GSU police from Kisumu came in a full lorry, the police from Maseno also came in one full lorry, and they had guns. When the two lorries arrived at Ramula they found where I was baptizing, [and] they met a very large group, more than they had expected. And in the middle of prayer I was sent a message that I was needed by the policemen who were waiting there. Even though I had seen them I was not scared, [so] I just went ahead with my work as usual without any fear.

198 When they realized that I was just going ahead baptizing people (because there were hundreds of people), [and] that I was taking long because there were many people (the children and the adults; [it took me] until around 3:00 PM) there, they again sent me a

message. And I just refused, [believing] that I could not stop the work of God to go and talk to the police. I said that there was nothing wrong I had done; I was not a criminal. They could talk to me when I would have finished the work, whether I [would] finish at 7 pm or at 6 pm or at whatever time. I just went ahead with the work.

199 When they had waited and waited and heard all the words I was speaking, and [when they saw] how the people were calm and peaceful [and] how the people were praising the Lord, then the lorry that came from Kisumu with guns just went back, and there remained the lorry that came from Maseno. Then we just went ahead until we finished our prayer (after 4 PM), and then they talked with me. I told them how I was baptizing people, how we were preaching love, and how we were earlier members of the Anglican Church, but we later left it for the reasons I explained to them. They were accompanied by some Anglicans, [and] they then took the Holy Communion cup away with them. There was no one who was arrested among us, neither was there any bad thing that they did to us, and we just arranged for another meeting elsewhere.

200 After, when Assistant Bishop Olang' had chased us away from Maseno, we then received the suspension letters which stopped me from work and padre Owira, and also our secretary, Benson Otieno (who was also the secretary of the Maseno CMS hospital), he also received the suspension letter that stopped him from work. Then, when we told people what had happened, they became harsh and they did not want to hear that word. [It happened] that our suspension made many people to join us. When I was suspended I was robbed of the robe and the certificate, [and] all these I returned to Maseno as they required. And after this was when we went ahead with work more than before. We made our own clothes as we required, and the work just went on more than usual.

201 Let me say that when we had worked and got our registration they [the Anglicans] returned those robes in the middle of the year 1958, but they did not return the license. They also returned the Holy Communion cup which they had taken away with them. But later, we bought our own cups and our own robes.

202 [We then] started a more serious preaching of the gospel here in our land, [and] I could address two to four meetings a day. That means I could address one meeting in the morning, one in the afternoon, another in the evening, and the other at night. We were traveling in a very long convoy of bicycles, and the bicycles were

not getting punctures or [being] twisted. We were really visiting the parts of Luoland.

203   We were [also] traveling up to Western Province, the land of foreigners, until we reached the home of Mulama, the son of Mumia, who was the paramount chief. When we went to Mumia's home, at a place now called Mumias, I was with Owira and padre Nyende (who later became our bishop), and there [were] also other people in our team. Mulama blessed the Church of Christ in Africa. He said that he had blessed the Church of Christ in Africa (Johera), and it should multiply. He blessed the Church of Christ in Africa to spread in Kakamega, on the land of Western Province, [and he said] that the Church of Christ in Africa should reach all corners of the world, and [hoped that it] may not face any shortfalls. We were welcomed with the animal skins, and then he prayed that the Church of Christ in Africa should expand. Even though we were members of the Church of Christ in Africa, we also had among us some Luhyias even [on] that day when we were being suspended from Maseno, and therefore the Church of Christ in Africa spread into the Luhyaland very fast. We then had many churches in Luhyaland. But the majority [of] members in the Church of Christ in Africa at present are the Luos, followed by Luhyias, and then we have a few other tribes.

204   During those days we were still under the British, [and] it was the British people who controlled both Uganda and Tanzania. There was only one currency, there were no problems at the border [so] people were moving very freely. That is the reason why there are many Luos in North Mara (Tanzania), and they are mixing together with foreigners there at South Mara, Susoma, Bugembe, Geita, and other places around the lake shore. The Luos are there fishing, [and] they have married some of these tribes they are living together with; they have married from these people. We preached the gospel up to Tanzania, until many Luos became members of the CCA and also other tribes.

205   I can remember that the assistant chief from the village where the former president of Tanzania, Dr. Nyerere, was coming [from was] a member of CCA. Wanjage, who was the brother of Nyerere, was a strong supporter of the CCA and was giving all support; he was also in our team. These were the people from the clan called "Wachemake," [but] the other tribes were also with us.

206   We also started to spread the gospel very strongly in Uganda, [because] in Uganda there were very many Nilotic people. When we were coming back we left the last group of the Nilotes which was called Padhola, who were living at a place near Busia.

The Johera Narrative

207   God chose the Jews when he chose Abraham and his wife Sarah. Again, in Genesis chapter 12:3,4 God says that from you, Abraham, all nations will have blessings. That was why the Lord Jesus preached this, [for] he was born among the Jews. He told that woman that he was sent first to the group of Israel, [and] that was why he performed a tough job among Israel so that they may become God's people. But he said that he came to save the whole world, but also where he was born, since charity begins at home. He first worked so hard among his people, [and] some accepted him while others did not. He was speaking to a group of people when a woman approached him for assistance. He told her that a group of Israel should [have no dealings with her, but] that woman told him that even dogs can feed on the leftovers. Jesus worked for the benefit of many people, and we realize that after his death many people got saved.

208   Many times when I preach I tell the Africans that we are not far away from that Kingdom. When there was a great famine in the world Abraham and his wife Sarah just got the rescue here in Africa. God knows Africa! During the period of great famine that killed many people during the time of Jacob, God made a great plan when he sent Joseph to become a King in Egypt. Then Jacob and all his sons were evacuated to get relief in Egypt. Yes, the Lord knows Africa! Moses was born here in Egypt; that is here in Africa. And Moses released his people, [and] he was given a good education under the King of Africans, the King of Egypt, until he grew into an adult and achieved the right knowledge that is in Africa. And when Moses had achieved full knowledge, the Lord revealed himself to him, that he should release his people who were being persecuted, who were being given hard labor, who were being killed, so that they may go back to the promised land where God had promised their grandfathers, Abraham, Isaac, and Jacob. He removed the children of Israel with the power of God. Again, the daughter of the King, the daughter of Africa, was the one who brought Moses up in the house of the King. Africa did all the work!

209   When we look at the time [before] when Jesus was born, Ruth, the daughter of the Moabites was the daughter of the people. When they had lost hope, Malon and his brother together with their grandmother came back to Israel. That's the lineage where Obed was born, where David was born, and where Jesus was born. God had long brought the nations together for the salvation of the entire world.

210   We have the right to claim Jesus. When Jesus was born and the Jews wanted to kill him, when the Romans wanted to kill him, when people wanted to kill him, God on his heavenly throne saw that a safe place where he could hide his child who will save the whole world was Africa. He told Joseph and Mary to stand up and take the child and go and hide him in Africa. Jesus was hidden here in Africa until some of those who wanted to kill him had died.

211   God loves Africa! When Jesus was arrested and people ran away (even his disciples ran away when he was going to be crucified), Simon of Cyrene (Cyrene is in the north of Africa here) [was there to help him]. Had the Muslims not swept away Christians and demolished churches, the north [of] Africa, which is now Islam dominated, would have been all Christians. Simon from Cyrene helped Jesus carrying the cross. There was no America [then], [and] there was no whitemen or an Indian or an Arab who helped Jesus to carry the cross. It was an African who identified himself with Jesus and helped Jesus carrying the cross. What kind of love was that? God loves Africa, and that is why we should not backslide. Sometimes Africa fails to have an immediate understanding of this, and that is the reason why the gospel went back to England and later came back here.

212   During the period when all these things were happening the people from Europe or Asia were not aware that these things were happening. Jesus stepped on the African soil before he stepped in Europe, [and] before he stepped in America. That is the reason why the Africans should know very well that God loves them, and that they are in the history of salvation for the whole world, [and] that those Jews who accepted Jesus were Jews from the Jewish territory.

213   During those days Greek was the language spoken in the Mediterranean Sea just the same way Kiswahili is the national language here, or just as English is spoken. The Jewish people and the Greek people who accepted Jesus were those from places like Athens [and] Corinth, and when they accepted the Lord [they] became saved Christians (that is where you find the Greek Orthodox Church). Were they calling themselves the Greek people? No! They were saying that when the Jews here accepted Jesus, then they (the Greeks) should also accept the Lord and call themselves Christ's people.

214   During the time Jesus was born it was the Romans who were the rulers of the Empire. And since Rome was the capital city where the government was living, the important leaders of the church (such as the bishops who were also staying in Rome) took advantage

because they were living in the capital. (We also witness the same thing even here in Kenya. The Mayor of Nairobi considers himself more important than other mayors elsewhere in the country, and he calls the meetings of mayors in his office.) Then, when the Roman bishop was living there in the capital, that was the time when Rome began to expand. When the Italians accepted Jesus, they did not call themselves Jews or Greek-Italians, but they just called [their church by] the name of their big city. [They] called [it] Rome. That's the Roman Catholic Church, and when you find people fighting, claiming to belong to the Romans, and others [saying] that they belong to other people, you can really wonder. This is because of the little knowledge amongst the Africans!

215   These people just started these churches according to the names of their capital city, which was Rome, [and] that is the [beginning of the] Roman Catholic Church. Since it was the capital city of the government the major important church functions and other functions started to take place there. That is why the big churches, such as the St. Peter's Basilica and others, were found there, because they were people who knew how to build. Even the Greek people also knew how to build, and the Jews also knew how to build. Those places have very big houses for God.

216   It [is] also these Romans who preached the gospel to the Englishmen. When they were coming across the arrested Englishmen, they were sympathizing with their good children. The Englishmen were wealthy people, and the Romans thought that in such a situation, when these people were preached the gospel, they could possibly become Christians. Then preachers were sent to them, but the Englishmen had evolved into very dirty things, until King Henry wanted to divorce his wife. When the Pope refused, that marked the beginning of the Church of England. Henry came to loggerheads with the Pope because of marriage. Then the Englishmen started saying that they were not going to allow other people to rule them on their land, and therefore [they said] we, the Englishmen, we should have our own church, [and] that is the Church of England.

217   It is from the Church of England where CMS emerged, [and] it was the one that preached to me. It was the one that taught me many things until now, and we really thank it for this. But, it did not call itself that it was [the] Roman church, for the Jews or for the Greeks, but [rather] the Church of England.

218   But what crime is there if we, the Africans, have our own church? Why are these whitemen following us? It's God who

divided this world that is surrounded by water, and He didn't make us whitemen. He did not put us in the other parts of the world, and therefore our peoples should know this, and the whitemen should also know this: we are not inferior! There is no third class Holy Spirit that is given to the black people, [for] there is no second class Holy Spirit, [and] there is no first Holy Spirit. There is only one Holy Spirit that is given to those who accept Jesus. It's the [same] Holy Spirit that is given to the Africans, and why then do these whitemen look down upon us? Have they not become Christians? Do they have the same opinion that Peter at first had, when he said that the Jews cannot mix freely with the other people and such like things?

219   Jesus [said to Peter] in his dream that one should not disrespect what had [been] made holy by God. And when they went to Cornelius, the Holy Spirit came down to these people, and Peter was surprised and asked if those people could just receive the Holy Spirit the same way we (Peter's group) could? [He realized that] there is no difference, that there is no special Holy Spirit for them and that for the Jews. He then said that these people have the right to be baptized because they have been given the Holy Spirit the same way we (the Jews) have been given it.

220   When I explained this, even now when I explain this to the Africans (I repeat this to my people where they are meeting), many understand and say that it is true. But it is true! And that is why we know that when we are praying here in Africa our prayers reach heaven. And even the Romans, when they are praying there in Rome their prayers reach the same place. And the Englishmen, when pray their prayers reach there, and the Americans the same. But somebody should not say that we should pray through Rome or through England or through elsewhere, [for] God is omnipresent.

221   Therefore, the thing that happened to Peter (whatever he saw in his dream) really strengthened me, [so that] even though I [was] being threatened that I would be arrested, even though I was threatened that I would be taken to the place where Kenyatta was detained (that I would be taken there), [and] even though the police were following with a gun all over, I wholly agreed that God loved Africa, and that He must have preachers here in Africa, even if those big churches for the whitemen accept it or not.

222   When God was sending Abraham to Africa, He did not ask the whitemen about it. When He was sending Joseph and the house of Jacob to come to Africa, He did not ask the whitemen about it. That is why the whitemen belong to God, and the blackmen also belong to

God. But I should say that the black people are closer to God than others, [because of] the above brief history I have given.

223   In my sermons I have preached to say that whenever I am walking, I am very happy with what the missionaries had done. That is, the Jews preached the gospel, the Greeks preached the gospel, [and then] the Romans preached the gospel to the Englishmen. They [the Englishmen] were also given the gospel [that] they should also bring it to us. Others who went to America were also preached the gospel, [and] they should also preach the same gospel to us, for there is nothing bad in that. They are only paying for what God had done for them. We are happy with the work they did and really happy when God has now revealed Himself to the people of Africa. That is why Jesus is ours the same way he is for the others.

224   During those days I sent the layreader, David Ochuodho, and other people to go and preach the gospel at Kericho Tea Estate. The overall manager, whom I think was called Harrison, [lived] in the town of Kericho. [He] refused that these people could not preach the gospel, [for] there was no other church allowed in Kericho because those that were already there were enough. These people talked with him but he refused. Some elderly black people who were there also talked to him (those who wanted to join the Church of Christ in Africa, Johera), but he refused.

225   But when these people brought the message to me I left for Kericho to see the general manager. I told him that when my people came he refused them to preach the gospel, and yet I wanted us to do so. That whiteman really shouted at me, saying that many churches had come there, and there was no more permission granted to other simple churches to preach there in Kericho. He really shouted at me, and again said that if someone is preaching there and he finds some money, he has to let him know how much he has received. Then I told him that I had with me the layreader, David Ochuodho, and our secretary-general, Benson Otieno. I again told him that the Church of Christ in Africa was a registered church (that was in January when we had been registered), and for that reason we wanted to preach the gospel there. But he told me that you will not!

226   Then I told him that the registration that we had been given covered Kericho. It covered the whole [of] Kenya and Kericho was also within Kenya. And [I said that] if you refuse us to preach, then write us a letter to that effect, and I [will] take it to the government. But those days the government was still under the Englishmen. [Yet, I said write us a letter] so that I take it to the government, and [I will] tell them that the manager at Kericho has refused us to

preach the gospel. Write us the letter now [and] we [will] take [it] with us!

227 He was shocked and then he asked me, "Where did you learn?" Then I quickly told him that I had just learned locally here. He again asked, then I told him that I learned at St. Paul's Theological College and that I have just learned locally here [in] Maseno and Yala. And then he asked the layreader, David Ochuodho, "Where did you go to school?" Then David answered him that he went to St. Philip's Bible School in Maseno. Then he asked Benson Otieno, "Where did you go to school?" Then Benson told him that he [was] just a secretary, [and that] he did not go to have theological training anywhere. He shouted at Benson when telling him that they were the people spoiling others. He asked him how could he preach the gospel of God and yet he had not studied the word of God? I told him that we were the ones who had sent him as our secretary, and again that he was a saved man of God. He could not preach something which could spoil someone.

228 Later on he cooled down and told us to go ahead preaching the gospel, but cautioned us that when we were preaching, we [must] make sure that the money we receive, we had to let him know how much it was. I again asked him if the Roman Catholic Church, which was there, was letting him know how much money they had collected or [were they] taking their collection to him? The Anglicans who were there and other churches which were there, did they really bring their collections to him, and if not, why then [should] we be the first one to do that? He had nothing to say. He told us that you go and preach and that was how the word of God entered Kericho.

229 After that we headed for the Rift Valley. Our people that we had found in towns then started preaching the gospel outside the town, in the farms. We went up to Elmolo, Alfega, and other places like Gilgil, Njoro, and others.

230 [One day] we arrived at Subukia at the farm of Michael Bloundell at around 12:00 noon. When we arrived there the workers told us that he was there, and [that] we had to go and request him permission; we went. When we went and he saw me in collar we told him, "Sir, we wanted to preach the gospel here in your farm." He asked me what type of people we were, [and] I told him that we [were] members of the Church of Christ (Johera) which was a new church. Then he told us to wait there. And as he entered the house he just went to call the police and the Nakuru District Commissioner.

231   He stayed for awhile and when he returned he told us that he had allowed us to preach, and requested us to tell people not to steal anything in the farm and that they should work hard. And I told him, "Thank you sir, and we are going to do what you have told us." He again told us to sit down so as to give us something to eat because it was lunch time. Bloundell brought meat and bread and we really ate there. When we had eaten we found that he was very fluent in Dholuo, [and that] he was calling himself Onyango the son of Alego. Then he told us to go and preach, and he requested us to go and tell people not to steal anything there in the farm, but [rather tell them that] they should work very hard. We told him, "Thank you, sir" [and] we opened very many churches.

232   When we went to Molo we met John Bell. We went to every part, [and] we went to the whitemen first. When they had realized that we were a registered church they were allowing us to preach to people, [and] we opened very many churches in the Rift Valley. Most of our members there were Luos, then Gikuyus, and then the Kalenjins were also there and the Abaluhyias also. And the gospel was really preached.

233   After that we went to Nairobi, [and] in Nairobi I can remember we first prayed with seven people. (Buy now we have so many people, thousands of people, and we have almost 25 churches in Nairobi city alone. We also have churches in other towns.) There we went up to the governor's home where his servants were Luos, and there we opened a church. We tried to visit the very important persons at their residences so that we could open churches there. After opening churches at such places we now got the courage to open churches elsewhere. (In Nairobi we first prayed at Starehe, then Kaloleni, and then to many other places.)

234   When we had gotten the registration we sat down to plan how our work should be programmed. As per the leadership of the church, we resolved that we should have the catechists, [and] we should have the layreaders for the church. [These] should be the saved people and [they] should serve the responsibilities such as: praying for the women who have given birth (thanksgiving), [and] assisting the main padre when they give the Holy Communion and during the baptisms. We also said that we should have deacons, those who are saved and have the collars, who may baptize the children, and also assist the main padre giving the Holy Communion. We said that we should have priests (the padres) who could give the Holy Communion, preside over weddings and preside over other church events. We also resolved that we should have bishops, we

should have other posts like rural canons [and] councils, which we call areas and not the deanery (but we call it areas).

235 We also passed that we shall have the area diocese, which means we group many areas into a diocese. We agreed that we shall have bishops, we agreed that we shall have robes, [and] we also said that we shall continue with the prayers in the Prayer Book. And the things which are not in keeping with our traditions we shall throw them away. But those in keeping with our tradition we should keep and use in our prayers. We also resolved to write our own prayer book. We continued to use the Anglican prayer book for a short while, and [also Anglican] hymns, but the Holy Spirit was revealing new songs for praising the Lord.

236 We then found the things to revive the hearts of people, because when we were in the Anglican [Church], people were very cold. They were singing cold songs, [there was] cold preaching, and almost everything was cold. And then [we came to believe that] if we have received the Holy Spirit, then people should have warm preaching, strong and warm praying, and lively songs (because in the Anglican Church we were not clapping while singing). Now we were aggressively clapping when we were praising the Lord with songs as it [is] required by Psalms (David's).

237 And then the Anglicans started to throw insults at us. [They said] that we were singing like the people of the world, and that we were clapping as people performing wedding rituals (Jondaria), but we had a lot of pride in us. For instance, the Lord has given me some gifts, one of which is that I know music, and therefore I started to compose these songs into set pieces, and arranging them in order. We made a lot of them, but I had only a little money, and therefore only a few of them were printed (above one hundred, but we are still organizing them because they require a huge sum of money). And it is this that we are now singing here in our church. We also sing other good Christian songs, but our own songs that were started or composed by the CCA, some of them we have put in the books that we use, but others we shall still put in the books.

238 We had also planned to organize our churches in this order: one church is a church with its teacher, and two, three, or four churches like this we shall call a pastorate. But some few pastorates (three to four) we shall call an area, but about three to four areas we shall call the area diocese. And when all these area dioceses are merged together, we shall call it [a] diocese. Then, the presiding bishop is the head of the diocese, the assistant bishop [is] to head the area diocese, and pastors under them, etc.

The Johera Narrative

239   And at this time that I am talking we are about one million people in the Church of Christ in Africa. We have about 800 churches here in Kenya. CCA is also registered in Tanzania, but the "Kijiji cha Ujaama" that was brought by the former president, Nyerere, made the church lose many people in Tanzania, since many people crossed the border into Kenya, and others went to other villages (Kijiji). But we still have some churches in North Mara, South Mara, and other places where we are registered. We are also registered in Uganda, but during the time of Amin the churches were closed, and our church was one of them. He only left the Anglican Church, the Catholic Church, the Orthodox Church, and Islam. But when Amin closed [the] church, and then by the time Obote returned to power, we went back and registered the church. Those many wars interfered with our churches, but there are still some churches. We have our headquarters in Kampala, and we have people in other towns. In Tanzania we have our headquarters at Musoma and also have our plot there. We are also registered in Zaire, [and] we are registered in Zambia. Those are the places where CCA is (but we also have friends in other countries here in Africa).

240   For this reason when we had settled down to start the work after the registration, we thought that first we should have our Bible College. The CCA has a Bible college which is called St. Matthew's Masogo Bible School which is in Gem. It has not faired on well, because those who teach theology are few. It was forcing me to go and teach there, and a few elders were also helping me there, and therefore it doesn't regularly operate. We often teach our people here at the headquarters, Kisumu, which is called "Dala Hera." Therefore, those whom we find (with whom we left the Anglican Church, who were layreaders), many of them we were training and [they] were later being confirmed as deacons.

241   Before I go ahead with the church issues I would like to briefly tell how we first wrote several letters to the Archbishop of Canterbury, the Right Honourable and Most Reverend G. F. Fisher, the primate of all England and Metropolitan, Lambeth Palace, London. This letter [which I will now read] was written in the year 1958 in March (that was when we had received our registration in January). In all those letters which we had written, some of which I have talked about above, there was never any fruitful agreement. But this letter I wrote in English and that is why I will read it like so:

[Here he reads the entire letter of 27 March, 1958 addressed to the Archbishop of Canterbury, G. F. Fisher.]

242   The Archbishop of Canterbury replied me on August 13, 1958. This was his reply from a letter addressed from Lambeth Palace:
[He here reads the letter of 13 August, 1958.]

243   You can see that when we presented our complaints to the Archbishop of Canterbury, [and] after trying for a long time to bring unity after several meetings here, [still] the Archbishop of Canterbury just continued to praise his archbishops here, Beecher and Olang'. [He said] that they were the best men who could assist us in all ways, more than anybody else. [He also said] that they are the ones endowed with the best wisdom and leadership and guidance that is required [to assist us].

244   But when I received this letter I presented it before the elders of the Church of Christ in Africa. But after this letter had been read the elders were not happy, even a little, because it was these people [Beecher and Olang'] who had all along persecuted us, [yet] the Archbishop also sided with them. Instead of questioning us about the matter, meeting us or just doing something about it, he refused.

245   That was why we took a different step. We replied back [in] the letter to G. F. Fisher, the Archbishop of Canterbury, Lambeth Palace. And this is what we told him:
[Here he reads the letter of 24 October, 1958.]

246   When we had read this letter from the Archbishop of Canterbury [we wondered] that he could still support those people who had troubled us, [but] we then resolved that our God would hear and support us. We had also seen that when Moses was called to the ministry there wasn't any ceremony held for him, nor was there any supper organized for him. Nobody laid his hand on him, [for] it was God who called him, who blessed him and sent [him] to work. We also find God telling Jeremiah that you should not fear that you are still young. [God said to him], "Before you were created and born I knew you when you were still in your mother's womb. I have chosen a man of God and a preacher. Therefore, you go and you will meet the adults and the youth. You will meet the rich and the poor, and you will plant and uproot, you will destroy and build, and I myself, I will go with you."

247   When the elders had read all these they again read where Jesus appointed the disciples, [where] He was calling them and blessing them. Then the elders appointed me to be the leader of the Church of Christ in Africa. And it was that name of the church which kept on lingering in my mind all the time, all those years, even that time when we [were] writing those letters. Nobody was helping me write

them, but it was God who was directing on what to write, even while we were still members of the Anglican Church.

248   Now that the elders had appointed me their leader, they prayed for me, and they also prayed for all of us. Then we started leading this church, knowing that it was God who had called us. I, for one, was among the first deacons who were ordained and laid hands on at the All Saints' Cathedral in Nairobi, because [until that time] it had belonged to the whites alone. I was ordained by the Bishop of the Anglican Church who was a whiteman, and when I was again made a priest, I was made the priest of the main CMS in Luoland which was called Ng'iya, and it was the Archbishop of the Anglican Church who ordained me. Therefore, our people and myself did not see me as a man from no background, [and] I was a man who grew in faith. Even when it was the [doctrine of] apostolic succession [that was in question], we were the people who passed through the right church and through clear procedure.

249   Then we started planning for the church, and thereafter we started to walk from place to place when we were opening new churches, appointing leaders in the old ones, and when we were organizing for our meetings.

250   I can remember that [in attendance at] our first synod meeting for the year 1958 there was an Anglican Church padre by the name of Heson Rachier who [was] the pastor in [the] church of Masogo. (This man came with the police to arrest me). [In] that period they [(the police)] were whitemen. As these other whitemen [(the police)] were coming to where we were meeting, the others including the main padre for the Anglican Church had remained in the vehicle. These other whitemen who had come to me told me that I was required in Kisumu. I asked them what I was needed in Kisumu for and yet I had a meeting that time. I asked them if I could call off that meeting? They insisted that I was needed in Kisumu, and I told them that I could not go with them that moment. [I said] that I would follow them the following day since I was not going to run away. The elders at the meeting also refused [to allow me to leave], and as others started to leave they said that I [should] go ahead and follow them in Kisumu.

251   When we were leaving after the meeting we realized that the main padre of the Anglican Church, who had come with them, was left in the vehicle outside. People shouted him and later left him to go. We then preceded with a lot of force, and when we had preached I slept, and then went to Kisumu the following day (that was to the police station). I was accompanied by some of my people.

252 The main thing we were told was that it is being said that we were taking churches by force, and that we were fighting in the churches. I then asked him, "Where that was? Where have we beat someone in the church? Where have we taken a church by force?" Then he refused to give an answer to these my questions, [and] they then left me and only cautioned me not to cause any more problems.

253 Then we met and planned how to reorganize the church. We organized for the teachers, preachers, deacons, priests, and I [was chosen] as the presiding bishop. I was one bishop but my assistant was called Meshack Owira, who was one of the padres with whom we left the Anglican Church. Both of us were saved. We also had padre Philip Okungu, who was also one of the padres from the Anglican Church. We also had padre William Ogada with whom we were in the Anglican Church. We had some of the padres who had retired from the Anglican Church, such as padre Simon Nyende, who later served as the Bishop here in the Church of Christ in Africa; padre Isaiah Ndisi; and later on, padre Mathayo Owino. All these were people who had retired [from the Anglican Church] and were resting at home.

254 We started to restructure the inside of the church, [and] we started having departments of women. In the Church of Christ in Africa we have women['s] department. We started four departments: 1) the workers' wives, [and] these were wives to the padres and the lay readers and the bishops. They had their own group, which was called the workers' wives. They had their chairperson and secretary and their treasurer, right from the diocese up to the level of the church; 2) we have the widows, the women whose husbands have died. We group them as a team. They also have their chairpersons and other leaders right from the church level to the diocese level; 3) we have the women in development group. These women [are] train[ed] [in] weaving, pottery, knitting, tailoring, cookery, and such things. These women also have their leaders from the church level to diocese level; 4) we have the diocese women. These are general women whose duty is to strengthen the issues pertaining to the diocese. Since there were so many people, those who had stayed longer with us, we were giving them chances to work or preach. Then we came up with two new groups of women: the young women became sisters, just as we read from I Timothy 5:1, [and] the old women [became] as mothers.

255 On the side of men we said that the middle-aged men should be brothers [and] the old men fathers. On the side of youths we have youth organization, and we divide the youth into two groups.

Sometimes they become one group, but sometimes they break into two groups. They were called the Church of Christ Youth (CCY). There is male CCY and female CCY.

256   There is a visiting program for these women [where] they go round visiting all the dioceses. They go visiting in twos [or] threes, when they preach the gospel outside for one week or for one week and a half. [This is] when they preach the gospel and collect money and gifts and stress the work of women once in a year. We also have the youths' visits which comes only once in a year; that is both female and male Church of Christ Youths. During this they preach the gospel, they teach the youths songs, and collect money from their fellow youths.

257   In our church every church has twelve elders whose chairman is the teacher. That's the old men and women. In the pastorate is the pastorate meeting where the pastorate padre is the chairman, but the representatives all come from the churches. We have the area meeting where those who attend this meeting come from every pastorate. In the church, pastorate, or the area are their leaders. The chairman represents the pastor there, the teacher represents the church, and senior pastors represent the area. There are secretaries, there are treasurers, and there are also other leaders. There is a [person] in charge in the area diocese who is usually the Assistant Bishop. He also has his secretary and treasurer and other leaders. In the diocese we have the Presiding Bishop, who is myself, Matthew Ajuoga. And there we find representatives who come from all these departments: the youths are there, the bishops are there, the archbishops are there, and members from each area. The languages that we use, these are Dholuo and Kiswahili, and other issues are discussed in English.

258   The Church of Christ in Africa grew up very healthy. [Yet] when a child is healthy he may [still] develop some problems. In the middle of 1960 my deputy, who was called Meshack Owira, broke away from us. This was the cause of the fight:

259   Some padres had bad relationships with women [and] the church punished them. But when they were punished by the church, [some observed that] they were people from this side of Kisumu where my deputy, padre Meshack Owira, was coming from. Then the people from the East said [that because] I come from Siaya then their sons can't be punished [by me or anyone from Siaya]. [They said that] when Ajuoga has to punish them then we have to break away from Ajuoga. Therefore many people from the East broke away and many others remained with me. The Church of Christ in

Africa is larger in Kisumu than the group that ran away, just as it is larger in Siaya [than in the other Nyanza districts].

260   Then these people took me to court. [They said] that I had insulted them [by saying] that they commit adultery with women, [and they said] that I was punishing them for no reason. There was a serious case in the court. At first I called the Luo elders; I first called the late Oginga Odinga, pastor Omer, Ombino, [and] Kogola Jeel Omino (that found [him] when he was the mayor here in Kisumu). And many other important Luo men also came to bring peace between us. These old men gave a wise judgement when they threw away Owira and his followers, but they refused to [listen to] these old people's call and just went ahead with their division.

261   They later took me to court [and] we had a serious case. They remain with some few churches, but we managed to remain with more churches in the Church of Christ in Africa. Many of the Masogo people (who had made us call ourselves the diocese of Masogo) were now supporting Owira and were [now] calling themselves the Masogo diocese, [yet] we were also still calling ourselves the Masogo diocese, [and this created problems]. After cheating people for a long period of time [by saying] that they were the Church of Christ in Africa, they again renamed themselves the "Holy Trinity Church." But this was locally known as "Nyamgutu," where the word "nyamgutu" means something that has left the home compound and is now found behind the home.

262   But through bad luck most of these people have now died, and those who are surviving are divided. The most unfortunate part of it is that the padre, Meshack Owira himself who had been the bishop for those separatists (who were the HTCA), was struck by lightning after some days there, and we were really shocked to hear that. We continue to live as strong members of the CCA, but the health of those who separated from us has not been so well. That someone can see by himself.

263   When it reached 1975 the Luhyas had two bishops, Nathan Silas Awuor and Elijah Magokha. They thought that the Luos were misusing them and that the Luos were their leaders, and [yet] they (Luhyas) were calling themselves members of the Church of Christ in Africa (Johera). They were also on the verge of starting their own church, the Luhya church, and call it "Mirembe." Many Luhyas followed those their two sons and later called themselves "Mirembe Church." Through God's grace, as the years were advancing most of those HTCA came back to join us, and many more are still coming up to now. Through God's miracle (that [was] last year) the members

of Mirembe returned to CCA in a large number, almost all of them. Now we have so many people, [more] than those who are still counted as members of Mirembe. [They] are very few. For that I really thanked God, for this work he performed to those who were separating.

264 Those people were asking themselves, that since the time we separated from the Luos where is even a single church which has been built? Where is even a single office that has been built? Where is any development that has taken place? There is none. Therefore to us (the Luhyas) we see no racial discrimination in God. We have to go back to Kisumu, [and] a Luo by the name Ajuoga is going to lead us. And they came back almost all of them. We really thank God for this, and we are really progressing very smoothly with them. I can now see some churches are being built, the number of people are also multiplying so well, and the Lord is revealing himself to many people.

265 In our diocese synod we have additional committees. First, we have [several] standing committees of twelve people. We have financial committee of twelve people, we have building committee of twelve people, and we also have development committee of twelve people. We also have education committee where we also have board of governors which runs our two schools.

266 The CCA has done a lot of development. First, we have a house craft training centre, [and] this home craft training is divided into four departments. The first is cookery department where women are trained how to cook and [to do] other domestic work. The second is the department of knitting, [and] the third is the department of tailoring and dressmaking. The fourth is the department of tie and dye. They have been doing quite well for a number of years, because some of them were started as early as 1960. However, some of them may not be doing quite well [at this time].

267 In this work of training we have attended so many shows, here in Kisumu, Homa Bay, Kakamega, Nakuru, and the International Show in Nairobi. At some of these places we have taken positions one, two [and] three, while at others we have not managed to take any number. All these we were doing because there are women who have nothing to do at home. There are [also] children who have finished school, standard eight or form four, [and] some of them are drop outs. But then we think that when one gets training, he/she can use this knowledge in the house or somebody may employ them. And many of those who have trained here [have been employed],

[and] some have employed themselves. The women and young ladies have tailoring shop, sweater shops, and so on, and they really make us happy.

268   On the side of pure education we have nursery schools, we have primary schools, [and] we have three secondary schools. The first one is situated here in Kisumu (Dala Hera), [and] it has form one to form four. Many people who have achieved their education here are now working in various departments, [and] some of them work as top civil servants in the government, and all these really please us. Many people have left our secondary schools and join university. Even now there are three who had gone though here and are now graduates and are teaching here at our school.

269   This school is composed of different people. The school is registered with the government from the year 1971, but it is being managed by the CCA. In this school we take people from all denominations, [and] people from all races, but the majority are Luos, followed by Luhyas, and then Kisiis, Gikuyus, Kambas, and Kalenjins. We have taught people here from different parts of the country. This is why we thank God for his provisions, so that we may also do the little we can afford, because we do not get any other financial assistance either from the government or through fundraising. Whenever we call for fundraising nobody from outside comes to join us. It is only ourselves, the church members, who bear this burden.

270   Sometime back, when the government realized that we were doing well in the examination (for instance, the Kenya Junior Secondary Examination, when our students were performing well, after their form two) they were taking them to government secondary schools. Then later on they accepted to assist us with teachers, but that is [only] up to last year, 1992. They removed all their teachers, so the remaining teachers now are our own employees, and we are the ones paying for their salaries. But we have seen a great change since those whom we were being given [by the government] were people from different denominations. Some of them had been rejected while a few of them were righteous people.

271   This was a very bad mixture, and since we did not want to see this happen here at our school, we started to teach people three programs so that those who go through our school should be spiritual, intellectual, and should be physically fit. This was why we started this school, because many schools say that there is no God, and therefore there has been a big problem. But the schools where the child listens [to] the word of God are so important.

272 In Kisumu District we built one school which is called Nyanza Christian College. In Siaya District we built one school called Christian Secondary School, which is also doing just as good as the Nyanza Christian College. They were doing so well in Kenya Junior [that] some of them were being taken by the government, and sometimes the government was assisting us with two or more teachers (but later [they] withdrew them). Now the teachers we have are purely our employees. In the past few years we have been taking one, two, or three of our students to the university. Last year alone, we had three qualified students to join the university from Nyanza Christian College, and two from Christian Secondary School.

273 One time a certain education officer really bothered us. [He asked] why we were calling our schools "Christian" schools. But I told him that we wanted to identify ourselves with Christ and His Church. I again asked him why were they only following us? There are also Muslim schools, there are Methodist schools, and such like schools. That is why we Christians, when people tend to forget their Christ, we would not want to forget our Christ. And that is why all these our schools must bear the name of Christ.

274 We Luos have three districts, and therefore we thought that before we go out [to help others] (charity begins at home) we could start from here at home first. We built the third school, which we called Rachuonyo Christian Secondary School there at Kodera, which is a few miles from Oyugis turn. But there, since people in the surrounding [areas] were SDA and Catholics, they showed a lot of jealousy and refused their children to go to this school. But people in those places have not quite welcomed education, [for those] people do not take education seriously. Therefore, we [saw that] that school [was] not doing well, and so we closed it temporarily. We have a lesson of the experiences we encounter [in this case], and have the feeling to start it again on a very strong note.

275 The thing that impresses both the church and me is the fact that now the headmistress of Nyanza Christian College is a graduate of this school, [where] she was a student up to her form four. She went for her high school in Kikuyu, and later went to Daystar University for her degree program. And upon completion she came back and is now the head of this our school here. Sometime ago she was here together with the other two people who had passed through this school and later became graduates of Nairobi University. Now the government has taken one of them and has given [him] a job, but others are still here. This school has produced doctors, administrators (such as the DC, the DO), and many other such kind

of people. It has [also] produced ministers and padres for various churches.

276 These schools are helping those our padres. Since we lead the people who are poor, many may not be able to raise money to pay these padres. Again, we have not trained ourselves to give right from our former churches, and that is why we don't receive in abundance. Therefore, we thought that [we could not] let our pastors' children miss education and [yet] it is something [we can] afford to offer. That is why the children of our pastors, who learn [or go to school], just receive it [free] without any problem, because we have secondary schools where they can go.

277 There is a development that the Church of Christ in Africa has come up with: we have opened four clinics. One of these four clinics was started by the drugs we received from England. We received two boxes of these drugs and then started a clinic here at Dala Hera to help the children, the Christians, and those who are here at the headquarters (and the outsiders who are within the surroundings of this home). Our brethren from Luhyaland of Kakamega requested that we give them one box of the drugs, because there was not enough health care where they come from. We gave them one box, and we then went to open Chekalili Health Centre at a settlement scheme. We also opened another clinic in Siaya, and the other one [we opened at] Rachuonyo Secondary School.

278 Through bad luck, that is because of lack of money which we can use to run all these clinics, there is only one clinic that is operational. [This] is Rachuonyo clinic, but the one at Siaya closed down. The one in Kisumu here [also] closed down, and the same [is true of] that at Chekalili. However, we have the faith that we shall, if we are able, open these places (especially at this time when treatment has become a primary requirement) so that people may get help.

279 In the last few days we thank Christians from America, especially for the few drugs they brought us. We used some of them here (Kisumu), and sent others to our clinic at Rachuonyo.

280 In the past days we opened a farm where we had three hundred chickens, [and] there were three-grade cattle. We had a German who was one time a member of the Anglican Church, but when his contract expired, we took him and he stayed with us for a period of five years. [During this time] he was caring for our chickens, caring for those cattle, and was also treating people using traditional African herbs. He continued for just a while, and he later

left because we lacked the resources to keep these programs running. After he left these programs could not run, because we did not get well-trained personnel in this area. Again, he did not want to train someone who could take his place when he left. We have also realized that this is quite common with many missionaries, that when they are doing something they don't want to train local people, so that by the time they leave they [(the local people)] could take up the responsibility. But instead they do their things in a hidden manner, so that when they leave the work should also stop.

281 Now we have the farm there but nothing good is happening there. But we still have the hope to have such a farm [again], because it trains people to plant and reap, just as we planted vegetables there. People could come and train themselves here, and later they [could] go and do the same at their places of residence for their personal gains.

282 In the past few years we opened a polytechnic to help in teaching people electrical engineering, motor vehicle mechanics and motor engineering, carpentry, masonry, and a section to assist our accounts department. Because the lady students at the secondary section would also want to get trained in typewriting, we then transferred the full secretarial section to the polytechnic. Those who were in the polytechnic section were also doing quite well in the government trade tests. You may find that those who have been trained here in either typing or accounting are now working in many different parts of the country, and I can see even the Catholics or missionaries are sponsoring some students here.

283 In these various departments some are doing quite well while others are not doing well. But what I have also realized is that our people also fear manual work. Our children have been subjected to bad training, [for they think] they only need the white collar jobs, and the white collar jobs are no longer available. This is the reason why we are trying very hard to open these centres as to help our children who have left school, together with men and women, so that they may find a way of getting self-employment.

284 We have at these centres enough sewing machines, [and] we have enough typewriting machines. However, we don't have enough tools (but we have a few of these), and these are the things that the Church of Christ in Africa is trying to do so as to help its Christian members, other Christians, and the people of this country. We don't close the doors to outsiders since even the Muslims are also taking courses here. We have also seen some people from other big churches who come to be trained here, so that they can also go and

open similar centres elsewhere in their churches. We really thank God for this.

285   In this church we try to be self-supporting. We make our own money to support ourselves, we sew clothes for our pastors, we sew uniforms for the students here, and many other such things. Much of the carpentry work we also do by ourselves here. We try to do this and we find it quite helping, but it is only that we don't have enough funds.

286   The Church of Christ experienced a serious war starting from the main churches. But when things calmed down a few churches started to side with us, because they could see that what we were doing here was now being copied by other churches. We could as well see [that] those who were being denounced by the main churches were doing what we people were doing. We see that what we were doing here was now being copied by the so-called "main churches." That is why I agreed that the Lord had called [me] to this ministry to serve the young and the old churches.

287   Working together with other churches I can [say] that we [have] become an ecumenical society or faith, because [we] were trying our level best to work together with the NCCK [National Council of Churches in Kenya]. But since permanent leaders of this council were from the Church of England (that is the CMS or CPK [Church of the Province of Kenya]), the Methodist Church, and the Presbyterian Church, these three churches have prevented even the American churches to freely work with them. These three churches refused to freely work with the indigenous churches. When you ask to become a member then you are asked so many things. But we really thank God because you can now find a few [such] churches becoming members of NCCK. We also tried to be registered as members of the NCCK, but we later withdrew our membership.

288   What made us withdraw in the year 1965 [was because of the following]. First, when I left the country to tour Europe I went to England, and when I got into the office of the CMS I found some missionaries there who had been here (in Africa) before, such as Dr. Leakey. I saw Greenshaw there, [and] I found [a] sister-in-law of Dr. Leakey there. However, Taylor, who had been the general secretary, really welcomed me, but those other missionaries who had worked here in Africa seemed not to be free with me. The general secretary, Rev. Taylor, gave me a warm welcome and I told him the whole story of how things were, and he gave me an appointment to go and have dinner with him. However, I think these missionaries spoilt everything, [for] when I had left that dinner was cancelled.

289   I again wanted to see the Archbishop of Canterbury face to face, and they agreed to arrange for the appointment. I really stayed in England for almost one month, but I left without seeing the Archbishop of Canterbury. Even up to now I [am] still waiting that our appointment which we planned for in 1962 will materialize, and that I will one day be called to see the Archbishop of Canterbury.

290   There, as I admired the development of the youths I kept on visiting the Selly Oak [Colleges], and I talked quite a lot on how I really wanted the church to have a well- organized Sunday School for our youth. They accepted and gave me scholarships in the Selly Oak [Colleges]. I then sent one of my pastors who went to the Selly Oak [Colleges] for one month, where he learned how to conduct Sunday School for the youth, and I really thanked them.

291   When I left there I went to other parts of the world like Germany. When I went to Stuttgart I met a woman there by the name of Elizabeth Obick, and she took me to the leaders of the churches in Stuttgart. When I told these people how much I required a Bible school, they accepted that they were going to build for me a small Bible school, and these people accepted that they would finance us. But when I came back here, they asked the NCCK and the Anglicans [about us], and when they did this those people really talked bad about us. The man by the name of Mr. Kamau and the Anglican leaders really spoilt our names, [for they said] that we were not a church. Those people (from Stuttgart) sent 17,000 Shillings as their first disbursement, which I used to set up a Bible school. But later I could not finish this Bible school because I did not have any more funds to build.

292   The NCCK and the Anglicans have really spoilt our names to the extent that the Germans stopped the aid they had pledged to give for building this Bible school. How sinful this was!

293   [We have problems in training our people because]: first, [in trying to put them] through those missionary schools so that we could be able to send our people to be trained has become a real problem. They don't want to accept us. Secondly, we don't have very qualified people. Thirdly, we don't have churches that have money to pay school fees at those big schools. Why when, [when] we want to build ours, instead of helping us, they speak bad about us to those who are willing to help (and the money is not theirs)?

294   Then when they had spoilt our names like that, the World Council of Churches sent their delegation from Geneva to come and assess us. [They came] to find out about that big church they have heard about [that was supposed] to be splitting. [They wanted to

know] whether or not it is really existing, and what type of a church it was. When they came they interviewed our people, they interviewed me, and we told them what had caused the split. We told them how we preach, we told them what we confess, and our faith. They saw with their own eyes, and when they went back they recommended us.

295 Later I told them that I had the interest to go and study the word of God, [and] during that time when I left for England, I went up to Jerusalem, where we shared a room with another pastor who was the chaplain of American forces. I told him how I was eager to further my education. Although I had gone through St. Paul's Theological College, Limuru, [still I believed] if we had to effectively lead the modern churches well, we have to achieve better education. As he was leaving for America this man accepted my request. (As I can remember he was called Samson.) We later found that he had written to the World Council of Churches to inform me that they were willing to give me scholarship. Then I was given scholarship through the World Council of Churches. But when the World Council of Church contacted the NCCK here, those people were not happy about that and they really complained. But another missionary man, whom I think was Mr. Storolt, told me that my scholarship was there but some Kenyans and the NCCK people were sitting on it. When I went to check with them, they were trying to hide the truth about it. But when I remained stubborn and wrote to the WCC, I was told that my scholarship was there with the NCCK. I then became even more stubborn with them until that scholarship was released.

296 Now I was selected [as] an ecumenical student, and I went to Union Theological Seminary, New York, near Columbia University. There were people who were selected from India, Pakistan, [and] England. There we were with another famous lady in the ecumenical movement in England who was called Miss Webb. There we had people from Canada [and] America, [but] from Africa we were only two; it was myself from Kenya, and a man from Ghana.

297 That's why when I came back I decided to withdraw our membership from the NCCK.

Appendix 2

A Chronology of Significant Events

1844	Church Missionary Society begins work in Kenya
1877	Church Missionary Society begins work in Buganda
1895	British Protectorate declared over Kenya
1895-1901	Uganda Railway Built
1899	Two Anglican Dioceses formed in East Africa Protectorate; Nyanza becomes part of Uganda Diocese
1902	Roman Catholics (Mill Hill Fathers) begin work in Kisumu, Nyanza; American Friends' Industrial Mission established in Nyanza
1906	Church Missionary Society begins work at Maseno; Seventh Day Adventists, the Salvation Army, and the African Inland Church all begin work in Nyanza
1910	First Anglican Baptisms in Nyanza (15 school boys)
1911	Publication of Mark's Gospel in Dholuo

A Chronology of Significant Events

1913	Mumbo Cult established in South Nyanza
1914	First Luo AIC, Nomiya Luo Mission, founded by Johana Owalo in Nyanza; Church of the One Almighty God founded by Malaki Musa Jjakawa in Uganda
1916	Roho (Holy Spirit) movement within the Anglican Church begun among the Nyanza Luo by Alfayo Odongo
1918	Walter Owen arrives in Nyanza
1920	Kenya Becomes a Crown Colony
1921	Young Kavirondo Association formed; Nyanza transferred from Uganda to Mombasa Diocese
1923	Kavirondo Taxpayers Welfare Association formed
1925	Abednego Matthew Ajuoga born, 25 December, in Siaya District, Nyanza
1926	Dholuo New Testament Published
1929	African Orthodox Church founded by Reuben Spartas in Uganda
1933	Alfayo Odongo et al. massacred in midst of Anglican controversy in Nyanza
1934	Odongo's Followers form Dini ya Roho (Religion of the Holy Spirit) in Nyanza
1936-1941	Matthew Ajuoga attends Primary School in Nyanza
1937	First East African Revival Fellowship convention in Kenya, at Kabete, near Nairobi; 15,000 attend
1938	East Africa Revival Arrives in Nyanza
1942-1946	Matthew Ajuoga attends Secondary School in Nyanza

A Chronology of Significant Events

1946-1947	Matthew Ajuoga teaches Primary School in Nyanza
1946	Bildad Kaggia leaves Anglican Church in Central Province, Kenya to begin Kuhama (separatist) sect
1948-1950	Matthew Ajuoga works for Kenya-Uganda Railways
1948	Matthew Ajuoga's Conversion and Call; Ishmael Noo forms Christian Universal Evangelical Union in Nyanza; Reuben Kihito forms the Friends of the Holy Spirit Church among the Kikuyu in Central Kenya; Elijah Masinde founds Msambwa (ancestral spirit) cult in Western Kenya
1948-1952	Climax of the East Africa Revival in Kenya
1949	Publication of the controversial "Beecher Report" on African education, authored by Leonard J. Beecher; invokes widespread negative reactions from Africans
1950-1954	Matthew Ajuoga trains for the Anglican Priesthood at St. Paul's Theological College, Limuru, Kenya
1951	First Maseno Convention of the East Africa Revival Fellowship; 6,000 attend
1952	Johera Established; Dini ya Mariam (Religion of Mary) formed from the Roman Catholic Church in Nyanza; "Mau Mau" Begins
1952-1955	State of Emergency in Kenya
1953	Dholuo Old Testament Published; Leonard J. Beecher becomes Bishop of Mombasa
1953-55	Festo Olang' is Rural Dean in Nyanza
1954-57	Matthew Ajuoga is Rural Dean in Nzoia, Rift Valley Province, Kenya

A Chronology of Significant Events

1955	Bildad Kaggia's followers in Nyanza found the Voice of Worldwide Salvation and Healing Revival Festo Olang' becomes Assistant Bishop for Nyanza; Wahamaji (Separatists) return to the Anglican Church
1956	Matthew Ajuoga writes "The Light"; Second East Africa Revival Fellowship Convention at Maseno, 12,000 attend
1957	Matthew Ajuoga returns to Nyanza; Johera officially leaves the Anglican Church
1958	6 January, The Church of Christ in Africa-Maseno is registered; 27 March, Matthew Ajuoga seeks recognition for Johera from the Archbishop of Canterbury; 13 August, in a letter to Matthew Ajuoga the Archbishop declines to recognize Johera
1960	Meshack Owira leaves Johera to form Holy Trinity Church
1963	Kenya becomes an independent nation
1964-65	Matthew Ajuoga receives a World Council of Churches scholarship to study at Union Theological Seminary, New York City, USA
1975	Mirembe (Peace) Church splits with Johera
1982	Matthew Ajuoga becomes Chairman of the Organization of African Initiated Churches, Nairobi
1983-85	Matthew Ajuoga is an external student at the International Bible Institute and Seminary, Orlando, Florida, USA; earns Doctor of Divinity degree
1993	14 May, the *Johera Narrative* project officially begins

Endnotes

Chapter One: Introduction

1. In this study the term "African Instituted Churches" will be used rather than the other, more common designation of "African Independent Churches." This is because it is the name chosen for themselves by the large association of these Christian communities headed by Matthew Ajuoga, the Organization of African Instituted Churches.
2. Ajuoga's reluctance to speak freely and openly resulted primarily from perceived Luo alienation from the Kenyan political process; see Chapter 5.
3. While Ajuoga gave limited cooperation to Welbourn and Ogot (1966) and Barrett (1968), he did not relate his complete story.
4. Welbourn and Ogot's volume (1966), as it relates to this study, is reviewed in Chapter 3.
5. Barrett's study (1968) is further analyzed in relation to this study in Chapter 3.
6. At the time of this research, the Church Missionary Society's archives had been opened only to 1949.
7. While Ajuoga himself is very critical of Welbourn and Ogot's and Barrett's interpretations, it seems to me that he is nevertheless flattered that men of such repute should have given him their attention. Criticism *is* a form of flattery!
8. This view is also put forward by the Nigerian scholar E. A. Ayandele, who observes that "disproportionate attention [has been] given to the causes of the rise of African Churches... ." He argues that this is a tactic Western scholars have used to discredit AICs (1979, 221).
9. This is primarily due to the closure of the CMS archives for the relevant period. Consequently, the "official" CMS perspective is not presently available and therefore a balanced historical analysis is not currently possible.
10. Ajuoga's lack of explicit focus on his inherited religious past is extremely significant, and is discussed in Chapter 7.

11. My use of the word "intermediate" is based on the work of Sallie TeSelle (1975a).

Chapter Two: Towards an Inside Understanding of the Johera Narrative

1. Turner's general approach to the study of African religious movements is also summarized in (1979, 63-77).
2. Harold Turner's debt and contributions to the phenomenology of religion are detailed in Walls and Shenk (1990, 1-34).
3. My introduction to African Instituted Churches came in 1983-84 during my post-graduate African Studies. Then, from 1985-89 I was formally involved in Bible teaching among Akan churches in greater Abidjan, Ivory Coast. When I moved to Kenya in 1990, my contact with AICs was less formal and more restricted, yet I maintained regular involvement, primarily with the Church of Christ in Africa- Johera.
4. Ajuoga was aware of my ministry among African Instituted Churches in Abidjan, mainly through our mutual acquaintances.
5. The reasons for this suspicion are outlined in Ngada (1985).
6. I detail the nature of my participation in the lives of Matthew Ajuoga and the CCA in the following chapter.
7. These are detailed in Chapter 4.
8. In this regard Turner has noted,

> To make all these influences clear to himself is the most that the investigator can do to reduce the ways in which his own religious, cultural, and historical position may affect his study of an African church (1979, 45).
>
> This awareness of all the factors involved in the parties concerned is the major step not only towards objectivity but also towards the relative detachment that is essential in theological evaluation (1979, 46-47).

9. Such as his primal past and allegations of tribalism leveled against him.
10. Ajuoga's notoriety outside Kenya is illustrated by my first view of an old CCA calendar bearing the wedding photo of Matthew and Milcah Ajuoga—not in Kenya—but in the Central Library, Selly Oak Colleges, Birmingham, England!
11. This Ajuoga argues based upon his relative standing in his graduating class from St. Paul's United Theological College, his standing as an acting Rural Dean when the difficulties with the Anglican Church became severe, his good physical and mental health, and upon his age and years in ministry.
12. Although this is an issue which is addressed in Chapter 10.
13. Ajuoga's involvement in ecumenism is outlined in Barrett and Padwick (1989) and is also discussed in Chapter 10.
14. This view has been communicated to me on numerous occasions by various people from Kisumu and Nyanza, Ajuoga's home area.

15. "Qualitative methodologies refer to research procedures which produce descriptive data: people's own written or spoken words and observable behaviour" (Bogdan and Taylor 1975, 4).

16. Even so, the extensive reference list appended to this study illustrates my use of many "non-theological" sources, for example those by Terence Ranger and Peter Berger and his colleagues. Thus, this study is multi-disciplinary in its awareness, but primarily religious in its focus.

Chapter Three: Sources Available for the Study of the Johera Narrative

1. The qualitative method seeks not the facts or causes of a phenomenon, but rather an understanding of that phenomenon (Bogdan and Taylor 1975). Because I am limiting my focus to an understanding of Matthew Ajuoga's experience as expressed in the *Johera Narrative*, supplementary source materials have been limited to those which serve this purpose.

2. A major difficulty Ajuoga faced in providing source materials from inside the CCA was in locating them. Matthew Ajuoga has stored his many years of correspondence and writings in one small room in his house, where they are not readily accessible.

3. Ajuoga's disillusionment with the Anglican Church is discussed in Chapter 6 below.

4. Large portions of Ajuoga's fifteen page pamphlet are reproduced in (Welbourn and Ogot 1966, 45-52).

5. These themes in Ajuoga's theology are discussed in Chapter 10 below.

6. My methods described here are those advocated by Jan Vansina for the study of oral performances (1985, 33-67). Vansina cautions that the researcher should seek minimal input, thus not "disrupting the normal flow of events" (1985, 59-61).

7. "The first requirement, therefore, is that the researcher 'accept' the informant and give priority to what he or she wishes to tell, rather than what the researcher wishes to hear" (Portelli 1983, 103).

8. The major difficulty I experienced in relation to these sources was location. Due to the CCA's lack of an official archives, these materials had to be collected from various sources.

9. pages 12-16 and 254-263.

10. Barrett calculates the tribal zeitgeist of the Kenya Luo to be 13 out of a possible 18 (1968, 309), and in his list of 227 African tribes only 18 have higher zeitgeist ratings (1968, 305-312). Consequently, according to Barrett's theory it is not surprising that, as of 1967, there were at least 60 separate AICs with an estimated 240,000 adherents among the Luo in Kenya and Tanzania (1968, 14). This almost equals the estimated 250,000 membership for the combined Catholic and Protestant communities in the same year (1968, 9).

Chapter Four: The Gestation of the Johera Narrative

1. At the time of this writing the average life expectancy for males in modern Kenya is barely 59 and rapidly declining (*Daily Nation*, Nairobi, 3

November 1995). While 67 is not necessarily considered to be an advanced age in the West, in Kenya when that age is reached, one is aware of "living on borrowed time."

2. For the role of the *griot* in various African societies see Vansina (1985, 37ff).

3. For a detailed discussion of the traditional role of Luo elders, as well as how they were perceived by one young man, see Odinga (1992, 1ff).

4. In the creation and preservation of oral traditions, the audience or "public" who receives the tradition is extremely significant; see Vansina (1985, 34ff).

5. I must express my gratitude and indebtedness to these two men, John Okoth Okelo and Keta Peterson Midida. Although both are originally from Nyanza, Ajuoga's home province, John and Keta are from a different district. Ajuoga comes from Siaya District and John and Keta originate from an area further south, the Migori District. Although John and Keta were aware of Ajuoga, before this project they had never met him, and while both were sympathetic towards the CCA, neither had direct or even indirect affiliations to Ajuoga's ministry. These factors allowed John and Keta to participate in this project with an emotional distance which was extremely valuable, and their insights should consequently be noted as valuable sources for the completion of this study. Their Kenya Luo, yet modern and external observations provided several perspectives absent from my other sources.

6. "The crucial relationship between collecting evidence and its interpretation is, after all, nowhere more intimate than when the historian uses oral sources" (Henige 1982, 3).

7. The importance of the *Johera Narrative* for the study of oral literature is discussed in Chapter 9.

8. These impressions have been formed from my reading of those who have most aggressively argued for the recognition of the validity of oral sources, and who, in my judgment, often overstate their case. See, for example, Henige (1982), Lummis (1987), Portelli (1981), Thompson (1988), and Vansina (1985).

9. This is illustrated by the attention given to oral theology in the report of the Documentation, Archives and Bibliography Network of the International Association for Mission Studies, Mission Studies 5:2 (1988): 134-145.

10. This tendency has been noted and challenged by Terence Ranger (1987, 31ff; 1993, 182ff).

11. The objectives of accuracy and authenticity in oral accounts are discussed in detail in Allen (1982).

12. In my recording of the *Johera Narrative* I have drawn heavily upon the practical advice offered by Curtin (1968) and Yow (1994).

13. The relationship between recording methodologies and the freedom of the informant are discussed in Curtin (1968, 376ff), Lummis (1987, 42-43), and Yow (1994, 56ff).

14. For the collector's responsibility to preserve oral materials in ways that maximize their value for future use, see Curtin (1968, 369).

15. For example, this method was widely used in collecting the materials published in Curtin (1967).

16. It has been argued that "oral testimony will never be the same twice" (Portelli 1981, 104).

17. Even though the CCA is currently multinational, multi-ethnic, and therefore multilingual, still the vast majority of Johera are Luo.

18. Ajuoga's use of the vernacular represents his attempt to merge the "popular" theological world of the people and his own, more "academic" theological world. The relationship between these two realms of Christian experience, here expressed in the tensions between language and theology, is extremely significant for the study of African Christianity (cf. Hastings 1984, 371ff). The vernacular issue in African Christianity has recently been explored in depth by Lamin Sanneh (1989 and 1993) and Kwame Bediako (1995b, 59-73).

19. The process of reducing a taped account into writing introduces varying degrees of interpretation. This is due to the necessary introduction of punctuation marks, paragraphing, and sentence structures that are either not present or are unclear on the tapes. Additionally, the tone of voice, hesitations, and the emotional expressions of the narrator are impossible to reproduce. For these difficulties relating to the transcription of oral texts, see Portelli (1981, 97ff).

20. At the time of this writing the original tapes, copies, and the Dholuo transcription are held by Matthew Ajuoga at his home, Dala Hera, Kisumu, Kenya.

21. Essentially, four English versions of the *Johera Narrative* emerged: the first, literal, word for word translation; the more grammatically correct version; the version edited by Ajuoga; and finally, the version appended to this study, which reflects my further editorial efforts.

22. Matthew Ajuoga is a graduate of St. Paul's United Theological College, Limuru, Kenya, and he also studied at New York City's Union Theological Seminary (pars. 10-11).

23. While it will be, I hope, universally agreed that Ajuoga's account is a "narrative," it may be argued that his text is more about himself than about Johera. However, from my own understandings of Ajuoga's intentions for the text, it is clear that he believes he is telling the story of all Johera. Here can be seen the tensions between individual and communal history, and between the private yet corporate nature of religious experience. Because these dimensions cannot be separated without fundamental damage to the text, I have selected the full title: "Matthew Ajuoga's *Johera Narrative*," to communicate that this is Ajuoga's private version of the story of Johera.

24. I was also influenced by the fact that Janzen and MacGaffey (1974) had employed this method of organizing oral materials arising from African religious experience.

25. The transmissive procedures described in this chapter raise questions about the *Johera Narrative's* orality. Considering that the text as presented in Appendix 1 is the product of the transcription, translation, and editing of four individuals, the nature of the text's orality must be clarified.

First, throughout this study the *Johera Narrative* is referred to as an "oral text," expressing that the narrative originally existed in oral form, yet it has been reduced to writing, thus it is a "text." Second, as an oral text, Ajuoga's narrative represents a significant type of theological material, one described as "oral theology in translation" (see Chapter 9 below). Third, the orality of the *Johera Narrative* derives primarily, not from its syntax which has been altered in the transmissive processes, but rather from its forms, genres, and contents, all significant representations of oral literature (see Chapter 8 below).

Chapter Five: The Kenyan Legacy

1. For ease of expression, in this chapter, I will use the general term "historical" to include the social, political, and economic dimensions of the text's setting.

2. A discussion of this debate in second century Graeco-Roman culture is found in Bediako (1992). An excellent example of more recent Roman Catholic thinking on this issue is Shorter (1988), and Taber (1991) provides an historical overview of Protestant approaches to the role of culture in missiology.

3. For a discussion of the issue of Gospel translation, see Sanneh (1989).

4. Throughout the remainder of this study, I will use the terms "crisis," "stress," and "tension" more or less synonymously in regard to the historical and religious contexts of the *Johera Narrative*. "Crisis" is here understood to be "a deeply felt frustration or basic problem with which routine methods, secular or sacred, cannot cope. Any massive helplessness at a critical juncture may be a crisis..." (La Barre 1971, 11).

5. This thesis, I believe, is not only supported by the contents and tone of the *Johera Narrative*, but also by my conversations with Matthew Ajuoga.

6. An excellent and lengthy, yet dated, bibliographical essay of the literature related to the role of crisis in social and religious change is La Barre (1971). This paradigm is also used by Wallace (1956), and specifically in regard to Christianity in Africa by Bureau (1968).

7. For example, La Barre (1971).

8. A classic example is Baeta (1962).

9. While numerous excellent volumes relating to general Kenyan history are available, the two most helpful for the completion of this study have been by Ochieng' (1989b and 1992). Their value is primarily due to their recent and local, even Nyanza Luo, interpretations; Ochieng' is Nyanza Luo.

It will be noted that in writing this section I have relied heavily upon the interpretations of Bethwell A. Ogot (1963). This can be justified by the fact that Professor Ogot is a veteran scholar with an international reputation, and his article represents the only available detailed analysis of the effects of British administration in Nyanza. His interpretations of these and other events, rather than being discounted by more recent scholarship, have actually been accepted as fundamental. Additionally, I have found Ogot's interpretations especially relevant for this study because they reflect popular Nyanza Luo interpretations. Not only is Professor Ogot himself Nyanza Luo, but he and Matthew Ajuoga have a long-standing friendship. Given that people act upon their perception of the facts, I believe Ogot's interpretations are most helpful in recreating and understanding the crisis among the Nyanza Luo during this period.

10. Ogot (1963, 258) provides an example of one popular Omera verse:

> Oh, the Lindi road was dusty,
> And the Lindi road was long
> But the chap w'at did the hardest graft,
> And the chap w'at did the most wrong,
> Was the Kavirondo porter, with 'is Kavirondo song.
> It was "Porter, njoo hapa!"
> It was "Omera, hya git!"
> And Omera didn't grumble,
> He simply did his bit.

11. Walter Owen served in Uganda from 1904 to 1918 (Hewitt 1971, 140).

12. An excellent description and interpretation of Owen's Nyanza career is Spencer (1983).

13. Matthew Ajuoga's impression that Walter Owen "appealed" to England on behalf of the Luo probably relates to the fact that much of Owen's campaign in East Africa was published in the Manchester Guardian (Hewitt 1971, 169). For Matthew Ajuoga's own appeal to England in 1958, see Appendix 1, paragraph 241.

14. A recent testimony to the forceful and enduring impact of missionary modeling in Africa is Nthamburi (1992). Indeed, a crucial part of Jonathan Bonk's argument (1992) is based upon the local impact of what is observed as opposed to what is heard. In my own missionary experience, I have often been surprised and humbled by African perceptions of my overall lifestyle, which usually focus more on attitudes, behaviour, and bearing than upon my stated positions. Thus, what is caught is often more significant than what is taught.

15. My interpretation of this period as one of mounting crisis is based, in part, upon Berman and Lonsdale (1992a and b). These volumes have provided crucial background information to the general social climate in Kenya during this period.

16. The article by Zeleza (1989) provides a detailed description and analysis of the economic conditions during and after the Second World War.

17. According to B. A. Ogot, the relative ineffectiveness of the Kenya Africa Union in Nyanza was due to Gikuyu dominance of the organization, and its inability to effectively organize itself among the Nyanza Luo (1963, 269-270).

18. The literature related to Mau Mau is now vast and diverse. The treatment by Buijtenhuijs (1971) represents the initial scholarly interpretation of Mau Mau as a purely Gikuyu political phenomenon, and Furley (1972) provides an excellent introduction to the breadth of later scholarly approaches and analyses. Buijtenhuijs (1982) offers a detailed bibliographic essay of Mau Mau scholarship from the 1950's to the early 1980's, and Furedi (1989) details the social basis of the movement. Berman (1992) and Presley (1992) are

examples of recent revisionist interpretations of the wider significance of Mau Mau. For the purposes of this study, however, the article by Lonsdale (1990) has been most valuable, because of its interpretation of Mau Mau as a product of the stresses present in post-war Kenya.

19. Oginga Odinga's political philosophy and career are detailed in his autobiography (1992).

20. Johera's split from the Anglican Church as understood within the paradigm of crisis resolution is discussed in Chapter 10.

21. The paradigm of mental and social stress for understanding African initiatives in post-war Kenya is the thesis of Lonsdale's article (1990).

22. Of the 297 paragraphs contained in the *Johera Narrative*, only 67 (23%) are not directly related to the late Kenyan colonial period, 1939-1963. The paragraphs not related to this period are: 3, 11, 15-22, 24-25, 58-66, 89, 239-240, 254-297.

23. According to the 1989 Kenya census as cited in *The Standard* (Nairobi), dated 12 March 1994, the Luo, who form the majority in Nyanza, are the third largest ethnic group in Kenya. The Luo number 2,653,932, while the Gikuyu number 4.45 million, and the Luhya 3.08 million.

24. See note 22 above.

Chapter Six: The Christian Legacy

1. Because of the scarcity and nature of the available sources relevant to the work of the CMS in Nyanza, because the CMS has had and most certainly will have further opportunities to offer its perspectives on these events, and because of this study's desire to move toward an "inside" interpretation and offer Johera's perspective, this section will seek to interpret these events based upon my understanding of the *Johera Narrative* and other Johera materials, and from private conversations. This presentation, consequently, will differ from the CMS version, and will provide a necessary counterbalance to the "official" CMS versions of these events.

Because of the closure of the CMS archives for the period most crucial for this period (post-1949), I have had to rely upon less specific sources which do not focus exclusively on CMS efforts among the Nyanza Luo; sources specific to CMS efforts among the Nyanza Luo are not currently available.

Nevertheless, the available sources have been consulted. The most informative are all "in-house" interpretations (Church of Province of Kenya 1994, Hewitt 1971, Murray 1985, Omulokoli 1981, Stock 1899, 1916), and because of their broad, non-Luo, and frequently hagiographic perspectives, these have been of only limited value. Grove's classic chronicle (1954, 1955, 1958) was useful, and additionally several monographs have also been consulted (Oliver 1952, Strayer 1978, Temu 1972).

2. The other Anglican missionary societies were the Society for the Propagation of the Gospel (SPG) and the Society for the Promotion of Christian Knowledge (SPCK).

3. In fact, at its founding the CMS was called "The Society for Missions to Africa and the East." However, the society's popular name, "The Church" missionary society became official in 1812 (Murray 1985, 8).

4. Taylor's (1958a) classic study is still the best comprehensive assessment of early CMS work in Buganda. A concise, more recent summary has been offered by Ward (1991b).

5. An excellent interpretation of Henry Venn and his policies is Shenk (1983).

6. "Kavirondo" was the name originally given to the area east of Lake Victoria by Swahili-speaking traders. The CMS officially used this term until the region was transferred to the Mombasa diocese in 1921, when "Nyanza" was used (Hewitt 1971, 138).

7. Ajuoga records his years at Maseno school in paragraphs 5, 22 and 23. Oginga Odinga's experiences at Maseno as both student and teacher are detailed in his autobiography (1992, 30-60). Although Odinga's criticisms reflect his anti-Western evaluation, Ajuoga's praise and appreciation for early CMS educational policy (pars. 65-66) more accurately reflects the popular, grassroots sentiment.

8. The CMS was not alone in sending its least able missionaries to Africa. According to Andrew Walls, "The heavy artillery of the missionary movement was deployed in Asia...," and the "celestial cannon fodder" was left for Africa (1996, 184).

9. Paragraph 62 expresses the fond familiarity the Luo developed with J. J. Willis. His popular nickname, *Ogore*, is allegedly a result of Willis's frequent mispronunciation of the informal Dholuo greeting, *Oyawre*, a mistake made during his early days of language learning.

10. The significance of Maseno for the CCA is further explored in Chapter 10.

11. From Kisumu, Mombasa is an exhausting and expensive overland journey of approximately 600 km., yet it is a relatively cheap and easy ferry trip of roughly 280 km. to Kampala. The major cities of Eastern Uganda (Mbale and Jinja) are even more accessible from Nyanza.

12. In early 1949 the Kenyan colonial government appointed a committee, chaired by CMS missionary and then Archdeacon Leonard J. Beecher (later to become Archbishop of the newly formed Province of East Africa [1960]), to make recommendations for African education in Kenya for the coming decade. The recommendations, popularly known as the "Beecher Report," were published in November 1949. This report was controversial, even among some Europeans, and was generally despised by Africans. It recommended only primary education (8 years) for Africans, with secondary schooling to be restricted to only a few elite; only sixteen secondary schools for Africans were to be created by 1957. This report, not only was understood to be a reversal of previous CMS and government policy, but was also considered by many to be racist and paternalistic, aimed at perpetuating colonialism and the servile position of Africans in Kenya (Anderson 1970, 39, 139; Church of the Province of Kenya 1994, 89-90).

I was never successful in locating a copy of the "Beecher Report." However, among the available CMS archival materials (Overseas Division-Africa 1935/59 G3A5 e1) was a letter of Alfred Stanway to the African Secretary, CMS, London (5 September 1949) which offers a detailed overview of the contents of the Report. This report confirms the popular African disdain.

13. These societies and the dates of their establishments in Nyanza are: 1902, American Friends; 1904, Mill Hill Fathers; 1906, Church of God, Seventh Day Adventists, Nilotic Independent Mission, Apostolic Faith Mission; 1911, African Inland Mission (Rosberg and Nottingham 1966, 17).

14. Strayer (1978, 79-159) offers an excellent discussion of the nature of African Christian frustrations, not with Christianity, but with "missionary absolutism" (1978, 158). These conditions are demonstrated by the appearance of Christian independency throughout Kenya during this period, an issue examined in the next chapter.

15. Despite widespread Anglican allegations of Ajuoga's arrogance, his letters to the authorities in Kenya portray a very different spirit. Their contents are reasonable, and the tone is humble. I detect no insolence or insubordination, unless the very act of sincerely asking questions is so interpreted. Should not a Rural Dean express pastoral concern?

16. Regardless of my numerous sincere attempts to discover a thoughtful CMS analysis of these issues, I was never successful in locating an informant who could rise above a cursory assessment which failed to seriously address Ajuoga's concerns.

17. Ajuoga's construction of the shared identity of himself and Johera, based upon this tradition of reform, is further discussed in Chapter 10.

18. While Jocelyn Murray (1975) has provided the most comprehensive bibliography on the East African Revival to date, I have nevertheless experienced difficulties in the writing of this section related to the nature of these sources. The available materials are all limited in scope, and consequently at the time of this writing, no comprehensive chronicle or assessment of the East African Revival was available. Consequently, basic facts were obtained from the monographs noted within the text.

Once again the perspective presented here is my reconstruction of Matthew Ajuoga's interpretation, a version which provides an inside African view of the darker side of the revival.

Most of the published interpretations of the East African Revival are less than balanced, either because of a romantic tendency (e.g., Church 1981 and Langford-Smith 1954), or due to limited and distant knowledge (e. g., Warren 1954). Given the preeminence of such sources which fail to seriously address the moral and doctrinal excesses of the Revival and their significance, Matthew Ajuoga's perspectives are especially welcomed. His narrative of the contentions produced by the Revival—and others like it—while unsavoury and controversial, must be considered if a balanced understanding of the lasting significance of the East African Revival is to be gained.

19. The anti-church effect of the East African Revival is highlighted within the *Johera Narrative*, and will be examined later in this chapter.

20. In my opinion, the most serious study of the schismatic effect of the East African Revival is still that of F. B. Welbourn (1961). This vestige of the Revival and its significance continues to be, perhaps surprisingly, widely ignored. This reflects a myopic, Euro-centric, and "white-washed" approach to the history of African Christianity, in which only the structures and histories of the ecclesiastical "establishment" (mission-founded) at their best are given serious attention; the stories and experiences of the "dissenters" are treated as insignificant.

21. The 126 paragraphs which explicitly relate to the Revival are 1, 12-13, 24-57, 67-131, and 152-175. This personal experience of the East African Revival offers an interesting comparison and counterbalance to that of Joe Church (1981).

22. The Wahamaji were accepted back into the Anglican Church in 1955 (pars. 78, 93; Welbourn and Ogot 1966, 41).

Chapter Seven: The Luo Legacy

1. My use of the terms and concepts of "inherited" and "adopted" in describing Matthew Ajuoga's dual religious heritage is borrowed from Andrew Walls (1980). Kwame Bediako (1995b, 91-108) is my source for the term and concept "primal imagination."

2. This term is borrowed from Cox (1996, 69).

3. Andrew Walls's understanding of religious "translation" is based upon the process and impact of Bible translation in the spread of Christianity. Walls's views are expressed in (1990b), and examples of others who share this understanding of the nature of primal religion and Christian interaction are Bediako (1995b, 109-125) and Sanneh (1989, 1993, 1994). A view of translation originating from the other, Christian end of the process, can be found in Kaplan (1986, 170-172).

4. An excellent overview and evaluation of these views is provided in Cox (1996, 64-69).

5. These three overlapping stages which precede and necessitate the period of revitalization are: "the steady state," "the period of increased individual stress," and "the period of cultural distortion" (Wallace 1956, 268-269).

Though originally articulated forty years ago, Wallace's views are still considered foundational for the understanding of many types of social and religious movements (e.g., see Adas 1987).

6. The literature reflecting the relationship between social stress and religious response is vast, yet an excellent bibliographic essay of related literature is La Barre (1971), and more specific studies of religious crisis responses are found in Lanternari (1963) and Turner (1968). Specifically related to Africa, three excellent studies are the classic by Horton (1971), Bureau's (1968), and the one by Assimeng (1978).

7. For example, see Baylis (1988), J. Brown (1984), and Schmidt (1988).

8. Mbiti (1981, 1989) and Parrinder (1969, 17-97).

9. Excellent descriptions of the Luo primal religious world are found in Dirven (1970, 30-35), Hauge (1974), Ocholla-Ayayo (1976), Odinga (1992, 1-16), and p'Bitek (1971).

10. A basic explanation of Luo genealogy is found in Ochieng' (1992, 18-20).

11. An elaboration of the role of land in the production of Luo identity is found in Cohen and Odhiambo (1989, 9-42).

12. Examples of primal Luo prayers and a discussion of Luo sacrifices can be found in Hauge (1974, 101-107).

13. My use of the term "mantic" is borrowed from Anderson and Johnson (1995a), and is used to refer to any of the primal religious specialists who were believed to possess esoteric religious knowledge. These would include diviners, seers, oracles, ritual experts, spirit mediums, witch-doctors, and prophets (Anderson and Johnson 1995a, 2).

14. A representative overview of the belief in the afterlife in African primal religion can be found in Mbiti (1989, 149-165).

15. For a more detailed discussion of primal Luo beliefs in the afterlife, see P'bitek (1971, 42-43), and for the Luo understanding of the role of the ancestors, see Hauge (1974, 71-77) and P'bitek (1971, 10-40).

16. An excellent description and interpretation of the primal Luo understanding of daily and seasonal time and history is found in Dietler and Herbich (1993). Cohen and Odhiambo (1989) present several modern examples of how the present is guided by the past among the Luo.

17. John Mbiti (1981, 31-39) provides a general summary discussion of African ideas of the universe, and his introduction to the role and use of religious objects in African primal religions can be found in (1981, 141-149).

18. A discussion of the meaning and significance of Luo naming customs is found in Dietler and Herbich (1993, 250ff).

19. For example, see Ajuoga (1956b).

20. The two major schisms within the CCA, referred to in pars. 258-264, were to a large extent a result of Ajuoga and the CCA's Christian conservatism.

21. For example, this attitude is clear from his sermonette, recorded in pars. 207-223.

22. For example, Ajuoga's separation with the Anglican Church, in part, was due to his greater toleration for polygamy, a position which he still maintains (see Chapter 10).

23. Matthew Ajuoga's translation of a concern for "holy place" is evident in the symbolism of Maseno, an issue taken up in Chapter 10. The Luo primal monistic view of life has contributed to the CCA's concern for wholistic ministry; see pars. 266-286.

24. The specific focus of Anderson and Johnson's investigation (1995b) is East Africa. However, because of the diffusion and sharing of the prophetic traditions among the peoples of East Africa, including the Luo, the existence and significance of the prophetic traditions among the Luo's neighbours is particularly significant for this study. Waller (1995) discusses this common mantic tradition, as well as the development of the prophetic tradition among the Maasai and Gikuyu. David Anderson (1995) describes the mantics among

Endnotes 309

the Kalenjin and Maragoli, and Ambler (1995, 233) notes the presence and significance of more trans-ethnic African prophets in Nairobi. An earlier study by Jackson (1972) examined the prophetic tradition among the Kamba.

25. The rise of prophets outside East Africa during the colonial era has been examined, for example, by MacGaffey (1983) and Sundkler (1948).

26. The continuing importance of the East African prophetic tradition in the present is examined by Lonsdale (1995). Anderson (1995) documents the rise of prophets among the Kalenjin and Maasai in the nineteenth century, Ambler (1995) notes the rise of prophets in central Kenya during the same period, and Jackson (1972) examines the same phenomenon among the Kamba.

27. For Ajuoga's narration of his initial "call," see pars. 7-11. Yet, Ajuoga's interpretation of this call must be understood within the context of his life's work as recorded throughout his text.

On different occasions, I questioned Bishop Ajuoga about the significance of his name, *ajuoga*, and his consistent answer illustrates his synthesis between his two religious traditions. Ajuoga maintains that his name was given to him in memory of his grandfather, who was an *ajuoga* in the primal sense, yet Matthew does not see himself—at least consciously—in that primal role. However, while he does not understand himself to bear the title *ajuoga* with all its primal content, he nevertheless serves as a Christian *ajuoga*, leading his people in times and personal and communal crisis. While the content has been modified, the basic structure has been translated.

28. Matthew Ajuoga's major theological innovations are discussed in Chapter 10.

29. These issues are further examined in Chapter 10 below.

30. Perhaps the classic example of this Afro-centric approach to the history of Christianity in Africa is Sanneh (1983).

31. This figure is my own estimate based upon the available yet incomplete statistics.

The earliest AICs among the Luo and proximate areas, with their dates of formation, are:

   1907: Nomiya Luo Mission (Luo)
   1913: Mumbo Cult (Luo and Abagusii)
   1913: Malakite Church (Uganda)
   1916: Roho Movement (Luo)
   1927: *Dini ya Roho* (Southern Luhyia)
   1929: African Orthodox Church (Uganda)
   1934: Gospel Furthering Fellowship (Luo and Luhyia)
   1943: *Dini ya Msambwa* (Luhyia and Luo)
   1948: Christian Universal Evangelical Union (Luo)
   1952: *Dini ya Mariam* (Luo)

The most helpful sources for this section have been: Barrett (1968 and 1973); Barrett and Padwick (1989); Church of the Province of Kenya (1994); Maxon (1989); Ochieng' (1992); Rosberg and Nottingham (1966); Were (1972); and, Wipper (1977).

32. Bildad Kaggia's story is recounted in his autobiography (1975).

Chapter Eight: A Literary Survey

1. Many attempts have been made to categorize the different forms of oral messages. For example, Finnegan (1970, 55-76) lists three major forms: poetry, prose, and special forms; then, each major form contains several more specific types of messages.

2. Because personal accounts may become group tradition over time (Vansina 1985, 17), I believe that Ajuoga's account will eventually form the basis for the more "official" and communal story of Johera. My interaction with various members of Johera lends support to this belief.

3. These issues are discussed further in Chapter 10.

4. My use and understanding of the synonymous terms "Documents of Life" and "Life Documents" comes from Plummer (1983, 13-38).

5. Bertaux (1981, 7) makes a further distinction between a "life story" and a "life history," however, for the purposes of this study his distinctions were not relevant. Even so, his general discussion of the value of life stories has been extremely helpful.

6. The importance of Ajuoga's text for the study of Narrative Theology is detailed in the following chapter.

7. paragraphs 1-23; 8% of the narrative is devoted to this topic.

8. paragraphs 17-22.

9. paragraphs 24-66, 166-168; 16% of the narrative is devoted to this topic.

10. Both these topics are discussed further in Chapter 10.

11. paragraphs 176-199, 202-206, 224-240, 247-249, 253-257, 265-285; 25% of the narrative is devoted to this topic.

12. paragraphs 67-82, 162-165, 169-175, 200-201, 250- 252, 258-264, 286-297; 16% of the narrative is devoted to this topic.

13. paragraphs 207-223; this represents 6% of the total narrative.

14. paragraphs 83-161, 241-246 are devoted to this topic; this represents 29% of the total narrative. The three letters on which Ajuoga comments are Ajuoga (1956b, 1958a, 1958b), and the pamphlet is "The Light" (Ajuoga 1956c).

15. Vansina provides a detailed discussion of the various roles played by oral literary genres, and of the cultural specificity of various genres (1985, 79-83).

16. A good general discussion of *pakruok* as a literary genre is found in Amuka (1992). The prominence of this genre in Luo history is seen in Ogot (1967) and examples of its use in traditional oral literature is found in Liyong (1972, 57- 65).

17. Often during informal conversations Ajuoga would speak of his Luo heritage, and of his concern for his people in the present economic and political climate. And, while he is able to criticize some of the traditional practices perpetuated by his people (e.g. wife inheritance), he clearly is proud of most of his heritage.

18. At the time of this writing a general debate is on-going between those Kenyan leaders considered to be "nationalists" and those labelled as "tribalists." Ajuoga sees himself, and is widely seen, as being a "nationalist." An example of Ajuoga's political involvements and his popular acceptance as a Luo spokesman is his leadership of the Church and State Cooperation and Development Committee. This committee, formed in 1995 by President Moi, is an attempt to foster better relations between the KANU government and the Luo. Matthew Ajuoga was chosen by both the President and his Luo peers to serve as Vice-Chairman of this committee.

19. It must be noted that, in its earliest Christian usages, *apologia* was intended to be a defense of the faith in general, and not primarily a justification of the personal faith of the individual apologist. Even so, it should be recognized that any attempt to defend *the* faith is in fact an exposition of one's personal understanding and appropriation of that faith. Thus, in focusing on his personal faith Ajuoga is still operating within the ancient tradition of the first Christian apologists.

20. A good discussion of the generic genre of confession is found in Spender (1980).

21. This general knowledge of Christian history is illustrated by Ajuoga's references in pars. 123-125 and 211- 217.

22. These observations are based upon my broad familiarity with evangelical Kenyan Christianity through my affiliation with Daystar University. In Kenya, evangelical Christians from all affiliations tend to evaluate the quality of personal faith on the basis of the presence or absence of one's testimony. It is commonly said, for example, that "s/he has a wonderful testimony," or alternatively that "s/he professes but has no testimony.

Chapter Nine: A Theological Assessment

1. At the time of this writing, a Daystar colleague, Kenya Luo, and CCA member James Kombo, is considering carrying out his own linguistic analysis of the text.

2. It is conceded that, while oral theologies might be enigmatic and obscure to the uninitiated, they are clear and authoritative for the members of those communities from which such theologies originate.

3. The rarity of oral theological source materials was one of the primary factors in the IAMS' call for the intensive gathering and preservation of such materials (IAMS 1988, 153).

4. Because of the innate inter-relatedness of all theological reflection and praxis, it is conceded that often it is difficult to determine the direction of the theological process. Nevertheless, my scrutiny of Matthew Ajuoga's *Johera Narrative* convinces me of the validity of the position being argued here, and my experiences in observing Matthew Ajuoga's ministry also supports this contention. If Ajuoga's experience had been shaped primarily by his theology, then he might never have formed Johera!

5. These insights have benefited from the writings of Sallie McFague TeSelle (1975a, 1975b). While these writings technically focus on Narrative

and Biographical Theology in the West, I have found them helpful in approaching Ajuoga's oral theology in translation. I have discovered that the Western theological approach most fruitful in understanding African oral theology is that of Narrative Theology. These issues are discussed in more detail later in this chapter.

6. See Bediako (1989, 1992, 1995a, 1995b). It will become evident that I have drawn heavily upon the writings of Kwame Bediako for the insights expressed in this chapter, and this is primarily so for two reasons. First, Bediako's thinking is more recent and reflects the "cutting edge" of various issues related to African Theology. Second, Bediako's thinking is fresh, building upon the theologizing of the past without being imprisoned in its quagmires. Rather, Bediako blazes new theological trails, which in my experience, more accurately reflect the concerns of the grassroots.

7. Molyneux notes that "the two theologies [oral and written] need each other, whereas all too often they are mutually out of touch." While oral theology keeps written theology relevant, written theology keeps oral theology balanced and universal (1993, 378).

8. An example of this contribution of cutting-edge and mostly relevant written theologies by those actively involved in African Church life is Schreiter (1991).

9. It is noted that all academic theology, not just that in and of Africa, tends to be the specialized reserve of an elite. It might also be argued that Matthew Ajuoga, himself, is a member of an elite, primarily because of his education, travels, and social position. While it is conceded that "elite" is a relative term, I want to argue that because of his long experience at the grassroots level, as opposed to working in a strictly academic setting, Matthew Ajuoga's theology more closely resembles that of his grassroot church; in a very real sense he does speak and theologize for an "actual life" Christian community.

10. For example, see Mugambi (1989a and 1989b) and Nyamiti (1984).

11. For example, see Appendix 1, pars. 85, 86.

12. Based upon the more general thinking of Andrew Walls (1980), the significance of identity for African Theology has been more closely examined by Kwame Bediako (1989, 1992, 1995b) and Gordon Molyneux (1993).

13. My use of the term "religious worlds" is taken from Paden (1988), whose thoughts have provided helpful stimulation for my understanding of Matthew Ajuoga's religious synthesis.

14. The beginnings of this shifting focus can be seen in Ajayi (1965), and a later illustration of the completion of this process is Sanneh (1983).

15. Johera's differences with both the Wahamaji and the CMS in Nyanza were discussed in Chapter 6.

16. Due to the nature of most AICs it is impossible to arrive at an accurate representation of their numerical strength on the continent. However, an enlightened estimate for 1985 (Barrett and Padwick 1989, ii) offered the figures of 7170 separate denominations in 43 African countries; 74,000 places of worship with over 32.7 million adherents. These numbers represent an addition of 850,000 new members per year, and they together illustrate the significance of AICs for a balanced understanding of Christianity in Africa.

17. An excellent survey of the early approaches to the study of African Instituted Churches is Fernandez (1964 and 1978). An example of the condescending and paternalistic perspective towards AICs is Jassy (1973), and Barrett's (1968, 269ff) comments are representative of those studies which saw the origins of African Christian Independency in terms of the "failure of missions." A survey of the many early studies of these phenomena from one non-religious perspective is presented in the comprehensive bibliographic essay by La Barre (1971).

18. While exceptions exist for all the following general observations concerning studies of AICs, I nevertheless believe they accurately portray the general trends of the past literature, as well as the current need for additional focus on materials from the inside. Examples of this most distant approach to the study of AICs are Barrett (1968) and Welbourn and Ogot (1966).

19. Examples of this second, less distant approach to the study of AICs are Sundkler (1948) and Turner (1967a, 1967b).

20. Examples of studies which utilize information from inside AICs, yet employ outside and imposed categories, are Nussbaum (1985), Oosthuizen (1967), and Turner (1965).

21. Examples of efforts to allow AICs to speak for themselves, in their words and categories are Hexham (1994) and Krabill (1989).

22. For an example of the continuation of the early preoccupation with the origins of AICs and the use of dated materials, see Antunes da Silva (1993); and, for an example of the perceived ability of dated AIC studies to communicate the current state of AICs, see Nthamburi (1991, 54-61). Additionally, in my experience within the Kenyan evangelical community, I continue to be amazed at just how formative and final the very preliminary and general conclusions of Barrett (1968) remain for both African and non-African academics, as well as for Western missionaries.

23. A more detailed examination of the *Johera Narrative's* diachronic narration of legitimization is offered in the following chapter.

24. For example, Alward Shorter (1974, 93) prophesied the eventual movement towards each other of the AICs and the "mission" churches, as did John Mbiti (1970, 34ff). Andrew Walls (1979, 51) also foretold that, over time, the distinctions between "older" and "independent" churches would become less meaningful. This trend was later observed in Liberia by Paul Gifford (1993, 196ff).

25. The more recent discussion of the theological value of narratives stems from the thinking of H. Richard Niebuhr (1960). An excellent overview of the types, problems, and benefits of Narrative Theology is found in Stroup (1981, 70- 97), and the entire October 1983 (37:4) edition of *Interpretation* is devoted to an analysis of this approach. An excellent overview of Biographical Theology is McClendon (1974), and Fowler et al. (1980) illustrates the value of this focus.

26. An examination of the role of the Bible in the *Johera Narrative* as it relates to Johera's restitutionism is presented in the following chapter.

27. A recent example of this method of African theological expression is Schreiter (1991).

28. Gwinyai Muzorewa (1985) provides an excellent overview of this approach.

29. Stephen Crites's article (1971) provides a lengthy presentation of his argument for the essential narrative quality of all human experiences.

Chapter Ten: A Listener's Guide

1. "New Religious Movements should be taken seriously, and not be viewed as marginal and curiously eccentric groups on the periphery of Christianity, as they were often regarded in the past" (A. Anderson 1995, 286).

2. The abiding significance of the theme of primitivism in the history of Christianity, especially in the United States, is illustrated by the 1991 conference, "Christian Primitivism and Modernization: Coming to Terms with our Age," held at Pepperdine University (CA) and funded by Pew Charitable Trusts. The papers of this conference are published in Hughes (1995).

3. Two examples of the Western relevance of missiological insights gained from non-Western lands are Leslie Newbigin's "Gospel and Our Culture" movement, and the 1996-97 "Missiology and Western Culture" project sponsored by the Pew Charitable Trusts.

4. I am indebted to James Krabill (1989, 391-412) for this quote from Sundkler and its usefulness here.

5. It is significant that Matthew Ajuoga's use of the "legal-rational" method for establishing legitimacy was primarily directed at missionaries and other, predominantly Western, audiences outside Johera (see Ajuoga 1956b and Chapter 6).

6. The official CCA position regarding polygamy and the sacraments is documented in Welbourn and Ogot (1966, 70-71). An excellent interpretation of the significance of this issue within the CCA is also offered (1966, 145-146).

An interesting survey conducted in 1969 among Kenyan Anglican clergy found "...that the clergy of the ex-CMS dioceses are in full cry at the head of the movement to baptize polygynists" (Newing 1970, 139). Accordingly, this survey confirms that Johera's position and practice regarding polygamy, while opposed to that of the CMS and most Western missions, was consistent with grassroot African opinion, even "faithful" Anglican clergy.

7. The CCA's ecumenical efforts are highlighted in Barrett and Padwick (1989). While Barrett and Padwick do not use the term "legitimacy," they do recognize that the conciliar efforts of AICs are related, at least in part, to their desire for "recognition" (1989, 12). This acceptance by more universal bodies, however, has a definite legitimizing effect. So, while we are not here suggesting that the efforts of the CCA or other AICs in ecumenism are entirely motivated by their desire to formulate legitimacy, this intention is still present and crucial for the churches' more recent development.

8. An excellent, concise overview of the abiding significance of the motif of restitutionism in Protestant Christianity is Allen (1988). An indication of the importance of this theme in the universal Christian story was the decision of the American Academy of Religion to devote the entire March 1976 issue of their

journal, the *Journal of the American Academy of Religion* (44:1), to studies of Christian restitutionism.

Reference List

Adas, Michael. 1987. *Prophets of Rebellion: Millenarian Protest Movements against European Colonial Order.* Cambridge: Cambridge University Press.

African Spiritual Churches' Association. 1985. *Speaking for Ourselves.* Braamfontein, South Africa: Institute for Contextual Theology.

Ajayi, J. F. Ade. 1965. *Christian Missions in Nigeria 1841-1891: The Making of a New Elite.* Evanston, IL: Northwestern University Press.

Ajuoga, A. Matthew. 1955. Letter from Eldoret, Kenya to Reverend R. Peaston, 15 November. Typed transcript privately held by Matthew Ajuoga. A copy has been desposited in the Harold W. Turner Collection, Selly Oak Colleges Central Library, Birmingham, U. K.

──────. 1956a. Letter from Eldoret, Kenya to The Right Reverend L. J. Beecher, Bishop of Mombasa, 13 February. Typed transcript privately held by Matthew Ajuoga. A copy has been deposited in the Harold W. Turner Collection, Selly Oak Colleges Central Library, Birmingham, U. K.

──────. 1956b. Letter from Eldoret, Kenya to the Reverend R. Peaston, 5 July. Typed transcript privately held by Matthew Ajuoga. A copy has been deposited in the Harold W. Turner Collection, Selly Oak Colleges Central Library, Birmingham, U. K.

_____. 1956c. *The Light*, letter/pamphlet from Eldoret, Kenya to the Vicar General, the Venerable P. G. Bostock, 1 June. Typed transcript privately held by Matthew Ajuoga. A copy has been deposited in the Harold W. Turner Collection, Selly Oak Colleges Central Library, Birmingham, U. K.

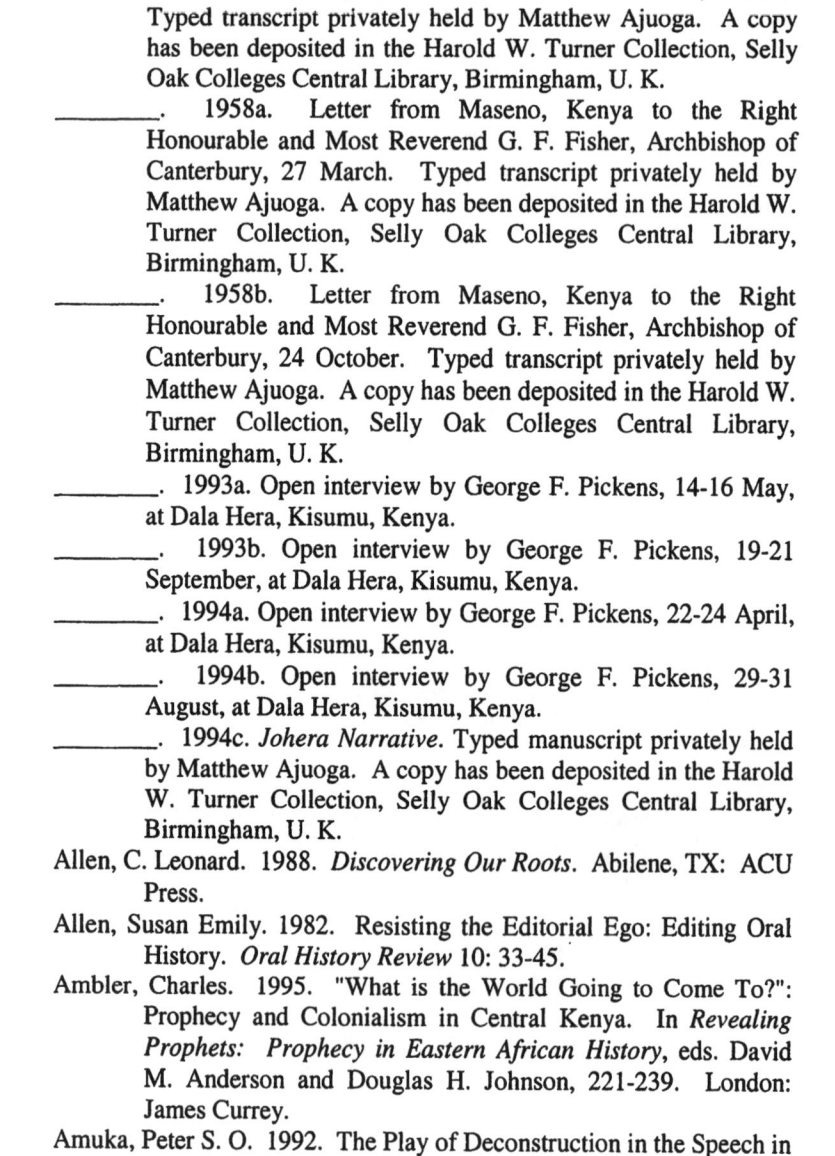

_____. 1958a. Letter from Maseno, Kenya to the Right Honourable and Most Reverend G. F. Fisher, Archbishop of Canterbury, 27 March. Typed transcript privately held by Matthew Ajuoga. A copy has been deposited in the Harold W. Turner Collection, Selly Oak Colleges Central Library, Birmingham, U. K.

_____. 1958b. Letter from Maseno, Kenya to the Right Honourable and Most Reverend G. F. Fisher, Archbishop of Canterbury, 24 October. Typed transcript privately held by Matthew Ajuoga. A copy has been deposited in the Harold W. Turner Collection, Selly Oak Colleges Central Library, Birmingham, U. K.

_____. 1993a. Open interview by George F. Pickens, 14-16 May, at Dala Hera, Kisumu, Kenya.

_____. 1993b. Open interview by George F. Pickens, 19-21 September, at Dala Hera, Kisumu, Kenya.

_____. 1994a. Open interview by George F. Pickens, 22-24 April, at Dala Hera, Kisumu, Kenya.

_____. 1994b. Open interview by George F. Pickens, 29-31 August, at Dala Hera, Kisumu, Kenya.

_____. 1994c. *Johera Narrative*. Typed manuscript privately held by Matthew Ajuoga. A copy has been deposited in the Harold W. Turner Collection, Selly Oak Colleges Central Library, Birmingham, U. K.

Allen, C. Leonard. 1988. *Discovering Our Roots*. Abilene, TX: ACU Press.

Allen, Susan Emily. 1982. Resisting the Editorial Ego: Editing Oral History. *Oral History Review* 10: 33-45.

Ambler, Charles. 1995. "What is the World Going to Come To?": Prophecy and Colonialism in Central Kenya. In *Revealing Prophets: Prophecy in Eastern African History*, eds. David M. Anderson and Douglas H. Johnson, 221-239. London: James Currey.

Amuka, Peter S. O. 1992. The Play of Deconstruction in the Speech in Africa: The Role of *Pakruok* and *Ngero* in Telling Culture in Dholuo. In *Reflections on Theories and Methods in Oral*

Literature, ed. Okoth Okombo and Jane Nandwa, 74-96. Nairobi: Kenya Oral Literature Association.
Anderson, Allan. 1995. Challenges and Prospects for Research into African Initiated Churches in Southern Africa. *Missionalia* 23 (November): 283-294.
Anderson, David M. 1995. Visions of the Vanquished: Prophets and Colonialism in Kenya's Western Highlands. In *Revealing Prophets: Prophecy in Eastern African History*, ed. David M. Anderson and Douglas H. Johnson, 164-194. London: James Currey.
Anderson, David M., and Douglas H. Johnson. 1995a. Revealing Prophets. In *Revealing Prophets: Prophecy in Eastern African History*, ed. David M. Anderson and Douglas H. Johnson, 1-26. London: James Currey.
Anderson, David M., and Douglas H. Johnson, eds. 1995b. *Revealing Prophets: Prophecy in Eastern African History*. London: James Currey.
Anderson, John. 1970. *The Struggle for the School*. London: Longman.
Antunes da Silva, Jose. 1993. African Indpendent Churches: Origin and Development. *Anthropos* 88: 393-402.
Assimeng, Max. 1978. Crisis, Identity, and Integration in African Religion. In *Identity and Religion: International Cross-Cultural Approaches*, ed. Hans Mol, 97-118. London: SAGE Publications, LTD.
Ayandele, E. A. 1979. *African Historical Studies*. London: Frank Cass and Company.
Ayandele, E. A., and J. F. Ade Ajayi. 1979. Writing African Church History. In *African Historical Studies*, E. A. Ayandele, 230-252. London: Frank Cass and Company.
Baeta, C. G. 1962. *Prophetism in Ghana*. London: SCM Press.
Barrett, David B. 1968. *Schism and Renewal in Africa: An Analysis of Six Thousand Contemporary Religious Movements*. Nairobi: Oxford University Press.
_____. 1971. Interdisciplinary Theories of Religion and African Independency. In *African Initiatives in Religion*, ed. David B. Barrett, 146-159. Nairobi: East African Publishing House.
Barrett, David B., and T. John Padwick. 1989. *Rise Up and Walk*. Nairobi: Oxford University Press.
Barrett, David B., et al. 1973. *Kenya Churches Handbook: The Development of Kenya Christianity 1498-1973*. Kisumu, Kenya: Evangel Press.

Baylis, P. 1988. *An Introduction to Primal Religions*. Edinburgh: Traditional Cosmology Society.

Becken, H. J. 1992. I Love to Tell the Story: Oral History in the Nazaretha Church. In *Empirical Studies of African Independent/Indigenous Churches*, eds. Gerhardus Oosthuizen and Irving Hexham, 29-48. Lewiston, NY: Edwin Mellen Press.

Bediako, Kwame. 1989. The Roots of African Theology. *International Bulletin of Missionary Research* 13 (April):8-65.

_____. 1992. *Theology and Identity: The Impact of Culture upon Christian Thought in the Second Century and Modern Africa*. Oxford: Regnum.

_____. 1995a. The Significance of Modern African Christianity—A Manifesto. *Studies in World Christianity* 1:1: 51-67.

_____. 1995b. *Christianity in Africa: The Renewal of a Non-Western Religion*. Edinburgh: Edinburgh University Press.

Berger, Peter L. 1967. *The Sacred Canopy: Elements of a Sociological Theory of Religion*. Garden City, NY: Doubleday and Company.

Berger, Peter L., and Brigitte Berger. 1983. *Sociology: A Biographical Approach*. New York: Basic Books, 1972; reprint, Harmondsworth: Penguin Books (page references are to reprint edition).

Berger, Peter L., and Thomas Luckman. 1975. *The Social Construction of Reality*. First published in the U. S. A., 1966; reprint, Harmondsworth: Penguin Books (page references are to reprint edition).

Berman, Bruce. 1992. Bureaucracy and Incumbent Violence: Colonial Administration and the Origins of the "Mau Mau" Emergency. In *Unhappy Valley: Conflict in Kenya and Africa, Book Two: Violence and Ethnicity*, 227-264. London: James Currey.

Berman, Bruce, and John Lonsdale. 1992a. *Unhappy Valley: Conflict in Kenya and Africa, Book One: State and Class*. London: James Currey.

_____. 1992b. *Unhappy Vallley: Conflict in Kenya and Africa, Book Two: Violence and Ethnicity*. London: James Currey.

Bertaux, Daniel. 1981. Introduction. In *Biography and Society: The Life History Approach in the Social Sciences*, ed. Daniel Bertaux, 5-15. Beverly Hills, CA: SAGE Publications.

Bogdan, Robert, and Steven J. Taylor. 1975. *Introduction to Qualitative Research Methods: A Phenomenological*

Approach to the Social Sciences. New York: John Wiley and Sons.

Bonk, Jonathan J. 1992. *Missions and Money: Affluence as a Western Missionary Problem.* Maryknoll, NY: Orbis Books.

Bosch, David J. 1991. *Transforming Mission.* Maryknoll, NY: Orbis Books.

Brown, J. E. 1984. Religion in Primal Societies: North American Indian Religions. In *A Handbook of Living Religions*, ed. J. Hinnells, 392-412. Harmondsworth: Penguin Books.

Brown, Robert McAfee. 1980. Starting Over: New Beginning Points for Theology. *Christian Century* 14 May, 545-549.

Bruner, Edward M. 1986a. Experience and Its Expressions. In *The Anthropology of Experience,* eds. Victor W. Turner and Edward M. Bruner, 3-30. Urbana, IL: University of Illinois Press.

_____. 1986b. Ethnography as Narrative. In *The Anthropology of Experience,* eds. Victor W. Turner and Edward M. Bruner, 139-155. Urbana, IL: University of Illinois Press.

Buijtenhuijs, Robert. 1971. *Le Mouvement <<Mau-Mau>> Une Revolte Paysanne et Anti-coloniale en Afrique Noire.* Paris: Mouton.

_____. 1982. *Essays on Mau Mau: Contributions to Mau Mau Historiography.* Paper No. 17. Leiden: African Studies Centre.

Bureau, R. 1968. Influence de la Christianisation sur les Institutions Traditionnelles des Ethnies Cotieres du Cameroun. In *Christianity in Tropical Africa,* ed. C. G. Baeta, 165-179. London: Oxford University Press.

Christie-Murray, David. 1990. *A History of Heresy.* London: Oxford University Press, 1976; reprint, London: Oxford University Press (page references are to reprint edition).

Church, J. E. 1981. *Quest for the Highest: A Diary of the East African Revival.* Exeter: The Paternoster Press.

Church of the Province of Kenya. 1994. *Rabai to Mumias: A Short History of the Church of the Province of Kenya, 1844-1944.* Nairobi: Uzima.

Cohen, David William, and E. S. Atieno Odhiambo. 1989. *Siaya: The Historical Anthropology of an African Landscape.* Nairobi: Heinemann.

Cox, James L. 1996. The Classification "Primal Religions" as a Non-Empirical Christian Theological Construct. *Studies in World Christianity* 2:1: 55-76.

Crites, Stephen. 1971. The Narrative Quality of Experience. *Journal of the American Academy of Religion* 39 (September): 291-311.
Curtin, Philip D., ed. 1967. *Africa Remembered.* Madison, WI: University of Wisconsin Press.
_____. 1968. Field Techniques for Collecting and Processing Oral Data. *Journal of African History* 9 (3): 367-385.
Daneel, M. L. 1984. Towards a Theologia Africana? The Contribution of Independent Churches to African Theology. *Missionalia* 12 (August): 64-89.
_____. 1993. African Independent Church Pneumatology and the Salvation of All Creation. *International Review of Mission* 82: 143-166.
Denzin, Norman. 1989. *Interpretive Biography.* Newbury Park, CA: SAGE.
Dickson, Kwesi A. 1984. *Theology in Africa.* Maryknoll, NY: Orbis Books.
Dietler, Michael and Ingrid Herbich. 1993. Living on Luo Time: Reckoning, Sequence, Duration, History, and Biography in a Rural African Society. *World Archaeology* 25: 248-260.
Dirven, Peter J. 1970. The Maria Legio: The Dynamics of a Breakaway Church Among the Luo in East Africa. *Doctorate in Missiology* diss., Pontifica Universitas Gregoriana.
Fackre, Gabriel. 1983. Narrative Theology: An Overview. *Interpretation* 37 (October): 340-352.
_____. 1984. *The Christian Story: A Narrative Interpretation of Basic Christian Doctrine.* Grand Rapids, MI: Eerdmans Publishing.
Ferm, Deane William. 1988. *Third World Liberation Theologies.* Maryknoll, NY: Orbis Books, 1986; reprint (page references are to reprint edition).
Fernandez, James W. 1964. African Religious Movements: Types and Dynamics. *Journal of Modern African Studies* 2: 531-549.
_____. 1978. African Religious Movements. *Annual Review of Anthropology* 7: 195-234.
Finnegan, Ruth. 1970. *Oral Literature in Africa.* Oxford: Oxford University Press.
Fisher, G. F. 1958. Letter from Canterbury to A. Matthew Ajuoga, 13 August. Typed transcript privately held by Matthew Ajuoga. A copy has also been deposited in the Harold W. Turner Collection, Selly Oak Colleges Central Library, Birmingham, U. K.

Fowler, James W., Robin W. Lovin, et al. 1980. *Trajectories in Faith: Five Life Stories.* Nashville: Abingdon.
Furedi, Frank. 1989. *The Mau Mau War in Perspective.* London: James Currey.
Furley, O. W. 1972. The Historiography of Mau Mau. In *Politics and Nationalism in Colonial Kenya,* ed. Bethwell A. Ogot, 105-133. Nairobi: East African Publishing House.
Gensichen, Hans-Werner. 1976. Church History in Context. *Lutheran World* 23 (October): 252-261.
Gifford, Paul. 1993. *The Church in Doe's Liberia.* Cambridge: Cambridge University Press.
Githige, Renison Muchiri. 1982. The Mission-State Relationship in Colonial Kenya: A Summary. *Journal of Religion in Africa* 13: 110-125.
Goldberg, Michael. 1982. *Theology and Narrative: A Critical Introduction.* Nashville: Abingdon.
_____. 1983. Expository Article on Exodus 1:13, 14. *Interpretation* 37 (October): 389-391.
Gray, Richard. 1968. Problems of Historical Perspective: The Planting of Christianity in Africa in the Nineteenth and Twentieth Centuries. In *Christianity in Tropical Africa,* ed. C. G. Baeta, 18-30. London: Oxford University Press.
Greschat, Hans-Jurgen. 1990. "The Founder" of Prophet Movements and the Phenomenology of Religion. In *Exploring New Religious Movements,* eds. A. F. Walls and Wilbert R. Shenk, 19-27. Elkhart, IN: Mission Focus.
Groves, C. P. 1954. *The Planting of Christianity in Africa.* Vol. 2. London: Lutterworth Press.
_____. 1955. *The Planting of Christianity in Africa.* Vol. 3. London: Lutterworth Press.
Hastings, Adrian. 1976. *African Christianity: An Essay in Interpretation.* London: Geoffrey Chapman.
_____. 1979. *A History of African Christianity, 1950-1975.* Cambridge: Cambridge University Press.
_____. 1984. On African Theology. *Scottish Journal of Theology.* 37: 359-374.
_____. 1994. *The Church in Africa, 1450-1950.* Oxford: Clarendon Press.
Hauerwas, Stanley, Richard Bondi, and David B. Burrell. 1977. *Truthfulness and Tragedy: Further Investigations in Christian Ethics.* Notre Dame, IN: University of Notre Dame Press.

Hauge, Hans-Egil. 1974. *Luo Religion and Folklore.* Oslo: Scandinavian University Books.
Henige, David. 1982. *Oral Historiography.* New York: Longman.
Hewitt, Gordon. 1971. The Problems of Success: A History of the Church Missionary Society, 1910-1942. Vol. 1, In *Tropical Africa, the Middle East, at Home.* London: SCM Press.
Hexham, Irving, ed. 1994. *The Scriptures of the Amanazareth of Ekuphakamen.* Calgary: University of Calgary Press.
Hill, Samuel S., Jr. 1976. A Typology of American Restitutionism: From Frontier Revivalism and Mormonism to the Jesus Movement. *Journal of the American Academy of Religion* 44 (March): 65-76.
Hollenweger, Walter J. 1989. The Future of Mission and the Mission of the Future. *Occasional Paper,* Number 2, Selly Oak Colleges, Birmingham.
Hoopes, James. 1979. *Oral History: An Introduction for Students.* Chapel Hill, NC: University of North Carolina Press.
Horton, Robin. 1971. *African Conversion.* Africa 41 (April): 85-108.
Hughes, Richard T., ed. 1995. *The Primitive Church in the Modern World.* Urbana, IL: University of Illinois Press.
International Association for Mission Studies. 1988. Some Concerns and Pointers from the Conference. *Mission Studies* 5: 150-153.
Irvine, Cecilia. 1976. The Documentation of Mission in the19th and 20th Centuries. *Missiology* 4 (April): 189-205.
Isichei, Elizabeth. 1977. Ibo Worlds: *An Anthology of Oral Histories and Historical Descriptions.* London: Macmillan.
_____. 1995. *A History of Christianity in Africa: From Antiquity to the Present.* London: SPCK.
Jackson, Kennell. 1972. *An Ethnohistorical Study of the Oral Traditions of the Akamba of Kenya.* Ph.D. diss., University of California, Los Angeles.
Janzen, John M. and Wyatt MacGaffey. 1974. *An Anthology of Kongo Religion: Primary Texts from Lower Zaire.* Lawrence, KS: University of Kansas Press.
Jassy, Marie-France Perrin. 1973. *Basic Community in the African Churches.* Translated by Sister Jeanne Marie Lyons. Maryknoll, NY: Orbis Books.
Jenkins, Paul. 1986. The Roots of African Church History: Some Polemic Thoughts. *International Bulletin of Missionary Research* 10 (April): 67-71.

———. 1988. Archives Report in Documentation, Archives and Bibliography Network. *Mission Studies* 5: 141-143.

Kaggia, Bildad. 1975. *Roots of Freedom, 1921-1963*. Nairobi: East African Publishing House.

Kalu, Ogbu U. 1993. African Church Historiography. In *African Historiography*, ed. Toyin Falola, 166-179. Harlow: Longman.

King, N. Q. 1968. The East African Revival Movement and Evangelism. *Ecumenical Review* 20 (April): 159-162.

Kitshoff, M. C. 1992. Aspects of the Concept "Church" as Understood by a Group of African Independent Churches. In *Empirical Studies of African Independent/Indigenous Churches*, eds. Gerhardus Cornelius Oosthuizen and Irving Hexham, 49-64. Lewiston, NY: Edwin Mellen Press.

Krabill, James. 1989. *Dida Harrist Hymnody 1913-1949: A Historico-Theological Study*. Ph.D. diss., University of Birmingham, UK.

Kritzinger, J. J. 1994. The Past 25 Years of Missiology in South Africa: A Stock-taking Exercise. *Missionalia* 22 (August): 147-162.

La Barre, Weston. 1971. Materials for a History of Studies of Crisis Cults: A Bibliographic Essay. *Current Anthropology* 12 (February): 3-44.

Langford-Smith, Neville. 1954. Revival in East Africa. *International Review of Missions* 43 (January): 77-81.

Lanternari, Vittorio. 1963. *The Religions of the Oppressed*. Translated by Lisa Sergio. London: MacGibbon and Kee.

Liyong, Taban lo, ed. 1972. *Popular Culture of East Africa*. Nairobi: Longman Kenya.

Lonsdale, John. 1989. The Conquest State, 1895-1904. In *A Modern History of Kenya, 1985-1980*, ed. W. R. Ochieng', 6-34. Nairobi: Evans Brothers.

———. 1990. Mau Mau of the Mind: Making Mau Mau and Remaking Kenya. *Journal of African History* 31: 393-421.

———. 1995. The Prayers of Waiyaki: Political Uses of the Kikuyu Past. In *Revealing Prophets: Prophecy in Eastern African History*, eds. David M. Anderson and Douglas H. Johnson, 240-291. London: James Currey.

Lummis, Trevor. 1987. *Listening to History: The Authenticity of Oral Evidence*. London: Hutchinson.

MacGaffey, Wyatt. 1969. The Beloved City: Commentary on a Kimbanguist Text. *Journal of Religion in Africa* 2: 129- 147.

———. 1983. *Modern Kongo Prophets: Religion in a Plural Society*. Bloomington, IN: Indiana University Press.

Maxon, Robert. 1989. The Years of Revolutionary Advance, 1920-1929. In *A Modern History of Kenya, 1895-1980*, ed. W. R. Ochieng', 71-111. Nairobi: Evans Brothers.

Mays, James L. 1983. Editorial. *Interpretation* 37 (October): 339.

Mbiti, John S. 1969. *Concepts of God in Africa*. London: S. P. C. K.

———. 1970. The Future of Christianity in Africa (1970- 2000). *Communio Viatorum: Theological Quarterly* 13: 19- 38.

———. 1981. *Introduction to African Religion*. Nairobi: Heinemann, 1975; reprint (page references are to reprint edition).

———. 1986. *Bible and Theology in African Christianity*. Nairobi: Oxford University Press.

———. 1989. *African Religions and Philosophy*. Nairobi: Heinemann, 1969; reprint (page references are to reprint edition).

McClendon, James William, Jr. 1974. *Biography as Theology: How Life Stories Can Remake Today's Theology*. Nashville: Abingdon Press.

McLoughlin, William G. 1978. *Revivals, Awakenings, and Reform*. Chicago: University of Chicago Press.

Mead, Sidney E. 1956. The Rise of the Evangelical Conception of the Ministry in America. In *The Ministry in Historical Perspectives*, eds. Richard H. Niebuhr and Daniel D. Williams, 207-249. New York: Harper and Brothers.

Mishler, Elliot G. 1986. *Research Interviewing: Context and Narrative*. Cambridge, MA: Harvard University Press.

Mitchell, Robert Cameron. 1970. Religious Protest and Social Change. In *Protest and Power in Black Africa*, eds. R. Rotberg and A. Mazrui, 458-496. New York: Oxford University Press.

Mojola, A. Osotsi. 1993. Vernacularization and the African Independent Churches' Cross-Cultural Encounters: Some Preliminary Observations from Close Quarters. *Africa Theological Journal* 22 (July): 130-146.

Molyneux, K. Gordon. 1993. *African Christian Theology: The Quest for Self-hood*. San Francisco: Mellen Research University Press.

Mugambi, J. N. K. 1989a. *African Christian Theology*. Nairobi: Heinemann.

Reference List 327

———. 1989b. *African Heritage and Contemporary Christianity.* Nairobi: Longman.
Murray, Jocelyn. 1975. A Bibliography on the East African Revival Movement. *Journal of Religion in Africa* 8 (April): 144-147.
———. 1985. *Proclaim the Good News: A Short History of the Church Missionary Society.* London: Hodder and Stroughton.
———. 1994. *Letter from London, 8 November.*
Muzorewa, Gwinyai H. 1985. *The Origins and Development of African Theology.* Maryknoll, NY: Orbis Books.
Newing, Edward G. 1970. The Baptism of Polygamous Families: Theories and Practice in an East African Church. *Journal of Religion in Africa* 3: 130-141.
Niebuhr, H. Richard. 1960. *The Meaning of Revelation.* New York: Macmillan, 1941, reprint 1960 (page references are to reprint edition).
Ngada, N. H. 1985. Preface to *Speaking for Ourselves*, by African Spiritual Churches' Association. Braamfontein: Institute for Contextual Theology.
Nthamburi, Zablon. 1991. *The African Church at the Crossroads.* Nairobi: Uzima Press.
———. 1992. Foreward to *Missions and Money: Affluence as a Western Missionary Problem*, by Jonathan J. Bonk. Maryknoll, NY: Orbis Books.
Nussbaum, Stan W. 1985. *Toward Theological Dialogue with Independent Churches: A Study of Five Congregations in Lesotho.* Doctor of Theology Thesis, University of South Africa.
Nyamiti, Charles. 1984. *Christ our Ancestor—Christology from an African Perspective.* Gweru: Mambo Press.
Nyanza Christian College. 1976. *Annual Magazine.* Church of Christ in Africa, Kisumu, Kenya.
———. 1984. *Annual Magazine.* Church of Christ in Africa, Kisumu, Kenya.
Ochieng', W. R., 1989a. Independent Kenya, 1963-1986. In *A Modern History of Kenya, 1895-1980*, ed. W. R. Ochieng', 202-218. Nairobi: Evans Brothers
———, ed. 1989b. *A Modern History of Kenya, 1895-1980.* Nairobi: Evans Brothers.
———. 1992. *A History of Kenya.* Nairobi: Macmillan Kenya, 1985; reprint (page references are to reprint edition).

Ocholla-Ayayo, A. B. C. 1976. *Traditional Ideology and Ethics among the Southern Luo*. Uppsala: Scandanavian Institute of African Studies.

Odinga, Oginga. 1992. *Not Yet Uhuru: An Autobiography*. Nairobi: Heinemann, 1967; reprint (page references are to reprint edition).

Ogot, Bethwell A. 1963. British Administration in the Central Nyanza District of Kenya, 1900-60. *Journal of African History* 4: 249-273.

_____. 1967. *History of the Southern Luo*. Nairobi: East African Publishing House.

Olang', Festo. 1991. *An Autobiography*. Nairobi: Uzima Press.

Oliver, Roland. 1952. *The Missionary Factor in East Africa*. London: Longmans, Green and Company.

Omulokoli, Watson A. 1981. *The Historical Development of the Anglican Church Among Abaluyia, 1905-1955*. Ph.D. diss., University of Aberdeen.

Oosthuizen, Gerhardus Cornelius. 1967. *The Theology of a South African Messiah: An Analysis of the Hymnal of the "Church of the Nazarites."* Leiden: E. J. Brill.

_____ and Irving Hexham. 1992. Introduction. In *Empirical Studies of African Independent/Indigenous Churches*, eds. Gerhardus Cornelius Oosthuizen and Irving Hexham, 1-10. Lewiston, NY: Edwin Mellen Press.

Paden, William E. 1988. *Religious Worlds: The Comparative Study of Religion*. Boston: Beacon Press.

Parrinder, Geoffrey. 1969. *Religion in Africa*. Harmondsworth: Penguin.

P'bitek, Okot. 1971. *Religion of the Central Luo*. Nairobi: Kenya Literature Bureau.

Plummer, Ken. 1983. *Documents of Life: An Introduction to the Problems and Literature of a Humanistic Method*. London: George Allen and Unwin.

Pobee, John S. 1989. Oral Theology and Christian Oral Tradition: Challenge to our Traditional Archival Concept. *Mission Studies* 11 (January): 87-93.

Portelli, Alessandro. 1981. The Peculiarities of Oral History. *History Workshop* 12: 96-107.

Presley, Cora Ann. 1992. *Kikuyu Women, the Mau Mau Rebellion, and Social Change in Kenya*. Boulder, CO: Westview Press.

Pretorius, H. L. 1995. *Historiography and Historical Sources Regarding African Indigenous Churches in South Africa*. Lewiston, NY: Edwin Mellen Press.

Ranger, Terence. 1975. Introduction to Part One. In *Themes in the Christian History of Central Africa*, eds. Terence Ranger and John Weller, 3-13. London: Heineman.

———. 1978. Personal Reminiscence and the Experience of the People in East Central Africa. *Oral History* 6: 45- 78.

———. 1987. Taking Hold of the Land: Holy Places and Pilgrimages in Twentieth Century Zimbabwe. *Past and Present* 117 (November): 158-194.

———. 1993. New Approaches to the History of Mission Christianity. In *African Historiography*, ed. Toyin Falola, 180-194. Harlow: Longman.

———. 1994. Protestant Missions in Africa: The Dialectic of Conversion in the American Methodist Episcopal Church in Eastern Zimbabwe, 1900-1950. In *Religion in Africa*, eds. Thomas D. Blakely, Walter E. A. van Beek, and Dennis L. Thomson, 275-313. London: James Currey.

Regional Report on Central African Christian Council. 1975. By A. Matthew Ajuoga, Chairman. Kisumu, Kenya: Central African Christian Council.

Rosberg, C. G. and J. Nottingham. 1966. *The Myth of "Mau Mau" Nationalism in Kenya*. Nairobi: East African Publishing House.

Sanneh, Lamin. 1983. *West African Christianity: The Religious Impact*. Maryknoll, NY: Orbis Books.

———. 1989. *Translating the Message: The Missionary Impact on Culture*. Maryknoll, NY: Orbis Books.

———. 1993. *Encountering the West: Christianity and the Global Cultural Process: The African Dimension*. Maryknoll, NY: Orbis Books.

———. 1994. Translatability in Islam and Christianity in Africa: A Thematic Approach. In *Religion in Africa*, eds. Thomas D. Blakely, Walter E.A. van Beek, and Dennis L. Thomson, 23-45. London: James Currey.

Schmidt, R. 1988. *Exploring Religion*. Belmont, CA: Wadsworth Publishing Company.

Scholes, Robert and Robert Kellogg. 1981. *The Nature of Narrative*. New York: Oxford University Press, 1966; reprint (page references are to reprint edition).

Schreiter, Robert J., ed. 1991. *Faces of Jesus in Africa*. Maryknoll, NY: Orbis Books.
Shenk, Wilbert R. 1983. *Henry Venn—Missionary Statesman*. Maryknoll, NY: Orbis Books.
_____. 1996. Toward a Global Church History. *International Bulletin of Missionary Research* 20 (April): 50-57.
Shorter, Alyward. 1974. *East African Societies*. London: Routledge and Kegan Paul.
_____. 1988. *Toward a Theology of Inculturation*. Maryknoll, NY: Orbis Books.
Sparks, Allister. 1990. *The Mind of South Africa*. London: Heinemann.
Spear, Thomas. 1981. Oral Traditions: Whose History? *History in Africa* 8: 165-181.
Spencer, Leon P. 1982. Christianity and Colonial Protest: Perceptions of W. E. Owen, Archdeacon of Kavirondo. *Journal of Religion in Africa* 13: 47-60.
Spender, Stephen. 1980. Confessions and Autobiography. In *Autobiography: Essays Theoretical and Critical*, ed. James Olney, 115-122. Princeton: Princeton University Press.
Spindler, M. R. 1990. Writing African Church History: A Survey of Recent Studies. *Exchange* 19 (April): 70-87.
Stanley, Brian. 1978. The East African Revival—African Initiative within a European Tradition. *Evangelical Review of Theology* 2 (October): 188-207.
Stock, Eugene. 1899. *The History of the Church Missionary Society*. Vol. I. London: Church Missionary Society.
_____. 1916. *The History of the Church Missionary Society*. Vol. IV. London: Church Missionary Society.
Strayer, Robert. 1976. Mission History in Africa: New Perspectives on an Encounter. *African Studies Review* 19 (April): 1-15.
_____. 1978. *The Making of Mission Communities in East Africa*. London: Heinemann.
Stroup, George W. 1975. A Bibliographical Critique. *Theology Today* 32 (July): 133-143.
_____. 1981. *The Promise of Narrative Theology*. London: SCM Press.
Sundkler, Bengt G. M. 1948. *Bantu Prophets in South Africa*. London: Lutterworth Press.
_____. 1976. *Zulu Zion and some Swazi Zionists*. London: Oxford University Press.

Taber, Charles R. 1991. *The World is Too Much with Us.* Macon, GA: Mercer University Press.

Taylor, John B. 1976. Introduction. In *Primal World-Views: Christian Involvement in Dialogue with Traditional Thought Forms*, ed. John B. Taylor, 1-14. Ibadan: Daystar Press.

Taylor, John V. 1958a. *The Growth of the Church in Buganda.* London: SCM Press.

———. 1958b. *Processes of Growth in an African Church.* London: SCM Press.

Temu, A. J. 1972. *British Protestant Missions.* London: Longman.

TeSelle, Sallie McFague. 1975a. *Speaking in Parables: A Study in Metaphor and Theology.* Philadelphia: Fortress Press.

———. 1975b. The Experience of Coming to Belief. *Theology Today* 32 (July): 159-165.

Thompson, Paul. 1988. *The Voice of the Past.* London: Oxford University Press.

Thompson, T. Jack. 1996. Re-membering the Body: Discovering History as a Healing Art. *Studies in World Christianity* 2:2: 127-144.

Turner, Harold W. 1965. *Profile Through Preaching.* London: Edinburgh House Press.

———. 1967a. *African Independent Church, Vol. I, History of an African Independent Church, The Church of the Lord (Aladura).* London: Oxford University Press.

———. 1967b. African *Independent Churrch, Vol. 2, The Life and Faith of the Church of the Lord (Aladura).* London: Oxford University Press.

———. 1977. Primal Religions and Their Study. In *Australian Essays in World Religions*, ed. Victor C. Hayes, 27-37. Adelaide: Australian Association for the Study of Religions.

———. 1979. *Religious Innovation in Africa.* Boston: G. K. Hall and Company.

Turner, Philip. 1971. The Wisdom of the Fathers and the Gospel of Christ: Some Notes on Christian Adaptation in Africa. *Journal of Religion in Africa* 4 (January): 45- 68.

Turner, V. W. 1968. *The Drums of Affliction.* Oxford: Clarendon Press.

Vansina, Jan. 1981. Oral Tradition and its Methodology. In *UNESCO General History of Africa. Vol. 1, Methodology and Africa Prehistory*, ed. J. Ki-Zerbo, 142-165. Berkeley, CA: University of California Press.

_____. 1985. *Oral Tradition as History*. Madison, WI: University of Wisconsin Press.

Wallace, Anthony F. C. 1956. Revitalization Movements. *American Anthropologist* 58: 264-281.

Waller, Richard. 1995. Kidongoi's Kin: Prophecy and Power in Maasailand. In *Revealing Prophets: Prophecy in Eastern African History*, eds. David M. Anderson and Douglas H. Johnson, 28-64. London: James Currey.

Walls, Andrew F. 1972. African Church History: Some Recent Studies. *Journal of Ecclesiastical History* 23 (April): 161-169.

_____. 1979. The Anabaptists of Africa? The Challenge of the African Independent Churches. *Ocassional Bulletin of Missionary Research* 3 (April): 48-51.

_____. 1980. Africa and Christian Identity. In *Mission Focus: Current Issues*, ed. W. R. Shenk, 212-221. Scottdale, PA: Herald Press.

_____. 1982. The Gospel as the Prisoner and Liberator of Culture. *Missionalia* 10 (November): 93-105.

_____. 1987. Primal Religious Traditions in Today's World. In *Religion in Today's World*, ed. F. Whaling, 250-278. Edinburgh: T. and T. Clark.

_____. 1990a. Building to Last: Harold Turner and the Study of Religion. In *Exploring New Religious Movements*, eds. A. F. Walls and Wilbert R. Shenk, 1-17. Elkhart, IN: Mission Focus.

_____. 1990b. The Translation Principle in Christian History. In *Bible Translation and the Spread of the Church*, ed. P. Stint, 24-39. Leiden: E. J. Brill.

_____. 1995. Christianity in the Non-Western World: A Study in the Serial Nature of Christian Expansion. *Studies in World Christianity* 1:1: 1-25.

_____. 1996. African Christianity in the History of Religions. *Studies in World Christianity* 2:2: 183-203.

Walls, Andrew F., and Wilbert R. Shenk, eds. 1990. *Exploring New Religious Movements: Essays in Honor of Harold W. Turner*. Elkhart, IN: Mission Focus.

Ward, Kevin. 1991a. "Tukutendereza Yesu": The Balokole Revival in Uganda. In *From Mission to Church*, ed. Zablon Nthamburi, 113-144. Nairobi: Uzima Press.

――――. 1991b. A History of Christianity in Uganda. In *From Mission to Church*, ed. Zablon Nthamburi, 81-112. Nairobi: Uzima Press.

Warren, M. A. C. 1954. *Revival: An Enquiry*. London: SCM Press.

Welbourn, F. B. 1961. *East African Rebels*. London: SCM Press.

Welbourn, F. B., and B. A. Ogot. 1966. *A Place to Feel At Home: A Study of Two Independent Churches in Western Kenya*. London: Oxford University Press.

Were, Gideon S. 1972. Politics, Religion and Nationalism in Western Kenya, 1942-1962: Dini ya Msambwa Revisited. In *Politics and Nationalism in Colonial Kenya*, ed. Bethwell A. Ogot, 85-104. Nairobi: East African Publishing House.

White, Hayden. 1980. The Value of Narrativity in the Representation of Reality. *Critical Inquiry* 7 (Autumn): 5-27.

Wipper, Audrey. 1977. *Rural Rebels: A Study of Two Protest Movements in Kenya*. Nairobi: Oxford University Press.

Yow, Valerie Raleigh. 1994. *Recording Oral History: A Practical Guide for Social Scientists*. London: SAGE Publications.

Zeleza, Tiyambe. 1989. Kenya and the Second World War 1939-1950. In *A Modern History of Kenya, 1895-1980*, ed. W. R. Ochieng', 144-172. Nairobi: Evans Brothers

Index

Abidjan, 298
Abraham, 210, 229, 271, 274
Abuodha, 241
academic theology, 166, 196, 312
adopted past, 145
Adoyo, Julius, 246
Africa, 329
African Christian community, 3, 4, 14, 145, 163
African Christian experience, 5, 7, 24, 127, 165, 170, 190, 193, 212, 218
African Christian independency, 6, 9, 14, 19, 24, 25, 33-34, 42, 130, 137, 144, 158, 173, 175, 176, 179
African Christian scholarship, 4, 5, 162, 168
African Christian theology, 157, 165, 211
African Christianity, 2, 4-5, 9, 27, 38, 100, 104, 109, 132, 147, 164, 168-173, 178, 182-183, 186, 206, 213, 301, 307, 319, 322, 325, 328, 331
African Church history, 165
African District Association, 73
African Independent Churches, 18, 297, 324, 325, 331
African Instituted Church, 1-4, 6, 10-11, 19, 20-21, 25, 42, 47, 133, 142-144, 152, 164, 167, 173, 202
African Israel Church Nineveh, 33
African Orthodox Church, 309
African Spiritual Churches Association, 18
African Studies, 298, 320, 321, 327, 329
Agola, Evans, 238
Aguko, Phanuel, 263
AIC, 1, 9-10, 56, 126, 136, 152, 167, 175-180, 184, 211, 313
Ajuang', Jennifer Claris, 222
Ajuoga, Matthew, 1-6, 9, 11, 13-58, 63-64, 67-69, 73-75, 77-78, 81-82, 85-88, 92-93, 95-101, 105-109, 111-112, 114, 116-117, 124-133, 135, 136-137, 139-153, 155-156, 158-160, 162-167, 170-173, 175-181, 183-185, 187, 189-193, 197, 198, 199-214, 217-219, 221, 224, 237, 260, 283, 285, 297-303, 305-312, 314, 316-317, 321, 328
Akan, 298
Akoko pastorate, 242, 244
Aladura, 11-15, 17, 330
Alaka, Peter, 226
All Saints' Cathedral, 281
Amin, Idi, 279
Amoke, 226-228, 244
Amoke, Musa, 226

Index

Anderson, 128-130, 204, 305, 308-309, 314, 317-318, 324, 331
Anderson, Allan, 22
Anglican Church, 1, 19, 29-30, 73, 74, 82-83, 91, 93-97, 99-100, 107-109, 133, 136, 145-146, 208, 210, 214, 221-223, 225, 229-232, 234-235, 237-238, 240-243, 246-251, 256-257, 260-266, 269, 278-279, 281-282, 288, 298-299, 304, 307-308, 327
Anglican Primary School, 222
Anglicanism, 31, 88, 93, 99-100, 107-108, 131, 136, 190, 210, 213-214
apartheid, 94, 255
apologia, 150, 311
apostolic succession, 281
Apunda, Eliakim, 263
Archbishop of Canterbury, 29, 98, 251, 279-280, 291, 317
Archbishop of York, 237
archives, 3, 31, 297, 299, 304
Athanasius, 99, 249
Awuor, 236, 238, 256, 284
Awuor, Nathan Silas, 29, 238
Balokole Revival, 100, 331
baptism, 245, 267-268
baptisms, 83, 268, 277
baptize, 267, 277, 314
baptized, 86, 91, 226, 231, 266, 267, 268, 274
baraza, 224
Barrett, 3, 24, 34, 101, 132-133, 135, 136, 206, 297-299, 309, 312-314, 318
Barrett, David B., 1-3
Bediako, Kwame, 5-6, 111, 113, 116, 125-126, 161-164, 166, 168-169, 178-179, 186, 200-201, 212, 301-302, 307, 312, 319
Beecher Report, 91, 93, 305, 306

Beecher, Leonard, 91, 93-95, 97, 236-239, 250, 256, 259-260, 266, 280, 305-306, 316
Bell, John, 277
Bembei, 242
Bible, 93-94, 134, 156, 166, 181, 182, 210, 222-223, 228-229, 232, 234, 237, 240, 246, 250-251, 253, 256-258, 261, 264-267, 279, 291, 298, 307, 313, 325, 331
Bible used in African Theologizing, 181
Biographical Theology, 180, 312, 313
Bishop, 29-30, 83, 85, 89, 92, 94-95, 97, 99, 221-223, 236, 238-239, 247, 250, 256-257, 259, 266, 269, 281-283, 309, 316
Bishop of Mombasa, 29, 89, 92, 94, 250, 256, 316
bishops, 83, 108, 229, 241, 247, 252, 272, 277-278, 282, 283-284
Bloundell, 276-277
Boers, 255-256
Bostock, 238-240, 317
British, 57-60, 62-67, 69-70, 95, 144, 270, 302, 327, 330
Buganda, 57, 82-83, 305, 330
Bugembe, 270
Busia, 270
Carey, 250
Carey, W. H., 239
Carrier Corps, 62
Central African Christian Council, 31, 328
Central Nyanza Deanery Council, 248
charismatic authority, 128
Chekalili Health Centre, 288
Christian identity formation, 22, 212
Christian Secondary School, 287
Christian Universal Evangelical Union, 136, 309

Church and State Cooperation and Development Committee, 311
Church Missionary Society, 3, 31, 65, 82-83, 225, 297, 323, 326, 329
Church Missionary Society (CMS), 3, 31, 32, 82, 83-96, 99-101, 109, 146, 172, 193, 205, 208, 210, 214, 222, 225, 232, 234-235, 237, 239, 246, 257, 259, 269, 273, 281, 290, 297, 304-306, 312, 314
Church of Christ in Africa (CCA), 1, 2, 3, 4, 5, 6, 13, 14, 15, 16, 17, 19, 20, 21, 24, 27, 28, 29, 30, 31, 32, 33, 34, 36, 42, 74, 77, 78, 88, 98, 100, 125, 126, 133, 137, 145, 146, 147, 208, 209, 210, 211, 213, 214, 219, 221, 223, 258, 264-268, 270, 275, 278-280, 282-284, 285, 286, 288-289, 298, 299, 300, 301, 305, 308, 311, 314, 326
Church of Christ in Asia, 265
Church of Christ in Galatia, 265
Church of Christ in Rome, 265
Church of Christ Youth (CCY), 283
church of God at Maseno-Kogore, 257
Church of Scotland, 234, 264
Church of the Lord (Aladura), 12
Church of the Province of Kenya, 87, 95, 100, 102, 105, 290, 305, 309, 320
Church, Joe, 101, 307, 320
Churches of Christ, 201, 265
clinics, 288
CMS, 83, 95
colonial administration, 57, 59-60, 63, 65, 71, 73, 95, 134
colonial government, 60, 63, 71, 72, 94, 255-256, 266, 305
commission of inquiry, 254
community, 2-3, 12-17, 19-21, 31, 36, 52, 55, 72, 75, 77, 85, 94, 96, 98, 100, 118, 128, 129, 130, 142, 144-145, 162, 165-167, 171-172, 176, 178, 190, 194, 204, 208-210, 213-214, 312-313
constitution, 84, 246, 263-265
Cornelius, 274, 324, 327
Coward, John, 264
Cranmer, 250
Cranmer, Thomas, 99
crisis, 54-58, 61-64, 68-73, 75, 77-78, 81-82, 92-95, 107, 109, 115-116, 120, 128-130, 137, 147, 163, 173, 190, 197, 201, 204-208, 211-212, 302-304, 307, 309
Cyrene, 272
Dala Hera, 32, 279, 286, 288, 301, 317
Daneel, 178, 321
Daneel, M.L., 174
Daystar University, 40, 287, 311
Dholuo, 1, 40, 45-48, 62, 65, 91, 148, 155, 219, 224, 277, 283, 301, 305, 317
Dini ya Jesu Kristo, 136
Dini ya Mariam, 309
Dini ya Msambwa, 134-136, 309, 332
Dini ya Roho, 136, 309
Diocese of Eastern Equatorial Africa, 83
Diocese of Masogo, 263
Diocese of Mombasa, 89-91
Diocese of Uganda, 83, 85, 89
divorce, 233, 266, 273
Dunde, Onyango, 133
East Africa, 31, 57, 58, 59, 64, 83-84, 86, 100, 102, 104, 128-129, 131-132, 155, 221, 223, 225, 231, 237, 258, 303, 305, 308-309, 321, 324, 327
East Africa Protectorate, 57-58
East African Revival, 1, 82, 85, 93, 100-107, 109, 150-152, 153, 193, 206, 209, 225, 257, 306-307, 320, 324, 326, 329
ecumenism, 103, 211, 298, 314

education, 19, 59, 86-88, 91-94, 144, 161, 205, 222-225, 234-235, 246, 256, 260, 266, 271, 285-288, 292, 305, 312
elders, 36, 60, 71, 85, 88, 225, 238, 249, 279, 280-281, 283-284, 300
Eldoret, 268, 316, 317
Eliot, Sir Charles, 57
England, 68, 82, 87, 108, 146, 208, 210, 221-223, 234, 236, 239, 250-251, 256, 260, 264, 266, 272-274, 279, 288, 290-292, 298, 303
English Reformers, 250
Eurocentrism, 196-197
Father, 267
First World War, 62, 69
Fisher, 98, 279, 280, 317, 321
Fisher, G.F., 29
Forum for the Restoration of Democracy (FORD), 76
Geita, 270
Geneva, 291
Gestation, 35
Ghana, 292, 318
Gikuyu, 64-65, 72, 136, 234, 243, 303-304, 308
Gikuyuland, 65
Gilgil, 276
God, 2, 6-7, 12, 17, 22, 26, 38, 54, 102, 107, 117-120, 122, 126, 129-130, 133, 146, 151, 153, 167, 170-171, 189-190, 202-205, 207, 210-211, 213-214, 218-219, 221-222, 225-226, 228, 230-235, 237, 239-240, 242, 244-246, 253-254, 257-258, 261, 264-265, 267, 269, 271-276, 280-281, 284-285-286, 290, 292, 306, 325
God-Talk, 2, 6, 7, 17, 22, 26, 54, 189-190, 202-205, 207, 211, 214, 218-219
Gospel Furthering Fellowship, 309
government capitulations, 63
Greek Orthodox Church, 146, 272

Greschat, Hans-Jurgen, 11-12, 322
Hannington, James, 83
Hastings, Adrian, 1, 101, 103-105, 161, 165-166, 169, 174, 203, 301, 322
Hawse, Peter, 236
heresy, heretic, 192, 194, 198, 249, 320
heretical, 107, 194
heretics, 109, 192, 194
Heywood, R.S., 89
Holy Communion, 225-227, 243, 245, 266, 268-269, 277
Holy Spirit, 102, 136, 222, 241, 251, 267, 274, 278
Holy Trinity Church, 284
Homa Bay, 285
HTCA, 284
human brotherhood, 255
Hymns of the Nazarites, 203
independence, 19, 57, 69, 71, 73, 75, 77, 84, 89, 161, 172, 261, 265
India, 82, 292
inherited past, 145
inside interpretation, 4, 14, 17
inside understanding, 12, 14-15, 22-23, 26-27, 32
Inside Understanding, 9, 299
institutional legitimacy, 208-209
International Association of Mission Studies, 157
interviews, 18-19, 30, 43
Islam, 90, 115, 272, 279, 328
Israel, 33, 271
Ivory Coast, 13, 298
Jeremiah, 280
Jesus, 106-107, 109, 136, 210, 221-222, 225-227, 229-232, 235, 237, 240, 242, 244-246, 248, 251, 258, 266-267, 271-272, 274-275, 280, 323, 329
Johera, 1-6, 9, 11-58, 63-64, 67-69, 73-74, 77-78, 81-82, 85, 87-88, 91-94, 96-100, 105-107, 109, 111, 114-115, 117, 124, 127, 129, 131, 133, 135-137,

139-144, 146-156, 158-160, 162-167, 169-173, 175-184, 187, 189-190, 192-195, 199, 202-214, 217-219, 221, 223, 231-232, 235-236, 238-240, 250, 257-259, 262-263, 265-266, 268, 270, 275-276, 284, 298-302, 304, 306, 310, 312-314, 317
Johera Narrative, 2-6, 9, 11-32, 34-35, 37, 39-58, 63-64, 67-69, 73-74, 77-78, 81-82, 84-85, 87, 92-93, 97-100, 106-107, 109, 111, 114-115, 117, 124-127, 129, 131, 133, 135, 137, 139-153, 155-156, 158-160, 162-173, 175-199, 202-204, 206, 208-214, 217-219, 221, 299-302, 304, 306, 311, 313, 317
Jokogore, 233
Jondaria, 278
Joremo, 2, 106-107, 235
Kaggia, Bildad, 136, 243, 310, 324
Kagika, Stanley, 243
Kakamega, 270, 285, 288
Kalenjin, 309
Kaloleni, 277
Kalu, 170, 324
Kalu, Ogbu, 2, 25, 169
Kamba, 309
Kambare, 221-222, 228
Kampala, 90, 279, 305
Kano Kobura, 263
Kariuki, Obadiah, 222
Kato, Byang, 125-126
Kavirondo, 57-58, 64-66, 89, 303, 305, 329
Kavirondo Taxpayers Welfare Association, 66
Kawango, 241
Kenya, 1, 19, 20, 31, 33-34, 40, 45-46, 49, 55, 57-58, 61, 63-66, 69-73, 75-77, 82, 86-87, 89-96, 99-101, 103, 105, 107, 109, 128-129, 132-133, 144-145, 148-149, 151-152, 155, 211, 221-223, 225, 227-228, 244, 254, 273, 275, 279, 286-287, 290, 292, 298-301, 303-306, 309, 311, 316-320, 322-328, 332
Kenya Africa Union, 71, 303
Kenya African National Union, 76
Kenya Junior Secondary Examination, 286
Kenyatta, Jomo, 71, 73, 75-76, 243, 260, 274
Kericho Tea Estate, 275
Kihito, Reuben, 136, 243
Kijiji cha Ujaama, 279
Kikuyu, 64, 96, 287, 324, 327
Kikuyu Association, 64
Kisumu, 32, 76, 91, 224, 234, 260, 263-264, 268-269, 279, 281, 283-288, 298, 301, 305, 317-318, 326, 328
Kisumu Karaten'g, 232
Kodera, 287
Krapf, Johann, 82
labour camps, 61
Lake Victoria, 83, 85, 133-134, 305
Latimer, Hugh, 99, 250
Latin American Liberation Theology, 159
lay readers, 244-245, 253, 282
Leakey, Dr. Richard, 290
legal-rational authority, 209
legitimacy, 20, 42, 146, 163, 167, 179, 192, 193, 195, 208-214, 314
legitimacy through identification, 210
legitimization, 20, 141, 208-211, 213, 313
letters, 17, 29, 87, 97, 99, 141, 146, 248-249, 269, 279-280, 306, 310
Limuru, 223, 229-230, 236, 292
Lonsdale, John, 57, 72, 303-304, 309, 319, 324
love, 1, 74, 99, 106, 107, 222-223, 227, 229-232, 237, 246-248,

256, 258, 260, 261, 262, 265, 267, 269, 272
Luhyias (Abaluyia), 244, 270
Luo, 33-34, 36, 40, 46, 48, 57-73, 75-77, 84-101, 106, 111, 117-130, 133-135, 137, 144-145, 147-150, 152-153, 155, 190, 200-201, 205, 207, 210, 212, 214, 219, 256, 268, 284-285, 297, 299-305, 308-311, 321, 323, 327
Luo diaspora, 64
Luo Union, 71, 73
Luoland, 226, 232-233, 247-248, 258, 260, 263, 270, 281
Luther, Martin, 10, 99, 240, 250
Maasai, 308-309
MacGaffey, Wyatt, 36, 301, 309, 323, 325
Magokha, Elijah, 284
Malakite Church, 309
Mango, Alfayo, 241, 246
mantics, 121, 129, 308
Maragoli, 309
Maranda School, 228, 244
marriage, 94, 222, 273
marry, marriage, 106, 227-228, 234, 250
Maseno, 86, 88, 91-92, 100-101, 133, 214, 222-225, 232-233, 235-239, 246-248, 250, 253, 256-260, 268-270, 276, 305, 308, 317
Maseno boys' school, 86
Maseno CMS Hospital, 232
Maseno Secondary School, 222
Masinde, Elijah, 134-136, 243
Masogo, 263, 281, 284
Mau Mau, 72, 93-96, 100, 105, 209, 243, 248, 262, 265, 303, 319-320, 322, 324, 327-328
Mbiti, John, 25, 117-120, 123, 156-158, 160, 161, 182, 307-308, 313, 325
Mboya, Tom, 76
Meru, 234

Methodist Church of East Africa, 251
Methodist Church of England, 251
methodology, 6, 9, 11, 22, 28, 30, 35, 45, 53, 170, 199, 203, 217
microcosm/macrocosm scheme of legitimacy, 209
Milcah, 298
Mirembe, 284
Mirembe Church, 284
missionary methodology, 207
missionary schools, 88
Moi, Daniel Arap, 75-76, 311
Molo, 277
Moses, 210, 231, 257-258, 271, 280
motivation, 18, 28, 69
Msambwa, 134-135
Mudhiero pastorate, 241
Mugambi, J.N.K., 312, 326
Mulama, 270
Mumia, 270
Murray, Jocelyn, 82, 84, 89, 94-96, 101, 105, 136, 194, 304-306, 320, 326
Musambwa, 243
Musanda, 241
Musanda Anglican Church, 241
Muslim, 287
Muslims, 272, 289
Musoma, 279
Mwan'gombe, Peter, 238
Nagenda, William, 226
Nairobi, 13, 30, 32, 64, 72, 75, 89, 90, 92, 96, 97, 100-101, 222, 225, 237, 238, 244, 247, 253, 259-260, 264, 273, 277, 281, 285, 287, 299, 304, 309, 318, 320, 322, 324, 325-328, 331, 332
Nairobi Detention Camp, 253
Nakuru District Commissioner, 276
Nandi, 58
Narrative Theology, 180-187, 310, 312-313, 321, 329
National Church of Kenya, 265

Index

National Council of Churches in Kenya (NCCK), 146, 211, 290-292
Nazaretha hymns, 10, 203
Ndisi, Isaiah, 263, 282
New Religious Movements, 213, 314, 322, 331
Ng'iya, 281
Nilotes, 270
Njoro, 276
Nomiya Luo Mission, 133
Noo, Ishmael, 108, 136, 225, 242
Northey, Sir Edward, 65
Nthamburi, Zablon, 303, 313, 326, 331-332
nursery schools, 286
Nyaera, 234
Nyakach, 234, 260, 263
Nyamgutu, 284
Nyamninia, 263
Nyanza, 1, 19, 30-33, 57-68, 70-75, 77-78, 81-82, 84-101, 105-109, 116, 133-137, 145-146, 172, 193, 205, 207, 208, 210, 213-214, 221, 236, 248, 251, 256-257, 259, 284, 287, 298, 300, 302-306, 312, 326-327
Nyanza Christian College, 30, 287, 326
Nyanza Ex-Soldiers Association, 71
Nyanza Luo, 19, 60-64, 66, 71-73, 75, 77, 85, 92, 99, 302, 304
Nyanza Province, 1, 57-58, 221
Nyasaye, 120
Nyende, Simon, 270, 282
Nyerere, Julius, 270, 279
Obick, Elizabeth, 291
objectivity, 14, 22, 144, 298
Obonyo, Levi, 241
Obote, 279
Ochieng', W.R., 64, 70, 75-76, 134, 302, 308-309, 324-326, 332
Ochuodho, David, 263, 275-276
Odinga, Oginga, 71, 73, 75-77, 86, 118, 148, 284, 300, 304-305, 308, 327
Odongo, Alfayo, 135, 136, 241, 246
Ogada, William, 236, 282
Ogot, Bethwell, 1-3, 29, 33-34, 57-63, 65-66, 68, 70-72, 78, 116, 136, 297, 299, 302-303, 307, 310, 313-314, 322, 327, 332
Oguna, 63, 67, 144, 224
Okungu, Philip, 229, 236, 282
Olang', Festo, 95, 101, 103, 236-238, 256-257, 259-261, 269, 280, 327
Oliver, Roland, 84, 90-91, 304, 327
Omino, Kogola Jeel, 284
Omulokoli, Watson, 85-86, 304, 327
Onguko, 226
Oosthuizen, G.C., 10, 78, 174, 176, 203, 313, 319, 324, 327
Oral Historiography, 323
oral history, 23, 36, 140-141, 144
oral sources, 23, 37, 42, 44, 300
oral theology, 38, 42, 156-160, 300, 302, 312
Organization of African Instituted Churches (OAIC), 1, 19, 211, 297
orthodox, orthodoxy, 21, 87, 107, 108, 163-164, 194
Osere, Shadrack, 242
Otieno, Benson, 232, 259, 263, 269, 275-276
Owalo, John, 133
Owen, Walter Edwin, 65-69, 95, 210, 256, 303, 329
Owino, Mathayo, 263, 282
Owira, Meshack, 32, 146, 229, 236-237, 260, 263, 269-270, 282-284
Padhola, 85, 270
Padwick, John, 132-133, 298, 309, 312, 314, 318

Pakistan, 292
pakruok, 148-150, 152-153, 310, 317
participant observation, 12, 32
participation, 13-15, 17, 19, 26, 43, 66, 103, 298
partnership, 15-17, 26, 88, 119, 198-200
Paul, the Apostle, 19, 222-223, 229, 231, 240, 249, 251, 258, 267, 276, 292, 313, 322-323, 329-330
Peaston, Rev. R., 97, 238-239, 316
Pentecostal [Church of] Norway, 265
Pentecostal Assembly of Canada, 264
Peter, the Apostle, 229, 231, 249, 274
phenomenological methodology, 18
phenomenology, 4, 11, 12, 14, 142, 144, 298
phenomenology of religion, 11-12, 298
Piny Owacho (the Voice of the People), 66
Pittway, R.A., 246
police, 261-262, 265, 268-269, 274, 276, 281
polygamy, polygyny, polygamous, 87, 145, 208, 210, 233, 267, 308, 314
polytechnic, 289
preparation, 35, 37, 40, 59, 86
Presbyterian Church of East Africa, 251
primal past, 5, 125, 126, 201, 212, 298
primal religion, 5, 111-124, 130-131, 135, 161, 165, 196, 200-201, 307-308
primary schools, 286
primitivism, 201, 213-214, 314
prophetic tradition, 128-131, 134-135, 137, 212-213, 308-309
Psalms, 278

qualitative, 17, 22, 28, 30, 39, 43, 299
Rabuor, 263
Rachier, Heson, 281
Rachuonyo Christian Secondary School, 287
Rachuonyo clinic, 288
racial relationships in the church, 255
Ramba, 228-229, 235, 257-259
Ramogi African Welfare Association, 71
Ramula Pastorate, 268
Ranger, Terence, 25, 41, 43, 170, 171, 214, 299-300, 328
Rearward-Looking Christian Identity, 211
recording, 35, 38, 43-45, 47, 300
religious dimension, 25, 208
religious experience, 17, 22-23, 25, 42, 78, 103, 113, 143, 203, 211, 301
religious self-determination, 202
restitutionism, 147, 165, 179, 201, 213-214, 313-314
restorationism, 201, 213-214
revival, 2, 29, 101-102, 107, 151, 198, 202, 206, 208, 223, 225-228, 231-232, 235, 237-240, 242, 244-248, 250, 258-259, 306
Ridley, Nicholas, 99, 250
Rift Valley, 276, 277
ritual practices, 233
Roho Movement, 309
Roman Catholic Church, 146, 264, 266, 273, 276
Roman Catholics, 225
Rubaga, 82
Ruoth, 60, 77
rural deans, 97-98, 108, 229, 235-238, 244, 246-247, 253, 256-257, 298, 306
Sakwa, 242
Salvation Army, 234
Samson, 292

Index

Sanneh, Lamin, 194, 301-302, 307, 309, 312, 328
schism, 1-3, 29, 31, 33-34, 146, 202
Scriptures, 146, 151, 181-182, 203, 261, 323
Second World War, 69-70, 303, 332
secondary school, 225
Secondary School, 222, 287-288
secondary schools, 254, 286, 288, 305
Selly Oak Colleges, 298, 316-317, 321, 323
Seventh Day Adventists, 266, 306
Shembe, Isaiah, 10-11, 203
Shenk, Wilbert, 169, 298, 305, 322, 329, 331
Shorter, Alyward, 302, 313, 329
Siaya, 221, 283, 287-288, 300, 320
Simon of Cyrene, 272
siro, 228, 245
Smith, Langsford, 247
Smith, Shergold, 82
social sciences, 25, 141, 208
sources, 2, 6, 11, 13-14, 16-17, 23, 27, 28, 30-32, 34, 38, 40, 42, 49, 53, 56, 98, 117, 140, 146, 156, 163, 165, 167, 170, 175-177, 182, 191, 196, 217, 299-300, 304, 306, 309
South Africa, 10, 176, 255, 316, 324, 326, 328-329
South Mara, 270, 279
South Nyanza, 134, 234
Spanish influenza, 63
St. Mary's Yala Secondary School, 225
St. Matthew's Masogo Bible School, 279
St. Paul's United Theological College, 223, 298, 301
St. Peter's Basilica, 273
St. Philip's Bible School, 276
Stanley, Henry, 82, 101-102, 151, 243, 322, 329

Starehe, 277
Stovold, Archdeacon, 235, 239, 246
subjectivity, 22-23, 144
Subukia, 276
Sunday School, 225, 254, 291
Sundkler, Bengt, 9-11, 18, 22, 24, 169, 203, 309, 313-314, 329
Susoma, 270
sympathy, 12-14, 17, 38, 42, 66
Tanzania, 223, 270, 279, 299
Taylor, John V., 30, 34, 83-84, 102, 112-113, 290, 299, 305, 319, 330
Tetzel, John, 240
The Light, 30, 97, 108, 136, 240, 256, 310, 317
theological studies in Africa, 24, 155-156, 180, 187, 202, 218
Thirty-Nine Articles, 229
Thuku riot, 65
Thuku, Harry, 64
totemic animals, 124
traditional authority, 209
transcription, 43-44, 46-48, 51, 301
translation, 43-44, 48-49, 114-116, 126-127, 130, 159-160, 185, 191-192, 200, 301-302, 307-308, 312
transmission, 6, 17, 35, 40-41, 43-45, 52, 218
tribalism, 33, 94, 298
truth, 18, 23, 62, 249, 261, 292
Tucker, Alfred, 83-85
Turner, Harold W., 9, 11-18, 22, 25, 56, 112-113, 117-120, 122-123, 130-131, 182, 298, 307, 313, 316-317, 320-321, 330-331
Uganda, 58-59, 65, 82-86, 89-90, 92, 99, 101, 109, 132-133, 210, 214, 222-223, 226-227, 270, 279, 303, 305, 309, 331-332
Ugenya, 241
Union Theological Seminary, 223, 292, 301

United Theological College, Limuru, 223, 239, 301
unity, 74, 94, 108, 122, 186, 249, 255, 261, 280
University, 287, 292, 314, 316, 318-332
University of Birmingham, 324
veneration of the ancestors, 122
Venn, Henry, 83, 305, 329
Wachemake, 270
Wahamaji, 29, 87, 97, 106-108, 125, 131, 172, 193, 208-209, 229-230, 235-236, 238, 240, 242, 244, 247-248, 251, 254, 257, 260, 263, 307, 312
Wallace, Anthony, 115-116, 302, 307, 331
Walls, Andrew, 6, 11-12, 112-116, 145, 147, 163, 168, 169, 179, 194-195, 198, 211-212, 298, 305, 307, 312-313, 322, 331
Wanjage, 270
Ward, Kevin, 100-101, 305, 331
Warren, M.A.C., 102-105, 151, 306, 332
Welbourn, F.B., 1-3, 29, 33-34, 102, 105, 136, 206, 297, 299, 307, 313-314, 332
Were, Gideon, 135, 309

Western, 13, 20, 48, 58, 64, 75, 117, 125, 126, 133, 135, 156, 163, 171, 185, 191, 193-195, 202-204, 209, 225, 244, 270, 297, 305, 312-314, 318-320, 326, 331-332
white settlement, 57, 61
wholistic ministry, 127, 210, 308
Willis, John J., 85-86, 88, 92, 210, 233, 235, 305
Wilson, Charles, 82
witchcraft, 232-233
wives (multiple), 224, 226, 228, 233-234, 242, 244, 253, 255, 282
women's meeting, 254
women's meetings, 254
World Council of Churches, 211, 223, 291, 292
written African theology, 160
written sources, 27
Yona Mondo, 226
Young Kavirondo Association, 65-66
Young Kikuyu Association, 64
youth organization, 282
Zaire, 223, 279, 323
zeitgeist, 3, 34, 299
Zulu, 9, 10, 24, 329

About the Author

George F. Pickens is Professor of Mission and Intercultural Studies and Chair of the Department of Intercultural Studies at Kentucky Christian College, Grayson, Kentucky. He holds a B.A. from Kentucky Christian College (Biblical Studies, 1980), an M.A. (African Studies, 1984) from Ohio University, and a Ph.D. (Theology, 1997) from the University of Birmingham, England. Dr. Pickens has lived and conducted research in both Ivory Coast and Kenya.

Made in the USA
Middletown, DE
08 December 2017